AF393285

GINO DE DOMINICIS

edited by Gabriele Guercio

GINO DE DOMINICIS
A READER

Verlag der Buchhandlung Walther und Franz König

Contents

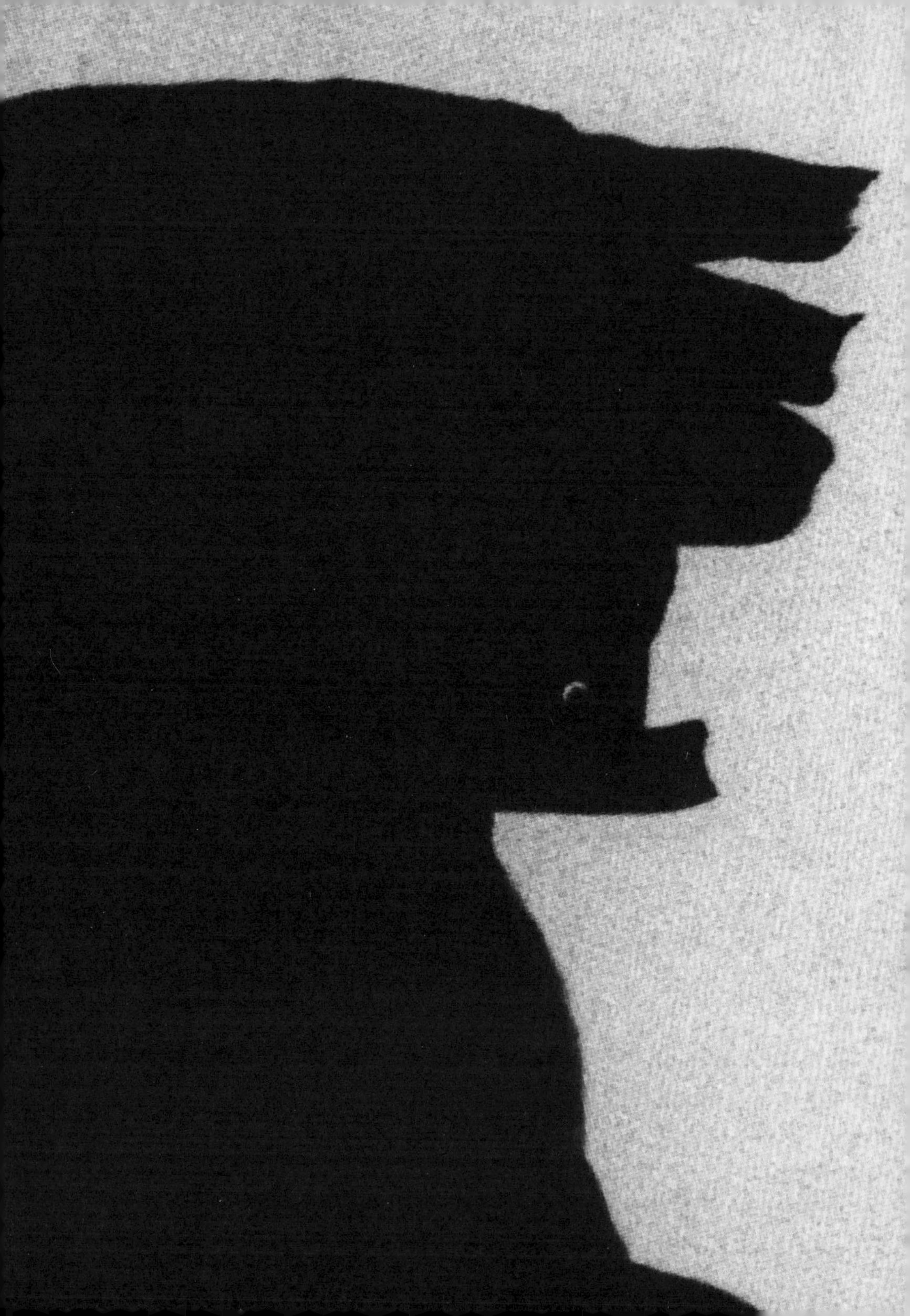

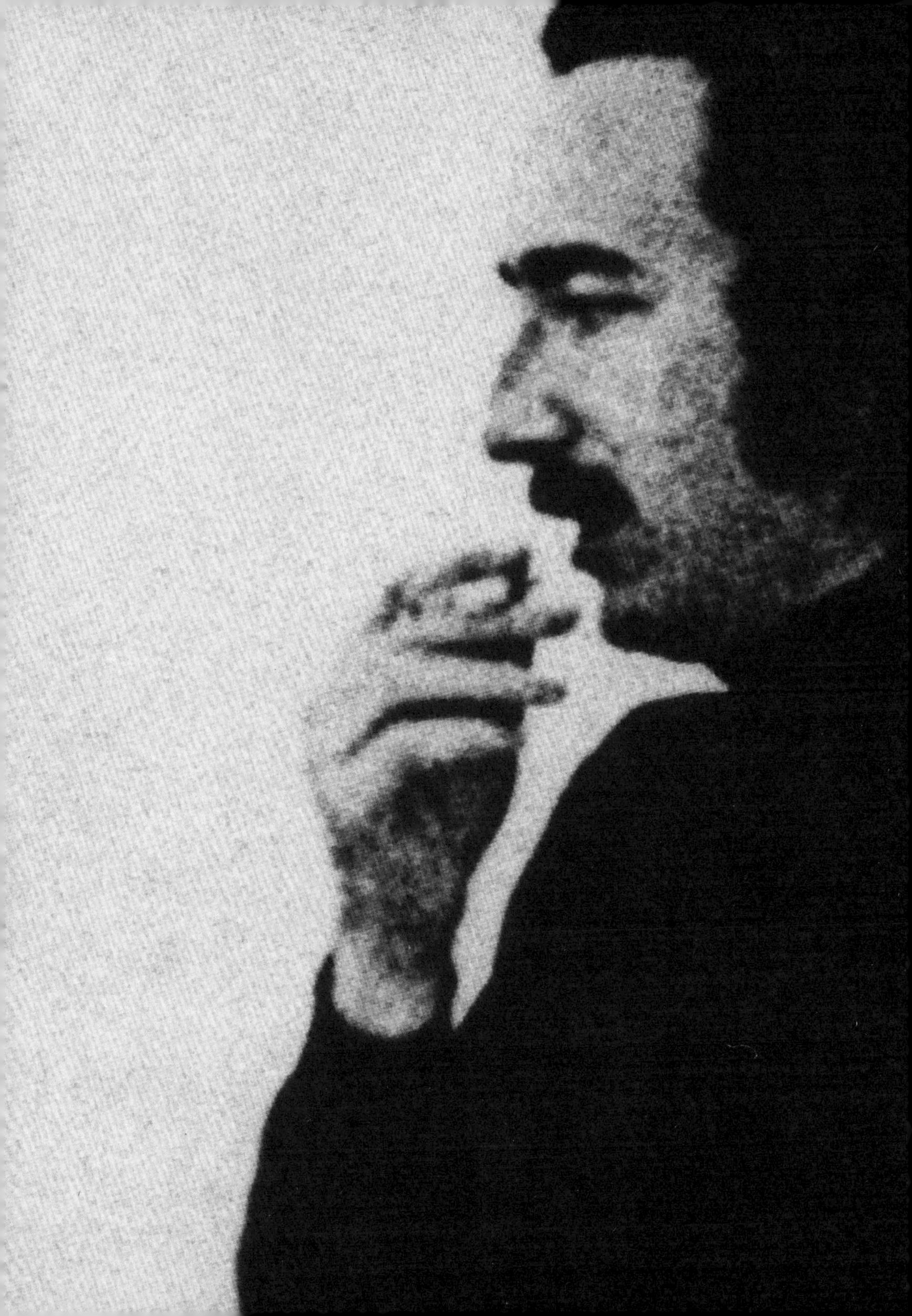

Against Finitude: An Introduction

Gabriele Guercio

Beginning with a solo show in his native town of Ancona in 1966, the career of Gino De Dominicis (1947–1998) spanned three decades. Every now and then, always cautiously selecting the places and people involved, he exhibited his artworks in Rome (the city where he would spend most of his life), throughout Italy, and abroad. His oeuvre mainly consists of drawings, paintings, three-dimensional objects, and "invisible" works, with the latter category deemed by the artist particularly germane to his practice. While De Dominicis considered himself a painter, sculptor, and architect, he proudly claimed that his work remained independent from mainstream culture and the artistic trends of his time. He liked to compare himself to a *cantautore* or singer-songwriter, inventing his own themes and motifs. For him, artistic creation and spiritual revelation, skillful manual execution and the elaboration of meaning, the growth of mental awareness, and the recognition of an auratic image or object, were all part of a single experience. He denied the usefulness of photography as a means of circulating his artworks and maintained that reproductions should only be credited to the photographers, never the artist. He even went so far as to argue that works of art do not need to be seen in order to exist.

Evidently, De Dominicis took an unusual stance both artistically and in his personal behavior. Not only did he make works of art but he also lived an artistic life, which is often a harder accomplishment. Perhaps it was for this reason that he was an artist loved by other artists. This emerges in the tributes from his contemporaries published in this volume, particularly Anselm Kiefer's recollection of De Dominicis in Venice and Marina Abramović's anecdote about their encounter in Rome. Courted by important gallerists around the world, he would decline their invitations by insisting that his works did not feel like inhabiting their spaces. His eccentric behavior, however, should not be misconstrued: it was art and only art that mattered to him; all the rest was just noise.

De Dominicis entrusted art-making with the capacity to create entities endowed with lifelike properties, if not a life of their own. He felt that a work, once finished, should always surprise him and give back more energy than he had put into making it. Indeed, at the innermost core of his practice lay the belief that works of visual art may be true models for the achievement of bodily immortality. Arguably, by virtue of their characteristic stillness, silence, and materiality, they channel a desire to overcome decay while affirming the primacy of being over negation, entropy, and death.

De Dominicis's concept of immortality is not strictly based upon Aristotle's assumption that we may live forever through our ability to perceive and conceive ideas that exist beyond the temporal boundaries of our lives. Nor is it the prospect of a never-ending life secured by the existence of the eternal soul or the resurrection of the body at the end of time, as is the case with Judaism, Christianity, and Islam. It cannot be clung to by imagining the immortality of the species rather than the individual, with each of us as one part of a long chain of being and reincarnation, a supposition traceable to the Vedas and resurfacing in modern authors such as Schopenhauer and Keats.

For De Dominicis, immortality refers to the possibility that we may stop in time and finally begin to live forever, here and now. The artist's view resonates with the struggles of the eponymous hero of *The Epic of Gilgamesh* (ca. 2600 BCE), the oldest surviving text to narrate a quest for bodily immortality. From the late 1970s onward, Gilgamesh and the Sumerian civilization became a beacon in De Dominicis's life and work. Giovanni Pettinato's essay examines this ancient and key myth, casting fresh light on the artist's unusual interest in it. Jean-Christophe Amman, on the other hand, focuses specifically on a signature work by the artist that features the epic king, in the twinned profiles of Urvasi and Gilgamesh.

Ultimately, however, it was the making of art itself that inspired and kindled De Dominicis's mindset, especially regarding immortality. He found that works of visual art possessed the unique faculty of embodying and encapsulating being, over and above any hint of nonbeing or threat of extinction or corruption. He intuited that the artworks that gave back energy were living entities. Both the maker of the artwork and those standing in its proximity may feel that there is no regress or progression and that time is not an arrow that travels in a single direction. They may instead see time, sub specie aeternitatis, as a creative unfolding.

Even though De Dominicis put forward no formula for an elixir of eternal life, he did not hesitate to imagine what its consequences would be for humanity. His faith in immortality as a concrete mode of human existence, foreshadowed by the timelessness of art, sharpened his sense of his own historical position. He was quick to downplay the hegemony of the so-called art world, observing that "there has never been an 'art world,' just artworks in the world." While De Dominicis as an artist distanced himself from the hubris of contemporary art, creating works that aimed to exist in the world without any mechanisms of reflection and integration with their audience, De Dominicis the man interacted with dealers, critics, and collectors while never deferring to them. Always insisting on complete artistic control, he would occasionally go so far as to do fantastic interviews, such as his memorable appearance on the television show *L'Angelo* (discussed here by Marco Senaldi in his essay on the artist's video works), in which he sat at a floating desk, in midair, painting an invisible work.

Conceding that "to get by, a painter may need to sell his work," the artist was nonetheless far from accepting that artistic value could be measured by monetary value or that contemporary art was inextricable from its market (an attitude that became especially prevalent in the 1980s, justifying the booming art industry). Against this backdrop, De Dominicis's ideas stand apart. In addition to considering interdisciplinary crossovers between different media a "senile fashion" of the day, he was convinced that his era was one "of standardization and a planetary craving for communication" against which only the "anti-ephemeral" major arts of architecture, painting, and sculpture could remain immune.

However, it would be misleading to conclude that De Dominicis's stance harbored nostalgia for some past, long-lost harmony. The often anachronistic imagery in his works is not pure escapism but, rather, emblematic of a quest that led him to investigate the mysterious realm of time and confront the abiding questions that haunt the human species. The artist rejected the illusion of progress and endeavored to envisage the origin of all matter, over and above any predetermined coordinates of time and space; his works not only became the sites of timeless values, they launched an implicit but poignant attack on the twentieth-century doxa of artistic fragmentariness, nomadism, and relativism. De Dominicis's stance challenges our understanding of the visual arts and prompts us to consider that the merits of artists' works may not necessarily be accounted for in historical and art historical terms alone.

The present book is meant to provide an introduction to the art of Gino De Dominicis. It comprises a miscellanea of texts by various authors, along with a selection of the artist's writings, statements, and interviews. Contributions offer a wide range of approaches and insights. They concern De Dominicis's works as much as his public persona and personality, and periodically return to the pivotal aspects of his oeuvre: death, immortality, femininity, and the mysteries of time.

Many of the essays sprang from the Italian context and some have been translated into English for the first time. Andrea Bellini's and Laura Cherubini's texts were written on the occasion of the retrospective exhibition *Gino De Dominicis*, which they co-curated in 2007 at the Centre National d'Art Contemporain de la Villa Arson. Via Cherubini in particular, the reader will find detailed accounts of exhibitions and episodes in De Dominicis's career. The vividness of Italo Tomassoni's essay is the result of an ongoing exchange between the critic and the artist, while Duccio Trombadori writes about the artist with the affectionate candor of a close friend. Germano Celant's characteristically sober prose provides a very useful overview, modeled for the international audience of contemporary art (it originally appeared in *Artforum* in 1986), and Achille Bonito Oliva (writing after the artist's death) blends impressions which go back to the 1960s with new insights, bearing witness to the three decades Celant and Bonito Oliva spent engaged in discussions about that fickle nexus between art and criticism.

It has been rewarding to read the contributions of foreign authors who do not belong to De Dominicis's original milieu. Norman Bryson identifies the important implications of the blend of Western and Eastern pictorial styles in the artist's likenesses, while Richard Shiff perceives the tantalizing consequences of dimensionlessness in De Dominicis's poetics, invoking the work of the American philosopher Charles S. Peirce. The theme of the feminine is addressed by Ombretta Celeste and Octavia Stocker, by way of De Dominicis's "Letter on Immortality." Andrea Cortellessa turns to the metaphysics of de Chirico to better understand De Dominicis. Finally, Creighton Gilbert, momentarily taking leave from his usual area of study, provides not only an original interpretation of some of De Dominicis's works but also foregrounds the artist's peculiar form of Platonism.

Considered both individually and collectively, the texts gathered here allow readers to appreciate the manifold facets of De Dominicis's legacy. Users of the present volume should be advised, however, that there are puzzling inconsistencies in his oeuvre and just as many riddles in his biography and career. They will find that it is open to speculation whether De Dominicis planned and crafted his interviews, possibly even inventing the names of the interviewers themselves. More mystifying still is the "Letter on Immortality," first published in 1970, of which there are different versions reporting conflicting dates as to when it was written. It is unclear whether this should be explained away as a mistake on behalf of the printer or if there is more to it. Indeed, the issue was further complicated by De Dominicis himself who, years later, claimed that he had written the "Letter" in 1966 and that it had been subsequently stolen and published without his consent. Whatever the case, the conflicting provenances of the "Letter" succeed in disturbing our conventional sense of the flow of time. One wonders how it came to be that the English version of the document predates the Italian version. Was the artist deliberately trying to confound us by reversing the chronology? It certainly casts doubt on the reliability of historical accounts while ultimately questioning our presumed ability to identify and sort any kind of record in an intelligible sequence. But the uncertainty acquires yet another connotation as soon as one remembers that it is a text expressing the author's desire for immortality and eternal life.

The possibility, however, that these inconsistencies were willed and astutely facilitated by the artist himself is reinforced when one considers his oeuvre, in particular the subjects and titles of some of his works. Occasionally De Dominicis repurchased his works from collectors, altered them, or even destroyed them; in other cases, he alluded in conversation to pieces that have remained untraceable. Moreover, particularly from the late 1970s onward, he made a number of paintings that he simply named *Untitled* or *With Title*. Works can be difficult to identify given that their themes and images are not always easy to decipher and that De Dominicis discouraged the publication of catalogues of his works: images were seldom reproduced and always under his tight editorial control when they were. Moreover, the same work may be referred to under different titles or even mistaken for another, similar work. For this reason, wherever possible, the works mentioned in the essays have been identified with the title and reference number assigned to them in the first edition of Italo Tomassoni's catalogue raisonné (2011), which is, to date, the most reliable source for the study of De Dominicis's works. Also, in the essay margins, the reader will find plate numbers referring them to the relevant page or pages in the plates section, "All works of art are contemporary."

Nonetheless, the question remains as to what motivated the artist's seeming nonchalance, even disdain, toward the fruits of his own labor. Perhaps we have to bear in mind De Dominicis's belief in the auratic, sacred nature of the visual arts. Conceivably, that belief not only motivated the artist's refusal to promote his works by means of publicity and the dissemination of reproductions but also led him to make a sort of bet on their chances of persisting in time and history. After all, as living entities, as he believed they were, his works could find their own niche in the world without having to depend upon external forces or modes of communication.

Whenever De Dominicis cultivated contradictions and ambivalence, it was never a prank or sheer provocation. With hindsight, a number of his odd, startling behaviors reveal the compelling implications of his own artistic slant. It is noteworthy that for his solo exhibition in 1969 at L'Attico, Rome—arguably his official entry into the international system of contemporary art—he made a poster announcing his own death. Not long after, selected by art historian Maurizio Calvesi for the volume *Segnalazioni Bolaffi 1972*, De Dominicis submitted as his self-portrait a photograph of a disturbed man with a mentally alienated gaze. In 1972, the artist invited Paolo Rosa, a youth with Down syndrome, to become the protagonist of his controversial *Second Solution of Immortality*. Years later, he still talked of Rosa with awe, referring to him as an extraterrestrial—which, for the artist, was the highest compliment.

By frustrating efforts to confine events within linear sequences of cause and effect, by hazarding that the intrinsic qualities of his works would on their own suffice to safeguard their permanence in the world, by standing with the aliens and those all too casually dubbed dysfunctional, and by asserting the existence of other forms of intelligent life in the universe, De Dominicis further confirmed his essential idea that artworks may signal the possibility of a time untouched by death and should therefore be regarded as true models of immortality. He rebelled against finitude by precisely, and paradoxically, vouching for the most finite kind of human endeavor: making works of art.

November 21, 2021

I

IN THE BEGINNING WAS THE IMAGE

A Futura Memoria

Andrea Bellini

He was a work of art—with nothing left over, from the beginning, mysterious and incessantly mystifying and secretizing himself.
Anselm Kiefer

An Inimitable Life

Gino De Dominicis could be considered one of the most emblematic and enigmatic figures in the history of postwar Italian art. In many ways, he is still something of a mystery, surrounded by a legendary aura. Because of his romantic impenetrability, it is difficult for writers to avoid the temptation to speak about his life and inimitable way of living it. Much of what has been written about him, in fact, wanders through meandering streams of mystifying anecdotes. Like a prince out of the distant past, elegant and remote, De Dominicis was surrounded by a kind of court throughout his life that, in true Renaissance style, included beautiful and virginal vestals, artists and scholars, merchants and saltimbanques.

In Rome, a city he loved above all others because it was eternal and impossible, De Dominicis enjoyed entertaining this odd assemblage with extraordinary conjurations. These tricks exalted the figure of the artist, benevolent if at times ferocious, and with them he would hypnotize his adoring public. In return, he demanded and received absolute devotion, unconditional love. Everyone, even people who were in his presence for only half an hour, has a story about him, an endless series of anecdotes and myths, of court intrigues and betrayals. Every aspect of his life, even his death in 1998, is enveloped in an aura of mystery and hagiography. Speaking to those who knew him, one will hear that Gino was a legendary and formidable lover, that he lived only at night like a Gothic count, that he was able to precisely predict the exact day of his own death, that he was planning to buy back all of his works in order to destroy them, and that perhaps he is not dead at all, but rather spends his days lying in the sun of a beautiful island in the South Pacific.

Gino De Dominicis the impostor, the apostate, the prince, and the extraordinary genius, generated a body of fantastic literature about himself, Rome, the Sumerian civilization, the myth of the artist, and the immortality of the flesh,[1] in which many people—including myself—loved to bask. But what has yet to be undertaken is a systematic, in-depth study of his work. There is not a single piece of writing on De Dominicis that does not mention the Sumerians, Gilgamesh, and the immortal gods who, he contended, had founded Rome itself. But to deny the centrality of these real

Epigraph   Anselm Kiefer, "Calling After Gino De Dominicis," in this volume, 101.
1   See Gabriele Guercio, "Arte visiva e immortalità del corpo," in *De Dominicis. Raccolta di scritti sull'opera e l'artista*, ed. Gabriele Guercio (Turin: Umberto Allemandi, 2001), 165–99.

and recurring themes—such as the immortality of the body, the mysteries of creation and human beauty, the unknown regions of the invisible, of the demonic, of occult traditions, of multiple points of view and upside-down perspectives, of the birth of the universe, and even of the ultimate sense and meaning of matter and its very existence—would contradict the work itself, as these themes reappear with extraordinary coherence in his drawings, paintings, and three-dimensional works, as well as in his writings, and represent the nexus and real truth of his poetics.

However, these themes in and of themselves are not enough to explain and describe the meaning and greatness of De Dominicis's work. It would be like trying to explain the importance of Giotto to the history of Western painting from the perspective of the Gospels or from the perspective of the Immaculate Conception and the teachings of Christ. What must interest us about De Dominicis's creative life is the extraordinary and autonomous language that the artist was able to construct, both in his "conceptual" pieces and in his pictorial works.[2] Rather than add to the copious writings about De Dominicis the man, the Sumerians, and the immortality of the body, I will attempt to explain, in brief, how the interplay of these themes engenders the extraordinary semiotic qualities of De Dominicis's paintings.

Three-Dimensional, Two-Dimensional, Homeopathic, and Invisible Works

In critical circles, the role of De Dominicis's style elicits much discussion. First of all, the artist belongs neither to the Arte Povera movement nor to the Transavanguardia, the two best-known Italian movements of the twentieth century's final decades, nor can De Dominicis be placed in any of the international artistic currents in vogue between the sixties and nineties. De Dominicis was and remains an isolated case, a complex personality who always turned his back on the logic of groups and movements, cultivating a superior, noble, and solitary notion of artistic creation. As Anselm Kiefer wrote, De Dominicis "proclaimed something like the Old Testament prophets, something worth far more than any valuable item that can be traded or exchanged: that thing is the possibility of an individual existence (and thus the possibility for every individual)—even outside of the crowd, of history, of time."[3]

The second issue concerns the grounds of his greatness. Critics, art historians, and his devotees in general are primarily divided in two groups: those who consider the first phase of his explorations—the period from the end of the sixties to the end of the seventies, erroneously described by some as "conceptual"—to be the crucial period, and those who consider his second, more "pictorial" phase to be more significant. The first phase includes a series of now famous masterpieces: his two films, *Tentativo di far*

·2 I use the term *conceptual* loosely, and despite the fact that Gino De Dominicis never considered himself a conceptual artist.

3 See Anselm Kiefer, "Calling After Gino De Dominicis," in this volume, 102.

formare dei quadrati invece che dei cerchi attorno ad un sasso che cade nell'acqua (Attempt to Form Squares Instead of Circles Around a Stone Falling into Water) [IT 83] (1969) and *Tentativo di volo* (Attempt to Fly) [IT 84] (1969), and the extraordinary sculpture *Il tempo lo sbaglio lo spazio* (Time, Mistake, Space) [IT 95] (1969), which consists of a human skeleton laid out on the ground with roller skates on its feet, the skeleton of a dog on a leash, and a lance; other pieces from this period are *Lo Zodiaco* (The Zodiac) [IT 105] (1970) and *Seconda soluzione d'immortalità (l'universo è immobile)* (Second Solution of Immortality [The Universe Is Still]) [IT 150] (1972), which was presented at the Venice Biennale in 1972. In this work, a young man with Down syndrome, Paolo Rosa, sat in a corner facing an invisible cube, a rubber ball suspended at the moment before bouncing, and a stone suspended before moving.

The second period is comprised of a smaller number of drawings and paintings, created over the course of two decades on wood, paper, and, in a few cases, canvas, that on the one hand extend and supplement the iconographic and thematic motifs of the previous period (the immortality of the body, beauty, esotericism, etc.), and on the other, reveal a new De Dominicis, trying in various ways to surpass even himself.

Which is his most interesting and fruitful period? In reality this is a false dichotomy: the act of dividing his work into two distinct periods and attributing a qualitative ranking to them is a gesture that has little bearing on the understanding of his creative trajectory, a trajectory that instead must be read as a complete act with a precise development. The artist himself, referring to his own work, said: "In the world there are—and have only ever been—two- or three-dimensional works, and some invisible works by Gino De Dominicis."[4] making it clear that he considered these diverse elements to be part of a single work. But within this progression, one can identify a specific turning point that provokes further inquiry.

In the latter half of the seventies, after creating his first series of masterpieces, De Dominicis began to develop a certain diffidence and dissatisfaction regarding the marketplace of conceptual and behavioral artists who filled biennials and exhibitions worldwide. Aristocratic, refined spirit that he was—he was almost conservative—he felt personally offended by the fact that girls had begun wearing jeans, in the American style. De Dominicis did not believe in "progress" in art, nor did he believe in "creative" critics who drew attention and space away from artworks, nor in nomadic, traveling artists, nor even in big exhibitions—in 1982, he famously refused an invitation to Documenta 7 in Kassel. Most of all, this curious and distant Italian artist never believed in Conceptualism; in fact, he poked fun at it in several interviews, seeing it as an overly facile way to fill shows and museums with objects that he did not consider to be real artworks. The sheer abundance and context of late sixties Conceptualism prompted many, including De Dominicis, to return to painting. Although De Dominicis had his first solo shows of paintings in 1964 and

1967,[5] during this second phase, painting became a path toward an even more solitary, refined, and elevated form than that which had preceded it. It is no coincidence that, in this period, the artist turned his back on some of his own works from the seventies, such as the sculpture *Madonna che ride* (Laughing Madonna) [IT 152] (1972) (which he destroyed) and *Mozzarella in carrozza* (Mozzarella in a Carriage) [IT 69] (1970),[6] which he described as a "homeopathic" work, or, in other words, a work that criticizes conceptual modes by recreating them.[7] For De Dominicis, painting became the thing that distinguished art from that which is not art.

26

4

In the Beginning Was the Image

Still hidden away and little known, to some extent by his own volition, the corpus of De Dominicis's pictorial works presents itself to us as one of the most extraordinary and enigmatic trajectories in Italian and European painting from the second half of the twentieth century. His painting style is meticulous and extremely reasoned, the fruit of constant concentration. In painting as in life, De Dominicis loved conjuring tricks, and like any good magician, he wanted to surprise himself most of all. The image must always be an epiphany; it must have a charismatic value and become a visible and archetypal fragment of an invisible universe, of a separate existence. What makes this series of works absolutely relevant is the artist's ability, with each new work, to accomplish a new pictorial inventiveness, a never-before-seen solution.

His paintings are fundamentally figurative and created from a few basic elements, such as tempera and pencil on board. They allude to a mysterious, archaic, and impenetrable condition of the human image. Urvasi and Gilgamesh, men with long noses, women-proboscises, solemn figures, or even giant shadows appear across diverse materials and media. The physiognomies of these solemn and unfathomable figures undergo strange compressions: elongated noses, eyes, mouths, and eyebrows become fine fissures, imbuing these faces with an extremely sweet and dreamy expression, and an interiorized accent that becomes the recurring element of all these works. Physical deformities—tiny forklike hands, huge, beaklike crania and noses, short arms that are out of proportion with the torso and legs—imbue these hieratic figures with the quality of caricature and grotesque, which is instilled with a multiplicity of psychic implications for which it is impossible to provide a single, definitive meaning. The images represent an autonomous, distant "elsewhere," with its own life, resistant to any univocal, standardized reading. De Dominicis, in fact, places us before his own cult of initiation, a world filled with strange alchemical and religious symbols—the cross, the pyramids, stars, geometric figures, and a series of symbols taken

5   For the 1964 show, see Laura Cherubini, "Perfect Living Object," in this volume, 40; for the Ancona show, see G. M. Farroni, "I Miti d'oggi nella pittura del giovane De Dominicis," in *La Voce Adriatica* (Ancona), May 10, 1967, reprinted in *De Dominicis. Raccolta*, ed. Guercio, 103–4.

6   Editor's note: *Mozzarella in carrozza* (literally, "mozzarella in a carriage") is a famous Italian dish made from a piece of mozzarella put between slices of bread and fried.

7   See Cherubini, "Perfect Living Object," 38–39.

out of their original contexts to be placed in the private and exclusive language of the artist. De Dominicis has written: "People must see, not know, must recognize the work of art for what it is and accept its effects."[8] This very impenetrability assures the work's timelessness and immortality; according to De Dominicis, art is not communication but creation, magic, and mystery, rendering its spectator superfluous. The basic assumption, in his work, is that there is no common, codified, and regulated language through which the artist communicates with others, nor should there be.

The work presents itself as an autonomous fact, as an ahistorical, creative, immortal product. Symbols, within De Dominicis's system of signs, cannot and must not correspond immediately with something in the world, but rather lie in the mythical substratum that the artist molds and reinvents at his pleasure, thus giving us the suggestion of, and even the hope for, immortality. Gino De Dominicis's artistic path proceeds under the banner of this titanic and solitary attempt to find a real and circumstantial nexus between the language of art and the undercurrents of a primordial, ahistorical, and infinite energy. In the context of this quest, painting performs a primary and extraordinary function, reaffirming the centrality of the artist as a demiurge.

Translated by Marina Harss
This essay was published in Italian, French, and English in a special issue of *Flash Art International* (June 2007): 14–31. This issue served as the catalogue for De Dominicis's solo exhibition curated by Andrea Bellini and Laura Cherubini at the Centre National d'Art Contemporain de la Villa Arson, Nice (June 29–October 7, 2007), Fondazione Merz, Turin (November 8, 2007–January 6, 2008), and MoMA PS1, New York (October 19, 2008–February 9, 2009).

8   Editor's note: No citation has been provided for this statement; however, the quote is very similar to a statement by Gino De Dominicis reported in a 1990 essay by Agnes Kohlmeyer, "Vedere e non sapere," in *De Dominicis. Scritti sull'opera e riflessioni dell'artista*, ed. Gabriele Guercio, 2nd rev. ed. (Turin: Umberto Allemandi, 2014), 201.

Art to the Power N

Germano Celant

In the West today, one of the few kinds of faith in immortality that remains vital is faith in art. Despite the view of certain artists and art movements as phantoms of significance, as the emperor's new clothes, art is generally viewed as something of great cultural value that will still be here when things contemporaneous with it are gone. This is not to disparage other sorts of artifacts but rather to speak of art as a deliberate choice of a vision whose life is lived not only through whatever renown it achieves or does not achieve when new but also through the renown realized long after its creator and original context have vanished. Artists who produce the unprecedented, who bring it into being for the future, resist classification—what one says about their work can be "accurate" in the context of the present but can become more and more "inaccurate" with the passage of the years. To understand such art fully, it would be necessary to live through all the cultures of the past millennia. Failing that, we can start by recognizing that art's undertakings bear witness to fragments of truths that change in both geography and time, incarnating vast extremes without actually bringing them within reach.

In the contemporary moment of crisis, in which we live with the prospect of decline or worse, the issue of death is ubiquitous—in art, in politics, in medicine, in science, in philosophy. One reason for its strong presence in the world of art is the anguish developing among artists from no longer having a role, from being no longer themselves, but lost. Since 1966, Gino De Dominicis has investigated art as a witness to death and immortality, and death and immortality as a witness to art. He began by posing the problem of verifying the very existence of things:

> *I don't think that things exist as such. A glass, a man, a hen, for example, are not really a glass, a man, or a hen but only the substantiation for the possibility of the existence of a glass, a man, or a hen. To truly exist, things would have to be eternal, immortal. Only in that way would they be not simply substantiations of certain possibilities but truly things.*[1]

In a work of his from 1970, the face and hands of a wristwatch are replaced by a mirror so that the wearer who consults it sees his or her own face where usually the passage of time is recorded (*Orologio* [Watch] [IT 113] [1970]). Here, one can literally see oneself aging. Beauty is the shadow of death, not in a romantic sense—both death and beauty are too cruel for that—but in a literal sense. Watching beauty disappear is watching it die. Beauty in all ancient and modern arts is a fleeting image. If "the 'history of beauty' might

17

---

[1] Gino De Dominicis, statement written in Ancona in 1966, and published in the catalogue for a show of the artist's work at L'Attico, Rome, November 1969. Editor's note: See Gino De Dominicis, "Letter on Immortality," in this volume, 59, 62.

be called the 'history of the judgments of those nearby and living on those distant and dead,'"[2] then the dead, to the extent that they have partaken of beauty, live on in the minds and eyes of those alive. De Dominicis, like the film director Ingmar Bergman, attempts continually to "touch" death and beauty, to understand these dynamics of existence in the moment they are realized, to step outside a view of time tied to our sense of the human body (just as our view of pictures may be subliminally tied to our sense of human scale) and into a different dimension, to fly with time instead of being run by it. "By fixing himself in time at an age he chooses and interrupting the process of aging, man would break the spell cast by the most mysterious dimension prevailing in the universe; and this would be the first step toward the possibility of a greater understanding of life."[3] All De Dominicis's work has tried, in one way or another, to visualize this impossible stopping of time, or flying with time, both of them paradoxical events, usually confined within the realm of the nonphysical and immaterial.

The "figures" of immortality and death emerge clearly in De Dominicis's recurring references to the story of Gilgamesh, the mythical ancient Mesopotamian king who tried to disentangle death from life by seeking the herb of eternal life. This Sumerian of the city of Uruk, two-thirds divine and one-third human, was born predestined to confront the immortal Utnapishtim, a progenitor of humanity (Utnapishtim and his wife alone survived the flood, in the Babylonian version of that myth). Gilgamesh's epic was probably written in the third millennium BCE, and despite his failure to find the herb of eternal life, to De Dominicis he is a symbolic figure, representing a being who crosses the bridge between two journeys—the journey of life and the journey of death. In addition, Gilgamesh epitomizes the seeker for the impossible goal—a metaphysical act.

Thus in *Senza titolo (Urvasi e Gilgamesh)* (Untitled [Urvasi and Gilgamesh]) [IT 200] (1979–80), originally a photographic work but recreated since in a variety of forms, the artist places two profiles in silhouette facing each other, one connoting Gilgamesh, one Urvasi, a goddess of beauty from the Hindu Vedas. Why Urvasi, a Hindu goddess? Like Beatrice and Laura for Dante and Petrarch, like Eurydice and Juliet for Orpheus and Romeo—in each case, the female figure precedes the male into the other world, accompanying him in the celestial journey—she is in touch with death. By setting the two shadow figures in the form of a "figure and ground illusion," De Dominicis establishes an osmosis between two different energies, representing two different times, genders, symbols, cultures, and histories. In the space between the two profiles, the space whose shape their outlines define, is a landscape image of the type that nineteenth-century travelers brought back from Egypt. It includes a pyramid—a concrete example of the constructions humans make around the idea of death, and the waiting room for a future life—and a flying disk. Between the two figures from myth, then, lie more myths, one historic, one futuristic, making

2   Gino De Dominicis, statement for a show at the Schema gallery, Florence, November 1972.
3   De Dominicis, "Letter on Immortality," 61, 64.

possible an infinite suspension. For his solo show at L'Attico, Rome, in November 1969, De Dominicis had posters printed in the form of an obituary that announced his death (*Manifesto mortuario* [Necrology (Mortuary Poster)] [IT 73] [1969]). And on the back of a photograph of himself from this period he wrote, "Gino De Dominicis was born in 1947 but no longer truly exists, being only an instrument of nature, which verifies certain appropriate possibilities through him." By "dying," De Dominicis set in motion a process of release from the concepts of fate and destiny—from their hideous shaping—and also revealed the anguish we feel about the inevitability of death. He began to develop an illuminated thought. To him, the artist, like Gilgamesh, stands opposed to predetermination in life and thus is privileged with the possibility of immortality. This is the symbolic meaning of what the artist represents to De Dominicis; the reality with which he identifies is the dandy, who also opposes the indiscriminate egalitarianism of death, which comes to all, by aestheticizing his own self in life. (Unlike death, immortality is not democratic—contrary to Christian culture's idea of the afterlife—but rather is the privilege of a caste, one member of which is the artist.) The artist can stage the impossible, and thus, in 1969, both ironically and seriously, De Dominicis began an attempt to fly, jumping off a low rock and waving his arms as if they were wings (*Tentativo di volo* [Attempt to Fly] [IT 84] [1969]); the idea of the piece was to make this attempt every day and later to teach the movement to his children, who would then teach their children, until one of his descendants would actually be able to take off. In another work from the same year, videotaped along with the flight piece, he threw a stone into a lake, trying to make square instead of circular ripples (*Tentativo di far formare dei quadrati invece che dei cerchi attorno ad un sasso che cade nell'acqua* [Attempt to Form Squares Instead of Circles Around a Stone Falling into Water] [IT 83] [1969]); and in yet another he built an "invisible" cube, pyramid, and cylinder, simply by marking their outlines on the floor.

Having died, De Dominicis was able to be reborn, and to declare his reappearance as an artist. A materialist might find all this rather delusional, or might assume that De Dominicis belonged in a spiritual, idealistic fold. In fact, his choices were both practical and enlightened, and had a vital relationship to contemporary art. The years 1966 to 1969, the period preceding De Dominicis's "death" and "birth," had seen what might almost be called a "conceptual" vertigo in art, a journey that at times seemed bound for a black hole, for art's self-extinction. In keeping with the group therapy to which society was submitting itself at the time and following Ludwig Wittgenstein, the artists of the "neo-Renaissance" forced themselves to justify every aspect of their role and work. What mattered in the art of these years was the discussion and enunciation of meanings. This X-ray force, which gained its energy from compulsive self-searching, had taken art to science, philosophy, and the politics of communication, to a country without images, a country whose existence was entrusted to words and possessed by the ecstasy of ideas. This was the result of passion but it also created an imbalance, a form of hara-kiri that ripped into the body of art as a visual practice in order to express its breath and voice—the word.

De Dominicis shared this same exorcism, living out the anguish of the reduction of the image in art to language—living out its possible death. He reacted by seeking not a return to the ways things were before, but a rebirth through a reduction of the word to image, instead of the other way around. Drawing a visual logic from words, he proposed them in nonverbal terms, as vision; to him, written and spoken terms were not to be thought of as independent of sight. In April 1970, again at L'Attico, he exhibited the zodiac (*Lo Zodiaco* [The Zodiac] [IT 105]), making the astrological signs material: the sign of Virgo was documented by a young girl, Leo by a real lion in a cage, Taurus by a live bull, Pisces by two dead fish lying on the floor, and so on. This crystallization of astrological signs into concrete images created a metaphysical suspension, a realization that a terrestrial constellation could embody magical forces. In November of that year, in the same space, he illustrated the term "mozzarella in carrozza" (the name of an Italian cheese dish) by setting a mozzarella cheese in the back seat of an old-fashioned *carrozza* or carriage (*Mozzarella in carrozza* [Mozzarella in a Carriage] [IT 69] [1968–69]). In 1971, he installed speakers in the empty space of L'Attico and broadcast a high-volume laugh; the invitation read *"D'io,"* a play on the Italian words for "God" and "of I." (*D'io* [Of I, God] [IT 127–28]). Through operations such as these, he gave embodiment to concepts and made physical the metaphysical, siting it in time and place. In these works, words escape their usual meanings, and art reveals the marvelous in them. If thought thinks images, images can also see thought. De Dominicis thus passed the word to the senses.

If words have a place in De Dominicis's work as an event of the imagination, so the spheres of entities thought to be unthinkable are real to him, and capable of being made perceptible and visible through a symbolic art. Fundamentally, the issue is that of making visible the inaccessible, giving it a point of reference. In 1972, at the Venice Biennale, having the preceding winter sent out a Christmas card that announced, "Gino De Dominicis wishes everyone immortality of the body," the artist presented *Seconda soluzione d'immortalità (l'universo è immobile)* (Second Solution of Immortality [The Universe Is Still]) [IT 150], in which a young man with Down syndrome sat on a chair in a corner facing one of De Dominicis's invisible cubes, a ball placed on the floor and labeled "rubber ball (falling from a height of two meters) in the moment right before bouncing back," and a rock labeled "waiting for a random one-directional molecular movement that could generate a spontaneous movement of material." In the same room sat twins, one behind a table in the symbolic role of the lecturer, the other—sitting among the chairs that were also included in the piece—representing the public. The twins connoted the sinister part of life. In some ancient cultures, twins were killed because their doubling was thought to represent something "unnatural," bad luck. They were sometimes associated with the devil, the dark, the unknown, the unthinkable that must be eliminated. Twins today are still mysterious in some ways, but they are no longer eliminated from culture. The man with Down syndrome, however, has much less social place. He represents the unthinkable, not only in ancient cultures, but also in ours. To De Dominicis, he exemplifies a distant realm of the mind, a bridge between the thinkable and the unthinkable. If we accept De Dominicis's view of art as the site of the unthinkable, the inexpressible, and also as the site upon which one can move these elements toward the thinkable and expressible, then the Down syndrome youth, whose presence upset much of the press— its defenses against such images led it to gauge the situation inaccurately as a manipulation—represented the autonomy of a different energy between life and death. To De Dominicis, the presentation in Venice concealed a revolution: by showing people and things on an unpredictable, uncontrollable course, he symbolized a way of thinking for which the culture has little framework, and showed it as a powerful potential force of internal energy. "If everyone," he wrote, "could imagine and desire their own salvation ... the 'second principle of thermodynamics' would no longer be valid, because it would be contradicted by the behavior of an organism that can project, without distraction (entropy), its own eternal condition as an 'isolated system.'"[4]

De Dominicis, in his work from 1972 through 1979, referred constantly to the territory of the "unthought of." In 1973, at the Lucio Amelio gallery, Naples, he showed a sculpture of a laughing Madonna, on a six-foot-high wooden base (*Madonna che ride* [Laughing Madonna] [IT 152]). She smiles, in De Dominicis's thinking, because, through her Assumption into heaven, she has been able to die without loss of her body. In 1975, for a show at the Galleria Lucrezia De Domizio in Pescara, the artist sent out announcements that "reserved entry to animals"; animals again, of course, are symbols of the mystery of thinking, of a framework of thought for which we don't have much of a key. In 1977, at the Incontri Internazionali d'Arte, in Rome, De Dominicis worked the symbolic miracle of making a person vanish. For a show beginning on January 14, 1977, at the Pio Monti gallery, Rome, he exhibited a large boulder inside an "invisible pyramid" (*Particolare 1967/69/77* [Particular 1967/69/77] [IT 187]) marked on the floor, and with a vertically suspended lance, a red ball, and a pair of delicate blue glass vases resting on or near it; for a show on January 14, 1978, in the same space, he exhibited exactly the same piece, which was not only an amalgamation of a number of his earlier works, thus keeping them alive, but specifically symbolized, because of its repetition in space and in time, the defeat of art's death. Doing the piece twice prevented it from aging and proved its ubiquity.

In 1979, at the Mario Pieroni gallery in Rome, he presented invisible statues—for example, by hanging a straw hat at about body height above a pair of slippers on a pedestal and leaving empty the space between (*Senza titolo [Statua invisibile]* [Untitled (Invisible Statue)] [IT 194–98]). The disappearance of the body is testimony to De Dominicis's interest in being "outside" the world—without gravity, a phantom, a shadow, in interplay be-

26

29

4   Gino De Dominicis, statement, Incontri Internazionali d'Arte, Rome, 1972. Editor's note: See Miriam Mirolla, "Immortality," in this volume, 74.

tween the real and the unreal. In a large untitled painting by De Dominicis from 1980, in tempera and plaster on board, two mysterious figures, again black silhouettes, watch Earth from somewhere in space. The vision of these beings (artists?) outside the world, exiled within the boundaries of the empyrean, flows from a sphere that has nothing above it to contain it. Their privileged placement, with all ties dissolved, is rooted in displacement. In 1982, in a show at the Galleria Sprovieri, Rome, De Dominicis set a metal outline of the profiles of Urvasi and Gilgamesh in an open window looking out onto the Piazza del Popolo (Urvasi and Gilgamesh [IT 204]). Inside the room, a constructed wall held a simple lens; looking through into a dimly lit space, the viewer could make out a painting of a large female head, an image based on a Sumerian sculpture from Uruk, and dating from the fourth millennium BCE (*Immagine della dea sumera Warka* [Image of the Sumerian Goddess Warka] [IT 189] [1977–83]). The eye sockets of the sculpture are hollow; De Dominicis gave the head contemporary life by adding bright eyes. One had the impression of having stumbled onto a sacred site, almost a crypt, the reliquary of an ancient culture. The way one saw the piece, through a hole in the wall, was not voyeuristic (despite the connection to Marcel Duchamp's libidinous *Étant donnés*, 1946–66); rather, it reflected the mystery of an ancient icon brought to light out of the dark obscurity of history. This rediscovery of an "elsewhere" addressed the fracture, caused millennia ago, between a culture of the marvelous and the Judeo-Christian civilization that conquered it. With this exhibition, De Dominicis made it clear that he had chosen his symbolic roots in the same way as he chose his subjects, the basic truths of death and life. Sumer was among the first complex civilizations, a basis for civilizations to follow. Its protagonists were warriors, and a 1983 painting by De Dominicis shows a one-eyed warrior whose red lance, glowing golden at the top, spreads a golden aura around his head, at the same time that it pierces a block of material of the same black that forms his own body (*Senza titolo* [Untitled] [IT 245]). This cyclopean figure is surely to be identified with De Dominicis—his face recalls the artist's profile. The reinforcement or affirmation here of the artist's role as a warrior is developed further in the large paintings that De Dominicis has been working on since 1983, and which he exhibited at the Galleria Emilio Mazzoli, Modena, earlier this year. Mainly stylized, long-nosed faces, again recalling the artist's own, they are very dark, often painted in blacks; like shrouds, these paintings are metaphors for an evolution from one state to another. The figures' long noses act to establish their roles as witnesses to invisible, immaterial forces. A sensorial organ like the eye, the nose here is hypersensitive, suggesting a kind of clairvoyance of the senses.

At times, De Dominicis's figures hold and observe sign-like forms, in particular one made up of symbols such as the Christian cross, the Greek cross, the swastika, and the Saint Andrew's cross, among others. This pattern of interweaving signs stands for a cosmos in which many cultures and perspectives, mystical and pagan, spiritual and solar, converge. The complex configuration, which De Dominicis designed in 1970, reappears in yellow—watched by the usual black witness, outlined in white and holding a single white cross—in a large canvas that formed part of a work shown at the Museo di Capodimonte, Naples, in a 1986 exhibition curated by Lia Rumma. On a wide band of blue that crossed the floor diagonally lay a rock, painted red, and the white-painted skeleton of a man on roller skates, holding a leash, which led to the white-painted skeleton of a dog.[5] (These two skeletons, in their unpainted state, were the parts of a work by the artist in 1969.) Two tall lances, colored black and yellow, stood vertically on their points within the blue stripe, while a third, in white, stood on the red rock. As in all of De Dominicis's previous works with lances, they stood "magically" erect, with no visible support. Behind and convergent with this arrangement was the canvas, also apparently freestanding, also on a diagonal, and also a broad expanse of blue with motifs in black, white, and yellow.

Death here was not static but dynamic; the skeleton figure was on the run—on skates. Yet his or her connection to the dog, its leash painted in black, served to underline the inevitability and faithfulness of death. The skeleton—diagonally across from the black-painted witness in the painting, and touching with one hand the black lance, thus possessing knowledge—was passing over the threshold between the known and the unknown, yet this character was still here, his lance held in balance. At the center of the composition was the red stone, pierced by the aerial lightness of the white lance. It was the Kaaba of creativity, the site of maximum concentration of the force and energy from which all intellectual and visual movement spring. Finally, the yellow lance, in an alchemic triad with the other lances, created a third moment in the transformation the work described, a hot, ardent moment, which cut across the blue ground like the sun. The color of light and gold is the color of transmutation. It is the force that allows communication in the cosmos of the material and immaterial.

The continuous movement in this work between horizontal and vertical, between second and nth dimension, served to show that the worlds described here—the worldly one below, the empyreal one above— are in reality one world. Its two flat surfaces touched at their vertex, forming a pluridimensional triangle. In addition to invoking the power of the alchemic and cabalistic number three, the triangle particularized the manner in which De Dominicis's work tends toward the harmony of opposites—past and future, accessible and inaccessible, surface and volume, open and secret, earthly and celestial. In a triangle, such oppositions cannot be total; the elements of this geometric figure are already set in tension, as if secretly attracted. In the Naples work, then, the real did not oppose the imaginary— each resolved the other. And this interweaving of parts suggested a further reality in which the thinkable and the unthinkable, life and death, dance together, as they really do.

This essay was originally published as "Art to the Power N: Vita brevis, ars longa, Gino De Dominicis" in *Artforum* 25, no. 4 (December 1986): 100–106.

5   Editor's note: See the installation view on p. 270.

The Gino De Dominicis Affair

Italo Tomassoni

The Gino De Dominicis affair was above all an enigma—a problematic situation. It is inevitable to wonder why this has finally surfaced, why the world of culture, after twenty years—despite the artist's unwillingness to cooperate and allow any interference with his practice—has decided to disclose information about his work and why several international observers are taking part. There may be many reasons, but there is only one explanation: over the years, Gino De Dominicis has made several memorable works that are outside or ahead of time. When a truly innovative artist appears, we must acknowledge from the very start that no one is able to penetrate the meaning of his work. Because this innovator overturns all our habits of perception; he establishes his own codes of reading, writing, and conduct; he pushes the world toward the movement of radical representational thinking, which is incompatible with the media precisely because of its radicalism. His art is defined by these full-speed oscillations that are so intense that, at best, the media can only misinterpret it.

This is what happened at the 1972 Venice Biennale. The only one to acknowledge the emblematic stature of Gino De Dominicis's work *Seconda soluzione d'immortalità (l'universo è immobile)* (Second Solution of Immortality [The Universe is Still]) [IT 150] was the poet Eugenio Montale, who discussed it in his Nobel Laureate lecture delivered some years later to the Swedish Academy, on December 12, 1975. Montale voiced his opposition to the military's forced closure of the gallery where De Dominicis's work was displayed and drew a connection between the artist's form of artistic expression and those practiced by Caravaggio and Rembrandt.

Heedless of the "art world," De Dominicis has developed a sense of cultural obscurantism and mourning, choosing not to integrate himself and his work into this growing "system." He does not trust *mass media* because art is the *mass medium* par excellence. While the world constructed itself according to the mechanical reproduction of images, he stated: "it is a mistake to put the name of the artist under the photographic documentation of a work of art. It is the name of the photographer who took the picture that should be there."[1] Since he did not accept photography as a means of documentation or publicity, he avoided building his work's history through catalogues and monographs.

Through his defiance of time, De Dominicis shows that the only way to be contemporary is to be free to create what is modern, rather than producing elaborations of the modern. And so, by accepting risks and hazards and practicing the unknown and the ungraspable alongside irony and adventure, he escapes the moralism of transgression. He breaks the boredom of the academy of newness and through a mastery of every artistic

1   See Gino De Dominicis, "Maxims, 1969–1996," in this volume, 93.

language, progresses with full autonomy, taking surprising steps and turns through suspended men, laughing Madonnas, paintings, drawings, apparitions, and dissolutions. In the era of postwar art, he is not coerced into participating in the tradition of newness. He does not play the positioning game that is typical of neo-avant-garde tactical maneuvers; rather, he strategically aims far and high. His works, despite being connected to each other as if they constitute a unified whole, each have their own respective formal innovations and autonomous universe. This is an exceptional fact, given their variety and number. When Italian art took its inevitable first steps in the international scene in the late sixties, Gino De Dominicis was elsewhere. As soon as he sensed that art was functioning as a kind of supplement, he avoided conformity and restored complexity to history through his art. In 1969 he took the art world by surprise and stirred up a debate on the great existential themes; he invented a new language made up of metaphysical and yet living and immobile people; long, obstinate, and complex titles; objects taken out of their temporal dimension; enigmatic drawings, etc., and shifted the focus away from the issue of space toward that of time, combining it with the themes of death and myth. He never, not even indirectly, took part in the argument about whether creativity was mostly driven by the rules of political economics; he entered history through the back door. In crossing these regal gates, he ventured into the uncharted territories of lost civilizations and found his home in a cosmic machine where he got to know the enchantment of a pre-Homeric vision, thus drawing on a different constellation of creation. In doing so, his freedom grew without limit because he drank from the headwaters giving rise to change without being an image of change itself. He paid no attention to the frantic activism surrounding him and came to the terrifying realization of art's finitude in complete solitude. A great nondenominational priest installed in an immobile space, as eternal and silent as genitality, he grasped Sumerian civilization. He recreated the zodiac (*Lo Zodiaco* [The Zodiac] [IT 105] [1970]) by materializing it with the splendor of an ecstatic universal art, like the eighth wonder of the world. He suspended human figures in the limbo of neutralized gravity; he vibrantly turned toward the origin of man's legend by making works that looked back on the first hero-artist in history with a language that was never literary.

    In 1964 he was in Rome. For over twenty years, nobody knew where he lived or worked; the only addresses he had left around were of hotels in the city center. The notorious impossibility of tracking him down, which still characterizes him, adds to the shadowy aura of quasi-novelistic mystery surrounding him. His coded playing with identity is ritualized, allowing us to rethink the repetition of gestures, habits, and words as false revelations that maintain the secret. In doing so, what comes into play is a way of life that is linked with the workings of thought, a way of life that raises the unlimited question of culture and which appeals to complexity. According to his perspective, Rome is one of those placeless places where one gets closer to the category of the impossible through art. This has nothing to do

15

with the idea of life as art. It is a sort of shocking and scathing anarchy at best, an obfuscation of those social conventions whose purpose is to dispossess the ego. Rather, it is a statement about the limitlessness of thought through the urgency of art. Just like clothing that enciphers an identity in a mask, his public persona has remained basically unaltered since his first portraits appeared in the 1960s. In those, he evoked the Count of Saint Germain: in 1970 he brought this man up directly to state that he is not him (*Io non sono il conte di Saint Germain* [I Am Not the Count of Saint Germain] [IT 112] [1970]), the count about whom Voltaire wrote, saying he had encountered him fifty years after his first meeting and found that he looked identical. Those who try to pin down De Dominicis fail; his demeanor changes like the images in a kaleidoscope and is all the more ungraspable for those who have tried to imitate him.

At the age of seventeen he had his first exhibition in Ancona, the city where he was born in 1947. After a few years spent traveling, he settled down in Rome, where, in 1969, he showed works made in the previous years and published his "Letter on Immortality." In 1972 the Venice Biennale invited him to show his works in a large room of his own. At Rome's *Contemporanea* (1973), he dismantled his exhibition after one day and left the space empty. At the Kunstverein in Munich, in 1971, he did not identify with the group of artists with whom he was included without his consultation and therefore chose not to show any work; he tore off the catalogue page documenting his inclusion and retitled the exhibition, hanging this on the wall in place of his work. In 1978 he was once again invited to show at the Venice Biennale; in 1980 he was at the Beaubourg in Paris with a dedicated room. He declined the invitation to Documenta in Kassel in 1982. He won the International Prize of the Paris Biennial (1985). In 1986 he had a solo exhibition at the Capodimonte Museum in Naples. For nearly twenty years he has exclusively shown works in solo exhibitions in Rome. Over the years, he has been called an "art genius," "outlaw," "self-proclaimed artist," and "the Scarlet Pimpernel of the art world."

The Italian anagrams that come from rearranging the letters of his name (*Godi! Cinsi Domine* and *Godi! Cinsi Demoni*, literally, "Enjoy! I encircled, lord" and "Enjoy! I encircled demons"), besides the exhortation to take pleasure in such language games, allow us to consider him as an artist with an aura of both sanctity and damnation, equally partaking in divine and terrestrial natures. He is the one contemporary painter for whom we can envision a romantic destiny; in the era of art's social climbers, one can describe him through the figure of Kean, found in Dumas's play of the same name: *désordre et génie*, unruliness and genius. This mixture of sanctity and damnation cannot be found in any other European artist since Rimbaud. When France presented him with an award at Paris City Hall, he was blessed. When he triggered the machine of inquisition and was tried for showing a "mongoloid" at the Venice Biennale, thus pushing art into "criminal" territory, he was profane. This radical and extreme act leaves an indelible mark on twentieth-century art. In the media, the innumerable commentaries coming from all over the world and the most disparate observers, including the Vatican City newspaper *L'Osservatore Romano*, ranged from cultural eclecticism to regime-like moralism. There are several anecdotes about his life, most of which are based on stories in the oral tradition, even though he was known to always refuse interviews. This is why a history of Gino De Dominicis always risks contradicting itself; what is verified about him does not bear verisimilitude, and often what appears to be true is not always verified.

A history rooted in endless conjectures is thus the opposite of what historiography is about. He actively reacts, for example, to the history of religions as well as the sciences. In a polemical article titled "We Will Not Achieve Immortality," scientist A. M. Liguori (*Corriere della Sera*, November 4, 1972) criticized De Dominicis for basing one of his arguments for immortality on the second law of thermodynamics. De Dominicis responded to this by organizing a cocktail party at Palazzo Taverna in Rome where he presented, among other things, a text objecting to the scientist's dogmatic stance.

> *If everyone could imagine and desire their own salvation, the preservation of their body for eternity, that would mean that finally there would be no mental dispersion (entropy). Therefore, the "second principle of thermodynamics" would no longer be valid, because it would be contradicted by the behavior of an organism that can project, without distraction (entropy), its own eternal condition as an "isolated system."*[2]

Later, the *Philosophical Magazine* (January 1985) acknowledged De Dominicis for leading to some discoveries in the field of the deflection of light in crystals. In the semantic deluge of our years, De Dominicis left some indelible signs. To contemporaneity, which is defined by an absence of enlightenment, he offers the intuition of a time for the immortality of bodies: a dream stemming from a kind of society that had imagined the prototype of the hero-artist. From his observation deck in Rome, De Dominicis peruses immortality with a dusty telescope and a foretelling, ironic, and disenchanted eye to capture its meaning as well as to shock his own times by drawing, once again, upon the striking power of illusion. This angelic gnosis bathes him in a kind of gloomy and skeptical light that has nothing to do with the Enlightenment and is not even concerned with the Romantic idea, which found its utmost embodiment in modern systems. This adherence to the mobility of things is the reason why, during these journeys into "myth," the sense of his work never crystallizes into a formal repertoire. He is mercurial by vocation, an ethnocentric and stationary globetrotter. One of the mysteries of his art is found in its ability to bring together the maximum of intellectual insight and the maximum of formal mobility by using objects, figures, and materials from the world to conjure up an ever-changing and surprising rhapsody. This game of making art spin at breakneck speed around several points of irradiation hinges on verticality, a primarily temporal verticality, which, through its being, conveys an axis of immortality too.

2   See Miriam Mirolla, "Immortality," in this volume, 74.

The immortality of the soul is postulated by many religions. Sumerians, for whom God is physical and immortal, are the only ones who postulate the immortality of the body. De Dominicis came across this mysterious civilization from the Near East whose main ideas have been subject to misinterpretation after its fall, and observed that Sumerian thoughts and works coincided with his own. It is by letting himself drift away with this thinking that De Dominicis hovers above the culture of his own era, contracting space and time until they are turned into immobile, physical concepts; giving freedom to figures that are as charming as hallucinations, almost like extraterrestrials that exist here and now as contemporaries or beings that were revived by a miracle of entropy, eternally sent back to the immanence of a previous life or a life that is constantly about to begin. No time separates us and no bond ties us to that image which, yesterday as today, from men sitting on "Chairs" (*Senza titolo [Immortalità]* [Untitled (Immortality)] [IT 124] [1971] and *Sospensione temporale* [Suspended Time] [IT 125] [1972]) to the Sumerian god, from the "Mongoloid" to the "Twins" (*Senza titolo [I gemelli]* [The Twins] [IT 173] [1973]), from the figures of the zodiac to Gilgamesh, materializes before our eyes, emerging from a time that is not a history. In making works such as the *Portrait of C. C. G.*, the *Madonna che ride* (Laughing Madonna) [IT 152] (1972), the untitled drawing dated 1970 (*Senza titolo* [Untitled] [IT 121]), the large panel including the Sphinx, the Tibetan woman, the Maja, the Madonna, and the Sumerian woman, he re-proposes women, female figures in art, as archetypes.[3] The "Letter on Immortality" is also a letter addressed to a mysterious woman:

> *Dear …*
>
> *I don't think that things exist as such … To truly exist, things would have to be eternal, immortal. Only in that way would they be not simply substantiations of certain possibilities but truly things.*[4]

In his art, the passage of time is neither experienced as linear nor cyclical. He offers himself as the interpreter of a tragic vision, evoking both the enigma of life and the stubborn and indulgent irony through which one can still contemplate the meaningless gem of death:

> *Life says to death: 'In order to exist, you need to do away with me and this is why you have always been hated. For me to exist, on the other hand, all that's needed is that you maintain the proper distance. There lies the difference.' Death, taken by surprise, says something in response and at that moment realizes that he can also exist autonomously. Life then …* (title of a 1983 tempera on panel).[5]

At any rate, his vision is never based on a ghost. His eye can be disillusioned and light, penetrating and insightful, dancing or steady, yet it always sees

3 Editor's note: Tomassoni refers here to a work made in the 1980s and later destroyed by the artist.

4 See Gino De Dominicis, "Letter on Immortality," in this volume, 59.

5 Mirolla, "Immortality," 72–73. Editor's note: The parenthetical addition by Tomassoni refers to an unidentified artwork.

what is presented before it as if for the first time. The eye that can see these objects or landscapes for the first time is unfamiliar with the alphabets conventionally used to convey such messages. This insuperability of the message is what grows into the sense of distance in him. His encounters are never close; they are always charged with deep hic et nunc focus but always with the suspension and boundless dilation of a kind of time and space that does not belong to everyday experiences but rather to a cosmic event.

The perspective from which De Dominicis observes his own work is an antediluvian perspective. Whereas man's fundamental attitude is to be static and annihilated as he stands before the cosmos, which is the true subject of the world, De Dominicis is instead tuned in to the order's variety and complexity. A perfectly slim and balanced vertical pole pointing down toward the ground is a recurring motif in his works. The 1967 version of it is golden and was eventually shown in Rome in 1969 and between the "Twins" in 1973; it is found in *Il tempo lo sbaglio lo spazio* (Time, Mistake, Space) [IT 95] (1969), in which a human skeleton on roller skates balances it on its finger while walking a dog's skeleton on a leash; again, the pole can be seen in Rome within *Piramide invisibile* (Invisible Pyramid) [IT 75] (1969); it is blue and topped with a star at Castello di Rivoli (1984); it is once again found in a drawing on a large panel with full–empty loving figures in vertiginous symbiosis (1984); it is held by a large black figure in 1983.

A work dated 1967 (shown in 1969) was also based on this kind of vertical tension, consisting of a silver chain "miraculously" hooked to the water inside a metal cylinder, which was thus lifted from the ground (*Secchio con acqua sospeso da terra con il gancio di una catena che fa presa sull'acqua* [Bucket with Water Suspended from the Ground, with the Hook of a Chain that Grips the Water] [IT 59]). This verticality was further evoked in the 1978–79 invisible statues of Urvasi and Gilgamesh looking over Piazza del Popolo in Rome from a window (1983) and in the monumental collection on display at the Capodimonte Museum (1986). A 1981–82 work (now found at MoMA, New York) is entitled *Con titolo (In principio era l'immagine; No!* (With Title [In the beginning was the image; No!]) [IT 238] (rather than "In the beginning was the word"). We should not forget that, before the big head, the artist placed a toilet in the middle of the room. Such an object, however, was not turned into a work of art; it was simply a toilet (as the author wished). In the cosmos of De Dominicis, the image is the first sign-producing entity, both when it manifests in an explicit and complete way (in the 1970 untitled drawings) and when it proceeds surreptitiously, through suspensions and evocations, as in *Tentativo di far formare dei quadrati invece che dei cerchi attorno ad un sasso che cade nell'acqua* (Attempt to Form Squares Instead of Circles Around a Stone Falling into Water) [IT 83] (1969), and *Dangerous Dying* [IT 95] (1969).[6] This is also the case both when the image seems to involve some kind of movement—*Poltrona per un viaggio*

---

6   Editor's note: Tomassoni is adopting here, with *Dangerous Dying*, the title that Maurizio Calvesi gave to De Dominicis's *Time, Mistake, Space* on the occasion of the exhibition *Fine dell'alchimia*, L'Attico, Rome, December 28–29, 1970.

nello spazio (Armchair for Space Travel) [IT 81] (1969); … *On the earth, which is not a sphere and is not part of the universe, which is neither expanding much less in a single direction*; or in the 1969 work *Attesa di un casuale movimento molecolare generale in una sola direzione, tale da generare un movimento spontaneo della pietra* (Waiting for a Random One-Directional Molecular Movement that Could Generate a Spontaneous Movement of Material) [IT 85–89]—and finally when the image is summoned up to question the identity principle ("I am not the Count of Saint Germain"), and in *"Io," "dopo," smemorato guardasala del museo mentre osservo le opere di un certo Gino De Dominicis"* ("I," "later," scatterbrained museum guard watching works by some guy called Gino De Dominicis) (1987), or such other works as *Senza titolo* (Suspended Men) [IT 124] (1970), *Piramide invisibile sospesa nel vuoto* (Invisible Pyramid Floating in the Void) (1987), and *Biglietto d'auguri* (Greeting Card for the Immortality of the Body) [IT 140], dated Christmas 1971.

This image is also central to the theme of time. *Palla di gomma (caduta da 2 metri) nell'attimo immediatamente precedente il rimbalzo* (Rubber Ball [Falling from a Height of Two Meters] in the Moment Right Before Bouncing Back) [IT 70] (1968–69) functions as proof of its own assumption. On the one hand, in De Dominicis's *Senza titolo (il giovane e il vecchio)* (Untitled [The Young and the Old]) [IT 101] (1969), the double portrait creates an impossible synchrony through the dissymmetrical relationship between the time of history and the time of fiction; on the other hand, the 1969 work *Tentativo di volo* (Attempt to Fly) [IT 84] ironically plays with anthropological evolution. In taking advantage of the sorcerous power of the image, De Dominicis exploits its psychic and ungovernable potential and looks for coincidences. In 1970 he singled out a figure between the leaves and fountain of Palazzo Taverna in Rome existing only in that brief moment, and illuminated it forever; in 1973 we find the work *Ovale eseguito a mano libera* (Perfect Freehand Oval) [IT 219]. Three years earlier he drew a little man in the middle of a large square sheet (*Senza titolo* [Untitled] [IT 120]). A seemingly banal picture serving as evidence of how a mark can be turned into an image with a light and delicate touch, there was, nevertheless, something in the sketch that struck him. He made it again, first as a sequence and then as a cycle: he found out that, if the drawing was linked twenty-two times, it would produce a perfect circle locking the space into a kind of rhythmical geometric sequence. That work had individuated a single possibility out of an infinite range, an almost vertiginous number considering that it was not a geometric drawing.

Beginning in 1964, he made several pen and pencil drawings in a small or miniature format. The last of these works is dated 1985 and was shown at the Paris Biennial that same year. In other works, a bunch of signs are spurted out, a technique that is reminiscent of psychic transmission (*Figure with Crossed Hands* [1965]). It is as if each image waited for a moment of revelation to then suddenly disappear (as with the "inexistent" black sculptures included in photographs of interiors, 1971–75); or, one can think of the time he made a person "disappear" during a memorable night in 1976 at

Palazzo Taverna, or of the piece *Macchina che fa sparire gli oggetti* (Machine Making Objects Disappear) [IT 62] (1968). Many of his works pertain to the power of materialization, such as those made in the seventies in which the body is seemingly predominant. This is also true of such works as *Bassorilievo della testa bidirezionale* (Bidirectional Head Bas-Relief) [IT 248] (1983), the large red figures on a black background and others made under the impulse of erotic references, the graphite and large tempera works dating back to 1985–86, his ... *di solito noi ricordiamo più bella una persona di profilo perché non poteva vederci* (Profile with Symbols on Glass) [IT 157] ("... we usually remember a person as more beautiful in profile because this same person cannot see us ...," 1972), and the ironic and "homeopathic" *Mozzarella in carrozza* (Mozzarella in a Carriage) [IT 69] (1970).

The 1972 cocktail party celebrating the refutation of the second law of thermodynamics (and responding to A. M. Liguori) was set in an ancient venue that was candlelit and celebrated a future event (2050) that was said to occur in the present. Mr. Paolo Rosa was disparagingly labeled by the mass media with an outdated name for his pathology—"mongoloid"—and just as disparagingly "gratified" by those photojournalists who marked his chest with a sign showing this inaccurate title (curiously enough, the Red Brigades would force them to undergo the same iconographic ritual). And yet, Paolo Rosa was a document within the "Second solution of immortality (The universe is immobile)," functioning as the very negation of the choice for representation. He is a body with no image, and who has never been faced with the possibility of representing himself. In that "mongoloid" (who brings to mind a "melancholy" iconography in his association with the ball, the stone, and the invisible cube in the overall composition), the loss of the ability to exit oneself obliterates the mirror stage that is meant to produce the loss of one's body. His real pathology is implosion, redundancy, the un-uttered word, the ablation of memory, the impossibility of escaping one's inertia, the flight from form and time and into darkness, and in that same conceptual darkness is situated the unprecedented exhibition that was only open to animals (Pescara, 1975). In the "Twins," materialization focuses on the body as a scene, starting from the gaze reflected upon it.

The death drive and the logics of the abyss allow for other perspectives from which to consider his work: the anticipation, out of an incalculable time, of the degree-zero found in life itself and the annihilation of the subject and the revelation of its damned side. The creative act ignites the spark of absolute occurrence. His *Senza titolo (Statua invisibile)* (Untitled [Invisible Statue]) [IT 195] (1979); his *Manifesto mortuario* (Necrology [Mortuary Poster]) [IT 73] (1969); the stones; the *Ubiquità dei vasetti* (Ubiquity of Jars) [IT 90–94] (1969), *D'io* (Of I, God) [IT 127–28] (1971),[7] the "trespassed" barriers (*Senza titolo* [Untitled] [IT 227] [1980]); the three-dimensional black or red long-nosed faces (1985–86), the silver drawings on a black background (1984–86), the one thousand colorful little men deco-

---

[7] Editor's note: This pun plays on the Italian word for god, *Dio*, which can also become *D'io*, which means "of I."

rating all the gallery walls (1973); the drawing of a woman (1970), the *D'io* (Continuous Laughter) [IT 127] (1970), the mirror watch (*Orologio* [IT 113] [1970]), the ring with an internally perfect geometrical stone (*Anello a perfezione geometrica interna* [Ring with Perfect Internal Geometry] [IT 138] [1970]); the large panels depicting the duo and trio with the city in the background (*Con titolo* [With Title] [IT 252, 1984] [1985–86]), the whole of those times and spaces on display at the Capodimonte Museum with the long work with merged figure and symbols (*Senza titolo* [Untitled] [IT 268] [1985]); and the secret of a space that is only visible from a small hole, in which a restored yellow-and-gold goddess on a blue background in an electric starlight looks at the present through human eyes (*Immagine della dea sumera Warka* [Image of the Sumerian Goddess Warka] [IT 189] [1977–83]). All these works, which gave rise to unexplored and alarming expressions, are no longer a scene. Neither are they the scene of a suspended moment. The same goes for the identical exhibition repeated one year later on the same day, at the same time, in the same street, in the same space, with identical invites (Rome, January 14, 1977, and January 14, 1978), the "Night-time" view on the sea with profiles and a bright entity in the sky (*Senzo titolo [Urvasi e Gilgamesh]—il notturno* [Untitled (Urvasi and Gilgamesh)—the Nocturnal] [IT 207] [1987]); the head of the white bas-relief (1987), *Con titolo* (With Title) (1972), the large yellow-and-purple one-eyed figure in the firmament [IT 265] (1985). Such is also the case for the mirror reflecting everything except for living things (*Senza titolo [Specchio che tutto riflette tranne gli esseri viventi]* [Untitled (Mirror That Reflects Everything Except Living Beings)] [IT 302] [1969]), and the painting that manifests in the so-called "devil" (*Senza titolo* [Untitled] [IT 277] [1986]) and then disappears forever (1987) only to appear again ([IT 326] [1989]), and when it does, it appears before the large red face (*Il guardiano dell'opera [Diavolo rosso]* [The Warden of the Work (Red Devil)] [IT 260] [1985]) as the work's warden. And so are all the other works that are impossible to name, and which testify to a form of art that does not derive from art. More than any other modern artist, Gino De Dominicis can situate himself, through art, in a charismatic domain that is both within and beyond language. He expressed a "powerful" idea that conveyed the tragically forgotten twentieth-century thought by playing with the talisman of immortality and put a human face to the enigmatic iconicity of those worn-out figures that were bound to represent the overwhelming difference of icons in the ensuing millennium. If we transported his works to other eras with the help of a time machine, and to other places, they would still, incredibly, retain all of their evocative potential, despite their unquestionably contemporary nature. We are walking in the steps of Gino De Dominicis.

And we shall keep spying on him.

Translated by Allison Grimaldi Donahue
This essay, titled "Il caso Gino De Dominicis," was originally published in Italian in *Flash Art*, no. 144 (June 1988): 38–41.

Perfect Living Object

Laura Cherubini

Dying is no more than not being seen.
Fernando Pessoa

Whatever the cost, Gino De Dominicis always thought, demonstrated, and put into practice the highest conception of the artist's role, against everything and against everyone if necessary, even in defiance of an art system that was sometimes weak, sometimes masochistic, and willing to retreat and give way on all counts. He always maintained the absolute centrality of art. We know how De Dominicis controlled every aspect and every characteristic of his work. We know what extreme attention he paid to the slightest of details. Now we face the problem of reconciling two pressing needs: respect for his thoughts and desires, and the wish to safeguard his extraordinary works, which, it must be said, live in splendid autonomy.

Oxymoron and Homeopathy

Drawing, painting, and "sculpture" are not traditional, but originary forms of expression. Therefore also future forms.[1]

From the beginning, De Dominicis drew, painted, and made three-dimensional works. By 1964 he had already shown about a hundred paintings and drawings. When galleries began to refuse to exhibit paintings, the artist managed to gradually reintroduce both drawing and painting into exhibition spaces. But quite apart from the problems of painting, the real adventure began in 1969, at Fabio Sargentini's L'Attico, a gallery that had become a reference point in those years when De Dominicis premiered a surprisingly lucid and self-assured exhibition. "With his invisible objects, Gino confused the issue with regard to Pino and Gianni, and the natural materials of Arte Povera," Sargentini said. The gallerist considered invisibility to be the great new frontier of De Dominicis's work, referring to the leading artists at the gallery up to that time, Pino Pascali, who died in September 1968, and Jannis Kounellis,[2] and to the revolutionary innovation of his work.

The poised golden rod, entitled *Asta in bilico (Equilibrio 1)* (Suspended Rod [Equilibrium 1]) [IT 47] (1967), was free and alone, suspended in space, appearing as a sort of generative line for the entire work.

---

1   This maxim appeared for the first time on the invitation card to the solo exhibition at the Nuova Pesa gallery in Rome, 1996. "Tradition interprets the origin," the artist told me when commenting on the phrase. See Gino De Dominicis, "Maxims, 1969–1996," in this volume, 96.

2   De Dominicis was probably struck by the innovative aspect of Pascali's work and by its physical nature, which was close to his idea that the artwork is always linked to its physical manifestation but with invisibility as one possible material. "With Gino we were really quite different, but for fifteen years we spent every evening together. Being different is a resource, not something to be condemned. We loved other artists—Ezra Pound, for example—who were also very different." Jannis Kounellis, interview by the author, November 2003.

Next to it were *Cubo invisibile* (Invisible Cube) [IT 45] (1967) and *Cilindro invisibile* (Invisible Cylinder) [IT 74] (1969): traced out on the ground, their bases form a circle and a square. Possibly, these two solids were chosen precisely for their different bases and for the dialectic between circle and square, which would return in his film *Tentativo di far formare dei quadrati invece che dei cerchi attorno a un sasso che cade nell'acqua* (Attempt to Form Squares Instead of Circles Around a Stone Falling into Water) [IT 83] (1969). A hook appears to hold a pail filled with water suspended in the air, as though water were solid and could be pulled up. Also, a nail—a minimal analogy of the rod—was suspended from a wall. Then the stone (*Aspettativa di un casuale movimento molecolare generale in una sola direzione tale da generare un movimento spontaneo del materiale* [Waiting for a Random One-Directional Molecular Movement that Could Generate a Spontaneous Movement of Material] [IT 85–89 [1969]]) and the ball (*Palla di gomma (caduta da 2 metri) nell'attimo immediatamente precedente il rimbalzo* [Rubber Ball [Falling from a Height of Two Meters] in the Moment Right Before Bouncing Back] [IT 70] [1968–69]).[3] Even though these two works consist of just two simple elements, their complexity is to be found in their double— and, in a certain sense, contradictory—status: on the one hand, in the way their invisible movement (which is virtual in the case of the ball and hoped-for in the case of the stone) is made transparent, and on the other hand, in the power art has to capture the moment of immobility. All of these works were sealed by a funerary poster announcing the artist's own death, the date of which, November 1969, was that of the exhibition.[4]

His work was erroneously considered by some to be "conceptual."[5] *Mozzarella in carrozza* (Mozzarella in a Carriage [an Italian fried sandwich]) [IT 69] (1970) formalized this conflict: here words took material, visual form. The work demonstrated the fact that mozzarella remains what it is even when it resides in a luxury coach, mocking imitators of Marcel Duchamp who believe that the gallery or museum has the power to transform any object displayed there into a work of art. De Dominicis exposes this mechanism by illustrating its ineffectiveness. Also, in his 1982 exhibition at Gian Enzo Sperone's gallery, the toilet remained what it is and was by no means miraculously transformed by being close to a painting.[6] These were, in

---

3   In Sargentini's opinion, the artist's finest work. Achille Bonito Oliva placed it on the cover of his book *Il territorio magico*, published by Centro Di in 1971.

4   "In 1969 we went together to Verano to look at the tombstones to find a mortuary script carved in a certain way," recalled Sargentini at the conference entitled *Che cosa c'entra la morte?*, curated by Giovanna Dalla Chiesa in October 2006 at the Accademia di Belle Arti in Rome. A summary of the three days was published in *Arte & Critica*, no. 50 (March–May 2007): 51. De Dominicis the man dies as a presence in the public registry and is born as an artist: Gabriele Guercio made some acute observations on this in "Arte visiva e immortalità del corpo," in *De Dominicis. Raccolta di scritti sull'opera e l'artista*, ed. Gabriele Guercio (Turin: Umberto Allemandi, 2001), 170.

5   "Originating in America, the term 'Conceptual Art' was very popular in Italy, perhaps because it reminded people of such common personal names as Concetta, Concezione, Concettina, etc. And it is continually being lazily used to label everything that, in art, is not immediately recognizable." Gino De Dominicis, "Maxims, 1969–1996," in this volume, 94.

6   *Con titolo (In principio era l'immagine; No!* (With Title [In the beginning was the image; No!]) [IT 238] (1981–82), a painting now at the Museum of Modern Art, New York.

the artist's words, "homeopathic" operations that criticize fashionable practices by duplicating them.[7] *Noi siamo le puntine* (We Are the Drawing Pins) [IT 183] (1975) was another of the artist's homeopathic operations: writing the title on the ground with the drawing pins themselves, ironically duplicating the minimalist tautology and reproducing the *ground-level* orientation of some works of Minimalism. When shown at L'Attico in a 1970 group exhibition, *Mozzarella in carrozza* caused a scandal. The artist maintained that it caused his ostracism from the art system and his exclusion from the important exhibitions of that time.

April 14, 1970, in the same garage, *Lo Zodiaco* (The Zodiac) [IT 105] materialized astrological signs in a semicircle. "The *Zodiaco* was stunning, with real animals," recalled his friend the artist Vettor Pisani. "Gino neutralized all symbolic meaning, and there was none of the esoteric aspect that appeared in Joseph Beuys's or my performances. He carefully avoided symbolism, and yet if we consider that his works appeared at L'Attico, in the same garage in Via Beccaria where just a few years previously Kounellis had shown his horses, we can see what a difference there was."[8] Here, the lion is not the equivalent of the horse, but a zodiacal sign and a constellation. The artist was certainly more interested in the cosmic aspect than in the symbolic. The elements—whether objects or living beings—come from a sidereal space, from an infinite, extraterrestrial distance. As Achille Bonito Oliva perceptively pointed out, the *Zodiaco* was, "for the first time in contemporary art, made outside the vitalistic convention of performance, by adopting living but static people in a position preestablished by the artist, as occurs with a mix of colors chosen by the painter, who is the overall author of the work."[9]

The View from Within

In 1972 a huge scandal occurred at the Venice Biennale with the work entitled *Seconda soluzione d'immortalità (l'universo è immobile)* (Second Solution of Immortality [The Universe Is Still]) [IT 150]. Simone Carella, an organizer of avant-garde theater in Rome and founder of Beat 72 who worked as Gino De Dominicis's assistant in Venice, recalled: "Gino considered the room a single work, as a sort of summation, though not arithmetical, of all that he had done until then. We arrived very early to choose the best room for what he had in mind. Then the work took shape and grew where it was. One of the reasons why the room was chosen was because it opened onto the garden, so it could be entered without going through the other rooms. There were skylights, which had been obscured, and the first thing that Gino asked, breaking into the conversation, was to remove the shades in order to allow daylight. That was how his adventure began: natural light and the door that gave onto the outside. The work was to be in con-

7 Laura Cherubini, "Gino De Dominicis," *Flash Art*, no. 199 (Summer 1996): 76–77.
8 Vettor Pisani, in conversation with the author, April 2007.
9 Gino De Dominicis, in *Vernissage — Il Giornale dell'Arte*, no. 40 (December 1986): 87–89; reprinted in Guercio, ed., *De Dominicis. Raccolta*, 133–37.

tact with the universe. Then he asked me to find someone who could represent this second solution of immortality—a young man who had not lost his childlike look."[10]

Immortality is made possible by shutting off time, the same aspiration recorded in the photograph documenting De Dominicis's participation in the seventh Paris Biennial. The artist wore the mask of an old man and a cassock and carried a placard with the inscription "Che cosa c'entra la morte?" (What has death got to do with it?) and, Pisani tells us, a transistor radio.[11] Quite apart from the subtle distinction between immortality and eternity, what the artist was interested in was what Carella described as "the fixity of the present moment, our perception of the instant." The person chosen embodied one solution of immortality; "since he has no memories, no recollections, no perception of the future," Carella said, "in an evident paradox, Paolo Rosa is immortal."[12] According to Renato Barilli, who had invited De Dominicis to the Biennale, Rosa was "a person who has overcome the 'cure,' in the Heideggerian sense, a mirror of virtue and a representation of the age of innocence. De Dominicis had some fixed ideas, overturning facts such as the principle of gravity and defeating time by reversing the laws of physics, but his ways of visualizing the concept were also capable of change."[13]

At opposite ends of the room, on two small chairs placed on high, were the figures of *il giovane* (the young man, impersonated by

22

10	"Finding the character was simple. When I asked in Strada Garibaldi in the Castello district, everyone said: 'el Pinin.' I spoke with his mother, one of those women who threaded beads with long needles, and we offered a fee. The only lie was that I said it was for the cinema because it would have been difficult to explain a work like *Seconda soluzione*. Paolo Rosa was sweet and Gino was very fond of him." De Dominicis later made a portrait of Paolo Rosa, which is extraordinarily intense as a painting: the mixtilinear frame encloses a painting that is gray on gray, but of huge variety and with a wealth of vibrations and with the head of Rosa, seen from the back of the neck up, in the bottom right-hand corner, similar to how De Dominicis preferred to be photographed. I believe there was a sort of identification of the artist himself with the figure of Paolo Rosa, which makes the testimony of Matteo Smolizza, found in the issue of *Quadri & Sculture* dedicated to the *Seconda soluzione*, all the more remarkable. According to Smolizza, De Dominicis for a long time had doubts about whether to exhibit this portrait of Rosa or a photo of himself as a child. These two pictures seemed totally different to Smolizza, although, for the artist, they were probably more linked to each other than one might imagine.
11	Editor's note: See the photograph reproduced in this volume, 308–9.
12	It is worthwhile recalling one of De Dominicis's childhood memories, which he told to a number of friends, of when he was on the beach in Ancona with a boy with Down syndrome. De Dominicis told me he had noticed how this child, the son of one of his mother's friends, spent hours staring at the same spot, as though he had no perception of time. The artist had sensed a scientific fact: people with Down syndrome have a perception of time that psychiatry refers to as being in "slides"—as though they were in front of a freeze-frame perceived as an eternal present. I owe this information to psychiatrist Geppy Tropeano.
13	According to Carella, the room was in perfect order; according to Barilli, however, the room had not been completely arranged when the dissenters broke in, and he believes the scandal had been set up. He also remembers the brave and unexpected defense of Francesco Arcangeli in the 1973 acquittal of De Dominicis when he was accused, with Carella, of "abducting a minor," and risked over twenty years in prison. In the light of this precious and direct evidence (even though, considering the artist's perfectionism, it is hard to imagine an unfinished state), the documentation acquires special importance, as an image designed by the artist to represent his own vision, the moment in which the object, visible for only a few hours, was looked at. Carella states that the incensed and embittered artist decided to close the room, while Gerry Schum suggested leaving a video with a close-up of the artist as testimony.

Carella himself) and *il vecchio* (the old man) [IT 124].[14] According to Carella, the rubber ball placed before Rosa is an artificial element, full of air, and alludes to an attempt to fly, while the stone is a natural element linked to the earth, waiting for a movement adherent to it. In addition to these objects, there was also the *Invisible Cube* in front of Rosa. It is clear that the room is a *magical territory* dominated by a circular form of vision. The artist himself spoke about the "viewpoint within the work." The room itself is built as an interior, as a noncommunicable situation, a theater of the mind, placed paradoxically on the stage not by the normal means of the theater—movement, words, texts—but by those of the visual arts. In the logic of his "Letter on Immortality," the three objects shifted from their status as "assessments" to that of "existing things" by entering the visual context of Paolo Rosa.

Motionless Odyssey

Gino De Dominicis returned to the subject of immortality and to the overcoming of entropy on December 18, 1972, at the Incontri Internazionali d'Arte at Palazzo Taverna: "on the occasion of the evening, an invitation card has been sent for a cocktail party to celebrate the overcoming of the Second Law of Thermodynamics. Refreshments are offered in crystal glasses and on porcelain plates. The table has been adorned with silver candlesticks and crystal chandeliers hang from the ceiling. Newspapers with sensational titles have been posted on the walls, announcing: 'Man has achieved the immortality of the body.'"[15]

In one of the versions of the "Letter on Immortality," De Dominicis writes: "Being unable to intervene directly to halt the inexorable course of his own 'internal time' and prolong his own life, man has invented means that make this time run faster. Intervening upon space, he has indirectly managed to intervene upon time. This operation would be justified,

14   In the Venice Biennale catalogue, Arcangeli wrote: "Why does Gino De Dominicis plan, if I am not mistaken, to have living people on high and below facing each other in the space allotted to him?" Also in the Biennale catalogue, Barilli stresses the fact that the artist pushed this behavior "until it acquires the category of the impossible." See *XXXVI Esposizione internazionale d'arte, Catalogo generale, 11 giugno–1 ottobre 1972* (Venice: Stamperia di Venezia, 1972), 93, 98. According to Carella, De Dominicis had also summoned the twins who performed the role of the Gemini from the *Zodiaco*, who were fitted with earphones. Carella, who, from his position on high, had a bird's-eye view of the room, says that the two of them were in the area closer to the Youth, while the scene with Rosa was in the left-hand corner of the room as one entered, underneath the Old Man: "One of the twins was sitting at a table, miming—as if he were presenting a paper—to a non-existent audience, indicated by the empty chairs in front of him. The second twin entered from the right wearing headphones and was dancing to nonexistent music, representing an inner world that cannot be communicated to others. Every now and then, the recorded laughter of *D'io* [IT 127] played in the room. In addition to the twins, Enrico Cattaneo's photographs document the twins in the room, a desk on which are photographs of the Youth and Old Man, and two photos of the young woman (IT 115) (1970). The same photos reveal the presence of the skeleton with roller skates (*Il tempo lo sbaglio lo spazio* [Time, Mistake, Space] [IT 95] [1969]) in Venice. Carella maintains that the skeleton had been removed by the time of the opening.

15   Daniela Lancioni, ed., *Cronologia* in *Roma in mostra 1970–1979. Materiali per la documentazione di mostre azioni performance dibattiti* (Rome: Joyce, 1995), 53. See also the exhibition catalogue *Incontri… Dalla collezione di Graziella Lonardi Buontempo* (Rome: Académie de France à Rome, 2003), 57. On this episode, see also Italo Tomassoni, "The Gino De Dominicis Affair," in this volume, 93.

however, only if space was finite and our imagination limited. Unfortunately, however, it is only a palliative and a very serious mistake." These words not only provide the best explanation for *Il tempo lo sbaglio lo spazio* (Time, Mistake, Space) [IT 95] (1969) but also provide a good introduction to another work he made for L'Attico: *Poltrona per un viaggio nello spazio* (Armchair for Space Travel) [IT 81] (1969). According to Sargentini, the artist modified a barber's chair with a ski-boot attachment to its feet and a sign that described the dual movement, rotation and revolution, of the earth. The person who sits on the chair takes a literal journey through space, a journey we are tied to with the movement of the earth.

In his 1975 exhibition, the public were forbidden from entering the Galleria Lucrezia De Domizio in Pescara. This was the *Mostra riservata agli animali* (Exhibition for Animals Only). We are told by Vettor Pisani that the spectators peeped in from the entrance and, on the threshold, an ox looked out, as did a donkey, a goose, a hen. Pisani said De Dominicis selected these animals as ones that have no consciousness of death. It is clear that De Dominicis was searching for alternatives to the destiny of mortals and to the paradigms of immortality of the body. Almost as though wishing to arrest time, De Dominicis performed a disappearance and reappearance at the Pio Monti gallery in Rome: "I remember two exhibitions, both exactly the same, repeated in my gallery exactly one year apart, on January 14, 1977, and January 14, 1978, with a huge stone, a balancing rod, two pots that represented ubiquity, and an invisible pyramid. Those who had been to the first exhibition in the same place found the same objects in the same positions: they were bewildered, as though time had indeed been brought to a standstill!"[16] In later exhibitions at the Monti gallery in the early eighties, the artist presented his *Lampadario antientropico* (Anti-Entropic Lamp) [IT 228] (1980) and *Senza titolo* (Untitled), known as "Sbarre violate" (Violated Bars) [IT 227] (1980). Without the dispersal of energy, there would be no entropy.

<u>Against Photography</u>

It is well known that De Dominicis did not like photography or the documentation of his work. In fact, over the years, he put into practice a vigorous strategy of resistance against documentation. Most likely, he probably perceived less energy and intensity in the photographs than in the actual works.[17] Through his words and writings, he always put us on guard against a passive acceptance of conventional market practices, suggesting they should be brought into question. His real strategy to subtract his own works from the substitutional tyranny of photography came with a pictorial technique so exquisite that it *almost* achieved nonreproducibility. While this was the general direction of his thoughts, he did allow photographs of his

16 Interview with Pio Monti at the *Che cosa c'entra la morte?* conference/event, Accademia di Belle Arti di Roma, Rome, October 4–6, 2006, curated by Giovanna Dalla Chiesa. The declaration is included in the summary of the first day, which appeared in *Arte & Critica*, no. 49 (December 2006–February 2007): 51.

17 All those who knew him well witnessed the artist faced with a Picasso monograph, pointing and declaring, "That's not Picasso, but a book of the photographer who took the photos of Picasso's paintings!"

work to be published on a number of occasions.[18] Thus it was not a mandatory rule, but an idealistic defense of his work and of his intention to lay bare and reveal the work and its reproduction. In 1973 De Dominicis was invited to show his works in a dedicated room at the *Contemporanea* exhibition organized by the Incontri Intemazionali d'Arte in the underground car park of Villa Borghese. In the room, there was a photograph of him taken by Elisabetta Catalano. It was a portrait that was not only authorized but used in a work of his own and on a number of occasions. In one picture of De Dominicis taken in 1975, he had himself photographed full-length by Buby Durini while hiding his face behind this portrait by Catalano, using it as a mask. De Dominicis replaces himself with his own portrait, a way of evading photographic depiction through photography itself.

Time and the Mirror

One example of the complex system of relationships De Dominicis establishes between the illusive space of representation and that of the real can be seen in the work shown in 1988 at Galleria Lia Rumma in Naples. Gabriele Guercio described it thus: "continuing the thread from his *Specchio che tutto riflette tranne gli esseri viventi* (Mirror That Reflects Everything Except Living Beings) [IT 302, realized in 1988 and later destroyed], the artist performed a total elimination of the public and of everything that moved in the exhibition space. In the dimly lit room, a projector illuminated a panel in black tempera, with Urvasi and Gilgamesh seen in profile, in silver-gray pencil, and a shining polyhedron at the level of their eyes. On the wall opposite the painting was an oval mirror, but when one went up to it, one could see that the 'mirror' reflected the room and the painting, but not the visitors. Discovering the trick is less important than grasping the outcome. The 'mirror,' which reflects everything except for anything that moves or is alive, removes and projects both works of art into a dimension that is alien to that of the spectators. By contrasting the permanence of the two paintings with the transience of the spectators, it strengthens the idea of art's timelessness."[19] De Dominicis's solution to the problem of *immortality* was beginning to take shape: it is the destiny of painting, not of man, and of the

32

---

18   These photographs appeared in such magazines as *Flash Art, Artforum, Il Giornale dell'Arte,* and *Quadri & Sculture,* but also in catalogues such as those for biennial and quadrennial exhibitions. De Dominicis wanted to control the quality, arrangement, and circulation of the image and gave very precise instructions. I remember a number of cases where he preferred to use Polaroid pictures, so that no copies could be made, but when, as commissioner for the Italian Pavilion at the 1990 Biennale, to which I had invited him, I told him it would not be possible to publish a full-page Polaroid, he did provide an excellent color photo. For the *Tutte le strade portano a Roma?* exhibition, he made a gigantic pictorial work almost seven meters tall, which was placed in the rotunda at the entrance, called *Fondazione Sumera di Roma* (Sumerian Foundation of Rome) [IT 401] (1990). When I was editing the catalogue, he wanted to publish a two-page picture of himself painting the great work and had an expensive color photo made especially for the purpose. When he saw the catalogues, he hugged both me and Lia Riposati of Carte Segrete, for the picture had been reproduced exactly as he wanted, with the gold paint clearly showing.

19   Guercio, "Arte visiva e immortalità del corpo," 178. Vittorio Sgarbi observes that De Dominicis "responds to mechanical reproduction systems by using mirrors." See Vittorio Sgarbi, "Il vero De Dominicis," *Quadri & Sculture,* no. 34 (January–February 1999): 74–75.

work, not of the artist. It is worth noting that, in a biography prepared by the artist, this exhibition is indicated as "a work that deforms time."[20] Everything gifted with movement has no chance of remaining in time, while the immobility of a work of art guarantees unlimited duration. It is not painting that is ephemeral and illusory, but what we consider to be real, ourselves. The living are condemned to mortality through their desire for movement, which leads them to make mistakes. The work of art, however, as the *perfect living object*, escapes this destiny.[21]

The Hanged Man

Drawing, painting, and "sculpture" are material, immobile, and mute; ontologically speaking, they are the very opposite of all other artistic languages.[22]

The artist was always opposed to "performance" in the strictest sense. He considered it a form of theater and not of visual art. Except in the case of his two films, De Dominicis never used movement in his work. Instead, he was the first to use living people that remained motionless, as in his *Zodiaco* of 1970 and as in the gallery at the Biennale in 1972. De Dominicis sometimes accompanied his works with motionless three-dimensional presences. It is another oxymoron, the juxtaposition of items of different natures, which produces difference and creates a visual short circuit. However, the fundamental oxymoron in De Dominicis consists of the fact that, in his works, he alternately used a system of presentation by using objects and living people, or a system of representation as is the case in his paintings, sometimes using the two systems at the same time, in the same period, or in the same exhibition.

This is true of the exhibition at La Nuova Pesa gallery in 1996, which occurred after the artist had not exhibited in Rome for thirteen years. In the first room, a large, three-meter-tall self-portrait in tempera was surrounded by spotlights. The position of the lights was reversed, so it was the painting that illuminated the public, an idea taken up in another of the artist's maxims: "It is the public that exhibits itself to art and not vice versa."[23] But hanging in front of the painting is a disturbing presence—a hanged man. Just when the desire to do away with the specifics of visual art emerged, "the death of painting and the painter," rigor mortis produced an erection of the brush, coming out of this hanged man's trousers and foreshadowing the alternative language of a future technological world. In actual fact, the painter was not dead, for hanging did not have this power over him and he was saved by his own technical expertise. In this case it was a living hanged man; the force of gravity should have been lethal but was neutralized. On a single panel there was the painting—a different form of self-portrait in the figure

20   The sentence was later erased by the artist, who also attributed an incorrect date to the exhibition, 1987.

21   "A perfect living object, a work of art can have an influence upon biological processes." See Gino De Dominicis, "Maxims, 1969–1996," in this volume, 96.

22   Ibid., 95.

23   Ibid., 93.

of the hanged man and a little man in gold and silver, placed on a plinth opposite and balanced on a crystal tip. Gravity becomes a supportive force, a theme that also exists in the gilded rod and the hanging objects.

In the second room, the figure of a woman five and a half meters tall was depicted resting in a display case and only the face, drawn in pencil, could be seen through an opening in the container. The bewitching face of the recumbent giantess is made up of countless signs through which, as though by magic, color appears. A drawing on glass was also displayed, alongside a self-portrait of the artist painting but seen from five points of view. So there were two figures typical of the work of De Dominicis in the show: the woman and the artist, who had already faced each other in the two profiles of Urvasi, the goddess of beauty, and Gilgamesh, the artist-king. The same two subjects appeared in the third room with another small self-portrait on glass and a stunning picture of a mother and child. Two luminous geometrical elements hung above their heads: a cube in reverse perspective above the woman and a sphere above the child, in a certain sense a return to the invisible cube and the rubber ball. De Dominicis's close focus on such fundamental themes as gravity and immortality is revealed iconographically by highlighting some essential figures. On the intellectual level, it echoes his striving to achieve extremely sophisticated painting by means of a few basic elements: the use of wood and the prevalence of apparently monochromatic colors and pencil. "Contemporary art and artists are considered (and consider themselves) to be modern. However, coming after everything that has gone before, they should know that they are the most ancient."[24]

Kali Yuga in Full Swing

In Indian philosophy, Kali Yuga is a calamitous era verging on collapse caused by a total loss of values. That De Dominicis gave the title *In pieno Kali-yuga* to his last exhibition, which opened at the Galleria Emilio Mazzoli in Modena on May 30, 1998, six months before he died, is indicative of what he felt was taking place in art and the world around him. In 1986 he had exhibited with Mazzoli what was considered the first important show of his work on, or involvement with, paintings: "Until that time he had exhibited only one painting, possibly with an object next to it ... Here, on the other hand, there were about fifteen paintings, and I also showed his first volumetric works."[25] De Dominicis had been working on a series of paintings that somehow combined two-dimensional and three-dimensional forms. His painting acquired depth and turned outward, combining different spatial qualities. This is how Bonito Oliva described the 1986 exhibition at Mazzoli: "Now the pictures appear to come from the future, figures with project-

24   Ibid., 96.

25   "The relationship was positive for me, rather like with Schifano—he was a character who intrigued me with his speed and irony, the way he lived the day and the night. He made some amazing comments ... Conversations with him were always on an upward note, never down. And of course I was only five years older than Gino, but I felt far older than that. I felt I could advise him, I always gave in to him ..." Emilio Mazzoli, interview with the author, in Achille Bonito Oliva, ed., *Italy 2000. Arte e sistema dell'arte* (Milan: Prearo, 2000), 88–89. Cf., in the same volume, the interview with Lia Rumma, 143–45.

ing noses and with their eyes in the center, sometimes alone, ready to occupy the space taken up by reason. These figures, made in various sizes and colors ranging from blue to red and black, suddenly produce anxiety and an unpredictable short circuit in our eyes."[26] Guercio states: "Many of the works were paintings of faces or figures with cone-shaped noses that lengthened out like beaks or trunks and are sometimes three-dimensional (modeled in clay and covered with paint). For example, in the violet and yellow figure on a black background, called *Senza titolo* (Untitled) [IT 265] (1985), the three-dimensional cone-shaped nose is almost as long as half of the subject's body. Flattened by the yellow garment, this body would lack depth and solidity if it were not for the inclination of the right arm, which, by burrowing into the garment toward the heart, indicates a depth and possibly the extraordinary ability of touching one's own heart with one's hands."[27] On the subject of Sumerian art, André Malraux talked of a "beak-shaped nose inherited from the prehistoric bird-man."[28] Agnes Kohlmeyer points out how, "for some populations, large noses are a sign of particular beauty."[29] The reference to Sumerian civilization is certainly plausible, but this element of the nose is, more than anything, a powerful intellectual invention. The frame becomes a sort of miniature architecture inhabited by a figure that becomes both painting and sculpture. The proportions between the whole and the part become far more important.[30]

What would be his final exhibition, *In pieno Kali-yuga*, was dazzling and harmonious, bearing no traces of Kali Yuga's calamitous definition. On the contrary, this 1998 exhibition seemed like an antidote to an age in decline.[31] There was a stunning series of portraits, which, with just a few essential lines, immediately made the sitter recognizable, and in which any deformations were immediately turned into beauty.

Next to these faces was one of the variations on the theme of the Sphinx that he was working on in those years—a sweeping red view and a still life in which the artist had experimented with silver. The intentional return to such conventional historical genres as portraiture and still life shows how even these subjects, which are apparently traditional, can be regenerated.

26 Achille Bonito Oliva, "Gino de Dominicis," in *De Dominicis. Raccolta*, ed. Guercio, 136–37.

27 Gabriele Guercio, "Arte visiva e immortalità del corpo," 183.

28 André Malraux, quoted in André Parrot, *Sumer: The Dawn of Art*, trans. Stuart Gilbert and James Emmons (New York: Golden Press, 1961), 30.

29 Agnes Kohlmeyer, "Vedere e non sapere," *Contemporanea*, no. 19 (Summer 1990): 64–69.

30 For example, one collector recalls that De Dominicis used a hammer to break a small work with a nose, suggesting that a bigger one should be made from it—which was to become the red nose that stands out in the light of the gold—precisely because it would have been of a more harmonious size.

31 "I went to the studio for the last time—it was a highly challenging exhibition and demanded a great effort. Right then I was almost afraid, but then I went out of the studio, stopped at the bookseller in Via Zanardelli and my wife said to me, 'Call him back.' I went back up, shook hands and left for that final exhibition, which in the end turned out to be a great success from all points of view … His death came out of the blue for me. If ever there was a positive-minded man it was him. He was the last person you could think anything might happen to." Emilio Mazzoli, interview with the author, in Bonito Oliva, *Italy 2000*, 89.

In his essay "On the Trail of Gilgamesh," the question Nicolas Bourriaud poses to himself—how to restore power to images without precipitating the ideology of the aura, which has fallen into disrepute in this "age of technical reproducibility"—finds its answer in De Dominicis. His work aims to reconstitute that incomparable, inveterate, irrevocable aura, but this time as art's solution to the problem of entropy: the dispersion of energy which art concentrates and cultivates in the gift of the work.

In a television program for the *Corto circuito* series, one can see Gino De Dominicis talking with a large painting of a female subject in front of him. In the end he turns to this figure and asks, "Is it true?" And the figure replies, "Yes."[32]

Translated by Simon Turner
This essay is an edited excerpt of a longer text that was originally published in Italian, French, and English in *Flash Art International*, special issue (June 2007): 32–85.

32   "The Masterpiece of the Next Millennium," broadcast on Canale 5 in 1996. While the likeness is painted, its face is reminiscent of Arianna De Rosa's, a dear friend of the artist and the model for most of his paintings.

The Prophet and Conjurer of Self-Deception

Duccio Trombadori

I became close friends with Gino De Dominicis in Venice during the 1990 Biennale. After that, we were never separated until the day of his death. I would visit him almost daily in the studio where he lived and worked, in the heart of Rome. We went out together in the evening and stayed up late in the trattorias and restaurants of which he was a fond patron. Gino did not love art critics: he considered them the children of a lesser god, capable of fabricating castles of words, but mostly incapable of giving form to works of art. He kept critics away from his world with few exceptions. He agreed to publish a few of his thoughts in the form of a dialogue between the two of us, entitled "Promemoria di fine secolo" (A Memo at the End of the Century).[1] That interview on contemporaneity contains what Gino had to say about art, and it can serve as a point of reference for anyone studying his work.

De Dominicis died at fifty-one, in 1998, at the end of November. In Rome and across the entire art world, a light went out; a sense of emptiness can still be felt to this day. I offered an account of our friendship, which touched on our human and moral affinities in the final decade of the twentieth century, in the book *De Dominicis amico pittore. Storia e cronistoria di un sodalizio* (De Dominicis, Painter Friend: History and Chronicle of a Brotherhood).[2] Since then none of the thoughts on the problems of aesthetics and criticism that my friendship with De Dominicis elicited in me have changed. Similarly, his influence on the chronicles of Italy's art scene in those years remains unchanged too.

More than twenty years have passed since my friend left us. His original virtue lay in his ability to best express, in various ways, with various visual accents, and yet with disarming simplicity, the question that always nagged him, and which every mind, albeit unconsciously, cultivates intimately: What does death have to do with it? The answer to this question stems from the fertile tree of his bizarre and disquieting oeuvre: paintings, written texts, environmental improvisations, and deceptive visual tricks.

I have clear in my mind a well-known photograph taken of the group of Italian artists who participated in the Paris Biennial in 1971: a young De Dominicis, twenty-four years old, appears with a mask over his face, standing to the side, like an unidentified and strange bugaboo amid the group. In the photograph, he upsets the entire sense of the image by holding up a sign on which you can read the crucial question, "What does death have to do with it?"[3]

1	Duccio Trombadori, "A Memo at the End of the Century," in this volume, 87–90.
2	Duccio Trombadori, *De Dominicis amico pittore. Storia e cronistoria di un sodalizio* (Falciano, San Marino: Maretti Editore, 2012).
3	Editor's note: See the photograph reproduced in this volume, 314–15.

Masking, doubling, disorienting, and disappearing: these are some of the recurring devices in De Dominicis's varied and versatile practice, which permanently repeat and suggest that internal question, sometimes veiling it and at other times revealing it. De Dominicis had a formidably informative and persuasive capacity that surprised and touched the innermost parts of human beings. For him, Marx's "dream of that very same thing" (the illumination of consciousness gained not through dogma but by consciousness itself) shed a fundamental clarity on the omnipresence of death, and how its intrusive and unsolicited interruption of life reveals the precariousness of existence.

What does death have to do with life, if life contains an intrinsic desire for eternal life and immortality? De Dominicis's was an ironic protest that posed a proud and pervasive question, which he carried within him from childhood and confronted and considered with all the answers that religion, science, and philosophy could offer. He was disappointed. "I'm not searching for the salvation of the soul in the afterlife," he would say, as a response to the dictates of faith. "I search for eternal life and the immortality of the living body, here and now. And all I see is death threatening life from every side; it degrades, undoes, and decomposes." He was not satisfied by the inquiries, methods, results, and conquests of science. Once convinced that the second principle of thermodynamics proved the universe's inevitable entropy, his opinion of scientific mentality lowered substantially. Descriptions of facts and phenomena can be obtained through scientific method, but these are partial remedies that delay but do not prevent the fatal destiny of life.

At the end of every unsolved inquiry came the rhetorical question, What does death have to do with it? And it was partly for this reason that, at some point, De Dominicis concluded in his "Letter on Immortality" that, insofar as they are mortal, things do not exist; rather, they are merely proof of a "possibility" of existence.[4] In his moral anxiety to grasp the fullness of "eternal life" De Dominicis had therefore severed himself from the strings of knowledge and the religious belief in the afterlife, recognizing, in art, a position of absolute creative freedom. This seemed to him the only form of human expression capable of condensing vital energy instead of dispersing it, of entrusting the vision of the artist with a metaphorical and desired immortality. A special credo of the artist as protagonist and hero was thus established. Art became the experimental verification of the limits of scientific and religious knowledge, as well as an occasion to go beyond any rational interpretation of reality.

If "things" do not exist, then hypothesizing the existence of another world is legitimate, a real world in which "things" and, with them, humanity, are but one imperfect and mortal reproduction. So De Dominicis predicted. The exercise of fantasy consisted in crediting paradox as truth. It was the key to a whole poetics that postulated the figuration of a world of immortal hyperuranian entities, shaped along the lines of Sumerian mythology and fanta-archaeology.

4   See Gino De Dominicis, "Letter on Immortality," in this volume, 59, 62.

It became possible, within the thaumaturgy of play and visual illusion, to answer the original question about the immanent invisible presence of death. (Life says to death: "In order to exist, you need to do away with me and this is why you have always been hated. For me to exist, on the other hand, all that's needed is that you maintain the proper distance. There lies the difference." Death, taken by surprise, says something in response and at that moment realizes that he can also exist autonomously. Life then…). This long title, affixed to a painting of 1983,[5] proves how pervasive his *meditatio mortis* was in the way he faced and enhanced the evidence offered by art. I do not know the extent of what is known about De Dominicis's unconditional admiration for Giorgio de Chirico's personality. De Chirico was the artist he respected most. He was influenced by de Chirico and picked up on his premonitory and enigmatic message—Cocteau's "secular mystery"—as an invitation to proceed along immortality's evocative path. A young de Chirico had titled his 1911 self-portrait *Et quid amabo nisi quod aenigma est?*, not without having first noted in a Schopenhauer book this symptomatic Latin phrase: "Meditatio mortis et somniorum magna semper poetarum et philosophorum delectatio fuit" (the meditation of death has always been a great pleasure for poets and philosophers).

This lesson was assimilated without necessarily being declared. De Dominicis internalizes and exalts the charge of bewildering irony contained in the mysterious aura of the work and in the enigmatic reference to de Chirico. However, De Dominicis's art is not so much defined by the minor tone of melancholy that had fed the imagination of the great metaphysicist, but rather it reenvisions an atmosphere of secular mystery in the major chant of a lively and paradoxical visual joy. This can explain and specify the common thread of so much of De Dominicis's oeuvre: a varied range of works that encapsulates everything from paradox, wordplay, and prestidigitation to spatiotemporal osmosis, duplication, and the disappearance of images, to a type of painting which associates archaic figures with cosmic visions that draw one's gaze toward unusual horizons of epochs and civilizations.

Pursuing the propitiatory method of keeping death "at an appropriate distance," De Dominicis built, over time, an entire poetic world to which he devoted his unshakeable faith until the end. Beyond mortal existence, the theory of the "real world" presented itself to his thunderstruck imagination. It was a place populated by the immortal Urvasi and Gilgamesh, by princesses and Sumerian divinities, by sidereal landscapes and ultra-terrestrial flying objects, sailing in space, whose silhouettes prompted him to pursue a visual translation alternated with elemental colors, like the primordial auroral echo: white and black, scarlet, silver and gold.

The world of paradoxical figures grew like a protective armor and justification of his creative freedom. And the first to convince himself of the alleged extraterrestrial truth was their author. "Marvel" became a work of art's first mark of quality: "a painter"—he used to say—"is like a conjuror

5   Editor's note: This work has not been identified.

who must succeed in astonishing himself with his tricks. That is where the complexity lies."[6]

Right from the beginning, De Dominicis distanced himself from categorization and from the contemporary trends of his time. And not by chance. He wanted to walk alone, with a fascinating visual production, persuaded as he was about reintroducing the parable of the Sumerian king Gilgamesh, in his attempt—which proved fatal—to unfurl and discover the secret of immortality. Art's thaumaturgy, artist's heroism: this mythical itinerary of salvation ("in arte salus") summarizes and illuminates the art practice of Gino De Dominicis, prophet and conjurer of self-deception.

Translated by Ombretta Celeste
This essay, commissioned for this volume, was originally titled "Il profeta e mago dell'autoinganno."

6   See Gino De Dominicis, "Maxims, 1969–1996," in this volume, 93.

II

THE THREAD THAT LINKS: GINO DE DOMINICIS ON GINO DE DOMINICIS

Letter on Immortality[1]

Gino De Dominicis

Rome, September 10, 1970

Dear…

I don't think that things exist as such. A glass, a man, a hen, for example, are not really a glass, a man, or a hen but only the substantiation for the possibility of the existence of a glass, a man, or a hen. To truly exist, things would have to be eternal, immortal. Only in that way would they be not simply substantiations of certain possibilities but truly things. In fact, by modifying themselves continually, they are used by "Nature," which, through their transformations, substantiates all the possibilities at its disposal. So, for example, the moment a hen performs its "natural duty" of laying an egg, it ceases to be a hen; it becomes solely the means by which "Nature" substantiates the possible existence of an egg, and thus of the world of feathered creatures. The same law is valid for the problem of space (both for the macrocosm and the microcosm). In a universe that is expanding, or at least moving, the planets and stars move; they occupy and "substantiate" the existence of new spaces that are adequate to their size (otherwise, they would change or disintegrate). Driven by the same "natural cause," man leaps from the earth and invades new spaces.

One of the properties that make an object what it is is the fact that its presence in a certain place prevents other objects taking that place. Given that there are no things that perpetually remain in the same space, they cease being objects to become substantiators of certain spatial possibilities—therefore, energy. And what, for objects, is a spatial problem, for men, is a temporal problem. When we perform an action—for example, running a race—we are not actually running; we are only substantiating the possibility of running and of the existence of the race, to then pass this stored experience on to "Nature." In fact, compared to the length of time that our spe-

---

1   Editor's note: "Lettera sull'immortalità (Letter on Immortality)" was first published in 1970 in the catalogue edited by Fabio Sargentini that accompanied De Dominicis's solo show at L'Attico (November 5, 1969–April 8, 1970). It was printed twice: in Italian at the front of the catalogue and in English at the back. The English contains three short sentences that do not appear in the Italian. The English text is given an earlier date (April 10, 1970) than the Italian (September 10, 1970), although it is very unlikely that De Dominicis wrote it in English first, or even at all. Shortly after, Sargentini edited and published *Album 9/68–2/71* (1971), which included an Italian version of the letter dated April 10, 1970, with fifteen sentences added. In the present volume are English translations of both the Italian letter as it appeared in the original catalogue published in 1970 and the second version with the additional sentences as published in 1971. All the additional parts of the second version of the Italian letter that do not appear in the first version are italicized. The entry for the "Lettera sull'immortalità" in Gino De Dominicis's catalogue raisonné (pp. 234–35) edited by Italo Tomassoni recounts how, in 1998, De Dominicis refused to allow the letter to be republished, arguing that "the text had been written by him in 1966 (aged 19) and published subsequently without his knowledge and against his wishes." It is unclear whether the conflicting accounts regarding the letter, its chronology, and motivations are the result of human error or a ruse on the part of the artist.

cies has existed, the time we have at our disposal during our own lifetime to take advantage of this experience is very limited. To truly exist, we should halt time, and then—finally—it would be we, ourselves, who were living; that is, it would be we ourselves, for ourselves, substantiating ourselves.

In other periods of history, humankind did not have our advanced science and technology, thus the prospect of tackling death with any probability of success was very limited. Man in the past spoke in ideal terms of eternal life. Nowadays, naturally, there is still talk of eternal life, but with the difference that we now have the chance of achieving it. In fact, we should direct all our efforts and all our capacities (particularly scientific and technological capacities) toward this single aim. What, for humans, were once only means (to emerge victorious from the eternal struggle against Nature) have nowadays become ends. We have lost our initial fear and the spontaneous reactions that went with it; we have become madmen running around on a ball wandering in space.

The fear of death was always sublimated or used by poets, philosophers, religions, and artists, but it was never faced with the necessary sangfroid. Most of the activities of man, which are today unjustified, would become logical for him only after having achieved immortality—because only then could we allow ourselves the fantastic and irrational objectives intended to give us joy (art, scientific research, etc.).

Nowadays biology has glimpsed a way of intervening in the cells that are at the root of the deterioration of the human body—that is, of the processes that inevitably lead to death. Unfortunately, only a very small number of people, compared to the whole population of the earth, is engaged in this research. We should all abandon some other activity—for example, space flight, artistic research, building weapons, etc. (excepting only those that make possible our survival)—in order to make our own contributions, either applying our own abilities or perhaps "inventing" other abilities for ourselves. With such a collective effort, one could defeat natural death within twenty years. Naturally, thereafter we would have to put a stop to births until we have found other planets or other possibilities for life on earth.

All of man's wars and resentments derive from an unconscious fear and awareness of death. Man began his evolution by defending himself against hostile circumstances and environments, he himself creating his means of defense. Curiously, after he managed to defeat the most obvious calamities, the gradual passage of time has made him get used to the idea of natural death as something inevitable, and his disregard of this final danger, this ultimate unresolved problem, has increased as he developed new interests. Each means of defense that man invents has always corresponded with a parallel instrument of threat. That precarious balance still exists today, with the difference that today those instruments are capable of destroying every form of life on earth. This is why it is more important than ever to focus all of our potential on an ideal that lies outside the usual sphere of man's impulses and aspirations. The fact of having children (one brings other things into the world because it is not possible to live forever, and perhaps that's impossible just because one brings other things into the world) is one way of achieving eternity, with the difference that, in this case, eternity is achieved by the human species and not by man. The awareness that we are already children should make us understand that we could be the ones using our experiences, we could be the ones making use of them in the future. For some time now, I have been more interested in the figures who have considered this problem—who have understood and interpreted the absurd and incomprehensible situation of man on earth—than in those who have sung the beauties and certainties of life. Besides, all men have always understood that living was worthwhile. Humanity has always created ideals in which to believe—that is, things that can give sense and meaning to life. Almost always these have been pretexts for the union of certain people with certain others, and almost always against or in favor of (possibly imaginary) others. Man has always pretended that it was not he who invented these motives, that they could not be fully controlled, that they were inevitably decided by Nature. These fantastic ideas in which he has pretended to believe have never united him with his fellow beings—precisely because he was unconsciously aware that they were fanciful ideals that were unlikely to offer him any real and durable advantages as a man. Only a higher—nonfatalistic, even if natural—ideal can unite all, without distinction, in an effort to achieve it.

By achieving immortality, man can—perhaps for the first time since his appearance on this earth—truly and indisputably distinguish himself from all other living species. By fixing himself in time at an age he chooses and interrupting the process of aging, man would break the spell cast by the most mysterious dimension prevailing in the universe, and this would be the first step toward the possibility of a greater understanding of life. I hope one day to take a glass, fill it with wine and drink it, to take a hen for a walk, and for it to be really me who is doing it.

Yours affectionately,
Gino De Dominicis

Rome, April 10, 1970

Dear...

I don't think that things exist as such. A glass, a man, a hen, for example, are not really a glass, a man, or a hen but only the substantiation for the possibility of the existence of a glass, a man, or a hen. To truly exist, things would have to be eternal, immortal. Only in that way would they be not simply substantiations of certain possibilities but truly things. In fact, by modifying themselves continually, they are used by "Nature," which, through their transformations, substantiates all the possibilities at its disposal. So, for example, the moment a hen performs its "natural duty" of laying an egg, it ceases to be a hen; it becomes solely the means by which "Nature" substantiates the possible existence of an egg, and thus of the world of feathered creatures. The same law is valid for the problem of space (both for the macrocosm and the microcosm). In a universe that is expanding, or at least moving, the planets and stars move; they occupy and "substantiate" the existence of new spaces that are adequate to their size (otherwise, they would change or disintegrate). Driven by the same "natural cause," man leaps from the earth and invades new spaces.

One of the properties that make an object what it is is the fact that its presence in a certain place prevents other objects taking that place. Given that there are no things that perpetually remain in the same space, they cease being objects to become substantiators of certain spatial possibilities—therefore, energy. And what, for objects, is a spatial problem, for men, is a temporal problem. When we perform an action—for example, running a race—we are not actually running; we are only substantiating the possibility of running and of the existence of the race, to then pass this stored experience to "Nature." In fact, compared to the length of time that our species has existed, the time we have at our disposal during our own lifetime to take advantage of this experience is very limited. To truly exist, we should halt time, and then—finally—it would be we, ourselves, who were living; that is, it would be we ourselves, for ourselves, substantiating ourselves.

Being unable to intervene directly to halt the inexorable course of his own "internal time" and prolong his own life, man has invented means that make this time run faster. Intervening upon space, he has indirectly managed to intervene upon time. This operation would be justified, however, only if space was finite and our imagination limited. Unfortunately, however, it is only a palliative and a very serious mistake. Culture, too—our desire for knowledge of the past, present, and future, of the "why" and the substance of things—is the fruit of a neurosis arising from our "limited" period here on earth. In fact, in these conditions, we must be the ones who move toward "things" in order to know them; while, in an ideal temporal situation, it would be the "things" that could move toward us to make themselves known in the way that was most natural to them. Aging is an internal illness, which, from around the age of twenty-six, begins to corrode body and mind. Then we think we have become used to the process and it seems inevitable to us; however, all man's actions have always been nothing but unconscious responses to this dramatic problem.

In other periods of history, humankind did not have our advanced science and technology, thus the prospect of tackling death *and aging* with any probability of success was very limited. Man in the past spoke in ideal terms of eternal life. Nowadays, naturally, there is still talk of eternal life, with the difference that we now have the chance of achieving it. In fact, we should direct all our efforts and all our capacities (particularly scientific and technological capacities) toward this single aim. What, for humans, were once only means (to emerge victorious from the eternal struggle against Nature) have nowadays become ends. We have lost our initial fear and the spontaneous reactions that went with it; we have become madmen running around on a ball wandering in space.

The fear of death *and aging* was always sublimated and used by poets, philosophers, religions, and artists, but it was never faced with the necessary sangfroid. Most of the activities of man which are today unjustified would become logical for him only after having achieved immortality—because only then could we allow ourselves the fantastic and irrational objectives intended to give us joy (art, scientific research, etc.).

Nowadays biology has glimpsed a way of intervening in the cells that are at the root of the deterioration of the human body—that is, of the processes that inevitably lead to death. Unfortunately, only a very small number of people, compared to the whole population of the earth, is engaged in this research. We should all abandon some other activity—for example, space flight, artistic research, building weapons, etc. (excepting only those that make possible our survival)—in order to make our own contribution, either applying our own abilities or perhaps "inventing" other abilities for ourselves. With such a collective effort, we could defeat natural death within twenty years. Naturally, thereafter one would have to put a stop to births until we have found other planets or other possibilities for life on earth.

All of man's wars and resentments derive from an unconscious fear and awareness of death. Man began his evolution by defending himself against hostile circumstances and environments, he himself creating his means of defense. Curiously, after he managed to defeat the most obvious calamities, the gradual passage of time has made him get used to the idea of natural death as something inevitable, and his disregard of this final danger, this ultimate unresolved problem, has increased as he has developed new interests. Each means of defense that man invents has always corresponded with a parallel instrument of threat. That precarious balance still exists today, with the difference that, today, those instruments are capable of destroying every form of life on earth. This is why it is more important than ever to focus all of our potential on an ideal that lies outside the usual sphere of man's impulses and aspirations. The fact of having children (one brings other things into the world because it is not possible to live forever, and perhaps that's impossible just because one brings other things into the world) is one way of achieving eternity, with the difference that, in this case, eternity is achieved by the human species, not by man. The awareness that we are already children should make us understand that we could be the ones using our experiences, we could be the ones making use of them in the future. For some time now, I have been more interested in the figures who have considered this problem—who have understood and interpreted the absurd and incomprehensible situation of man on earth—than in those who have sung the beauties and certainties of life. For a start, all men have always understood that living was worthwhile. Humanity has always created ideals in which to believe—that is, things that can give sense and meaning to life. Almost always these have been pretexts for a union of certain people with certain others, and almost always these unions have existed against or in favor of (possibly imaginary) others. Man has always pretended that it was not he who invented these motives, that they could not be fully controlled, that they were inevitably decided by Nature. These fantastic ideas in which he has pretended to believe have never united him with his fellow beings—precisely because he was unconsciously aware that they were fanciful ideals that were unlikely to offer him any real and durable advantages as a man. Only a higher—non-fatalistic, even if natural—ideal can unite all, without distinction, in an effort to achieve it.

By achieving immortality, man can—perhaps for the first time since his appearance on this earth—truly and indisputably distinguish himself from all other living species. By fixing himself in time at an age he chooses and interrupting the process of aging, man would break the spell cast by the most mysterious dimension prevailing in the universe, and this would be the first step toward the possibility of a greater understanding of life. I hope one day to take a glass, fill it with wine and drink it, to take a hen for a walk, and for it to be really me who is doing it.

Yours affectionately,
Gino De Dominicis

Both letters translated by Barry Schwabsky

"I should like to start by saying…"

Gino De Dominicis

I should like to start by saying that rather than a "history of beauty" I would call it a "history of the people living and near who are able to judge the people dead and distant." Normally someone is considered beautiful only if the person who is supposed to judge them looks at them very attentively. A person who is physically immortal does not have to look attentively. Beauty is only useful to those who run in order to make the journey seem longer. If a little boy is sad it means that he has young beautiful parents because they believed the opinion of an old person who was running. Beauty does not seem dangerous because it does not extend very far in space and time. Certainly a beautiful dead person in a photograph is less unpredictable than an ugly person who is alive. When a person says that someone is beautiful, it means that they need their ancestors. Seeing a person as beautiful means attributing temporal complications to them. An animal is beautiful when it is not being an animal. A plant is beautiful when it blocks our view of another plant. With not much time and a lot of space available it is preferable not to travel far but in the company of a beautiful person, who, because they resemble their parents, gives the impression of having traveled a lot. When someone dances they are beautiful if the music is beautiful, but the music is beautiful even if the person who is dancing is about to die. An old person is beautiful only for a young person. A sick person is beautiful only for nature. To see a person as beautiful you only have to remember them immediately and live in their company forever. Usually we remember a person in profile as more beautiful because they could not see us. Beautiful people can console and distract from their fundamental temporal anguish only the mad people who invented them. In actual fact, "beautiful" and "ugly" mean "would-be-beautiful" and "would-be-ugly." Usually nature makes more use of beautiful people because they are more grateful to nature; therefore, if death still exists, the beautiful are to blame. So I shall go out alone this evening.

Translated by Barry Schwabsky
Text of a talk given by the artist in November 1972 at the Galleria Schema, Florence, in the context of a conference on the theme of beauty. The text subsequently appeared on the invitation card for his one-person show at Lucio Amelio's Modern Art Agency in Naples, in April 1973.

A Brief Interview

Federica Negroni Manzini

FNM   For some time now, it has been interesting to observe a growing number of interviews, debates, and so on, in which artists set out their aims, problems, and aspirations, as well as the responses of critics who argue against some of them. Yet your own position in this remains unknown. Would you care to elucidate?

GDD   Yes. My position is standing when I make large paintings, drawings, and other works, and sitting for smaller ones.

Translated by Barry Schwabsky
This interview was originally published as "Breve intervista di Federica Negroni Manzini a Gino de Dominicis" in the catalogue of *La Biennale di Venezia. 46 Esposizione Internazionale d'Arte* (Venice, 1995), 363–64.

A Brief Interview

Domitilla S. Delfino

DSD   This is a really exceptional time! There have never been so many exhibitions and so many artists in the world as there are today, and never has there been such a problematic— not serene, but conflicted—relationship between the artist and the work of art, and this is positive. Art histories as detailed and fascinating as the Bible recount that "Rauschenberg begat Burri who begat …" and so on and arouse the interest not only of those who work in the field but also of an increasingly vast public. Today many "gallery owners," "critics," and "museum directors" feel that they are "something of an artist." They "express themselves" through the works of "their" artists and by mounting intriguing "group" exhibitions that succeed in arousing the curiosity of the public and in drawing them to places that are very often strange yet full of atmosphere but which, until then, had never been considered suitable for showing works of art. Very big exhibitions are being staged with hundreds of artists and works that "establish a dialogue" with each other as well as with "the space," and which serve to illustrate the visionary ideas of the "curators," who often want to anticipate prophetically what artists will do in the following decade, and this, too, is amazing and very original. So everything is "historicized live" without pointlessly waiting too long. There also exist countless instructive public collections, organized like a kind of natural history museum where works previously seen in galleries throughout the world are brought together. The works are selected without too many problems since the appointed venues notoriously have the power to transform into a work of art any object placed in their space. Today these works are dated to when they were first exhibited in public and not to when they were executed, and this is another novelty. Theories such as "the death of art," "going beyond the frame," etc. are also very positive and accompanied by original sophisticated terms that are very much in vogue such as "installation," "performance," "arrangement," "behaviorism," "conceptualism," "work in progress," "theme exhibition," "young artists," "curatorial operators," "fellow travelers," and "stables," which perfectly formalize a widespread understanding of the artist and his works. Very succinct but also useful labels have been coined that perfectly express the complexity of the various "trends": for example, "Pop Art," "Arte Povera,"

"Transavanguardia," etc., just as with the "historic avant-gardes." Then, even if it's not exactly close by, we often go into the "center" to get up-to-date on the latest novelties and the recent changes of "position" in the "art world," and this, as well as being fascinating, helps keep us from being so provincial. Finally, today many artists blithely skip over the stages necessary to the creation of a work by appropriating the results achieved by other artists, using them as a starting point for their own works, a method that has already been adopted in the field of science with excellent results. Today, the collective imagination mainly identifies with immaterial and mobile expressive languages and not with the material, immobile, mute "plastic arts." These came into being to contest transitoriness, perishability, and death, and to stop time, mainly through emotion and female beauty. This lack of interest in the visual arts is doubtless a great stimulus for today's artists, spurring them to produce more and more. Nor is it believed that the works of other periods are alive and are outside time, and it is for this reason that contemporary works of art quite rightly are compared only with each other. Objective and disinterested "sociopolitical" analyses have explained to us that at this "moment in history" it is "impossible to paint a picture" and the more intelligent and talented artists, in fact, "refuse to paint," aware of being in the "twentieth century" and that the future is just around the corner. It is also possible to appropriate and copy, by "quoting" works created by others, without having to worry about nonexistent copyright, which also gives one a very free hand. Recently a "new tradition" has shifted the center of gravity and greatly facilitated the possibility of expressing oneself without so many pointless problems, which has created great excitement. Why should galleries have to exhibit only visual artworks? The other languages have the right to be seen and followed too! Large, often very unconventional, alternative spaces have been taken over and are open to everything, and this, too, has been very entertaining and has contributed to creating an "international climate" and a great ferment. Visual art today is quite rightly considered a superstructure and we've overcome the extremely boring immobility of the works. They can finally move, as in the theater. Everything is also heading toward a pleasant symbiosis between art and life, toward naturalism and toward the long-hoped-for predominance of the word over the image. Usually the most interesting presentations are the most ephemeral ones that are executed "specifically for the space," by which they are often "inspired," where the only object that remains is a fine catalogue full of texts and photographs that often make the works appear more beautiful, like paintings. Bright, well-informed "art experts," who are bold and unprejudiced, confuse art with culture and spread a Western contemporary artistic model throughout the world, and this will certainly facilitate communication and understanding between nations immensely. This very unpredictable era has also overturned the concept of time; in fact, we consider today's art a young "modern" art, even though, since it comes after all that preceded it, it should be considered an ancient art, therefore more complex and not simpler. But for us who love horizontality, speed, and simplicity, this, too, is a good outcome. Fortunately—and today's artworks confirm this—we no longer believe in the "powers" and the "metaphysical quality" of the work, and works of art are considered much more simply as a special language that communicates through forms. It is their market price that gives them their level of credibility and importance and guarantees their "quality." Significantly, we also no longer believe that works of art would not even need to be seen to establish a relationship with the world and to exist. It's also very pleasurable and calming to be freed of the notion of the masterpiece; we have understood that the artwork is not the creation of the great artist's genius, but that all of us together contribute, each in his own way, to realizing the work of art. To be completely satisfied, we who participate in it so closely, need only be able to sign it, and why not let the public sign it too. Thus we contribute—and this is also most interesting—to creating the ideal conditions for completing the creation of a "figure" intermediate and alternative to that of the two poles of creation, woman and artist. In fact, this is the direction indicated by the "cultures" that have freely interpreted the original meaning. The boredom of the other periods has been avoided, art changes every ten years, first hot then cold or vice versa. All this and more is characteristic of the end of the twentieth century and it seems to prefigure a rosy future, and not just for the West. We would like to hear from you, De Dominicis, how you have managed and how you still manage today not to feel involved in all this? Don't you think that by dissociating yourself from all this, you will fail "to go down in history"?

GDD   Unfortunately, no.

Translated by Barry Schwabsky

This interview was originally published as "Breve intervista di Domitilla S. Delfino a Gino de Dominicis," in *Il Giornale dell'Arte*, no. 91 (July/August 1991): 32.

Some Impressions, Venice, June 15, 1993

Gino De Dominicis

The major arts have always been characterized by permanence and not by nomadism. As far as my works are concerned, the only nomadic thing about them is that they have been transported by truck from Rome to Venice. Moreover, painting, sculpture, and architecture, unlike writing, music, theater, cinema, etc., which unfold in space and time, are immobile creations. Western culture today mainly identifies with immaterial, mobile languages and forgets the high arts, which are material, mute, immobile, born from the desire to contest transitoriness, perishability, and death. The "artistic masterpiece" corresponds, in fact, to the "immortality of the body," and hence has nothing to do with the ephemeral. Moreover, since they do not exist in a temporal dimension, all visual artworks are contemporary. Given the universality of the visual arts, the concepts of internationalism and multiculturalism are implicit. The misunderstanding that there exists an "art world" rather than a "world art" has made possible an awkward attempt to shift the central focus from the work of art and the artist to those who deal with art, and, not by chance, some prizes at the Biennale were also awarded to non-artists; at this rate we will be giving prizes to the public as well at the next edition. As regards the West's cultural debts to other cultures, the main debt we all have in common is to the originary civilization. Art is confused with culture and vice versa; when art is creation and culture, by contrast, is the "history of creation." Even the concept of time has been reversed; in fact, contemporary art is thought of as being a young, modern art, whereas, since it comes after everything that preceded it, it should be considered the true ancient art. At the Biennale I noticed a very strange way of expressing oneself that harkened back to a mentality fashionable in the l960s and 1970s. Instead of celebrating the artworks, it was the spaces that were praised, the "rooms," the "arrangements," and it was no mere coincidence that a pavilion was awarded a prize instead of the artist exhibiting there. At the last Biennale they actually gave the prize for painting to a sculptor, the prize for sculpture to two photographers, and word was going around that they wanted to give the architecture prize to Alberto Moravia! Though it is disastrous, an anti-Art mentality seems to persist that has made it possible for nonartists to euphorically play a "creative," leading role. So that everyone can feel he is an artist, the work of art has been replaced by the problem of art or by an abstract sense of art; indeed, art is no longer considered the work of an artist but a product produced by the social elements that manage it. As regards mobility, interdisciplinarity, interrelationship, and breaking the boundaries between languages, there is misunderstanding here, too; in fact, all this is possible, but from "high" to "low" and not vice versa.

A great painter, apart from successfully transforming, if he needs to, something that lies outside that specific field into a work of art, could create a fine decoration, put on an interesting stage play, take a wonderful photograph, write an excellent critical text, win a table tennis championship, but never has a decorator, a theater director, a photographer, a critic, or a table tennis champion produced a painting. As regards the relationship between art and society, it is to be hoped that it is more than merely good and that they are both satisfied. The presence of three or four thousand "works," plus various kinds of spectacle, which is typical of mega exhibitions, only confuses and distracts the public from the few works of art on display. This Biennale seems to have wanted to celebrate its centenary by throwing a kind of big party, to mark the end of an era, I hope, and perhaps it is for this reason that "operatives" in other languages were invited to take part, such as musicians, directors, poets, journalists, photographers, dancers, ecologists, actors, critics, gallery owners, sociologists, playwrights, performers, philosophers, etc., who were often given more space—and this, too, is symptomatic—than the visual artists. The spectacular does not suit the visual arts; indeed, the artwork is alive and it would not even need to be seen to establish a relationship with the world. So the event was made more exciting and entertaining, in order to attract the general public and the mass media. And despite the fact that they are trying to make everyone believe that visual art is no longer indispensable for staging an exhibition of visual art, they have assured me that the true Biennale of visual art will most definitely be the next one!

Translated by Barry Schwabsky
This text was originally published as "Alcune impressioni di Gino De Dominicis" in *Il Giornale dell'Arte*, no. 113 (July/August 1993): 29.

Immortality

Miriam Mirolla

MM   Recently a large painting of yours, about seven meters long, titled *The Sumerian Foundation of Rome*, was exhibited in Rome. Do you think that Rome was founded by the Sumerians and not by Romulus and Remus?

GDD   Yes.

MM   The immortality of the soul is a postulate found in many religions. The ancient Sumerian civilization, which dates back to 4,000 BCE, defines God as physical and immortal and therefore alludes to the immortality of the body. Do you think that the subject of immortality is still relevant today?

GDD   Yes.

MM   In the Bible it is written that in the beginning was the word. By contrast, you entitled one of your exhibitions *In principio era l'immagine* (In the beginning was the image). So do you think that the image came before the word?

GDD   Yes.

By achieving immortality, man can—perhaps for the first time since his appearance on this earth—truly and indisputably distinguish himself from all other living species. By fixing himself in time at an age he chooses and interrupting the process of aging, man would break the spell cast by the most mysterious dimension prevailing in the universe, and this would be the first step toward the possibility of a greater understanding of life. I hope one day to take a glass, fill it with wine and drink it, to take a hen for a walk, and for it to be really me who is doing it.
Gino De Dominicis, "Letter on Immortality"

MM   In a famous exhibition twenty years ago, in an underground car park, the day after the opening, you suddenly dismantled the show leaving a vast empty room. How come? You didn't like the space?

GDD   Yes.

MM   There is a tendency to think that art should be more like science. Is it true that you think exactly the opposite, namely, that it is science that needs art?

GDD   Yes.

Life says to death: "In order to exist, you need to do away with me and this is why you have always been hated. For me to exist, on the other hand, all that's needed is that you maintain the proper distance. There lies the difference."

Death, taken by surprise, says something in response and at that moment realizes that he can also exist autonomously. Life then …
Gino De Dominicis, 1983[1]

MM   In the *Zodiaco*, which you exhibited in Rome many years ago, all the signs of the zodiac were represented by real figures and objects. For example, real twins for Gemini, a real bull for Taurus, a real ram for Aries, a real goat for Capricorn, real scales for Libra, and so on. It was a work that was concerned with myth and you showed it at a time when naturalistic and conceptual works were in fashion. Was the novelty of this work immediately understood by the art world?

GDD   Yes.

Dear …
I don't think that things exist as such. A glass, a man, a hen, for example, are not really a glass, a man, or a hen but only the substantiation for the possibility of the existence of a glass, a man, or a hen. To truly exist, things would have to be eternal, immortal. Only in that way would they be not simply substantiations of certain possibilities but truly things.
Gino De Dominicis, "Letter on Immortality"

MM   Is the zodiac as a symbolic image Sumerian in origin?

GDD   Yes.

MM   *Second Solution of Immortality (The Universe Is Still)* is a work that was shown at the 1972 Venice Biennale and which caused a scandal worldwide. Did you want to scandalize people?

GDD   No.

When we perform an action—for example, running a race—we are not actually running; we are only substantiating the possibility of running and of the existence of the race, to then pass this stored experience to "Nature." In fact, compared to the length of time that our species has existed, the time we have at our disposal during our own lifetime to take advantage of this experience is very limited. To truly exist, we should halt time, and then—finally—it would be we, ourselves, who were living; that is, it would be we ourselves, for ourselves, substantiating ourselves.

Being unable to intervene directly to halt the inexorable course of his own "internal time" and prolong his own life, man has invented means that make this time run faster. Intervening upon space, he has indirectly managed to intervene upon time. This operation would be justified, however, only if space was finite and our imagination limited. Unfortunately, however, it is only a palliative and a very serious mistake. Culture, too—our desire for knowledge

---

1   Editor's note: The title of an unidentified painting from 1983. See Duccio Trombadori, "The Prophet and Conjurer of Self-Deception," in this volume, 53.

of the past, present, and future, of the "why" and the substance of things—is the fruit of a neurosis arising from our "limited" period here on earth. In fact, in these conditions, we must be the ones who move toward "things" in order to know them; while, in an ideal temporal situation, it would be the "things" that could move toward us to make themselves known in the way that was most natural to them.
Gino De Dominicis, "Letter on Immortality"

MM   So you consider your work *Second Solution of Immortality*, a work of visual art that can be interpreted traditionally?

GDD   Yes.

MM   Unlike other artists who have a great many exhibitions and publish a great many catalogues, you have very few shows and have always refused to publish catalogues or books that document your work. Is this the consequence of a precise strategy?

GDD   Yes.

MM   So all this expresses your character and your mindset?

GDD   Yes.

If everyone could imagine and desire their own salvation, the preservation of their body for eternity, that would mean that finally there would be no mental dispersion (entropy). Therefore, the "second principle of thermodynamics" would no longer be valid, because it would be contradicted by the behavior of an organism that can project, without distraction (entropy), its own eternal condition as an "isolated system."
Gino De Dominicis, 1972[2]

MM   Women's faces often appear in your pictures and, in one sculpture in particular, you have made the face of a statue of the Madonna come to life. In traditional iconography the Madonna is always depicted as sad or in some cases smiling. Instead, you show her laughing. Is this perhaps to be interpreted as a liberating tribute to the traditionally oppressed female?

GDD   Yes.

MM   So are women the prime source of inspiration for your work?

GDD   Yes.

MM   Let's talk a bit about the present situation. Are you optimistic and do you think that Italy will have a better future given the rapid changes taking place at the moment?

GDD   Yes.

---

[2]   This text was written on the occasion of the *Cocktail per festeggiare il superamento del secondo principio della termodinamica*, organized by the artist at Incontri Internazionali d'Arte, Palazzo Taverna, Rome, on December 18, 1972.

MM   In some of your works there are figures that look like actual extraterrestrials. Do you believe that extraterrestrial civilizations exist?

GDD   Yes.

MM   The ancient Sumerians recount in their writings that they were initiated into culture and learned all they know from a civilization that came from outer space. Do you think all that is true?

GDD   Yes.

MM   Gino De Dominicis, have you ever been a member of or ever been interested in artistic groups or trends such as Pop Art, Conceptual Art, Arte Povera, and the Transavanguardia?

GDD   No.

MM   Gino De Dominicis, do you consider yourself the greatest living artist of the twentieth century?

GDD   Who knows!

Translated by Barry Schwabsky
This interview was initially broadcast as part of "Dedalo. Percorsi d'arte," RAI Radio 2, 1994, and subsequently published as "L'immortalità. Intervista a Gino De Dominicis" in *Flash Art International*, no. 214 (February/March 1999): 85–86.

The Unbearable Lightness of Art

Claudia Koll

CK   Gino De Dominicis, one of the most important contemporary painters, seems to get interested in a project only when it is strictly impossible. His enigmatic, impossible projects have addressed immortality and squaring the circle, among other things. It was impossible for Jean Clair to get him to participate in the next Venice Biennale. *L'Angelo* had also been pursuing an impossible project for quite some time: getting to interview him.

(The interviewer appears in side profile, walking in slow motion. The scene cuts to a shot of her from behind, pulling open a set of large doors.)

INTERVIEWER   Follow me, I will take you to meet Gino De Dominicis.

(Down the corridor, she pushes open a second, identical set of doors and rounds a corner. After the cut, as the camera pans right, past a wall, we see seated at a desk that floats in the air, Gino De Dominicis with a brush in each hand painting a canvas held on a desk-mounted easel. As the camera rotates around him, the work remains invisible as both brushes work at it. The camera cuts to a wider shot of De Dominicis smoking, suspended in the air with his desk.)

INTERVIEWER   Gino De Dominicis, why did you agree to appear on TV?

GDD   Well, there's actually been a mix-up, because a friend of mine who doesn't speak Italian that well picked up the phone, and then she told me some people were coming for a *visione delle tele* (a viewing of my canvases). That's what I thought it was, but it turned out to be *televisione*. Anyway, it's fine all the same.

INTERVIEWER   De Dominicis, you were invited to take part in the next Venice Biennale, the Centenary Biennale, with a dedicated room. You shocked everyone by turning down the invitation. What can you tell us about it?

GDD   It wasn't me who turned down the invitation, it was my works that didn't want to be in it. I just respected their wish …

INTERVIEWER   In your opinion, what is the difference between ancient art and modern art?

GDD   Well … There's a mix-up, I mean, what is considered ancient art is what came earlier, whereas what is made today is considered modern, young. It's actually the other way around, because time doesn't run backward, which is why earlier art is actually younger than our own art, and less ancient, by virtue of its coming earlier. The real ancient art should be the one that's made today.

INTERVIEWER Why do you make few exhibitions, and why did you never agree to publish catalogues or books on your works?

GDD Well, I make exhibitions … a few exhibitions compared to who and what? I just do what I feel like doing.

INTERVIEWER You made some invisible objects. Can you explain them to us?

GDD Invisibility is a kind of immortality and … any fast-moving object, very fast moving, vanishes from sight … so these invisible objects do exist. In the cosmos, too.

INTERVIEWER Gino De Dominicis, some newspapers have reported on some critics' attacks and statements against Italy's most important artists. What do you think about it?

GDD There's not much to think about. These … these are due to an inferiority complex toward the artists … They're a little jealous. It's always been the case. There's nothing to be done.

INTERVIEWER You refuse to be framed in any artistic movement such as Pop Art, Conceptual Art, Arte Povera, Transavanguardia, and so on. What is your position, then?

GDD My position is sitting when I make small-format paintings, and standing when I make large ones.

INTERVIEWER De Dominicis, you have been showing, among other places, at the Royal Academy in London, Naples's Capodimonte Museum, the Beaubourg in Paris, the Rayburn Foundation in New York, and next June you will represent Italy at the UN exhibition in Geneva. Do you see art as the expression of one particular culture, or is it international?

GDD Art isn't anything like … it's neither international nor anything else. It's a phenom—an issue that's concerned with the cosmos, it's a planetary and cosmic phenomenon.

INTERVIEWER What is the relationship between visual art and other media such as music, poetry, and cinema?

GDD Well, there's a tendency today to integrate all media into visual art, and that's linked with this thing they call contamination, this sort of stuff … They're actually all very different media, even though the popular imagination today tends to identify itself with these motion-based media … let's say, like music, theater, cinema, the TV and so on, whereas the language used in the major arts, the visual arts—painting, sculpture, architecture—is motionless, mute, and material. And so the relationship of other media with this … is very hard. They are all very different media, so there's this tendency that's really hard to understand … I mean, I can see why, they probably all want to feel a little bit like artists, painters … who knows why … Anyway …

INTERVIEWER In 1981 you made a work that was later bought by MoMA, New York's Museum of Modern Art, titled *In principio era l'immagine; No!* Why this title?

GDD Well, because there are several ideas about it; there are … I think the image comes before words and before numbers. There you go, first the image, then words.

INTERVIEWER A seven-meter-long painting by you was recently on display in Rome and titled *La fondazione sumera di Roma* (1990). Is it your view that Rome was founded by the Sumerians rather than by Romulus and Remus?

GDD Yes, that's how I see it, yes, it was founded before Romulus and Remus … by the Sumerians.

INTERVIEWER Should some of your works be regarded as performances?

GDD No, absolutely not.

INTERVIEWER *Seconda soluzione d'immortalità (l'universo è immobile)* is a work that was shown at the 1972 Venice Biennale, and which gave rise to a scandal all over the world. Did you wish to make a scandal?

GDD No way! Absolutely not …

INTERVIEWER And you didn't see this scandal coming?

GDD Of course not.

INTERVIEWER What's your opinion about the death of art and the theorization of art as a way to break the frame and get out of the painting?

GDD Well, these are … there's no such thing as the death of art … "Getting out of the painting" is just a phrase, because there's no way you can actually get out of the painting. You either make paintings or make something else.

INTERVIEWER And what do you think about American art?

GDD American art was very much influenced by Duchamp, mostly, and a little bit by Picasso too, and Duchamp did … he was taken literally, even things that Duchamp did as a paradox, as a joke … It was taken as a way of making art, this stuff, and this led to some problems, which I don't think they have figured out yet. Also, these trends, they … there's always "Art" attached to it, like Pop Art, Minimal Art, Conceptual Art … it's no coincidence that they always attach this term, "Art": it's a way to make it clear that it is art, because most of the time it's not that clear … not always, but still …

INTERVIEWER There is an economic crisis today that has also been affecting the art world. What's your opinion?

GDD Well, economic crises are started on purpose to make paintings cheaper. Also, visual art is self-evident, I mean the art object is, so paradoxically, visual art wouldn't even need to be seen, whereas other media need to be seen or heard or listened to in order to exist. Another distinctive element of visual art is that it doesn't address any one spectator in particular and there is no hierarchy of spectatorship, everyone is at an equal distance from the work. There are no experts. A kid's judgment is just as valid as a so-called expert's for the artist, there's no particular… Also because there's no such thing as an art expert because the only ones that are truly experts are the artists, all the others are just—they perceive art but they can't be experts, otherwise they would make it, they would know how to make it. Then there's this mix-up between creation and creativity. The artist is a creator, not a creative. There are creative people—they can be very nice, too, and talented—but one does not equal the other. Anyway this… that thing… with creatives, and artists, it all began in the late sixties when art dealers started to be creative, then came creative critics, and then came creative museum directors. And so it was an escalation which, you know, led to these Venice Biennale mix-ups, because they're made as if they were the director's own work. He feels like an artist and makes his exhibition by inviting the arti… a thematic exhibition, by inviting the artists to illustrate his theme, his core issue, with their works, and to me this is just insane. I'll now get back to trying to finish this ubiquitous work I've been working on for three years.

INTERVIEWER   Goodbye and thank you, then!

GDD   You're welcome, goodnight.

Transcribed and translated by Andrea Vesentini
This interview was originally aired on Italian national television, as part of Canale 5's art and culture program, *L'Angelo*, in 1995.

My Works Have No Wish
to Be Exhibited in the 46th
Venice Biennale

Gino De Dominicis

The director of the next Venice Biennale has been appointed to organize the exhibition of visual art, to celebrate the event's centenary with an exhibition on the history of the Biennale, and to ensure that all of the selected works and artists are presented in the most suitable way. From various communications and from the telegram informing me that I have been invited to take part, I gather that rather than an opportunity to offer a preview of my works with no interference, the Venice Biennale has become the director's personal event with a title, *Identity and Otherness*, invented by him. We thus have an exhibition of his set "theme" to be developed through works of art that constitute visual examples which serve to illustrate his theories, not to mention the involvement of fashion designers, set designers, and so on and so forth.

None of this is even original. Back in 1972, for example, the Documenta exhibition in Kassel was organized by a "creative director" along similarly bizarre lines.

The 1995 Biennale, like others before it, including the edition of 1993, is the result of the same mentality, one that for a long time now has been irksome not only to me but to the public at large.

A letter signed by numerous Italian artists was sent to the Venice Biennale on March 8, 1994, and published the following day in various newspapers. It expressed opposition to that mentality, to any preestablished theme, and to the obsession with self-advertisement of "curators" who make use of events and the works of artists to create "their own" exhibitions and thus feel that they, too, are artists to some small degree. This letter has evidently not been taken into due consideration.

What's certain is that no one has ever gone to the Venice Biennale out of curiosity about the ideas of its director, but rather out of a curiosity to see, with no attempt at indoctrination, previously unexhibited works of contemporary art. And it is also very strange that the director should be using the structure of the Biennale in order to "exhibit" and disseminate his theories, when a book would serve the same purpose.

Given the abnormal nature of the situation, my works refuse to take part in the show *Identity and Otherness*, which in 1995 will occupy the spaces of the Venice Biennale.

Translated by Barry Schwabsky
In this seemingly open letter to curator Jean Clair, the artist explains why he refuses to take part in the 46th Biennale di Venezia, *Identità e alterità: Figure del corpo 1895–1995*, June 10–November 5, 1995. There is no trace of this letter in the archives of the Venice

Biennale. In all likelihood, it was written by the artist but never sent. The archives do contain a copy of a telegram sent by De Dominicis, dated December 14, 1994, addressed to the President of the Biennale, Gian Luigi Rondi: "I thank you for your invitation in the telegram dated 30/11/1994 to participate in the exhibition 'Identità e alterità' for the next Venice Biennale. I must communicate, however, that my works do not want to be exhibited at 'Identità e alterità' and consequently I shall not participate in the exhibition either. Best regards etc." The following year, in an interview with Bernardino Cappello published by *La Repubblica* on June 19, 1995, De Dominicis refers to a letter he wrote titled "My works have no wish to be exhibited at the XLVI Venice Biennale," as he "could not adapt to a preestablished cultural operation."

Please Do Not Disturb the Artists

Franco Fanelli

We know that there is never a Biennale without controversy and the artists themselves have always been among those who criticize the Venice exhibition. For Gino De Dominicis, this began with his "live" room in 1972. When he was invited to the last two editions, in 1993, he said that his works had nothing to do with the Biennale, while this year he simply did not participate. Despite his idiosyncratic attitude to interviews, De Dominicis has agreed to answer the following questions.

FF   Mr. De Dominicis, you have recently underlined that certain disciplines have nothing to do with visual art. In your opinion, what canons should the identikit of the contemporary artist adhere to?

GDD   Despite the fact that important works of art are rarely found in the world today, only those who manage to establish a relationship that is not superficial and more respectful with the High Arts—painting, sculpture (three-dimensional works), and architecture—can understand and decide their future, present, and past. As far as the identity of the artist and art exhibitions are concerned, it must be said that every artistic expression is born of a special mentality and a desire that further distinguishes it from all other modes of expression. Painting, sculpture, and architecture, specifically, which are immobile, material, and mute, originate from a rejection of corruptibility and death. They create forms that resist time, and establish and perpetuate the desire for immortality. Whereas the other expressions take place in time, they move with it, and since they do not confront matter, they do not create a form.

FF   Who do you consider "artists" today?

GDD   Today it is thought that anyone, taking advantage of the opportunities provided by the art milieu, can enter and become part of the world of great artists; he will be seen in relation to them, even though he may express himself exclusively through performances, videos, multimedia installations, photographs, fashion, etc. Creation is confused with creativity. Recent editions of the Venice Biennale have invited directors, photographers, dancers, ecologists, journalists, set designers, poets, actors, critics, gallery owners, designers, sociologists, musicians, playwrights, performers, videographers, etc., who are often given more space than artists. It is also thought that the spaces assigned to visual art have the power to work the miracle of changing anything they exhibit into an artwork. And to finish it all off, the prize for the best painting was awarded to a video, the sculpture prize went to photographs and another painting prize went to a sculpture. Such absurdities show a lack of understanding and a lack of interest in visual artworks among those who want to deal with them. It's like a nightmare: in the spaces that should be devoted to art the public finds precisely those languages that currently dominate and routinely absorb the Western collective imagination—languages that are readily adopted by exhibition organizers so that they, too, can feel they are something of an artist.

FF   You made a name for yourself through research that some have described as conceptual. What thread links the De Dominicis who reemerged today as a sophisticated draftsman to the artist that exhibited a seated mongoloid man at the 1972 Venice Biennale?

GDD   It is more than obvious that my works have never had anything to do with so-called Conceptual Art—an artistic trend that triggered a response and aroused interest primarily in Southern Italy, perhaps due to it having the same etymological root as common Southern Italian proper names like Concetto, Concetta, Concettina, Concezione, etc. I never exhibited a mongoloid man. I created a work entitled *Second Solution of Immortality (The Universe Is Still)* that consisted of some works placed in front of Mr. Paolo Rosa (whom everyone crassly called "the mongoloid man," which is like calling someone who wears glasses "the shortsighted man" instead of using his name). Rosa, from within the work itself, observed these works from his particular and unique standpoint, which was the opposite of the viewers'. What an exaggerated scandal simply on account of nothing more than two different points of view! The thread that links my works is me.

FF   By the way, why do you have such fraught relations with the Biennale? Last year you strongly contested the exhibition, stating that your works had nothing to do with it; this year, you turned down the invitation—

GDD   A large number of Italian artists signed an article that was published in the *Corriere della Sera* with a title that referred erroneously only to the curator of last year's Biennale. Instead, the text pointed out the characteristics and the mentality that no subsequent director of the Biennale should have, the same characteristics and mentality that nearly all exhibition curators have had for the past years, including the curator of the previous Biennale, and also Jean Clair! It's for this reason that my works did not want to take part in "his" Biennale.

FF You have recently been named as the possible future president of the Quadriennale. How did that happen?

GDD Some rather optimistic people, without previously consulting me, put forward my name for president of the Quadriennale. I wanted to amuse myself for a few days by seeing what would happen. Then I sent a telegram saying that I withdrew my candidature, certain that it would never be accepted by the art personnel.

FF Though you are by choice one of the most reclusive artists active today, as the solitary artist par excellence you still have dealers, critics, collectors, and colleagues whom you feel—or who in actual fact—appreciate your work, don't you?

GDD I don't work; I never have enough free time to do so. I make art and I can do that alone.

FF How do you live in a milieu that demands that its protagonists put in personal appearances all the time?

GDD Well, I have noted that people from the so-called art world are never present on the most interesting occasions and in the most interesting places.

FF In short, why have you chosen to steer clear of the so-called circuit for years?

GDD The "circuit," among other things, periodically produces little personalities, all of whom would have greatly interested Sigmund Freud, who only want to experience the thrill of bugging artists. Now it's Bonito Oliva's turn. He does nothing but talk about me. If he goes on like this I'll have to cancel my subscription to *Eco della Stampa*[1] or else my studio will be swamped with clippings full of his platitudes.

FF What are your relations with the critics, museums, the market, prices, sales, and everything that makes art a job?

GDD I don't like exhibiting or selling my works, though every now and then I do. I've always tried not to become famous so that I could buy back my own works cheaply one day. Anyway, to exist and to have a good relationship with the world, works of art wouldn't even need to be seen, and as they are outside time, they are always contemporary.

FF Since you are an artist who appears very rarely in public and doesn't give interviews, our readers are hoping to learn something about your life. What artistic training did you have?

GDD You're wrong. I've appeared in public every day since I was little, and as you can see, I do give interviews. I have always painted and made drawings, and I have also produced three-dimensional works. When I was seventeen I had a one-

1 Editor's note: A newspaper clipping service.

man show of about one hundred works and they were all sold on that occasion.

FF   What are your future projects? What are you working on at the moment?

GDD   An extraterrestrial said to a Sumerian: "There has never existed and there never will exist a spaceship without a picture." I'll make some trips with Clementina.

Translated by Barry Schwabsky
This interview was originally published as "Gino de Dominicis. Si prega di non disturbare gli artisti" in *Il Giornale dell'Arte*, no. 136 (September 1995): 7.

He Is Too English for Me

Adriana Polveroni

AP   Francis Bacon has children and grandchildren in the art of this century who are sometimes found in the most unexpected places. Among his descendants are many performance artists who prefer working with the human body rather than the human condition. We therefore address the question of his legacy to an artist who, in his "mise-en-scènes of bodies," has taken to an extreme the human anguish that Bacon obsessively delineated in so many of his canvases. But is this really so? Let us hear what Gino De Dominicis has to say. Has Francis Bacon's lesson been important for you?

GDD   His works have never meant much to me. They remind me a bit too much of blurred photographs. Even the framing of his subjects is photographic in style and doesn't convince me. I'm sorry that Bacon never painted still faces, which is far more complicated to do than faces in motion. He himself spoke of this limitation in one of his last interviews.

AP   Do you recognize him as a great artist?

GDD   No, I prefer Ottone Rosai, who I have always thought influenced Bacon. Recently I was pleased to have confirmation that Bacon was very familiar with Rosai's works and considered him one of the greatest European painters. However, Bacon is still a good English painter.

AP   What do you mean by the adjective "English"?

GDD   England is a very big country and even people from other countries can like Bacon's paintings.

AP   Where does the similarity between Bacon and Rosai lie?

GDD   In their distortion of faces and figures they have in common.

AP   What do you think of the contemporary relevance of Bacon?

GDD   Being relevant is not the artist's problem, but the public's.

Translated by Barry Schwabsky
This interview was originally published as "Per me è troppo inglese. Colloquio con Gino De Dominicis" in *L'Espresso*, June 13, 1996, 122.

A Memo at the End of the Century

Duccio Trombadori

DT   The younger generations are probably not the most fortunate. The legacy of the twentieth century is no light burden. This may also be the reason that, not infrequently, we trust the myth of freshness and novelty represented by youth. In the visual arts we focus increasingly on young artists—

GDD   An artist's age is unimportant; his works are what counts. In fact, it's ridiculous to think of Raphael and Picasso when they were twenty as "young artists." The concept of youth is naturalistic and it isn't an inherent value. After every crisis or traumatic event in the world there's a physiological need to "start again" and therefore to feel "young." In the "modern" world even the perception of time has been reversed. In fact, what came before us is considered older, more ancient, and what comes after us is considered young, whereas in reality it is the exact opposite.

DT   In a relatively brief space of time, more or less thirty years, various aesthetic trends have been successful and succeeded one another in the hearts of the younger generation. I remember Pop Art, Arte Povera, Conceptual Art, and the Transavanguardia. It's a question of understanding what they have left us.

GDD   They have left their "works." I've never been interested in art in general; moreover, the adjectives used indicate a reductive attitude.

DT   However, we need to reflect on the fact that both the practices of the neo-avant-gardes and postmodern poetics refer to an idea of linguistic nomadism as the virtuous condition of aesthetic experience.

GDD   I like to repeat that the high arts are ontologically the opposite of all the other artistic languages, and one of their main characteristics is that they are stationary. "Nomadism," also in its psychological sense, is linked to languages that are immaterial and mobile. This era does not like visual art, but the "nomadism" of languages that "flow" in time and space: writing, music, cinema, television, etc. The many people who continue to deal with visual art with the sole intention of distorting its very foundations End rendering it homogeneous through those languages of the future that are at first more congenial to them only sow confusion and waste the time they never had. In an era of communicative, global, dematerialized, and abstract leveling, the only exceptions are drawings, paintings, and sculptures.

DT However, it is a fact that the proliferation of visual art-works seems to eliminate any possibility of synthetic analysis and evaluation. In order to be objective, exhibitions become a kind of inventory, listing an endless series of artistic expressions.

GDD Today, interdisciplinarity, breaking boundaries, and contamination between languages seem to be the fashion, although, in actuality, there is a tendency to replace the artist-creator with the figure of the "creative." If contamination between languages has ever existed, it has always been in one direction only: the various "artistic" languages have always copied or drawn from the high arts. Therefore it is the "creative" languages that have let themselves be contaminated by the high arts and not vice versa. The absurd idea of setting alongside the high arts languages that have nothing to do with them reached its peak at the most recent Venice Biennales, which will certainly go down in history for their stupidity. At these events the painting prize was awarded to a sculptor, the sculpture prize to two photographers, and then they couldn't decide whether to give the architecture prize to a video artist or Alberto Moravia!

DT The greater the disorder under heaven, the harder it is to find the right measure.

GDD In parallel to the Venice Biennale they should organize a Biennale for creatives (in Milan, perhaps) to which painters and sculptors should not be invited. In this case it would also be justifiable if someone a bit "creative" were to curate the exhibition. Prizes could also be awarded at this Biennale. For example, the Andy Warhol Prize for the Best Photographer, and other such prizes for the Best Performance, the Best Video, the Best Display, the Best Fashion Designer, etc. That way, everyone would be happy, especially those who would be absent—the painters and sculptors.

DT With ever-increasing insistence, artistic value and aesthetic significance are given to the speed of the message and of its transmission by the means of communication and telecommunication.

GDD A work of art cannot be translated into other languages such as photography, writing, etc. It must be seen "for real." Thinking that, by logging onto the internet or filling the house with catalogues, the public can become familiar with works of art from all over the world, is a mistake. It would be better if, instead of logging on to the net, the public and artists bought plane tickets and train tickets to go and see artworks in person. That would also give them at last the chance to be "nomads."

DT There are people who give a secondary value to the work of art as an object.

GDD For some time now everyone's been saying they're painters or that they want to be considered one, despite the fact that they don't paint pictures. Unfortunately for them, they are surrounded by very kind people who indulge them in this conviction. And because of this they happily go on believing they are painters.

DT I agree, but let's not forget Conceptual Art.

GDD I remember a unique phenomenon in the history of art: at the end of the 1960s, I noted that suddenly a large number of visual artists were wearing glasses. I was quite surprised, but then I found out that they were not painters or sculptors but "conceptual artists." In fact, the sense of sight was not so vital for these "conceptual artists" as it is for a painter. Their works analyzed art or the "problem of art." Another strange thing at the time was that "creative" gallery owners happily decided to make the spaces assigned to visual art available to any language and to anyone who had something to say.

DT It's said that Conceptualism was born with Duchamp.

GDD In America—and then back in Europe—they have taken Duchamp's "position" literally, thinking he was a model to be imitated and that his way of making art was alternative and modern. In fact, it was simply Marcel Duchamp's way of making art. One should never mistake an artist for a model, and still less a model, male or female, for an artist.

DT The lack of modernist certainties has created in many people a need to rethink tradition and revise the history of figurative culture. A typical aspect of the postmodern mentality is the "pleasure of citation." This too is a sign of the desperate search for a direction, in order to reestablish a table of values.

GDD Drawing, painting, and sculpture are not traditional but originary forms of expression. Today, we seem to confuse art with culture. Art is creation; culture is the account or re-elaboration of creation. Thinking to create a work of art by quoting or copying works of art that already exist means having a merely formal relationship with the work. It would be like finding a television in the future and copying its form without knowing its meaning or function. Even the copy of an African sculpture can never have the powers of the original. That is the difference between a work of art and an aesthetic object.

DT If the arts of painting, sculpture, and architecture are "originary," the problem arises of the autonomy of the form with respect to the "discourse" that situates it historically. It seems to me that, in general, the idea that the word and the critic are more important than the form and the artist is very widespread.

GDD   Here we are faced with another reversal. In fact, first came images, material forms, and then the words to name them. It is not merely by chance that Gilgamesh was a painter, sculptor, architect, and king of Uruk. Some millennia ago, however, it was decided that other social figures should take the place of the artist. So fantastical hierarchies were invented and reversals were effected, which in our era have gone as far as possible. All this was followed by a decline in knowledge. For example, the zodiac that was originally a Sumerian creation, which the greatest civilizations were linked to and inspired by, has today simply become the popular horoscope. Tarot cards, which were originally an Egyptian initiatory book, are now read as an individual social game. It is also symptomatic that the people most in vogue today are curators, organizers of exhibitions. Visual art too is now perceived as something quite different from what it principally is. What has been lost, among other things, is the knowledge of the work's powers. The visual art object is a living object and is not principally made to be seen. To be viewed in a museum is a secondary purpose. In any event it is the public who are exhibited to the work of art, and never vice versa. The artistic masterpiece is anti-entropic.

DT   Is the "art world" definitively paradoxical?

GDD   An art world has never existed and does not exist, there are only works of art in the world. Art is concerned with genius and its space is verticality. It doesn't move horizontally from right to left or vice versa, but it moves, immobile, from height to height. As my aunt also rightly thought.

Translated by Barry Schwabsky

This interview was originally published as "Promemoria di fine secolo. Colloquio sulla contemporaneità" in the catalogue *XII Quadriennale Italiana 1950–1990. Ultime generazioni* (Rome: De Luca, 1999), 30–31. The catalogue accompanied the exhibition held at the Palazzo delle Esposizioni, Rome, and the Ala Mazzoniana in Stazione Termini, Rome, September 25–November 25, 1996.

Get Thee Behind Me, Dear Creative!

Ela Caroli

"I've never been very interested in the Venice Biennales or in big exhibitions in general. Though I have participated in some Biennales, my works were never happy about it, and besides they were surrounded by masses of objects rather than works of art." Gino De Dominicis is speaking in his studio, just a few steps from Piazza Navona in Rome. The old rooms house the works that represent the thirty years' activity of this Italian artist, who is among the most highly valued internationally. His first exhibition was held in 1966 and since then De Dominicis has witnessed—though remaining mostly dissociated from them—the artistic trends that have succeeded each other over the last three decades, while he has been combining innovative expressions with an interest in ancient civilizations like that of Sumer. His drawings, paintings, and three-dimensional works have often triggered discussion and in one case actually caused a scandal when, at the 1972 Venice Biennale, he included a seated man with Down syndrome in one of his works. "I'm not interested in scandals," says the artist, "given that it's the public who are exhibited to the work of art and not vice versa." In 1995, De Dominicis refused to take part in the Venice Biennale curated by Jean Clair; earlier, he had declined an invitation to the 1982 Documenta at Kassel and refused to compete for the prizes at the 1993 Biennale. "I'm not very interested in modern or in ancient art, but rather in antediluvian art," he states. "Anyway, I don't like big exhibitions and this fashion of introducing into the specific field of the visual arts languages that have nothing to do with them. They are also trying to make us believe that there is no difference between creation and creativity."

EC   How do you define this difference?

GDD   Photography can reproduce immobile images, for example, of the forms of the human face and body, which are the way they are precisely because they are adapted to and designed for movement. And I think that's why those images are not alive and are fundamentally anti-aesthetic. This is also the limit of naturalism and realism in art. By contrast, in a painting, the painter uses matter to create forms that are right for immobility.

EC   What do you think about Germano Celant being appointed curator of the 1997 Venice Biennale?

GDD   I just heard a rumor today that Celant finally intends to mount a Biennale that focuses exclusively on the visual arts, without there being the contaminations of other languages such as photography, fashion, performance art, video art, and the multimedia in general. The best artists will be invited and each will have a room to himself. They will be free to show their works without having to follow a preestablished theme. So it will be a very simple Biennale to mount, without the pointless complications of the previous ones. This will finally please both the artists and the public, who previously thought they were going to see an exhibition of visual art and found themselves face to face with something quite different.

EC However, many critics and a section of the public think differently. They want to find something in exhibitions and museums that reflects the varied means of contemporary communication.

GDD The public and organizers often want to be entertained. So it would be an idea to organize a Biennale for creatives, in Milan, for instance, to which painters and sculptors would absolutely not be invited. Prizes could be awarded at this Biennale: the Andy Warhol Prize for the Best Photographer, for example, and others for the Best Performance, the Best Video, the Best Display, the Best Fashion Designer, and so on. That way everyone would be happy, especially those who are absent—that is, painters and sculptors.

EC In a society like today's, based on a surplus of aesthetic messages, how can we relate to contemporary art and how, on the other hand, can an artist formulate a new aesthetics?

GDD To begin with, we must not confuse art with culture. The visual artwork is a living thing that does not need to be seen to exist and relate to the world. The artistic masterpiece is anti-entropic. Instead of filling their houses with catalogues or logging onto the Internet it would be better if the public got a plane or train ticket to go and see artworks in person. In this psychologically nomadic era of dematerialized and abstract global communication, only anti-ephemeral works of art such as drawings, paintings, and sculptures are the exception and must be the exception. They are material, immobile, and mute, ontologically the opposite of all the other languages.

EC The new artistic expressions from the postwar years until today are still under the influence of America. How can we "liberate" ourselves from this, in your opinion?

GDD I have never succumbed to that influence. To protect yourself from "American influence" and artistic trends, I advise you to wrap up well in a knowledge of your origins. Of how, where, when, and why the first civilization was suddenly born on planet Earth.

Translated by Barry Schwabsky
This interview was originally published as "Caro creativo vade retro!" in *L'Unità*, December 9, 1996.

Maxims, 1969–1996

Gino De Dominicis

It is the public that exhibits itself to art and not vice versa.

Nowadays it is believed that the spaces dedicated to visual art have the miraculous power to make anything exhibited there into a work of art.

It is a mistake to put the name of the artist under the photographic documentation of a work of art. It is the name of the photographer who took the picture that should be there.

I am not very interested in modern art or even in classical art. I prefer antediluvian art.

My works have often refused to take part in large exhibitions.

Photography does not create; it reproduces or interprets what exists.

A painter is like a conjuror who must succeed in astonishing himself with his tricks. That is where the complexity lies.

Fashion shows would undoubtedly enjoy greater success if there were no clothes.

Instead of using works by artists—sometimes even dead artists—to illustrate and back up the theme of their collective or thematic exhibitions, critics should try to convince a publisher to print a book on the issue.

The myth of history leads to the belief that any artistic artifact or form of expression is, by the very fact of it having been produced, interesting, memorable, and worth collecting.

There are only a few artists who have not been conditioned by the religions to which, whether they know it or not, they belong. Their way of expressing themselves in art reveals this influence.

About two thousand years ago it was decided that women were inferior to men and that the visual artist was a superfluous figure, to be cut down to size. These are some of the innumerable lucky absurdities that have come down to us.

Just like drawing and painting, my "sculpture" is not bound by the force of gravity.

Long before Romulus and Remus, the city of Rome was founded by the Sumerians.

Those who think they can create their own work by "carrying on" the "research" of others have mistaken art for science.

The hurry to place contemporary art within history, within museums, in "real time" arises from a fear of the judgment of the future.

In the world there are—and have only ever been—two- or three-dimensional works, and some invisible works by Gino De Dominicis.

Art concerns genius and the space it occupies is a vertical one; it does not move horizontally, from left to right or vice versa. Instead, it shifts, immobile, from height to height.

The artists who create "installations" and "exhibition designs" have simply taken over the place of workmen.

Ephemeral histories of contemporary art in a biblical style tell us that "Rauschenberg begat Burri, who begat ..."

Originating in America, the term "Conceptual Art" was very popular in Italy, perhaps because it reminded people of such common personal names as Concetta, Concezione, Concettina, etc. And it is continually being lazily used to label everything that, in art, is not immediately recognizable.

In America—and then back in Europe—they have taken Duchamp's "position" literally, thinking he was a model to be imitated and that his way of making art was alternative and modern. In fact, it was simply Marcel Duchamp's way of making art. One should never mistake an artist for a model, and still less a model, male or female, for an artist.

The absence of a law governing the intellectual copyright of visual art means that it is possible to copy while claiming to be "quoting."

Alongside the Venice Biennale they should set up a "Biennale of Creatives" (in Milan, for example), to which painters and sculptors should absolutely not be invited. In such a case, one could justify entrusting the exhibition to a rather "creative" organizer. Such a Biennale could also give out prizes. For example, the Andy Warhol Award for "Best Creative Photographer," and other prizes for the Best Performance, or Best Video, or Best Display, or Best Fashion Designer, and so on. And everyone would be happy, particularly those who were absent—that is, the painters and sculptors.

The only trace of nomadism in my works is that sometimes they have been transported outside Rome for an exhibition.

Drawing, painting, and "sculpture" are material, immobile, and mute; ontologically speaking, they are the very opposite of all other artistic languages.

Among other things, 1968 gave us first the "creative gallery-owners," then the "creative critics," and more recently the "creative museum curator." We are looking forward to "creative collectors," "creative zoo directors," "creative surgeons," "creative station masters," and so on.

In an era of sameness, of relentless planetary communication, dematerialized and abstract, the only things that stand apart from this are the "anti-ephemeral" major arts.

This era does not love the visual arts; it identifies with the languages that unfold in time and space: writing, music, cinema, television, etc. A lot of those who continue to concern themselves with the visual arts do so solely with the intention of distorting their fundamental nature in order to make them homogeneous with those languages of becoming with which they feel more at home.

The mindless fashion for "crossing boundaries"—for the interdisciplinary and multimedia—has meant that the great art exhibitions have included as artists figures such as musicians, film directors, poets, journalists, photographers, dancers, ecologists, actors, critics, gallery owners, sociologists, playwrights, performers, philosophers, etc, etc....

There has never been an "art world," only works of art in the world.

Once it is finished, the work must surprise me, give me back more energy than I invested in the making of it. In this way a work is "anti-entropic" and contradicts the second law of thermodynamics. One thus reappropriates the problem of death and the immortality of the body, without delegating it to science and scientists, which would be a dangerous thing to do.

To live, the painter may need to sell his own work.

All works of art are contemporary. Otherwise, it would be like seeing a car from the 1920s approaching and deciding to cross the street anyway, thinking that you couldn't be run over because the car is from another era. But that's not how things are. And for the work of art it is the same thing: it is always "live."

Instead of subscribing to the Internet and filling their homes with catalogues and books, the public would do better to subscribe to rail or airline companies and go to see works of art "in the flesh."

"Video artists" should be put through a process of selection and—if they are interesting—invited to appear in a section of the Venice Film Festival.

Each artist is a great draftsman, a great painter or "sculptor," and has a special mark on his right foot.

The public prefers "the history of art" and "of artists" to the work of art and individual artists.

The case of my accountant is not unique. Today there are innumerable people working in the most varied fields and professions who are looking forward with impatience to the final breaking down of the boundaries of art by multimedia. Then they too can be artists, can put on exhibitions, can surf the Internet and share their own experiences with millions of other "artists."

Each language originates in a pressing need. Physical immortality is the pressing need behind the major arts, and the paradigm of its achievement is the masterpiece.

I am definitely more ancient than an Egyptian artist.

Among the many "reversals" that one sees nowadays, one perceives within art an overturning of time. Contemporary art and artists are considered (and consider themselves) to be modern. However, coming after everything that has gone before, they should know that they are the most ancient.

A perfect living object, a work of art can have an influence upon biological processes.

Drawing, painting, and "sculpture" are not traditional, but originary forms of expression. Therefore also future forms.

Translated by Barry Schwabsky
These maxims, written by De Dominicis between 1969 and 1996 and compiled by Cecilia Torrealta, were originally published as "Frasi di Gino De Dominicis, 1969–96" in *XLVII Biennale di Venezia* (Venice: La Biennale di Venezia; Milan: Electa, 1997), 66–67.

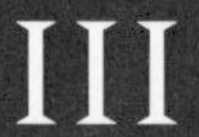

III

FOR IT TO REALLY BE ME: ARTISTS ON GINO DE DOMINICIS

Calling After Gino De Dominicis

Anselm Kiefer

We shout at someone, say a curse shouted after a driver who's sped past us while we're walking and splashed mud all over us, knowing full well that our intended listener can't possibly hear us and, even if he could, he can't be brought to justice since, in his car, he is so much faster than a pedestrian. Still, in an atavistically animist act, we shout at the vanishing man as a kind of magic spell, to bind him. We try to take him out of the normal physics of cause and effect to catch him—here, in the case of the inconsiderate driver, so that we can hold him accountable for his actions.

Now by eulogizing, calling after, Gino De Dominicis, we cannot summon or bind him, cannot call him back or hold him in place with a magic word. For it is *he* who has, on the contrary, long since put *us* under a spell. There is a beautiful German word coined by Novalis: *vergeheimnissen*, to make something secret or mysterious, give it a quality of mystery. For the philosophical system of the German Romantics, this word means glimpsing an interconnectedness in everything, one which may not always be graspable with rational means, but which can nonetheless be clearly indicated through art. This connectedness in all things is revealed not by analysis but, on the contrary, through "secretizing"—that is, things are removed from their false, banal places where a limited purpose has placed them and are repositioned in "the mysterious." We might also say, the question of the antinomy of art and life, which has become academic, is resolved by having lived and died as a work of art. Gino De Dominicis did not live for an idea, or for art, nor did he even create works of art. He *was* a work of art—with nothing left over, from the beginning, mysterious and incessantly mystifying and secretizing himself.

We don't know how large his latifundia were, an ancient inheritance he himself renounced, nor how many palazzi in Venice, Rome, Naples, Palermo he lived in. I saw only a few. Beautiful virginal vestals lived there, keepers of the white ashes. When someone had arranged to see him, he would send out two of his temple handmaidens to bring the visitor to one of his palaces; down in the canal there would be a small white boat waiting every night to take him to the casino. There, where people usually lose everything, he would generate more of himself with marvelous regularity. What for others was a kind of dissipation in his case brought in a royal income. In general, what for others was exceptional, even a kind of ecstasy, was for him everyday life. And looking on, you saw no sign of strain or fatigue from this constant stylization. Whether in Venice, Rome, or Naples, time spent with him was beautiful. Everywhere Gino went there was a vacant throne at the ready, which he would sit on for a short time. He avoided everything vulgar, the wellsprings of progress; never once did he set foot in the crowds of a public airport. And yet, so it seems, he weighed down Bourbon flags with a hammer and sickle.

I cannot call after Gino: he bequeathed nothing, left nothing behind.

Yet he did show us something, or better, proclaimed something like the Old Testament prophets, something worth far more than any valuable item that can be traded or exchanged: that thing is the possibility of an individual existence (and thus the possibility for every individual)—even outside of the crowd, of history, of time. (Not, please note, independent of history, time, etc. but outside of them.) Existence as ecstasy.

When I think of Gino De Dominicis, Symeon the Stylite comes to mind.

Translated by Damion Searls

This text, written in German and titled "nachruf auf gino de dominicis," was originally published with the title "Richiamo" in *De Dominicis. Raccolta di scritti sull'opera e l'artista*, ed. Gabriele Guercio (Turin: Umberto Allemandi, 2001), 60–62.

Translator's note: The German *Nachruf* means "obituary" but also, literally, "calling after" the person, with "after" meant in both senses: temporally later than, and spatially trying to catch up to. Thus Kiefer's title denotes both "Obituary for Gino De Dominicis" and "Calling After Gino De Dominicis."

(Hail Gabriele, Sighted Guercio.,. ecce echo of De Dominicis.,.)

Luigi Ontani

"GINO was my Indigenous name, as a child, androGino.,.
saying it to Gino De Dominicis, skeptical and scornful,
boss of the bone paradox,., IN the early
70s, night-owling, ironically asserted: /
.,. that American Art in order to make itself CREDIBLE.,.
needs the addition of the 'ART' label=
(pop Art, minimal Art, land Art, conceptual Art...)\?/
I was also a witness to the 'NEW Science'
in Via Vittoria, which with EMILIO PRINI,
involving and examining the artistic context
of Rome, put other artists to the test,
inviting them to PAINT with a BRUSH, RESETTING
the recognizable STYLISTIC FEATURES of language,=:
DESTROYING then the quantity
of CANVASES of several standard formats, \?/
except for 2 painted by 4 hands,
which were thrown into the trunk
of a Jaguar \?/ The same one
that on its way back from Naples,
spurting boiling hot water, later
on fire, was left on the highway
of the Sun, and some TWINS, dear Gods,
picked us up straight away.,. instantly.,. "
to the dear distinguished distant departed.,.
Long LivArt.,. "
Byeeeee

Rome, June 13, 2013

Translated by Barry Schwabsky
This text was originally published in Italian as "(Ave Gabriele, vedente Guercio.,. ecco eco di De Dominicis.,.)" in *De Dominicis. Scritti sull'opera e riflessioni dell'artista*, ed. Gabriele Guercio, 2nd rev. ed. (Turin: Umberto Allemandi, 2014), 73.

Pack of Cigarettes

Marina Abramović

I met Gino in 1971 in Rome at the Piazza del Popolo café. We met one another with a group of artists: Eliseo Mattiacci, Luigi Ontani, Jannis Kounellis, Mario and Marisa Merz, and Emilio Prini. I think it was Luigi Ontani who introduced me to Gino. My first impression of Gino was that he was different to all of us. He was the only one who wore a black suit, a white shirt, and a black tie. His face was very pale; his moustache was well maintained.

Observing him, I was questioning his profession.

I didn't have any idea what he was doing at the time.

I especially noticed his hands. He had long fingers and manicured nails. His black eyes were on fire.

He seemed extremely energetic and aware. He didn't speak much, but he observed, not only us but everybody at this café. I was guessing his profession. I thought that he could be a croupier from the casino or that he worked as a receptionist for a nightclub. Later on, I met him every time I was in Rome, and I started to love his work.

He was definitely a person of the night. I only met him once on the street during the day. I was so surprised when I noticed in the merciless sunlight how his black suit looked so faded and worn out. His shirt was not as clean as it had seemed during the night.

Gino's face was not just pale, but looked almost gray, and he had big black circles under his eyes, which testified to his many sleepless nights.

That day we went to get coffee, and he asked me for a cigarette.

I took the pack out of my bag to offer him one, but instead he took the whole package, opened it, and offered me one.

Then he took one for himself and put the pack in his pocket.

He did this with such elegance, grace, and generosity that I didn't notice anything until I returned home and realized my pack of cigarettes was missing.

Thinking back, this cigarette incident is still so vivid in my head. And I can relate this event directly to his work.

Not the fact that he took the pack of cigarettes, but the way he did it. He turned things around and made you see them from a different point of view and in a different light.

He created illusions around his actions, so that one would doubt oneself and one's sense of vision and judgment.

Did I see it?

Did this really happen?

Is it true?

Is it an illusion?

Can I trust it?

Gino is somebody who was always interested in exploring the fine line between the visible and invisible. Between time and timelessness. Between real and unreal, between mortality and immortality. He was aware of the right second, the right moment in space and time.

If you were not able to see his work, there was always some witness who would tell the story, and the story would grow into enormous proportions, even after his enigmatic death, like a stone thrown into the water that creates infinite ripples.

This text was originally published in Italian, French, and English in a special issue of *Flash Art International* (June 2007): 98–101. This issue served as the catalogue for De Dominicis's solo exhibition curated by Andrea Bellini and Laura Cherubini at the Centre National d'Art Contemporain de la Villa Arson, Nice (June 29–October 7, 2007), Fondazione Merz, Turin (November 8, 2007–January 6, 2008), and MoMA PS1, New York (October 19, 2008–February 9, 2009).

Gino De Dominicis

Daniel Buren

Graphism
Impertinence
Narcissism
Originality

Diabolic
Esthete

Dandy
Overconfident
Mozzarella in Carrozza
Indeterminable
Night Owl
Ineffable
Complex
Ironic
Solitary

Translated by Andrea Vesentini
This text was originally written in French and published as "Gino De Dominicis" in *De Dominicis. Raccolta di scritti sull'opera e l'artista*, ed. Gabriele Guercio (Turin: Umberto Allemandi, 2001), 32.

Clarity

Joseph Kosuth

The difficulty facing an existing individual is how to give his existence the continuity without which everything simply vanishes.
Søren Kierkegaard

I stuck to my idea and asserted that death was really the great organizing force of life.
Italo Svevo

How does the project of an artist's lifetime, one, in Gino's case, concerned with immortality, face the paradox of death? Is the work itself intended as a paradox, confronting the inevitable through a double face of denial and confirmation? Put another way, while the context of his project was the subject of immortality, his project, like the projects of all artists, was with meaning. Gino was an artist. The word *artist* is specific and says as much as is needed, given the full breadth of human activities. Artists do various things, some even use paint. However, whether they do or not means less than the totality of their activity. Within that totality, the *how* of an artist's production finds its actual meaning in the *why* which that work manifests. It has been clear for many years that there are "painters" and there are artists that occasionally use paint among other things. What must be understood, if one is to understand, is that artists work with meaning, that is their real material, and to produce that they *do what they can*. If one only paints, the total meaning of your activity is married to the tradition of painting itself and speaks of that more than what you as an individual artist might want to say, thereby losing the cultural and social value, and later historic value, that the life of one artist living and working *in the present* can offer. So, for an artist concerned with mortality/immortality, this takes on a particular significance.

Gino painted sometimes, among his other activities. For myself, I've always looked at the gaps between one work and another to "see" what an artist is saying because, there, one has a better view of the process of an artist's thinking. All the ways he worked articulate what he was saying, even that part which was unsayable. Painting was one important even if conservative option among several that delimited a kind of avant-gardist meaning and which, in yet another way, risked depersonalizing his statements on immortality. Such statements had to be rooted in the personal to be credible, referring as they do to the living and the present, which is also why he didn't *only* paint. One can perhaps argue that being immersed in the Italian art world of the 1980s and the impact of Transavanguardia, he was pulled further than he might otherwise have gone in a particular direction.

Certainly his maxims, which I remember as beginning at the same time as his paintings and which were published in their final form on the day of his death, represent a perverse and ironic, sometimes contradictory response to the thirty years of conversations we had together. Do I hear his laugh? Forgive me one and all, but I will take these statements as his last gesture in our particular game. But I can still speak, and I will: those that want to consider this artist a painter will have to eliminate most of his important work, works made of things appropriated, but that were constructions which held a meaning provided only through him. Indeed, this work, by using objects that have a life in the world, embraced reality and thereby empowered his questions about mortality since the questions were being asked in the midst of a life actually taking place. A painting, which by necessity relies on a fictive space, remains removed firstly for this reason, and further by the fact of its removal from the lived meaning of daily life to instead take its place among all other paintings that have ever been painted. If paintings are objects in the world, they are objects in self-denial, silencing each other with one voice.

Gino announced his death in 1969, in one sense to get it over with and thereby provide an "immortal" life, at least within the problematic of his work for the following thirty years. If you are "dead" but still around, you can't help but raise the question of immortality. This gesture was certainly more Duchampian than Gino would have admitted to, but it also wasn't as simple as that. Duchamp's act of "quitting" (another way of "dying" as an artist) was an external one; Gino's, internal. Gino was dead as a strategy of his work, comparable to the "living sculptures" of Gilbert & George from around the same time. Of course, the paradox is that no artist ever seemed more alive than Gino, no artistic institution more artificial and less alive than Gilbert & George. It has already been noted that Gino died exactly thirty years to the month from this announcement, and he did it in the "month of the dead." No one is casual about death, but this was an artist who was even less so because he had, through his work, integrated his life with his eventual death. His death would also be more than an ending or cutting-off of a process: it was inevitable that dying would be seen as an event *in* his work. Before he ever had to come to terms with actual death, he confronted the concept of death all of his working life. There is no place for romance in this story. It is simply one form clarity might take.

August 13, 2000

This essay was originally published in Italian as "Chiarezza" in *De Dominicis. Raccolta di scritti sull'opera e l'artista*, ed. Gabriele Guercio (Turin: Umberto Allemandi, 2001), 63–66.

Two or Three Uncritical Lines

Jannis Kounellis

I can write only two or three uncritical lines that are nonetheless tied closely together by a golden thread tied to my late friend. I don't want to say I like this or that; it's been known for a while what I think his images or sayings are that have attained a certain incisiveness. You can't change your mind after such a long time.

The arguments and polemics that took place in the bars around Piazza del Popolo and later near the Pantheon concerning the dramatic condition of the Italian artist, enmeshed in the body of a grandiose past that he had to acknowledge while standing before a present spangled with weaknesses as well as inconclusive and tragic dramas.

The effort to keep up this cultural identity, to accept it in spite of its burden, and the will to maintain this dialectic—although I must say that Gino never liked that word, *dialectic*.

This experience we shared as fellow artists and residents of this magic, grandiose, and terrible city, accomplices in an attack, players along with others wishing to bring new ideas to the theater of the art exhibition, to leave a mark that would cut deep, then another mark in another place and then again a mark in hopes of escaping our captivity, far away toward fullness, with a real painting, newly finished, under our arm.

Translated by Barry Schwabsky
This text was originally published as "Due o tre frasi acritiche…" in *De Dominicis. Raccolta di scritti sull'opera e l'artista*, ed. Gabriele Guercio (Turin: Umberto Allemandi, 2001), 67.

… side of life

Emilio Prini

… side of life in a Ginologickal key … Gino, Gene, Genome …

Translated by Ombretta Celeste
This text was originally published as "… lato di vita" in *De Dominicis. Raccolta di scritti sull'opera e l'artista*, ed. Gabriele Guercio (Turin: Umberto Allemandi, 2001), 85.

IV

A LANGUAGE BORN FROM A PRESSING NEED

Self-Portrait

Andrea Cortellessa

Dying is dangerous.
Gino De Dominicis

In the case of an artist as deeply enigmatic as Gino De Dominicis, one piece in particular, undated like many of his works but probably from the early 1990s, furthers his enigma: it consists of a tiny stone, roughly oval but irregular in shape, placed in a wooden box. The stone shines against the black-painted bottom of the box like a celestial body in a cloudless night sky. The siliceous concretions on its uneven surface are vaguely reminiscent of the moon's features, which are traditionally anthropomorphized. Unlike many of De Dominicis's works, this one is titled—*Autoritratto* (Self-Portrait) [IT 589]—and signed on the rear of the box. A second self-portrait-cum-stone is found among his works, *Opera non titolata* (Work without a Title) [IT 480] (1995–96). This work is made up of two interlocking pyrite blocks: a smooth cubic block inserted into another, much rougher block. Hand drawn on the latter block is a reproduction of the artist's first photographic portrait (or rather, one De Dominicis claimed to be his first): it portrays an approximately two-year-old child, bundled up in a heavy coat and beret, staring at something outside the frame at top left. The self-portrait-cum-stone "encapsulates the artist's thinking about permanence and eternity, the transience of human life, art's mythical origins, and the artistic process in general."[1]

At least one other untitled work, made earlier in his career, features a portrait of the artist as a child. The work is a photograph of him turning his back on the camera to look at a landscape painting, next to which we see a watch and a smaller photograph on a shelf, presumably a portrait of the artist as a child [IT 165] (1972–73). In 1973 this work was shown by Lucio Amelio alongside De Dominicis's untitled work consisting of a watch with a small mirror in place of its hands and dial (*Orologio* [Watch] [IT 113] [1970]). The display of these two works together functioned as a memento mori, not unlike De Dominicis's famous work *Il tempo lo sbaglio lo spazio* (Time, Mistake, Space) [IT 95] (1969), which falls in the traditional vanitas genre.[2]

One may suppose that, through the use of stones in his works, De Dominicis playfully and retrospectively brought an emblematic object into his own iconic universe. One of the objects on display at his first solo exhibition at L'Attico, in November 1969, which many consider the beginning of his artistic career, was a stone that, like other contem-

---

1   Cornelia Lauf, "La roulette e la storia dell'arte," in *De Dominicis. Raccolta di scritti sull'opera e l'artista*, ed. Gabriele Guercio (Turin: Umberto Allemandi, 2001), 70. All translations by Andrea Vesentini, unless otherwise indicated.

2   See Michel Butor, *Vanità: Conversazione nelle Alpi Marittime*, trans. Roberto Rossi (Milan: SE, 1991).

poraneous works, bore a convoluted title: *Attesa di un casuale movimento molecolare in una sola direzione, tale da generare un movimento spontaneo del materiale* (Waiting for a Random One-Directional Molecular Movement that Could Generate a Spontaneous Movement of Material) [IT 85–89] (1969). This stone was among the three objects featured in the profoundly psychical and, again, enigmatic temenos of the infamously shocking installation at the 1972 Venice Biennale, *Seconda soluzione di immortalità (l'universo è immobile)* (Second Solution of Immortality [The Universe Is Still]) [IT 150], which was withdrawn as soon as it went on display, due to public outcry.[3]

Besides, we might also read the all-too-physical, scandalous inclusion in the same work of Paolo Rosa, a young man affected by Down syndrome, as a secret avatar of the artist himself. In fact, the *Second Solution* was featured on the front cover of a special supplement to the journal *Quadri e Sculture* entirely devoted to De Dominicis and published on the day of his sudden death (November 29, 1998). As the journal's editor-in-chief, Matteo Smolizza, recalled, for a long time before its publication the artist had been hesitant about the cover, whether to use the image of Rosa or the photograph of himself as a child. "These two images looked totally different to Smolizza," Laura Cherubini has commented, "and yet they were probably more connected than we think in the artist's mind."[4] There is no question that the controversy around the 1972 Biennale made De Dominicis famous, but it also contributed to his public persona's somewhat devilish aura. One is inclined to agree with Fabio Sargentini when he suggests that, until his very end, De Dominicis was "haunted by the ghost of the mongoloid."[5] In retrospect, we might say that the so-called mongoloid—perhaps

3   On the work's composition, controversies, and the several instances on which the artist revisited it, see Eleonora Charans, *Gino De Dominicis: 2ª soluzione di immortalità (l'universo è immobile)* (Milan: Scalpendi, 2012). For an extremely articulate, profound, and philosophical reading of the work, and ultimately a key to understanding De Dominicis's entire oeuvre, see Gabriele Guercio, *L'arte non evolve. L'universo immobile di Gino De Dominicis* (Monza: Johan & Levi, 2015).

4   Laura Cherubini, "Oggetto vivente perfetto: L'opera di Gino De Dominicis," in "Gino De Dominicis," ed. Laura Cherubini and Andrea Bellini, special issue, *Flash Art International* (June 2007): 77. The issue was published on the occasion of the *Gino De Dominicis* traveling retrospective (Nice: Villa Arson; Turin: Fondazione Merz; New York: MoMA PS1, June 29, 2007–February 9, 2009). Cherubini's essay remains the most exhaustive and passionate overview of the artist's career; an edited version, "Perfect Living Object," appears in this volume, 40–50.

5   Fabio Sargentini, "Gino De Dominicis: il gusto dello scandalo," in *Gino De Dominicis. L'immortale*, exh. cat., ed. Achille Bonito Oliva (Milan, Electa; Rome, Fondazione MAXXI, 2010), 84. The exhibition was held at MAXXI, Rome, from May 30 to November 7, 2010. In another significant episode, De Dominicis, invited by Maurizio Calvesi to present himself to the public in the pages of the "National Bolaffi Catalog of Modern Art No. 7," *Segnalati Bolaffi 1972. 39 artisti scelti da 40 critici* (Turin: Bolaffi, 1971)—the chosen format for the publication being a double-page reproduction of a work followed by a photo-portrait of the artist—sent two photographs of the same person, a disturbed teenager who in the first image shows a broad smile and in the second laughs broadly (a caption recalls the work *D'io* [IT 127–28] [1971]), exhibited by Sargentini in the same year and revived, the following year, in the hall of scandal at the Biennale: "Gino De Dominicis, in the completely empty and illuminated gallery of L'Attico in Rome, exhibited, recorded, his strong laughter, which also resonated in the surrounding streets." Giuseppe Garrera recently elaborated on this episode in a conference dedicated to *D'io* on September 9, 2020, while *D'io* was installed at the *Editorial* exhibition curated by Luca Lo Pinto at MACRO, Rome.

unintentionally—grew into the artist's avatar and ghost; or, to use a less psychoanalytic term, his demon.

<u>Ubiequivocacy</u>
Besides, it's always the others who die.
Marcel Duchamp

In the case of an artist whose works are so labyrinthine and "secretly" interconnected, it is hardly advisable to embark on a metonymical detour, which would ultimately lead us to read his entire oeuvre as a "self-portrait." De Dominicis, who self-diagnosed his humorous skepticism toward "conceptual" practices as "homeopathic,"[6] had discouraged such a reading in a little-known work from 1970, consisting of a framed, nondescript sheet of white paper with "De Dominicis?" written across it in simple block letters [IT 123] (1970). This piece rules out any possibility that all his works should be seen as a manifestation of his own self, as somehow equivalent to his being.

Even so, it is undeniable that, as Anselm Kiefer wrote, "he lived and died as a work of art."[7] The making of his public persona was an integral and constitutive part of his work. Andrea Bellini dubbed this distinctive feature his "inimitable way of life,"[8] to use the words of one of Italy's most celebrated writers, Gabriele d'Annunzio.

Sargentini drew a different parallel when he wrote that "De Dominicis's demeanor and look (think of his moustache) have always been secretly modeled after Salvador Dalí."[9] Rather, I am reminded of another elusive night owl and dandy, a sarcastic and "metaphysical" character who, like De Dominicis, was also a gambler and wore a trademark moustache, the writer Tommaso Landolfi. However, the overall drive of De Dominicis's entire oeuvre undisputedly resided in his ability to keep his "real" identity *suspended* in an enigmatic and unresolved territory. Incidentally, I would suggest that this territory explains one of his most obsessive tropes: his tendency to literally *suspend* and levitate characters and objects in midair so as to remove them from the realm of an "ordinary" existence ruled by gravity and the second law of thermodynamics. In this respect, it is significant that De Dominicis, for his 1995 video interview for the television program *L'Angelo*, set up what could be described as yet another "self-portrait," by appearing to "magically" levitate while sitting behind a desk that hovered before him.

What is equally emblematic is his obsession with invisibility, found in a wide range of works from *Cubo invisibile* (Invisible Cube) [IT 45] (1967), another fetish first shown at L'Attico in 1969 and later in Venice, to

6   A more overt parody is found in his *Mozzarella in carrozza* [IT 69] (1970), shown at L'Attico on February 7, 1970, shortly before De Dominicis's break with Jannis Kounellis (see the commonalities between *12 cavalli vivi* [12 Live Horses] and *Lo Zodiaco* [The Zodiac]); as Sargentini recalled, Kounellis asked him to choose with these words: "It's either me or him." See Sargentini, "Gino De Dominicis: il gusto dello scandalo," 83.

7   See Anselm Kiefer, "Calling After Gino De Dominicis," in this volume, 101.

8   See Andrea Bellini, "A Futura Memoria," in this volume, 19.

9   Sargentini, "Gino De Dominicis: il gusto dello scandalo," 85.

Cilindro invisibile (Invisible Cylinder) [IT 74] (1969), which he made that same year, or in another lesser-known but just as emblematic self-portrait, his *Autoritratto di Gino De Dominicis, invisibile seduto nel suo studio* (Self-Portrait of Gino De Dominicis, Invisibly Sitting in His Studio) [IT 481] (1995–97), a photograph by Gianfranco Gorgoni taken circa 1995. Instead of listing each of the many artworks that De Dominicis entitled *Autoritratto*, one can generalize by saying that, starting from his seminal 1986 solo exhibition at Galleria Emilio Mazzoli, most of his paintings can be read as "presumed" self-portraits: in fact, such is the pseudo-title of one of them.[10]

De Dominicis's titles deserve a brief digression; the playfully sprawling ones of his early period are apparently no exception to the general rule that titles are the quintessence of any form of conceptual art. As such, they should be seen through a strictly orthodox "conceptual" lens as statements made by the author, which are meant to be juxtaposed with the artwork as a tautological self-confirmation or self-mocking counterpoint. However, the titling of his later works as *Senza titolo* (Untitled) or *Con titolo* (With Title)—the latter showing an even higher degree of tautology and self-mockery—sounds like a palinode of sorts, alluding to a break with tradition as well as with his own artistic background.[11] Further ambiguity is created by his habit of adding pseudo-titles or "nicknames," as I have previously dubbed them, which function like a quasi-esoteric lingo to be understood only by the "magic circle" of his closest aficionados. This practice should also be contextualized within his wider strategy of leaving his own work *suspended* in an undocumented or purposefully atemporal sphere and his aversion to photographic reproductions of his works, which should not be misread as an aversion to photography as a medium, since the artist used this technique whenever necessary, as Laura Cherubini has noted.[12]

The unmistakably "totemic element" which leads us to read "the unnamed and yet ubiquitous subject of De Dominicis's production throughout the 1980s" as his own presumed self-portrait is the nose/beak which, as Gabriele Guercio wrote, "rises to the status of an iconic résumé, catalyst, and self-projection."[13] It is also reminiscent of the birdlike imagery found in Sumerian art, an old favorite of the artist's, as well as Alberto Savinio's animal deities. This *sphraghis* could be read as a sapiential symbol but also as a clear phallic allusion that recurs alongside other elements in his oeuvre such as spears and poles. This latter reading is made explicit both in his *L'impiccato (Il pittore impiccator)* (The Hanged Man [The Hanged Painter]) [IT 482] (1996) and in a 1984 *Con titolo* [IT 253] that draws inspiration from Leonardo's so-called *Angelo incarnato* (Incarnate Angel).

10   A golden piece titled *Presunto autoritratto* was shown in November 1996 at the Severi Arte gallery in Bologna. Editor's note: This work remains unidentified.

11   One of De Dominicis's famous and often-cited puns is: "Originating in America, the term 'Conceptual Art' was very popular in Italy, perhaps because it reminded people of such common personal names as Concetta, Concezione, Concettina, etc."; see Gino De Dominicis, "Maxims, 1969–1996," in this volume, 94.

12   See Cherubini, "Perfect Living Object," in this volume, 46.

13   Gabriele Guercio, "Arte visiva e immortalità del corpo," in *De Dominicis. Scritti sull'opera e riflessioni dell'artista*, ed. Gabriele Guercio, 2nd rev. ed. (Turin: Umberto Allemandi, 2014), 315.

Generally, the concept of a presumed self-portrait, or what one may call a *suspended self-portrait*, refers to De Dominicis's main avatar as a painter: Leonardo. This interpretation is not so much based on Leonardo's adage that "every painter paints himself," but rather and more precisely on the hypothesis that the *Mona Lisa* is a self-portrait in drag. Such a reading of the painting emerged as early as 1913 and gained ground in 1987[14] but was finally popularized globally by Dan Brown's 2003 novel, *The Da Vinci Code*. De Dominicis's *Mona Lisa* was his quintessential fetish work. It is no coincidence that his obsession with Leonardo's portrait dates to the mid-eighties, when he developed a growing interest in the presumed self-portrait as a genre. At this stage, one must inevitably mention the avatar of Marcel Duchamp. Even in the early days of his career, the French artist's influence on De Dominicis was so apparent that De Dominicis felt the need to disclaim it, but his rebuttal became a confession, a Freudian denial of sorts.[15] In his account of his long-lasting friendship with the painter, Achille Bonito Oliva is reminded of *L.H.O.O.Q.*, the famous 1919 readymade in which Duchamp superimposed a moustache and goatee on a reproduction of the *Mona Lisa*.[16] As a matter of fact, the real prototype of De Dominicis's "electric moustache," as Sargentini described it when he first saw it at L'Attico, can be found in Duchamp's ominous addition to Leonardo's work; it is just as likely that Dalí used it as an inspiration for his own moustache. That De Dominicis's obsession with the prima donna of the Louvre began with Duchamp's alteration is further evidenced by an untitled work (*Senza titolo* [Untitled] [IT 313] [1988]), nicknamed *Piccola sfinge* (Little Sphinx) or *Vecchina* (Old Lady), first shown at Lia Rumma's gallery in July 1988. This piece is essentially De Dominicis's own rendition of the *Mona Lisa*, only in this case, she wears a Pulcinella mask. The omnipresence of female avatars throughout his work, whether in the guise of fashion models, interviewers, curators, coauthors, or authors, nicknamed with heteronyms such as "Domitilla S. Delfino," "Auronia," and "Delfina D.D.," echoes Duchamp's alter ego, introduced in 1920: Rose (later Rrose) Sélavy. It is worth noting that Maurizio Calvesi understood *L.H.O.O.Q.* as a further allusion to Leonardo's androgyny, which should not just be understood as gendered, but as a secret alchemical symbolism.[17]

As has been made evident, one could easily read all of the author's works as a form of self-representation by following the metaphysical threads stemming from his oeuvre. To cite a pun by a like-minded author, Corrado Costa, who wrote, "the Invisible Man / is not playing in many the-

14   See Lillian Schwartz, "Leonardo's Mona Lisa," *Art & Antiques*, January 1987, 50–55.

15   "In America—and then back in Europe—they have taken Duchamp's 'position' literally, thinking he was a model to be imitated and that his way of making art was alternative and modern. In fact, it was simply Marcel Duchamp's way of making art. One should never mistake an artist for a model, and still less a model, male or female, for an artist." Gino De Dominicis, quoted in Trombadori, "A Memo at the End of the Century," in this volume, 89.

16   See Achille Bonito Oliva, "Apologia del limite," in *Passo dello strabismo: Sulle arti* (Milan: Feltrinelli, 1978), 218.

17   See Maurizio Calvesi, *Duchamp invisibile. La costruzione del simbolo* (San Marino: Maretti Editore, 2016); and Calvesi, "Il sesso della Gioconda," *Art & Dossier*, January 31, 1989, 30–34.

aters / or / it is playing in many of them,"[18] the Invisible Man could be hiding anywhere. Alternatively, we might say he is *ubiquitous*, if we are to choose a word that evokes another of De Dominicis's primary spheres of interest. Or rather, *ubiequivocal*, to once again use Costa's accurate language; just like God. After all, we are all made in his image and likeness.[19]

<u>Prestidigitation</u>
Perfection and death are sisters
(Or maybe they're the same thing)
And both are disappointing
Tommaso Landolfi

The work entitled *D'io* (God, Of I) [IT 127–28], shown at L'Attico in April 1971, was made up of yet another sign/effigy displaying the pun in the title (a play on words between its literal meaning in Italian, "of I," and the near homograph *Dio*, meaning "God") and a looped recording of roaring laughter. The work, which was nicknamed "La Risata" (The Laughter), is key to understanding the structural ambiguity of De Dominicis's entire oeuvre. Although the recorded voice was not his own, the ubiquitous "laughter" heard around the gallery was ultimately the artist's way of ridiculing us as well as anyone and anything else. It is no accident that he once described it as "spine-chilling."[20] Such is the nature of his own temperament, *suspended* between his witty, scornful, irreverent, and annihilating humor and an endless inquiry into the transcendent and mystical implications of human transience. One is reminded of the overt interaction of such themes in his truly spine-chilling work *Madonna che ride* (Laughing Madonna) [IT 152] from 1972. Andrea Bellini has bracingly and brazenly divided the artist's cult into two factions, which were as fractious as the early Christians in *Monty Python's Life of Brian*. On the one hand, we have the champions of De Dominicis's sardonic and overtly humorous side found in the "conceptual" or "quasi-conceptual" objects and installations of the 1960s and 1970s; on the other, we have those who prefer the "sterner," mystical attitude of his paintings from the 1980s and 1990s.[21] However, the strength and complexity of the *Laughing Madonna* reside exactly in its being undecided and *suspended* between these two perfectly symmetrical

26

18 Corrado Costa, "L'uomo invisibile," in *The Complete Films* (Los Angeles: Red Hill, 1983); reprinted in Corrado Costa, *The Complete Films: Poesia Prosa Performance*, ed. Eugenio Gazzola (Florence: Le Lettere, 2007), 175. One of Costa's "visual prose" compositions, first published in *Nuova Corrente* in 1969, is titled *Ubiequivocità e descrizione della lotta operaia* (Ubiequivocality and Description of Workers' Struggle); see Costa, *The Complete Films*, 52–59.

19 A photograph taken from a 1970 video titled *Gino vi vede. Terza soluzione d'immortalità* (Gino Is Watching You: Third Solution of Immortality) [IT 122], no. 21, 238, is perhaps an allusion to the religious warning, "God sees you!" The phrase *Gino vi vede* (Gino sees you) was printed on the invitation to the exhibition *Videoaustellung colour videotapes* at the Videogalerie Gerry Schum, Düsseldorf, in June 1972; see Francesca Franco, "Schermo," in *Gino De Dominicis. L'immortale*, 146.

20 See Liana Bortolon, "Perché ho esposto un uomo," *Epoca*, June 18, 1972, 90–92, quoted in Francesca Franco, "Godi Cinsi Domine – Godi Cinsi Demoni. Scritti, interviste, testimonianze di G.D.D.," in *Gino De Dominicis. L'immortale*, 91.

21 See Bellini, "A Futura Memoria," in this volume, 20–21.

and yet contradictory souls. His installations always present an extremely accurate and unfaltering balance, both at a formal and an "architectural" level, whereas his paintings are clearly "a thing of the mind," to quote his putative "mentor" Leonardo.

There is no clear-cut transition between these two "periods," although the penchant for mystification grew more intense in the interviews (oftentimes, badly disguised self-interviews) and sardonic statements of his later period. There is, however, a sense of seamless continuity in his work's "metaphysical" quality, which emerges in the eerie laughter of his earlier period and the mystical but no less eerie iconography of his later, great paintings. Claudio Abate's photograph, capturing Giorgio de Chirico's inscrutable look as he walks out of a De Dominicis exhibition while De Dominicis is seen in the background, unusually wearing a white blazer, and watching de Chirico leave with an equally unfathomable expression (it's hard to say whether he looks disappointed or, once again, sardonic) prompts us to compare the two artists. One could start from their high-sounding surnames. According to de Chirico's brother, Alberto Savinio, their family name "certainly derives from the Ancient Greek word κῆρυξ, meaning 'herald,' 'announcer.'"[22] As for De Dominicis, there is no doubt his last name stems from the Latin word *dominicus*: "Lord's anointed" or "ordained," and thus his "messenger." The blatantly unrestrained humor observed in de Chirico's later years when he played cat and mouse with interviewers should not be seen as contradicting the "tragic nature of everyday life" found in his earlier works.[23] On the contrary, this same tragic nature takes on a novel meaning, as does the self-mocking character of his "neometaphysical" painting. Likewise, the "metaphysical" sternness of De Dominicis's later works, once again tackling the theme of human transience, is not at odds with the stellar Duchampian playfulness of his early years, as well as his penchant for disguise or pantomime. Examples of these can be seen when he first showed his work in Rome, with the carnivalesque *Laboratorio '70*, or when, in 1996, he staged the ritual execution of *L'Appeso*, a title that puns on the gallery's name, La Nuova Pesa. After all, he was born on April Fool's Day (April 1, 1947).

The two artists shared a taste for self-camouflage; in both de Chirico's famous self-portraits in disguise, dating back to the 1940s and 1950s, and in De Dominicis's iconic but fabricated persona. In 1970 De Dominicis issued a work entitled *Prestidigitazione* (Prestidigitation) [IT 116], and in one of his last interviews he stated, "the artist is like an illusionist, a prestidigitator; he should astonish himself with his own tricks."[24] The stage costume that he wore every night is reminiscent of that of a cartoon magician (e.g., Mandrake) or one from a traveling carnival, such as the Orson

22   Alberto Savinio, "Hermaphrodito," in *Hermaphrodito e altri romanzi*, ed. Alessandro Tinterri (Milan: Adelphi, 1995), 26–27.

23   *Il tragico quotidiano* is the title of a 1906 collection of short stories by Giovanni Papini, an intellectual who influenced de Chirico in his earlier years as well as "his putative Nietzschean brother"; see Maurizio Calvesi, *La metafisica schiarita. Da De Chirico a Carrà, da Morandi a Savinio* (Milan: Feltrinelli, 1982).

24   Marina Valensise, "L'arte è sempre in diretta," in "Gino De Dominicis," ed. Laura Cherubini and Andrea Bellini, special issue, *Flash Art International* (June 2007): 152–53.

Welles of *F for Fake*, the kind of magician whose mystifications and tricks reveal themselves through a cheeky smile. Often, these illusions are either a second-rate hoax or an artificially forced perspective: think of his rubber ball—*Palla di gomma (caduta da 2 metri) nell'attimo immediatamente precedente il rimbalzo* (Rubber Ball [Falling from a Height of Two Meters] in the Moment Right Before Bouncing Back) [IT 70] (1968–69), which, instead of being magically captured (in the moment before bouncing), is simply stuck to the floor, or his *Specchio che tutto riflette tranne gli esseri viventi* (Mirror That Reflects Everything Except Living Beings) [IT 302] (1988), which was merely a window looking onto a hidden replica.

In those same years, a text by like-minded author Giorgio Manganelli theorized the practice of "pseudonymity squared, which, as we all know, allows one to use a pseudonym that is exactly the same as one's real name."[25] De Dominicis's most impressive disguises are those I would describe as "tautological," such as the one from 1975: his collaborator, photographer Buby Durini, took a full portrait of him, in which his face is hidden behind an "official" portrait taken two years prior by Elisabetta Catalano. These tautological self-portraits are evocative of one of de Chirico's late masterpieces, in which his skills as a prestidigitator are made evident: the 1955 *Autoritratto doppio* (Double Self-Portrait), a mise en abyme in which the "real" author looks toward the viewer while his back faces another "fake," and thus masked, self-portrait, *suspending* any differentiation between real and fake. The most disturbing disguises, though, are seen in those asymmetrical works that decenter identity, such as those of Jim Dine, who, in the 1960s, titled some of his iconic unworn dressing gowns *Self-Portrait*.[26]

In de Chirico's incredible gallery of self-portraits, the most enigmatic of all is a 1914 painting that can be called a "presumed self-portrait." Although the title chosen by the artist is *Composizione metafisica* (Metaphysical Composition), which is little different from calling it *Senza titolo* given the ubiquity of metaphysical compositions in de Chirico's oeuvre, Max Ernst apocryphally called the work a "Self-Portrait" in 1938. Unlike the other titles concocted by the Surrealists to label de Chirico's works, the artist never bothered to disclaim this particular one; although he was unlikely to have picked it himself, it was a good match. In the painting, we see four objects set against the trademark background of cityscape with smokestacks: an egg, a recorder (or paper roll), and two feet that look like fragments of a classical statue. All these objects are lit from one side and placed on an inclined plane with a large *X* on a panel looming next to it. Where is the *artist's portrait* in all this?[27] Since the maker's face is not shown, we should shift our attention elsewhere to find it. While focusing on the petrified feet, a de Chirico motif, we cannot rule out the possibility that these appendages

25 Giorgio Manganelli, "(Pseudonimia²)," in *La notte*, ed. Salvatore Silvano Nigro (Milan: Adelphi, 1996), 12.

26 "The dressing gown is indeed an object, but also a projection of our self, an objective confession, a portrait not unlike the night portrait returned by our bathroom mirror." Alberto Boatto, *Pop Art* (Rome-Bari: Laterza, 1998), 88–89.

27 See Alberto Boatto, *Narciso infranto: L'autoritratto moderno da Goya a Warhol*, 2nd ed. (Rome-Bari: Laterza, 2005), 144–45.

are the artist's own. It is exactly this possibility of a *faceless self-portrait* that subdues and frightens us in this work.[28]

In much the same way, two late paintings by De Dominicis, "officially" titled *Autoritratto*, are among his most disturbing and outstanding works. One of them, made circa 1989 (*Senza titolo [Autoritratto]* [Untitled (Self-Portrait)] [IT 471] [1995]), depicts soft and sensuous skinlike ripples, at the center of which sits a hypnotic cavity or bump—it is unclear whether it folds in or out. In the ambiguity of convex or concave, we cannot help but fall into the depths of this navel/nipple/eye. The second is the self-portrait nicknamed *Cuore rosso* (*Autoritratto [Cuore rosso]* [Self-Portrait (Red Heart)] [IT 581] [1998]), which dates from the artist's last year and was first shown in 2010 at the MAXXI retrospective in Rome. In it, we see a featureless skull-like face that might just as well be a fleshy, livid, blood-pumping heart. Either way, organic and inorganic matter are intertwined, as they are in de Chirico's work. Essentially, the image consists of its question, the enigma it presents us with: there is nothing left to add. It violently addresses our fears and deepest desires, all of which we make out, perhaps for the first time, in its faceless gaze.

Gino, Two in One

So making paintings or literature would be like learning how to die, finding a way not to die by that stupid death, which others had in store for us but didn't suit us in the least, and so both are like making, arranging our own death and our wait for it to come, like making our life into our own death.
Michel Butor

There is one remaining question. Undoubtedly, another avatar De Dominicis wanted to evoke through his *Autoritratti presunti* was Pinocchio. Pinocchio is the quintessential long-nosed trickster, the undead hanged man, the fabulous liar who also proves to be an incurably wide-eyed fool: his gullibility runs perfectly symmetrical to the contrast of his compulsive, rather than vocational, propensity for mystification. In this respect, Pinocchio is not that dissimilar from De Dominicis, an unfettered mythmaker and enthusiastic devotee of fictional archaeology, ufology, and astrology, all of which, however, are merely self-imposed superstitions that overshadow his foundational superstition—immortality.

As a faceless self-portrait/presumed self-portrait, Pinocchio is a perfect match first and foremost because he is nothing but a mask. Hans Belting has written about the dialectical relationship found in representations of a person's face, all of which contrast the "real" identity of a subject with the one solidified in the life cast of a face. This solidification is merely one "mask." In Latin theatrical terminology, the mask was called *persona* as opposed to *facies*, which designates "the natural face, that is inseparable

---

28   See my "Autoritratto senza volto," in *De Chirico*, exh. cat., ed. Luca Massimo Barbero (Venice: Marsilio, 2019), 314–29.

from its wearer." The word *persona* has also been used to refer to one's liability in legal proceedings: the Italian language still differentiates between *persona fisica* (natural person) and *persona giuridica* (juridical person).[29] "Paradoxically, a portrait reduces the face to a concept of itself by creating a mask of it," Belting writes. "Only the mask can represent the essence of the face permanently, while a face can never come to rest and thus cannot be reduced to a concept."[30] Portraits can only perpetuate and codify the solidification of one's identity in the role the subject *impersonates* in its existence, regardless of whether this is an "official" or "unofficial" role.

As Ernst Kantorowicz evinced in his seminal study, *The King's Two Bodies* since the Middle Ages (and, overtly, since the 1500s), law and political science have understood a sovereign's "person" as one divided between a mortal, organic, statistically relevant body on the one hand and a "political" body on the other, the latter being imperishable and virtually immortal in that it is transferrable from one individual to the other.[31] This double person, in turn, is molded after the structural and functional model of Christ's dual nature as both human and divine. Many have highlighted the analogies between Pinocchio and Christ, and more generally between the popular children's character and Christian imagery tout court. Examples are found throughout the tale: Christ's sexless birth to a carpenter; his betrayal in exchange for money; his pleading for his father when he is hanged; the Jonah-like whale episode, and his eventual death and resurrection as a final metamorphosis.

De Chirico also used Pinocchio's mask as an inspiration when he made his Mannequins,[32] as has Luigi Ontani since the 1970s.[33] With an almost obsessive compulsion, Jim Dine has taken similar inspiration from Pinocchio in recent decades.[34] By the same token, Bartolomeo Pietromarchi noticed a recurring sense of familiarity with the popular character in the work of many contemporary Italian artists—such as Maurizio Cattelan and the Vedovamazzei duo—and dubbed it the "Pinocchio function."[35] The work of these artists is also proof of a profound interest in De Dominicis's art.

The reason why some artists, all of whom share a tendency to leave their own identity *suspended*, are drawn to Pinocchio can be traced to the same paradox that turned him into an incredibly popular character worldwide; namely, his dialectical dualism between plasticity and solidity.

29 Hans Belting, *Face and Mask: a Double History*, trans. Thomas S. Hansen and Abby J. Hansen (Princeton, NJ: Princeton University Press, 2017), 52.

30 Ibid., 93.

31 See Ernst H. Kantorowicz, *The King's Two Bodies: A Study in Mediaeval Political Theology*, rev. ed. (London: Oxford University Press, 1966), 43.

32 See my reading of de Chirico's works later in this text. Further evidence of his family's love for *The Adventures of Pinocchio* and its author is found in Alberto Savinio's investigative biography, *Collodi*, published in 1939, and reprinted in Alberto Savinio, *Narrate, uomini, la vostra storia* (Milan: Adelphi, 1984), 167–83.

33 See my "Being Luigi Ontani," *doppiozero*, May 21, 2012, https://www.doppiozero.com/being-luigi-ontani.

34 The last room of Jim Dine's large solo exhibition at Rome's Palazzo delle Esposizioni (February 11–June 2, 2020) was entirely devoted to his Pinocchios.

35 See Bartolomeo Pietromarchi, *Italia in opera: La nostra identità attraverso le arti visive* (Turin: Bollati Boringhieri, 2011), 78–81.

Many are fascinated by his restlessness and aversion to rules; Pinocchio is "the rebel, the Naughtiest Boy of All"[36] (in the words of Manganelli, one of his greatest fans), defying even the laws of physics and biology. His nature is metamorphic, resilient, and transient, marked by a radical, ontological, and invertible penchant for disguise: he is dressed up as "a boy like all other boys," or dressed down as a "donkey." And yet, the unbridled metamorphosis of "this mercurial creature" and his dromologically perpetual motion are trapped in a *solidified* body that is stiffer than the human body. Herein lies the profoundly uncanny significance of this character; after each adventure and metamorphosis, Pinocchio is no more than a "sarcastically hard piece of wood." He is the mask of masks because his ceaseless transformations and escapades merely reassert his fixity, turning it into an absolute condition. Pinocchio's essentially immutable *mask* is the very opposite of the mutability, plasticity, and *liveliness* of the human body and face; even better, it denies all these qualities with its dissimulation, opposition, and stiffness.

Such is the "irreparable" condition from which Pinocchio is unknowingly running away: "as long as he is a puppet, he cannot have a history, grow, or become someone else."[37] What is even more shocking is that, in order to escape the fixity of his own condition and "complete his initiation, Pinocchio must choose the only death he is allowed to choose for himself: suicide."[38] The author's choice, in turn, was due to the conservative moralism of his readers at the time, as Emilio Garroni explains in his seminal analysis, *Pinocchio uno e bino* (Pinocchio, Two in One).[39] By describing his death and rebirth as a suicide, Manganelli is disappointedly alluding to the end of the "dual" nature of Pinocchio as "one in two," that is, "the puppet's transformation into 'a proper boy.'"[40] He is far from being the only commentator to be disappointed by this. Pinocchio's paradox is found in the fact that, in order to access organic and social "life" as we know it, he must first let go of his previous "super-life" and "die," and thus relinquish his nonhuman condition as a puppet, a condition that is both within and beyond our human existence.

In fact, de Chirico was well aware of Pinocchio's profound nature, as signaled by what he wrote in his early years in the so-called Éluard Manuscripts: "to be really immortal a work of art must go completely beyond the limits of the human: good sense and logic will be missing from it. In this way it will come close to the dream state, and also to the mentality of children. I remember that often having read Nietzsche's immortal work *Thus Spoke Zarathustra*, I derived from various passages of this book an impression I had as a child when I read an Italian children's book called *The Adventures of Pinocchio*."[41] Pinocchio is a popular children's version of the

---

36   Giorgio Manganelli, "La morte di Pinocchio," in *Laboriose inezie* (Milan: Garzanti, 1986), 313.

37   Giorgio Manganelli, "Carlo Collodi: Pinocchio," in ibid., 311.

38   Ibid., 312.

39   See Emilio Garroni, *Pinocchio uno e bino* (Rome-Bari: Laterza, 1975).

40   Manganelli, "La morte di Pinocchio," 313.

41   Giorgio de Chirico, "Éluard–Picasso Manuscripts (1911–1915)," trans. Robert Goldwater and Louise Bourgeois, in *Metaphysical Art: The de Chirico Journals* 17/18 (2019), 41.

Übermensch in de Chirico (Nietzsche's influence on the artist is no secret), a puppet who is beyond good and evil and beyond *the limits of the human*. This is why he is *really immortal*.

It is not at all a far cry from De Dominicis's own paradox. His relentless, cheerful, yet tragic *attempt to achieve immortality* stemmed from a humanly unattainable need as well as a self-evident paradox. It is no coincidence that his first move as an artist was to announce his own death with a "death notice" that publicized his first solo exhibition at L'Attico. As Gabriele Guercio wrote, "man dies by becoming an author and the artist becomes an author by dying." Since "his works aim to transcend space and time … De Dominicis proclaims himself as their author by announcing the end of his existence as a statistically relevant individual."[42] In order to escape death, De Dominicis turned it into an a priori assumption by announcing it at the start of his career, and by later pursuing immortality in the form of a kind of ritual immobility before death, an exorcism of sorts. To use Joseph Kosuth's tersely illuminating words, De Dominicis's way of escaping death was to "get it over with."[43]

From the outset, the course followed by De Dominicis's art is perfectly consistent with this premise inasmuch as it carries on with this paradox. As Guercio explained, De Dominicis's art pursued the creation of an "immobile universe," sidestepping both history and the laws of physics, as a way to transcend human perishability.[44] However, by denying entropy, his art also denied movement, and therefore life as we know it. Since we are organic beings, life to us is nothing but a relentless process of constant decay, a slow and progressive death; to paraphrase the poet Giuseppe Ungaretti's famous lines, "la morte / si sconta / vivendo" (literally, "death is expiated by living"), we *count* the cost of our own lives in the days and hours lived that separate us from the end. We can summarize the temporal dimension's entropic collapse in one simple word: *aging*. It is worth noting that the major amendment made by the artist to the second version of his first written text, "Letter on Immortality," published for his second solo exhibition at L'Attico with inverted dates ("10 September 1970" for the show's opening and "10 April 1970" for its closing), consisted of adding the following passage to the initial version: "Aging is an internal illness, which, from around the age of twenty-six, begins to corrode body and mind. Then we think we have become used to the process and it seems inevitable to us; however, all man's actions have always been nothing but unconscious responses to this dramatic problem."[45]

His 1969 masterpiece, *Time, Mistake, Space*, is exactly an allusion to this never-ending paradox. In the work, we are not just presented

---

42   Guercio, "Arte visiva e immortalità del corpo," 302.
43   Joseph Kosuth, "Clarity," in this volume, 108.
44   This is the principal theme of Guercio's *L'arte non evolve*.
45   Editor's note: See "Letter on Immortality," in this volume, 62–63. I am unaware of the source on which De Dominicis bases his statement, according to which the "point of no return" can be "roughly" made to coincide with "the twenty-sixth birthday," but I cannot help noticing that his sudden death occurred when he was fifty-one and a half, and thus twice as old as this watershed.

with a man's skeleton, but also the skeleton of a dog lying next to it. In fact, moving across *time* and *space* on a horizontal (and thus progressive, straight, historical) line is an age-old *mistake* made by the organic sphere as a whole; hence the dog's skeleton. The mortal remains of both are laid out on this horizontal line. In man's case, such a *mistake* is exacerbated by his attempt to speed up this movement with the means provided by science and technology: it is no accident his skeleton wears roller skates. Incidentally, the powerful means of science and technology would take man as far as the moon that same year: a planetary and, according to some, catastrophic success for humankind.[46]

The artist indicated a path to salvation through the subsequent addition of a golden pole which counteracts the mortality emphasized in its horizontal composition. The pole points toward the vertical dimension. *L'Appeso* also reverses the relationship between the X and Y axes and once again creates an inverted symmetry. In this later work, the vertical axis, which is subject to gravity, is associated with death, while the paintbrush/phallus that rebels against death is on a horizontal axis. Likewise, Pinocchio was born into a form that was both within and beyond the human condition, and which "denied the possibility of time and growth."[47] Although he is not subject to entropy as he is not technically *alive* in a purely organic sense of the term, he makes a *mistake* too: he never stops running around and chasing a *proper boy*'s organic and social life and yet, once he finally gets hold of it, he is dead. Therefore, what we see in De Dominicis's skeleton is exactly this Pinocchio/Christ embracing his own sacrifice, transfiguration, and suicide. The artist's lifelong pursuit of a *suspended* and higher state of being, the attempt to counteract or at least correct and amend his human existence, is nothing but the same mistake, albeit inverted. Once he has finally reached the very top of these unparalleled heights and achieved perfect immobility, immortality is one and the same with death.

Translated by Andrea Vesentini
This essay, originally titled "Autoritratto," was commissioned for the present volume.

46 See my *Volevamo la Luna* (Fidenza: Mattioli 1885, 2019).
47 Guercio, *L'arte non evolve*, 64.

The Ancestral Objection

Gabriele Guercio

<u>A work without a public</u>
In June 1988 Gino De Dominicis presented his *Specchio che tutto riflette tranne gli esseri viventi* (Mirror That Reflects Everything Except Living Beings) [IT 302] (1969–88) at Galleria Lia Rumma in Naples. Conceived in 1969 and destroyed by the artist after the 1988 exhibition, *Mirror* defied widespread assumptions about the nature of a work of art. Effecting a double subtraction, it simultaneously made the public invisible and caused the painting(s) on view in the gallery to mysteriously appear to be located in two places at once.

Visitors to the gallery entered a darkened room where a light projector illuminated a painting hanging on the wall: a black panel showing, on the left and right sides respectively, profiles of a woman and a man traced with silver pencil and charcoal. The pairing of these two profiles is a recurrent motif in De Dominicis's oeuvre. It connects Urvasi, the celestial nymph whose beauty has been celebrated in Indian literature since the ancient Vedas, with Gilgamesh, the Sumerian king who went on a quest for bodily immortality. In the image shown in 1988, a multifaceted prism, foreshortened in the blackness and likewise traced in silver pencil and charcoal, floats between the nymph and the king. Visitors to the gallery would also notice an oval wooden frame with a shiny glass surface that hung on the far left of the wall opposite the painting. Approaching the frame, they would realize that it reflected the whole room: the light projector as well as the picture of Urvasi and Gilgamesh. *Mirror*, however, did not reflect the onlookers or anything else moving in the room.

It was quite a challenge to fathom the artist's trick—that a wall had been built in the gallery to make two symmetrical rooms, each containing a seemingly identical painting and light projector: what looked like a framed mirror was actually a window that allowed people to see into the other room.[1] The viewer was left to speculate on the implications of De Dominicis's mise-en-scène.

De Dominicis's *Mirror* conjures up a site exempted from human access—a pre- or post-human domain where there is no assured conjunction between the self and the other-than-self. *Mirror* engineers what could be called an "ancestral objection." In the modern West, the belief in a co-origination of humans and the world, in their being defined by their reciprocal codependency, has underpinned artistic culture as well as philosophical discourse in a number of ways.[2] The ancestral objection challenges this

---

1   To make the trick work, the painting visible within framed glass presented Urvasi and Gilgamesh, with the prism in a reversed position relative to the one in the room where visitors stood. After the exhibition, the artist destroyed the painting with the reversed image and kept the other, which is now part of the collection of the Castello di Rivoli Museum of Contemporary Art in Turin.

belief, arguing that co-origination or "correlationism" does not hold as an unshakable principle. Science posits an "arche-fossil," something that constituted matter prior to life on earth. The arche-fossil has no human witness. Its admissibility cannot be said to spring from a dynamic of co-origination between the perceiving subject and the perceived object, either at the time of the scientific discovery of the arche-fossil or, evidently, in the lifeless time-spaces of the ancestral realm.[3] With his 1988 mise-en-scène, De Dominicis seems to vindicate for the painting(s) of Urvasi and Gilgamesh a status akin to that of the arche-fossil. The "invisibility" of the gallerygoers construed by *Mirror* points to an ancestral past or a suspended future rather than to a correlational present. It nullifies both artist and public as agents located in fixed spatiotemporal coordinates while frustrating interpretations and preconceived manipulations from the outside.

The attempt to disengage the work of art from fixed space-time characterizes De Dominicis's modus operandi. It goes hand in hand with his pivotal idea that works of art are models of immortality. Already in 1969, De Dominicis issued an invitation to his first solo exhibition in Rome in the form of a poster announcing his death. The poster was meant to imply that the artist must go beyond his biographical identity and be faithful to the traces of the eternal contained in his works. While in his 1970 "Letter on Immortality," De Dominicis had called for a concentration of all human energies toward the goal of immortality,[4] the idea that works of art objectify that goal dawned on him soon afterward and has explicitly inspired his production since his paradigmatic *Seconda soluzione d'immortalita (l'universo è immobile)* (Second Solution of Immortality [The Universe Is Still]) [IT 150] (1972), briefly shown at the XXXVI Venice Biennale of 1972.[5] Since the 1960s, in fact, De Dominicis adopted heterogeneous means of expression such as drawing, painting, photographs, invisible works, and three-dimensional works to create images that could escape categorization in terms of progressive time and contextualized space.

2   In artistic culture, the belief is traceable to Johann Joachim Winckelmann's *Geschichte der Kunst des Altertums* (1764). Establishing a nexus between style and history, the evolution of the sculptural art and the life and culture of the Greek people, *Geschichte* marked the beginning of an art historical discourse. In the twentieth century, Marcel Duchamp contended that artists cannot fully grasp their own work because viewers have an equally relevant part in the process; see Marcel Duchamp, "The Creative Act," *Art News* 56, no. 4 (Summer 1957): 28–29. In philosophical discourse, the positing of a codependency between the self and the other-than-self is key, from Kant's transcendentalism to the various strands of twentieth-century phenomenology.

3   Speaking of an "ancestral objection," I am adapting a cogent argument by Quentin Meillassoux, who argues that post-Kantian philosophy is dominated by what he calls "correlationism," the often unstated view that humans cannot exist without the world, nor the world without humans. For Meillassoux, this devious maneuver allows philosophy to sidestep the problem of how to describe the world as it really is, prior to all human access; he terms this prehuman reality the "ancestral realm." See Quentin Meillassoux, *After Finitude: An Essay on the Necessity of Contingency*, trans. Ray Brassier (London: Continuum, 2008).

4   The "Letter" was originally published, without a title, in *Gino De Dominicis*, exh. cat. (Rome: L'Attico, 1970).

5   On the *Second Solution* and its controversial reception, see *De Dominicis. Raccolta di scritti sull'opera e l'artista*, ed. Gabriele Guercio (Turin: Umberto Allemandi, 2001), 111–30 and 195–96n11. See also Gabriele Guercio, "Apropos of Paolo Rosa," in "Gino De Dominicis," ed. Laura Cherubini and Andrea Bellini, special issue, *Flash Art International* (June 2007): 86–97.

The 1988 exhibition of *Mirror* therefore represented a new twist to De Dominicis's stance, further complicating and radicalizing it. Never before had De Dominicis so unequivocally indicated that works of art gain existence via subtraction and need not even be seen in order to exist. As he maintained: "It is the public that exhibits itself to art and not vice versa."[6] Through the device of a false mirror that, instead of framing or delimiting, paradoxically unbounds what it reflects, the painting(s) in the gallery are revealed as inhabiting a void in which the distinctions between now and then, seen and unseen, here and elsewhere, are blurred. *Mirror* intimates that "creation ex nihilo" happens. One cannot avoid being confronted with the enigma of "poiesis" or the occurrence of a coming-into-being in which being can be thought of as inextricable from nonbeing. The enigma of poiesis—poiesis as enigma—is arguably staged precisely by the work of art's faculty to resist whatever views and patterns of interpretation (historical, art historical, cultural, existential, etc.) may inform the situation prior to its appearance.

Making a hole in knowledge, a work of art takes on and fuels the idea that there is an "unconditional," by which I mean an experiential or cognitive surplus that one must accept without reservation—as one does with love, faith, a logical axiom of mathematics—because that surplus is a gratuitous extra. It cannot be described or understood by adopting the criteria of intelligibility currently used in the situation.[7] A work of art is a physical repository of the idea of the unconditional because it attests to the emergence of something that is not totalizable, that does not fit into a given state. Infringing upon the laws of causality and reason that presumably govern phenomena, a work of art hints at a self-contained, chaotic time. It is itself "invisible to" or "absconded from" viewpoints anchored in a determined world or dimension of being. Yet by virtue of its eluding time-space, a work of art may convey a desire to have and perpetuate lifelike qualities through means other than life.

Mirror raises numerous questions. For instance: What does it mean to see without seeing oneself seeing? Can such a seeing foster modes of vision that dispense with the co-originative intervention of a perceiving subject? Granted that *Mirror* is a device to achieve subtraction of both objects and subjects, do the painting(s) of Urvasi and Gilgamesh and the effects of *Mirror* mutually endorse each other? How and why does the site generated by *Mirror* promote the metamorphosis of bodies and minds that humankind has variously envisioned as immortality?

In addressing these and related questions, I will consider the 1988 exhibition of *Mirror* in light of De Dominicis's take on immortality and in connection with issues affecting artistic culture in the West. The spe-

6   See Gino De Dominicis, "Maxims, 1969–1996," in this volume, 93.

7   The philosophical pedigree of the idea of the unconditional may be traced back to German Idealism, to the writings of Immanuel Kant, Johann Gottlieb Fichte, and, most notably, Friedrich Wilhelm Schelling. The unconditional variously informed their questioning of whether and to what extent human reason is able to account for the absolute. For a suggestive discussion of these thinkers' stances and their attempts to investigate the very beginning of thought itself, see Massimo Cacciari, *Dell'Inizio* (Milan: Adelphi, 2001).

cial status that De Dominicis ascribed to artworks conflicts with accredited views, which hold that artistic phenomena are not only rooted in a time detectable as collective or individual, historical or art historical, but also forge a space of representation comprehensible in its visible, formal, and tactile components. Dispensing with these views, De Dominicis identified artistic creation with a breakthrough in a sense that upsets the realms habitually referred to as subjectivity, objectivity, and truth. While there seems to be no maker or user of art as a subject preexisting the appearance of the work of art, the latter poses itself as an everlasting object. Just as object and subject are not necessarily linked via reflective codependency, so the traditional notion of truth as correspondence between appearance and substance, language and reality, loses its credibility. Truth is instead tantamount to a surplus inexplicable within inherited structures of knowledge and experience. Truth may in fact be associated with whatever makes works of art the repositories of the idea of the unconditional.

<u>Seeing Without Seeing Oneself Seeing</u>

In the modern West, the art of painting has often been associated with a mirror's reflection. In *De Pictura* (1435–36), Leon Battista Alberti gave a seminal boost to this association when he called Narcissus the inventor of painting and asked, "What is painting but the act of embracing, by means of art, the surface of the pool?"[8] Significant works of art corroborate Alberti's assertion, either by depicting a mirror within the painted scene, as with Jan van Eyck's *Arnolfini Portrait* (1434), Diego Velázquez's *Las Meninas* (1656), and Édouard Manet's *Un bar aux Folies Bergère* (1881–82), or by alluding to the mirror's deceptiveness, as with René Magritte's *Le faux miroir* (1928). In so doing, these works probe into the scope of pictorial representation as crafty illusion, as poietical mediation between the artist and the world, and unremitting overture to its external context. Closer to our own time, Michelangelo Pistoletto's *Mirror Paintings* (a series begun in the early 1960s) consist of painted tissue paper glued on stainless steel bases so that each *Mirror Painting* shows stable figures along with the variable presence of the viewers and reflects every changing moment of its exposure. However, these works, from Van Eyck to Pistoletto, even while they explore the relationship between image and outside reality, nonetheless carry forward the interlocked assumptions that seeing is a self-reflective activity and that a liaison of some sort connects the perceiving subject, be it the maker or user of a work of art, with the perceived object, be it the work or its referent.

Both of these assumptions fail within the site of De Dominicis's *Mirror*. Because it does not reflect living beings, *Mirror* obstructs the identification of a perceiving subject that is so determinant in associating pictorial images and mirrors, representation and self-reflectivity. Visitors to the 1988 exhibition become "invisible" agents who could not but linger in the room containing the light projector and the painting or look at the

<hr>

8   Leon Battista Alberti, *On Painting and On Sculpture: The Latin Texts of* De Pictura *and* De Statua, ed. and trans. Cecil Grayson (London: Phaidon, 1972), 62.

other, identical room through the framed glass of *Mirror*. The whole setting voids any emulation of Narcissus's fate of endless self-identification. And it is not only the visitors who are freed from narcissistic viewing. Just as human agency is no longer essential to the artwork's fruition, so also the agencies of the painting(s)' maker need no longer be ascribed to a particular individual reflected within his or her own works. One is reminded that De Dominicis's artistic career in Rome started with the announcement of his death and also that the painting(s) in the room(s) can hardly be pinned down to, say, a world familiar or accessible to people living in 1988. Accordingly, the first remarkable feature of the *Mirror* site is its implication that, in the fruition as in the creation of a work of art, the perceiving subject may be able to repel the kind of scrutiny entailed by mirroring and self-reflectivity. This unavailability in *Mirror* encourages one to ponder whether a nonreflective seeing is possible and what it would mean to see without seeing oneself seeing.

The possibility of a nonreflective seeing is variously contemplated in De Dominicis's oeuvre, including in *Second Solution*. Due to the outcry it provoked, this work was visible only on the morning of June 8, 1972, at the opening of the Venice Biennale. Nevertheless a photograph signed and inscribed by De Dominicis as *(foto ricordo)* (souvenir photo) shows what people saw that morning. Paolo Rosa, a young man with Down syndrome, sits on a chair in the back corner while on the floor in front of him are arranged, from right to left, a stone, a rubber ball, and the perimeter of a white square. De Dominicis had shown these three works at L'Attico in Rome in 1969 as *Aspettativa di un casuale movimento molecolare generale in una sola direzione tale da generare un movimento spontaneo del materiale* (Waiting for a Random One-Directional Molecular Movement that Could Generate a Spontaneous Movement of Material) [IT 85–89]; *Palla di gomma (caduta da 2 metri) nell'attimo immediatamente precedente il rimbalzo* (Rubber Ball [Falling from a Height of Two Meters] in the Moment Right Before Bouncing Back) [IT 70]; and *Cubo invisibile* (Invisible Cube) [IT 45] (1967), an invisible cube whose base is traced with white paint. Each of these works posits a likelihood—that the stone will move spontaneously, that the ball is about to rebound, that an invisible cube sits on the floor—that holds only if, acknowledging the enigma of poiesis, one suspends disbelief and assents to the works' virtual proficiency as asserted by their titles. Rosa's position is that of the living agent, observer, and guardian of the works before him: he looks at them and he looks at us, inducing us both to return his look and to look at what he is looking at.

This looking resolves itself into a nonreflective seeing in that it cannot be translated into a knowing. Looking at Rosa, one has the same indescribable experience that one tends to ascribe to his unfathomable gaze. Seeing becomes tantamount to freeing the image and the viewer from the constraints produced by firm distinctions between seen and unseen, perception and conception, idea and vision. It is noteworthy that the *(foto ricordo)* features a woman beholding the scene. Her presence suggests that, demanding as it may be, a co-identification with the gaze of the young man affected by Down syndrome is possible. Such a co-identification is key to maintaining the multidimensional integrity of the three works on the floor. Rosa accords with their inclination to exist now and forever because his unfathomable gaze both implies and generates a nonreflective seeing that undoes chronological progression along with any supposition of a subjectivity tied to particular historical sequences and natural courses, such as are ruled by entropy alone. Impermeable to interferences, projections, and any arbitrary charges of meaning impinging from the outside, *Second Solution* aims at making everything stay as it is. It vindicates the notion that the shifting position of the stone is spontaneous, the ball is just about to bounce, the cube is invisible, and the young man is an ineffable subject (and object) of a perception overcoming the irreversibility of time and energy. At stake in *Second Solution* is the awareness of a perpetually still universe to which, until humanity achieves physical immortality, works of art can bear special witness. A nonreflective seeing affords glimpses of that universe.

Whereas the photograph of *Second Solution* shows two actual people typifying a nonreflective seeing consonant with the nature of the three works on the floor, *Mirror* pushes the implications of that seeing much further by suggesting that no viewer is needed to legitimize a work of art. Albeit indirectly, the 1988 exhibition uncovers the mechanisms of split and denial peculiar to the mirroring act. That act ties the agencies of an individual to an identification, a fictional form or ideal "I," symbolizing a mental stability that continuously diverges from the heterogeneous forces that make up the life of a subject.[9] Before a mirror, while becoming the other or seeking the other or oneself as another, one reduces otherness to one's own perspective. There can be no pure difference in a specular image because there is never a two.[10] Much of the mirror's spell lies in its denial that there is a two. De Dominicis's *Mirror* both disengages the perceiver from this spell and halts the self-reflectivity generated by a specular image. There is no longer a permanent subject (*hypokeiménon, subjectum*) sustaining its internal and external states while functioning as a medium of transference between the self and the other-than-self. *Mirror* robs the perceiving subjects of a firm seat. Unable to see themselves seeing, they cannot subdue the existent by naming and representing it in a self-reflective fashion.

Unframing what its frame circumscribes, De Dominicis's *Mirror* undermines not only the stipulation of a reality constructed by a transcendental guarantor—a mind or body or both instantiated via aprioristic categorizations of time and space, linguistic practices, and communicational agreement—but also the likelihood that subject and object are co-originative agents or transcendental guarantors. The "non-me" of the painting(s) suggests an image that, like an icon "not made by human hands,"

<hr>

9   See Jacques Lacan, "The Mirror Stage as Formative of the I Function," in *Écrits*, trans. Bruce Fink in collaboration with Hélöise Fink and Russell Grigg (New York: W. W. Norton, 2005), 75–81.

10   See Luce Irigaray, *To Be Two*, trans. Monique M. Rhodes and Marco F. Cocito-Monoc (New York: Routledge, 2001), 40–41.

does not stand for anything except its presentation of a likeness.[11] "What" one sees enhances the recognition that the existence of the painting(s) is irreducible to all the rest—to whatever data may be associated with the situation of the 1988 exhibition: author, public, institutional context, state of past and contemporary art, world affairs, and so on.

Gaining existence through *Mirror*'s double subtraction, the presence of the painting(s) is tantamount to something that might have happened or would have happened in time and space. This happening in an ancestral past or a suspended future would be, in fact, creation ex nihilo—a groundless happening of poiesis—because unsustained by a founding subject and unaccountable in a correlational present. But the sense of a subtracted stillness of the painting(s) is not only the result of *Mirror*'s device but also a characteristic of the painted image(s), to which I will now turn.

A Triadic Catharsis

The motifs of Urvasi and Gilgamesh in De Dominicis's oeuvre stem from his interest (since about 1977) in the Sumerians. From this ancient people of unknown provenance, De Dominicis drew confirmation of his intuition of a lost, yet still reverberating, origin of humankind's spiritual mission. From 3800 to 2000 BCE, the Sumerians developed an extraordinarily complex civilization in Mesopotamia, with artistic, urban, and political ramifications that foreshadowed myths, cultures, and religions to come.[12] De Dominicis also found in Gilgamesh, the eponymous hero of the Babylonian epic, the archetypal figure of the human aspiration to bodily immortality—the goal set in his 1970 "Letter on Immortality"—and did not hesitate to conjecture that Gilgamesh must have been an artist as well as a king.[13] As for the immortal Urvasi, in the poems narrating the love between the nymph and the mortal Pururavas—a legend traceable to an episode from the Rig Veda, a compilation of Indian philosophy dating to 3000 BCE—De Dominicis might have found the archetypal reference to immortality achievable through love. In one version of the poem, Pururavas defines love as a "super force" capable not only of binding the lovers but also of outliving their transient bodies.[14]

---

11 On the singular status of icons and their imperviousness to criteria of artistry and aesthetic and art historical worth, see Georges Didi-Huberman, *Devant l'image: Questions posées aux fins d'une histoire de l'art* (Paris: Minuit, 1990). See also Moshe Barasch, *Icon: Studies in the History of an Idea* (New York: New York University Press, 1992).

12 See, among others, André Parrot, *Sumer: The Dawn of Art* (New York: Golden Press, 1961); Samuel Noah Kramer, *History Begins at Sumer: Thirty-Nine Firsts in Recorded History* (Philadelphia: University of Pennsylvania Press, 1981); Harriet Crawford, *Sumer and the Sumerians*, 2nd ed. (Cambridge: Cambridge University Press, 2004); and Giovanni Pettinato, *I Sumeri* (Milan: Rusconi, 1994).

13 The conjecture has some grounds: Gilgamesh was an architect and a draftsman, and sources report that he drew the city walls of Uruk. On De Dominicis's references to Gilgamesh, see Giovanni Pettinato, "The Question of Immortality in the Gilgamesh Corpus," in this volume, 165–73. For Gilgamesh's late third millennium BCE epic, see also Andrew R. George, *The Babylonian Gilgamesh Epic*, 2 vols. (Oxford: Oxford University Press, 2003).

14 See Ramdhari Singh Dinkar, *Dinkar's Urvashi: A Saga of Human Love and Vedanta*, trans. Krishna K. Vidyarthi (New Delhi: Siddharth Publications, 1994), 69. On Urvasi, see Babu Ram Yadava, *Evolution of Urvaśī* (Aligarh: Vijñāna Prakāśana, 1986); and Krishna Kanta Handique, *Apsarases in Indian Literature and the Legend of Urvasi and Pururavas* (New Delhi: Decent Books, 2001).

De Dominicis's pairing of the Indian nymph and the Sumerian king suggests that Urvasi offers Gilgamesh another path to immortality via love and that the woman and artist constitute the two primary agents of creation. The pairing encompasses East and West, female and male, love and death. It sets up a clash of heterogeneous temporalities, cultures, and states of being. In the 1980 work, the black silhouettes of Urvasi and Gilgamesh violate historical concordance as they appear against a background showing, among other things, a pyramid and a mysterious flying disk.[15] This anachronistic configuration recapitulates a theme prominent in other works by De Dominicis—*Expectation* and *Rubber Ball*, for example—in which the image embodies more than one nowness. The possibility of such an embodiment was first noted by Leonardo da Vinci. In his comparison of poetry and painting, Leonardo maintained the latter's superiority, remarking that, unlike the poet, the painter can avail himself of the "visual virtue"—namely, painting's intrinsic power to capture a simultaneity of times and spaces in one representation.[16] Radicalizing the effects of the "visual virtue," De Dominicis could envision in his works not only themes, symbols, and figures that collapse temporal distance, but also the bodies of a species (pre- or post-human? extraterrestrial?) following an orientation of its own.[17] He could exploit the anachronism inherent in the production and reception of images.[18] Just as Giorgio de Chirico's "metaphysical" painting, by insinuating that reality hits humans visually rather than verbally,[19] upended chronographic complacency and interpolated conscious and unconscious sights, so De Dominicis's images characteristically shatter the order of things by indicating that the "non-me" of a work of art outstrips the reliance on linear history. It bears evidence of a multifaceted, effluent time.

Thus the theme of the painting(s) of the 1988 exhibition buttresses *Mirror*'s double subtraction, its suggestion that nothing in particular delineates here and elsewhere, seen and unseen, ancestral past and suspended future. Moreover, the triadic composition of the image(s) is especially noteworthy in its capacity to bind each element to the other two.

15   Germano Celant refers to this "disk" in "Art to the Power N," in this volume, 25–26. On this work and the pairing of Urvasi and Gilgamesh, see also Jean-Christophe Amman, "Ecstasy Between the Silhouettes," in this volume, 154–56.

16   See Leonardo da Vinci, *Libro di Pittura*, ed. Carlo Pedretti, vol. I (Florence: Giunti, 1995), esp. 146–48.

17   On these images of "another" species, see Norman Bryson, "The Buddha of the Future," in this volume, 157–60. See also Gabriele Guercio, "Arte visiva e immortalità del corpo," in Guercio, ed., *De Dominicis. Raccolta*, 163–99.

18   The anachronism of images was variously conceptualized in the twentieth century. It underpins Freud's discovery that the unconscious operates via condensation and displacement of images, Walter Benjamin's transference of the principle of cinematic montage to historical understanding, and Aby Warburg's search for transhistorical pictorial evidence of a discontinuous, folded time. See Georges Didi-Huberman, *Devant le temps: Histoire de l'art et anachronisme des images* (Paris: Minuit, 2000), and *L'image survivante: Histoire de l'art et temps de fantômes selon Aby Warburg* (Paris: Minuit, 2002). For a methodology of analysis attentive to the anachronistic mode of Renaissance artifacts and paintings, see Alexander Nagel and Christopher S. Wood, "Toward a New Model of Renaissance Anachronism," *Art Bulletin* 87, no. 3 (September 2005): 403–15.

19   See Giorgio de Chirico, "Discorso sul meccanismo del pensiero," in *Il meccanismo del pensiero. Critica, polemica, autobiografia, 1911–1943*, ed. Maurizio Fagiolo (Turin: Einaudi, 1985), 408.

Whatever we make of them, Urvasi and Gilgamesh confer meaning on the prism. Whatever we make of it, the prism qualifies who Urvasi and Gilgamesh are or become within the composition. This triunity suggests that neither co-origination nor transcendentality, what *Mirror* thwarts, suffice to explain Urvasi and Gilgamesh's meeting. Their encounter does not exhaust itself in either a mutual mirroring or a bifocal codependency. A triadic catharsis is in play in the painted image(s). The "two" of Urvasi and Gilgamesh is inextricable from the "third" element of the prism emerging out of the void. It is as if, facing each other against the background of the prism's emergence, Urvasi and Gilgamesh were exposed to, summoned, and defined by the prism. Their being two entails correspondences, ranging from their polar positions to the evidence of their encounter, as well as differences signaled by their sexual, temporal, and cultural heterogeneity. But above all it entails the recognition that another, supplementary element may attract, embody, and express the correspondence and the difference of their being two. In fact, they guard and ratify the reality of the prism, which in turn appears as a surplus (of light, energy) and as a remainder (of another space, time) that invests the nymph and the king while transfiguring and purifying them in their ecstasy.

Something of the kind was also envisioned by Picasso. For instance, in the graphic work for the *Suite Vollard*, taking up the motif of the artist and the model, Picasso imagined a trio in which a work of art, not necessarily the model's likeness, provides the third element in their relationship. De Dominicis himself often produced triadic images, as for instance with a wood panel on which a single line defines two faces merging together while the hand of the female figure holds a blue, vertical rod exemplifying the "third" between the two. In the painting(s) of the 1988 exhibition of *Mirror*, the third element of the prism does not simply qualify what happens between subjects and objects or subjects and subjects. It stands out as the "truth" of Urvasi and Gilgamesh. Rather than mirroring or having its referent in a state of things, truth must be understood here as an effluence that unsettles the seeming cohesiveness of the given. The prism epitomizes this effluence by signifying an "unconcealedness" within the blank or void of the canvas's blackness, a "subtraction" from all the rest except Urvasi and Gilgamesh, and an "event" whose resonance regards them alone by virtue of their being two.

Described in this way, the prism breeds views of truth akin to those developed in some strands of twentieth-century philosophy and psychoanalysis. For Martin Heidegger, truth is the revelation of being as such in its "unconcealedness." A work of art, originating from such a process, shows that truth stands between its disclosure and un-truth, the world's habituated order and its transformation prompted by the openness of truth.[20] For Jacques Lacan, truth bursts into reality through missing deeds, contradictions, and words outside rational control. It is what one grasps by put-

---

20   See Martin Heidegger, "The Origin of the Work of Art," in *Poetry, Language, Thought,* trans. Albert Hofstadter (New York: HarperCollins, 2001), 17–86.

ting to work one's own ignorance of what exceeds the order of signs. Halfway between language and subject, analyst and patient, truth emerges via the realization of its "subtraction," of its exposure of the chasm between the conscious and the unconscious, the symbolic and the real.[21] For Alain Badiou, truth occurs between the situation and what is indistinct and generic within the situation, the established knowledge and the elements escaping its computation. Irreducible to exact designations, truth is an "event" that implies the fidelity of those who recognize it and become subjects precisely by being true to it. Inventive, singular, and without factual basis, truth is a hazardous supplement that cannot be contained in any pre-given parameters of interpretation.[22] Conceiving truth as unconcealedness, subtraction, and event, these authors not only foster a sense of truth as the ubiquitous, unaided egress of a third that upsets and redesigns the given, but emphasize also qualities that characterize the triadic catharsis painted by De Dominicis.

The painting(s) of the 1988 exhibition can be seen positing the irruption of a "third" or "truth" in the image itself. But the sense of this irruption does not relate to the painted image(s) alone. It is the cipher of the revelation of a "non-me" that includes and defines the whole site of *Mirror*. In the painted image(s), truth is the prism between the pair of Urvasi and Gilgamesh. But the creation of the image is in turn thinkable as the third or truth issuing out of the pair formed by the encounter between artist and matter. The painting(s) can operate as the third or truth breaking into the site of *Mirror* and standing between the gallerygoers and the gallery itself, what is seen and what is unseen in *Mirror*, the mobility of the perceiving subject and the immobility of the perceived object.

That a logic/logique of the third may be applied to the site of *Mirror* means that the whole site is one of a triadic catharsis for objects and subjects. Absolved from the ties of co-origination and transcendentality, they yield to a multidimensional ubiquity. Objects and subjects can entertain a nonperspectival relationship with time and space—a relationship in which the third is the figure or carrier of places and moments hinting at ancestral pasts or suspended futures. Just as the pairing of Urvasi and Gilgamesh does not belong to any particular time and is arguably born in its exposure to the unforeseeable space construed by the sudden arrival of the prism, so maker and user of an artwork do not predate the latter and are arguably borne out of their exposure to the supplementary space construed

21   See Jacques Lacan, "Science and Truth," in *Écrits*, 726–45; "The Impotence of Truth," in *The Seminar of Jacques Lacan: Book XVII: The Other Side of Psychoanalysis*, trans. Russell Gregg (New York: W. W. Norton, 2007), 164–79; "La vérité surgit de la méprise," in *Le seminaire de Jacques Lacan. Livre I. Les écrits techniques de Freud (1953–1954)* (Paris: Seuil, 1975), 397–414; and "L'écrit et la vérité," in *Le Séminaire. Livre XVIII. D'un discours qui ne serait pas du semblant* (Paris: Seuil, 2006), 55–75.

22   See Alain Badiou, *Being and Event* (1988), trans. Olivier Feltham (London: Continuum, 2005), and *Logiques des mondes. L'Etre et l'Evénement* (Paris: Seuil, 2006). See also *Manifesto for Philosophy* (1989), ed. and trans. Norman Madarasz (Albany, NY: State University of New York Press, 1999); and "The Event as Trans-Being," "On Subtraction," and "Truth: Forcing and the Unnameable," in *Theoretical Writings*, ed. and trans. Ray Brassier and Alberto Toscano (London: Continuum, 2006), 99–136.

by the appearance of the non-me of a work of art. In the 1988 exhibition, the theme of the painting(s) and the device of *Mirror* mutually concur, so that the human beings' invisibility corresponds to the visibility of the painting(s) and vice versa. The parallel yet incomparable realms of space-time looming within and without *Mirror* force the recognition that a third is possible and that the very presence of the painting(s) in the gallery is the ultimate third or truth of the whole site.

Through various yet converging ways—inducing a nonreflective mode of seeing, presenting images that elude a set space-time, generating a chasm between the domain of the gallerygoers and that of the painting(s)—the site of *Mirror* suggests that the non-me of a work of art is uncanny and uncompromising because it resists understanding within the supposed totality of whatever informs or frames the situation prior to its advent. As a surplus and augmentation of energy, a work of art comes as a "surprise" for its maker.[23] And this surprise may await whoever exposes him- or herself to it. Maker and user of a work of art must surrender to their own ignorance of whatever lies behind the mirror and does not belong to a given state of affairs. Only via this surrender can they cope with the leap that, in a sense, constitutes creation ex nihilo and the groundless decisions it prompts. Achieving a double subtraction that ushers in a triadic catharsis, De Dominicis's *Mirror* immunizes a work of art from principles of causation (temporal and natural, historical and art historical) and shows that it may have a life of its own and cross through many dimensions. In the integrity of its plain, physical stillness, a work of art is a truth irrupting as unconcealedness, subtraction, and event.

De Dominicis felt his work to be more ancient than that of an Egyptian artist.[24] He believed that his trust in works of art as living entities corresponded to the Sumerians' recognition of the multidimensional agency of images and artifacts.[25] Accordingly, instead of casting a work of art as an object mediating between nature and culture, the outside world and the inner visions of the artist, *Mirror* triggers a circulation of agencies through the presentation and dislocation of an image that does not refer to an aprioristic artistic essence and cannot be slotted into classifications of works based on their semiotic features alone. With De Dominicis, the factual nature of a work of art, its material thereness, is no longer evidence of

---

23 "Once it is finished, the work must surprise me, give me back more energy than I invested in the making of it. In this way a work is 'anti-entropic' and contradicts the second law of thermodynamics. One thus reappropriates the problem of death and the immortality of the body, without delegating it to science and scientists (which would be a dangerous thing to do)." See Gino De Dominicis, "Maxims, 1969–1996," in this volume, 95.

24 Ibid., 96.

25 Irene J. Winter has indicated that, in the early Sumerian texts, the construal agent/patient supplants that of subject/object so that language can accord agency to a temple or statue and suggest the outward effects of an object projected into the world; see Irene J. Winter, "Agency Marked, Agency Ascribed: The Affective Object in Ancient Mesopotamia," in *Art's Agency and Art History*, ed. Robin Osborne and Jeremy Tanner (Oxford: Blackwell, 2007), 42–69. The ascription of agency to images and artifacts, characteristic of cultures that are extraneous to or predate Western modernity, is also pivotal for a radical rethinking of the anthropology of art; see Alfred Gell, *Art and Agency: An Anthropological Theory* (Oxford: Oxford University Press, 1998).

skill, taste, inventiveness, and transformations to be tested against art historical criteria. The factuality ex nihilo of a work of art is a nascence impervious to univocal determinations of being. In engineering this nascence, *Mirror* is neither a plea for art for its own sake nor an endorsement of the specificity of the pictorial medium. Whether or not one shares De Dominicis's belief in works of art as models of immortality, one cannot help recognizing *Mirror*'s indication that the fact of the painting(s) of Urvasi and Gilgamesh is unconditional and hence capable of reconciling thought and eternity while perpetuating life over and above its relative states of organic evolution and spiritual introspection.

A longer version of this essay was published as "Repositories of the Unconditional: Gino De Dominicis' 'Mirror' and the Work of Art as a Model of Immortality," in *Res: Anthropology and Aesthetics* 55–56 (Spring–Autumn 2009), 308–23.

Why a Woman?

Ombretta Celeste and Octavia Stocker

The opaque address which opens Gino De Dominicis's "Letter on Immortality" invites ambiguity into an otherwise blunt statement of intent. "Cara" (which translates into English as "dear") identifies the addressee as female and, combined with the letter's fond valediction "tuo affezionatissimo," perhaps suggests the existence of a preestablished bond between her and the writer.[1] The female presence might be that of an intended recipient, an ideal reader, or even an abstract feminine noun. In the visual arts, it is not always easy to untangle literal and figurative feminine figures, since the former are often allegorical stand-ins for the latter, especially for grammatically feminine virtues.[2] The question remains: Why did De Dominicis choose to open his argument for a paradigmatic shift, to bring immortality to humanity, with "cara," and how does the textually embedded presence of a reader alter our reading of it? Do the epistolary form and informal, gendered salutation introduce a layer of intimacy into an otherwise public manifesto? Or does it work to lift the "Letter" above the mundane and position it as a votive missive to a muse—perhaps even *Immortalità* herself?

In De Dominicis's catalogue raisonné, Italo Tomassoni states that, many years after the first publication of the "Letter on Immortality" in the catalogue for the artist's show at L'Attico, the artist declared that it "was not to be published, or at least not all of it, as the text had been written by him in 1966 [at age nineteen] and subsequently published without his knowledge and against his wishes."[3] This repudiation emphasizes how the epistolary form, ostensibly positioned as a text from one individual to another, jars with the genre of the publicly oriented manifesto. Just as epistolary fiction can sublimate authorship by re-presenting the act of writing as a discovery or editorial compilation, the form of the "Letter" accommodates the narrative of reluctant public authorship. This categorical evasion echoes the textual instability of the "Letter": three different versions were published in two catalogues by L'Attico in 1971, two of which bear conflicting dates. However, the language of all three versions is broadly that of the manifesto: proclamatory and universal, with nothing extraneous to its argument for immortality. The performative reticence does not contradict the strident language of the argument, but it does alert us to a discrepancy between form and content.

Throughout, De Dominicis never attempts to invite a dialogue or elicit a response; the addressee's silence is ingrained in its monologic vision. Therefore, does taking the unanswered "Letter" as a starting point place silence at the center of the artist's representation of feminine figures? And if so, what kind of silence? Silence can imply a lot of things: dis-

<hr>

1   See Gino De Dominicis, "Letter on Immortality," in this volume, 59, 62.

2   See Marina Warner, *Monuments and Maidens: The Allegory of the Female Form*, 2nd ed. (London: Vintage, 1996).

3   Italo Tomassoni, ed., *Gino De Dominicis. Catalogo ragionato* (Milan: Skira, 2011), 235–37.

agreement, resistance, mystical plenitude, vacuous absence, skepticism, reticence, obedience, or simply nothing. Since silence is not a sign, to sound it out we must turn to De Dominicis's works.

A quadriptych of photographs (shown at the Venice Biennale in 1972) show the same man, young and old, and the same young woman, who remains unchanged, *Senza titolo* (Untitled) [IT 115] (1970). In the double portrait of the woman, subsequently destroyed by the artist, she holds a single flower up to her chest in a pose as indebted to Mannerism as it is to fashion magazines. Her image is timeless and timely; the flower she holds is both a mid-twentieth-century symbol of liberated sexuality and a saint's emblem.[4] While the man remains an individual in and of the world, the woman's image is an archetype of femininity, of blooming grace. This atemporality is a kind of power when set against and alongside the quotidian representation of masculine aging, but the aesthetic richness of one and the civilian simplicity of the other have obvious consequences for the subjectivity of the individuals depicted. Together, the worldliness of the man and the otherworldly stillness of the woman indicate a scene in which femininity is divorced from experience (though she remains steeped in advertising's commercial visual language). While the entirety of a man's life spins out in the gap between the two photographs, nothing can be imagined in the pause between the repeated photographs of the young woman.

Reading this work alongside the "Letter" recalls a category of silence identified by Roland Barthes: *silere*.[5] As opposed to *tacere*, which is a silence that occurs within and interrupts language (a stutter, a pause, a break in communication), *silere* is the silence that predates, transcends, and exists independently from language. *Silere* presided before the first word and will fall again after the last has been spoken, and so, like the young woman in the photograph, it exists outside time.[6] De Dominicis linked the simultaneous fall in the cultural hierarchy of creation (an act he ascribed only to women and artists) with the rising prominence of writing, a statement full of longing for the prelapsarian idyll of *silere* and its offer of escaping language's fallen and always potentially mendacious medium.[7] That discourse has an oppressive function and that female subjectivity can also be silenced within and by language connects femininity to the artwork; both are sur-

4   The quadriptych was first exhibited at the 1972 Venice Biennale, where it was "placed on a table at which one of the twins in *Gemini* sat, read the *Letter on Immortality* and delivered a bizarre, incomprehensible lecture over a microphone to his listening brother"; see Tomassoni, ed., *Gino De Domincis*, 247. Editor's note: Cf. Simone Carella's very different description of De Dominicis's contribution to the biennale, in this volume, 44n15.

5   Roland Barthes, *The Neutral: Lecture Course at the Collège de France (1977–1978)*, ed. Thomas Clerc, Eric Marty, and Lawrence D. Kritzman, trans. Rosalind E. Krauss and Denis Hillier (New York: Columbia University Press, 2005), 21–29.

6   In particular, "the bud of tendril that hasn't yet opened up, the egg that is not yet hatched: *silet, sileunt*. In short, *silere* would refer to a sort of timeless virginity of things, before they are born or after they have disappeared (*silentes* = the dead)"; ibid., 22.

7   While there are many occasions in which Gino De Dominicis asserts the primacy of the visual over the verbal, in this instance, these two statements are particularly telling: "the two poles of creation, the woman and the artist" and "Some millennia ago, however, it was decided that other social figures should take the place of the artist"; see Domitilla S. Delfino, "A Brief Interview," in this volume, 69; and Duccio Trombadori, "A Memo at the End of the Century," in this volume, 90.

rounded and misunderstood by text. The silence of the addressee, like the stillness of the young woman in the photograph, may therefore be viewed as an imaginative encounter with the prelinguistic sovereignty of the feminine and the artwork, free from the oppressive function of discourse.

Muteness, immutability, and immobility—three qualities linked to the young woman—are aspects of painting and sculpture, the media which De Dominicis never hesitated to consider the "high" artistic forms.[8] He felt that these could produce clear models for immortality, unlike writing, music, and drama. By representing women in terms of silence, immutability, and immobility, he identifies femininity with painting, sculpture, and immortality. The silence of the addressee may be a link between femininity and the artwork, and, more specifically, to the kind of artwork that De Dominicis argued was capable of serving as a model for immortality. Although the "Letter" itself predates the connection between immortality and the artwork as a model for achieving it, it may be possible to understand the addressee as acting as a kind of theoretical bridge between the two ideas.[9] This possibility becomes clearer in works like *Senza titolo (Coppia con asta)* (Untitled [Couple with Rod]) [IT 267] (1985), which depicts a reclining female balancing a rod—an iteration of the recurring *asta* which often operate as mortal wounds or discrete miracles—on a luminous fingertip while an amorphous and amorous male figure bends toward her. It is the female figure that can carry the impossible object without harm.

There is a telling anecdote about Gino De Dominicis in which the artist, watching Livia Azzariti present a show on the television, turns to a companion and asks, "Do you see how she looks at me?"[10] It's a thought that echoes the fantastic embrace of *L'artista e il suo doppio* (The Artist and His Double) (1980) [IT 370] in which De Dominicis seems to take a stroll with one of his own invented figures who leans into him, wide-eyed, to point the way forward. In this playful moment, De Dominicis lends animating power to the image, suggesting it can look back while being looked at. But this can only happen as an exchange. The power of the image increases by divesting its subject of autonomy. If femininity does have a place in the poetics of immortality then arguably it works by a similar mechanism. Silence can be an open-ended communiqué, an attempt to pass over the limits of language, the place where paradigms dissipate, but only when it is accompanied by agency. When a silence has been scripted, as it has been in the rhetorical silence of the addressee, it is important not to preemptively dismiss the likelihood that obedience and (verbal) chastity have been assumed. Is silence a sign of sovereign subjectivity, beholden not even to language, or the marker of a malleable object? In this silence, can we read resistance, or only acquiescence?

50

8   Gino De Dominicis, "Some Impressions, Venice, June 15, 1993," in this volume, 70.

9   For the artwork as a model for immortality in Gino De Dominicis's works, see Gabriele Guercio, *L'arte non evolve. L'universo immobile di Gino De Dominicis* (Monza: Johan & Levi, 2015).

10   "Whenever she appeared on television he would stare like an enchanted child, sure that the feeling was reciprocated from the other side of the screen: you see how good she is, do you see how she looks at me?" Duccio Trombadori, *De Dominicis Amico Pittore* (San Marino: Maretti Editore, 2012), 111 (authors' translation).

63

Opera ubiqua (Ubiquitous Work) [IT 558] (1997) is a portrait of a woman in a state of meditative repose. Her features are elongated just beyond the reaches of realism, softly eroded and made palatable by an excess of sfumato. She looks like she has only ever been sculpted from stone and her aura of wisdom stems partly from an effect of material endurance and partly from her blindness, the inward-looking absence of a gaze. The fact that the *Ubiquitous Work* was replicated by De Dominicis across multiple and various works is not the sum of its ubiquity. The word *ubiquity* was first coined to reconcile the philosophical conundrum of an omnipresent, immortal God that can occupy a limited, mortal body; it is a concept that is in many ways the ideal solution to the problem identified in the "Letter," the problem of being and action, because it allows for both specificity and eternity.[11] The *Ubiquitous Work* can be in one place at one time without infringing on its immortality because it is simultaneously everywhere else too. Regarding female bodies, this idea of dual being was evidenced in the doctrinal change made for Elizabeth I during her reign; the introduction of the metaphysical ideal of the monarch's two bodies in which the imperfections and temporalities of Elizabeth, as a physical, aging woman were superseded, perhaps excused, by the "Body Politic" with which she ruled. Here was a woman conceived as both a temporal, immanent being and an atemporal, transcendent being.[12]

64

This dual presence, one physical and the other divine, is the dynamo of *Auronia D. D.* [IT 542] (1997). The work consists of a framed portrait of a reclining woman who looks like the woman in *Ubiquitous Work* and of a large transparent box on a plinth that contains a smaller transparent box floating alchemically in its center. Approaching *Auronia D. D.* with the knowledge of the "Letter," the transparent boxes look like a visual representation of silence. The title of this work, *Auronia D. D., uscita dal parallelepipedo di vetro, volteggia invisibile nella bacheca. Auronia D. D. a 99 anni in 99 luoghi* (Auronia D. D. leaves the glass parallelepiped, spins invisibly on a board. Auronia D. D. in 99 places for 99 years), tells us that it is from within one of these boxes that Auronia emerged and that she is now spinning invisibly while simultaneously spending ninety-nine years in ninety-nine places.[13] The transparent cases suggest a form anterior to her figurative representation; what is being visually represented and captured by the *Ubiquitous Work* (what is, in some sense, beyond or behind the work) is the silence of an atemporal immortality. There is also the contradictory description of impossible behavior in the title, the heady movement which works against the stasis of

---

11   "The omnipresence of Christ in his human nature, as maintained by the ubiquitarians; the doctrine of this omnipresence; ubiquity, n.," *Oxford English Dictionary*, s.v. "ubiquity, *n.*," accessed November 18, 2019, www.oed.com.

12   See Ernst H. Kantorowicz, *The King's Two Bodies: A Study in Mediaeval Political Theology*, rev. ed. (London: Oxford University Press, 1966).

13   Italo Tomassoni offers his own interpretation that positions Gino De Dominicis as the prime mover: "The artist never explained which of the two containers Auronia D. D. emerged from for her walk in space before finding herself again at rest in the horizontality of the austere black frame in which De Dominicis intended to keep her for one hundred years." Tomassoni, *Gino De Dominicis*, 481. There is, in this account, a paternalistic inference of feminine placidity and masculine domination which we would argue is not present in the original title.

the rest, articulating an essential part of the representation of feminine immortality: the knowledge that there is a mobile and lively aspect of De Dominicis's icons that cannot be represented visually. It implies there is always a remainder which cannot be depicted by the artist, a reticence in the subject. Susan Sontag identified artworks articulating silence as those that are "unresponsive before being seen, inviolable in their essential integrity by human scrutiny."[14] De Dominicis resonated with this sentiment when he stated that his artworks "have no wish to be exhibited."[15] There is something withheld, part of the artwork which resists exposure. This suggests that while the feminine is shown to wield the same spatial and temporal integrity as the immobile, material, and mute artwork, Auronia also outlasts, predates, and outbids it.

Silence and its causal stillness are aspects of immortality that the artist can depict through the representation of the feminine. In fact, the immobility, muteness, and immutability that come with total immortality look a lot like death; if immortality requires absolute stillness then perhaps it is only achievable in the afterlife. The strong presences of the intense gaze of the *Immagine della dea sumera Warka* (Image of the Sumerian Goddess Warka) [IT 189] (1977–83), of Urvasi's mountainous profile, and of the lovely frozen poise of the ageless model point conversely toward nonexistence. This contradictory duality encompassing both presence and nonexistence corresponds to the similar dilemma faced in attempts to define the female subject without using the Western philosophical tradition's othering rubric. Many would define the female subject negatively, by her nonexistence and inarticulability, rather than participate in what Gayatri Chakravorty Spivak calls "recognition by assimilation."[16] However, the similarities end there. De Dominicis's representation of women appeals to notions of a shared ahistorical and essential nature in which absence becomes a kind of freedom from the specificity of the mortal, active, desiring subject. Feminist thought countered this lack of a discursive female subjectivity by developing a concept of being which is relational, fluid, and multiple. It is interesting to think of these two different responses to nonexistence or inarticulability: one defined by its mobility and the other by its immobility, one singular and the other plural. The difference between the two recalls De Dominicis's critical division of contemporary art into "material, mute, immobile, born from the desire to counter transitoriness, perishability, and death" (i.e., painting, sculpture, and architecture) and "immaterial, mobile languages" (i.e., writing, music, theater, cinema, etc.).[17]

The artist represents a feminine that is already immortal in immobile artworks that can act as models for countering death. Immortal-

14   Susan Sontag, "The Aesthetics of Silence," in *Styles of Radical Will* (London: Penguin Classics, 2009), 14.

15   Gino De Dominicis, "My Works Have No Wish to Be Exhibited in the 46th Venice Biennale," in this volume, 80.

16   Gayatri Chakravorty Spivak, "Can the Subaltern Speak?," rev. ed., in *Can the Subaltern Speak? Reflections on the History of an Idea*, ed. Rosalind C. Morris (New York: Columbia University Press, 2010), 47.

17   De Dominicis, "Some Impressions," 70.

ity is the ultimate desire, but perhaps there's an understandable ambivalence about the absolute stillness that comes with it. The poetic logic of the Eternal Feminine, the ultimate muse, bestows upon women a trait that the artist both longs for and fears.

This essay was commissioned for the present volume.

On the Invisible Works

Creighton Gilbert

People in general, art critics and historians in particular, looking at a solo show, naturally find themselves drawn to unify everything shown via the artist's single personality. This is reasonable, since the bringing together of the varied objects has as its sole raison d'être their common authorship. Yet this perhaps does a disservice to the majority of artists. The works were not executed with the intent of being looked at together, but instead one at a time. Thus many solo shows, if they clarify the personality, make it seem repetitious and boring. With Gino De Dominicis, it is the opposite. His works differ from each other to an amazing degree, so much so that they can stand being grouped; they evoke a person of exceptional liveliness. The artist has clearly understood all this about himself as well as his relationship to viewers, when he remarks, on the one hand, that "il filo che lega fra loro le mie opere sono io,"[1] and, on the other, that the viewer should judge not a *mostra* but individual works. From any other artist these remarks would contradict each other; from De Dominicis, they do not.

The sibylline and paradoxical qualities of his remarks are a parallel art to that found in his visual work, possessing the rigor of a theoretical edifice. The artist, in another remark, classifies works of visual art as either two-dimensional, three-dimensional, or invisible, the latter being a rare category, produced only by himself.[2] From this variety I will omit the two-dimensional ones, paintings chiefly of heads, which, to my taste, are the least evocative. Naturally one wants to explore the invisible ones. Although De Dominicis does not explicitly state this, there seem to be no works placed totally within this category. Invisibility is only a quality of parts of works, of which other parts are three-dimensional. Indeed, in a quite natural and helpful way, the invisible parts tend to be inner components, bracketed by outer visible parts that serve to determine their character, whether through size or otherwise. However, these outer parts do not only function as frames. They have additional qualities as part of their capacity to express. A simple example of this is the invisible statue, with a straw hat on top and slippers below, *Senza titolo (Statua invisibile)* (Untitled [Invisible Statue]) [IT 198] [1979]. The slippers and hat are at first adopted by the viewer merely to establish the existence of a statue and its height, but they also delimit a quite particular identity and a certain kind of person, of whom this is a portrait. This clarifies why De Dominicis has been labeled as a conceptual artist and why the artist rejects the label with annoyance. In his works, there is a demonstrated preference for the elementary or vernacular, and the empirical particular image is always present as a thing in addition to the concept.

29

---

1   "The thread that links my works is me." See Franco Fanelli, "Please Do Not Disturb the Artists," in this volume, 83.
2   See Gino De Dominicis, "Maxims, 1969–1996," in this volume, 94.

But why should a statue be invisible? Why is it superior to a visible one? The artist's reason appears in another remark, in which he says that a glass and a hen (or other things) are not real, but merely verify the existence of a glass, a hen, etc.[3] By this, I understand that he is concerned with the perfection of a hen, or that which fully corresponds to the generic word *hen*, as against the particular imperfect example. No image of a hen can do this, but the invisible one can be so understood. If I understand correctly, we are being invited to partake in a new interpretation of the Platonic ideal, which might never be realized empirically, but is possible in theory.

Platonic idealism, more or less connected with Plato, has of course been a constant thread in Western culture and has had a special interest for artists; two periods in which it has been important can illustrate this. The revival of Platonism in the Florentine Renaissance, in which Michelangelo was much involved, stimulated his famous sonnet about the problem of making art; he begins by stating that the hand must obey the mind to realize a concept, but concludes that he was inadequate to draw it, and so produced the contrary, which was death, instead of beauty. In the Romantic period, painters might evoke the ideal through misty shadows or, more often, through figures given arbitrary allegorical names, and poets might do so more effectively, as when Percy Bysshe Shelley, in "Adonais," complained that "Life, like a dome of many-colour'd glass, / Stains the white radiance of Eternity." In all cases the active theme turns out to be the impossibility of attaining the ideal, and the restriction to a partially asserted surrogate. De Dominicis offers a new approach to this eternity when he frames the invisible with many-colored brackets.

As for Shelley, so for De Dominicis; the attempt to arrive at the idea involves not only the spatial but also the temporal ideal. The artist's general obsession with matters of time—shared by many artists before him, albeit through the strict limits of visualizing an instant—is perhaps most neatly shown in his modified watch (*Orologio* [Watch] [1970] [IT 113]). He removed the clockface and substituted a mirror. When you try to tell the time, what you see is your own face, which has grown older since the time before, and that is its only measure for time. This effect could not be produced by a mirror alone; the frame, the watch case, asserts the relevant context of time's passing. Thus again the frame, as with the invisible statue, contains the central motif, which makes time the leitmotif. The mirror in the watch also involves another of De Dominicis's statements, that art (in this case, the mirror) looks at us, not the other way around. The watch with a mirror thus turns out to bear little resemblance to Dada, as one might first guess (it is not a caprice of absurd conjunctions), but more to a philosophical seriousness.

Perhaps the most complex of the artist's images about time is clearly complex only through its title: *Seconda soluzione d'immortalità (l'universo è immobile)* (Second Solution of Immortality [The Universe Is Still]) [IT 150] (1972). It includes an observer, the much-discussed man with Down syndrome who observes the other parts of the work, again recalling

     See Gino De Dominicis, "Letter on Immortality," in this volume, 59, 62.

De Dominicis's statement about art being the one who observes; this viewer is the framing that brackets the work's central thematic focus. The eternal or immortal perfection of time reappears in *Lo Zodiaco* (The Zodiac) [IT 105] (1970), in which the artist replaces the usual twelve signs with real rams, real young women, etc. These objects of our physical world, vernacular documents like the straw hat, readily suggest to viewers their well-known metaphoric nonphysical equivalents, the signs of the zodiac, which form time in an endless circle and are therefore immortal, unlike the animals and humans we see here. In another use of vernacular material, we are shown a banal plaster statue of a laughing Madonna. This refers, it is explained, to the church doctrine that the Virgin rose to immortality in heaven with her body.

Immortality, thus, has unexpected corollaries and referents, immobility and a body. An immobile body cannot but suggest a dead one. Though that is hardly what we would first select as immortal, a continued presence of the body after death recurs in the artist's work in varied and surprising ways, from his exhibition of his own obituary to the skeletons included in his larger works. Death as a visible token, suggesting the existence of ideal immortality, is less of an oxymoron if we stipulate that, like the invisible statue as a token of an ideal form, we cannot actually possess the ideal image of the immortal, but only a physical reference that suggests it to us in our limited capacities. Our face in the watch mirror, by its changes, also moves toward death as we gradually understand.

If art is concerned with ideal forms and with the eternal, it is not surprising to be told by the artist that all art is contemporary. I was drawn to that statement because I had said so years ago in an argument with a friend. However, my vantage point was entirely different from that of De Dominicis: to combat some people's dismissal of art that was not new, by responding that past art confronts us without mediation whenever we look at it. That is a smaller point about immortality, ideal forms, or invisible works than the one I presume De Dominicis is making, and suggests that one's reading in such cases can well be wrong, so I offer mine about him with hesitation.

Meyer Schapiro, in a 1977 lecture rich with ideas, expanding outward from an initial discussion of Cézanne, discussed the many attempts to link art closely to philosophy. He rightly began by saying it is difficult to do, to "find equivalents to a philosopher's ideas without doing injustice to the qualities of the paintings ... the actual substance of painting."[4] De Dominicis, in what I would like to label his Platonism, has tried not to conquer but to circumvent this difficulty perhaps in part by employing another medium than painting: mixing solid forms, invisible works, and his statements.

A version of this essay, "Un possibile rapporto tra Gino De Dominicis e la filosofia," was originally published in *De Dominicis. Raccolta di scritti sull'opera e l'artista*, ed. Gabriele Guercio (Turin: Umberto Allemandi, 2001), 45–50.

4   Meyer Schapiro, "Cézanne and the Philosophers," in *Worldview in Painting: Selected Papers*, vol. 5, *Art and Society* (New York: George Braziller, 1999), 75–76.

GDD TV

Marco Senaldi

GDD TV #1

When one considers Gino De Dominicis's works as a whole, his relationship with technology hardly fails to surprise. Despite his work's countless references to myths, ranging from those of the ancestral Assyrian-Babylonian past to Pinocchio, it is clear that this fascination with mythology was not his primary aesthetic, something incontrovertibly proved by De Dominicis's use of modern technologies such as photography and video. Famously, he took part in a venture promoted by filmmaker Gerry Schum, *Fernsehgalerie* (Video Gallery), a project intended to create video art anthologies for public television. De Dominicis contributed two of his most celebrated works, *Tentativo di far formare dei quadrati invece che dei cerchi attorno a un sasso che cade nell'acqua* (Attempt to Form Squares Instead of Circles Around a Stone Falling into Water) [IT 83] (1969) and *Tentativo di volo* (Attempt to Fly) [IT 84] (1969). In both cases, video is used not merely as instrument, but within technology's metaphysical dimension.

Each of these works consists of the indefinite repetition of the same action: in the former, that of shaking the arms like wings in an attempt to fly, and in the latter, standing still at the edge of a pond, throwing stones into the water in an attempt to obtain concentric square ripples. While endlessly iterative repetition in response to mechanical reproduction is a concept already tied to avant-garde modernist films—for example, the famous sequence of the washerwoman who goes endlessly up and down the stairs in Fernand Léger's *Ballet mécanique* (1924)—in De Dominicis's two videos, this repetition is no longer a mere representation of the vision that arises from an abuse of technology. Rather, through the repetition of an absurd and clearly impossible action, designed to repeat the Same, what happens is that "something changes." Even though it is true that the action does not obtain the hoped-for result (the person seen from behind—none other than the artist—does not fly, nor does he obtain ripples other than normal circular ones), it does achieve an unhoped-for result. The action is transformed into something else. The result of the repeated action, in the words of Gilles Deleuze in *Difference and Repetition*, is not that the Same is repeated, for what happens is the Same as the Repetition. Repetition becomes the event itself.

If we observe the two videos from another point of view, not just purely from a "retinal" one, this becomes quite evident: by looking at the same repeated gesture for long enough, it becomes clear that the real "squaring of the circle" is actually the repetition of the attempt, the fact itself that, thanks to video, the number of stones that can be thrown into the water is unlimited. It can be repeated endlessly, just as by looking at the artist ineffectually flapping his arms in the wind, we might say that he "flies" because by being indefinitely broadcast, he goes "on air," ending up by "flying" through the ether, and achieving the "suspension" he so longs for.

GDD TV #2

In 1995 when I took part in *L'Angelo* (Canale 5), the first national television program devoted entirely to contemporary art, we thought of interviewing De Dominicis.[1] Since we were well aware of his almost paranoiac aversion to the photographic reproduction of his works (he had somehow managed to have the catalogues and almost every photographic record concerning him mysteriously disappear from the archives of the Venice Biennale and from the Galleria d'Arte Moderna in Rome), we naturally expected him to refuse. But, to our surprise, De Dominicis accepted. Even so, his conditions were quite unusual: he would not give an interview to us but promised to produce a video of about ten minutes in which he would interview himself. What he sent us was astounding and, miraculously, considering the ephemeral nature of television broadcasts, can still be viewed today. Seated behind a desk that apparently and impossibly floats in the air, De Dominicis, while miming the act of painting, answers questions posed by a female interviewer, herself rather surreal in her role, who is primarily off-screen. Shot from a peculiar angle and with the interviewee at a curious distance, the rather monotonous video, with no soundtrack, conflicted with the fashion of nineties television editing. In those days, videos were highly fragmented, packed with energy, with countless cuts, and, through music clips, often had intrusive sound and emotive music. Here the discontinuity adopted by the artist attains its full metaphysical value. Not only is the artist suspended, but the entire video constitutes a sort of alienating pause in the noisy and brusque flow of television images: an authentic "suspension." What is more, the artist's position in the frame makes it impossible to see the painting he works on, preventing the audience from seeing what their attention is actually drawn toward. His art is therefore obliged to occupy a space that is intrinsically off-screen—it becomes invisible in our range of vision, like the blind spots of our own eyes.[2]

When it was shown, De Dominicis's self-interview surprised many experts, among others, but few realized that the concept, the production, and the text were entirely his own work. Today, more than ten years since the broadcast, it is still important to stress that, since this was a self-production, this video should be considered a work by De Dominicis like the videos he made in the seventies. Indeed, its original location in a television program sheds light on those previous works of his, which can thus be considered less as separate video works and more as operations

1   *L'Angelo* (1995–96) was created by Gregorio Paolini (who had already devised such innovative programs as *Target*), who entrusted the studio management to Claudia Koll and the directing to Cristina Crocetti. See Joseph Baroni, *Dizionario della televisione* (Milan: Raffaello Cortina Editore, 2005).

2   The subsequent interview, which De Dominicis gave in 1996 for *Cortocircuito*, the cultural magazine of Canale 5 (also through the good offices of Cristina Crocetti), went along the same lines: the artist could be seen painting what he claimed was a "Gioconda," but only the back of it could be seen resting on an easel.

within the space-time dimension of the television program, where they were originally shown.

<u>GDD TV #3</u>
De Dominicis's particular notion of television as a non-place "place" can be seen in two other episodes. The first concerns an exhibition of De Dominicis's work at La Nuova Pesa gallery, where a hanged man who appeared dead—although real and alive—was hanging at the center of the show, wearing the black clothes normally worn by the artist. Unlike his usual approach to his shows' documentation, De Dominicis helped film the exhibition, indicating that he evidently did not consider video as "theft" or as an illicit reproduction of his works, but rather as something different, something with greater potential than just mere reportage. This extra something is certainly not due to the particular originality of the medium, but possibly to the fact that a television broadcast, which, by its very nature, is restricted to a very short period of time, normally just a few minutes, is naturally impermanent and transitory. It is something that passes by and is well suited to the ontological concept of frozen eternity that is typical of De Dominicis's work. After all, television perfectly embodies one of the artist's best-known beliefs, that "it is the public who are exhibited to the work of art"[3]: because, in the case of television, there is all the more reason to say that it is the audience, through its passiveness, that is "watched" by television. To an even greater extent today, television introduces a space-time concept that is quite out of the ordinary, for its uninterrupted flow and the "real time" of the eternal live broadcast embodies an entirely new form of eternity, something that is always on the brink of becoming unstoppable. This balancing act, this indefinite ontological suspension, is of the same type that we find in De Dominicis's video operations and installations, and it is a keystone that appears everywhere in his works.

Since we had a certain degree of autonomy in our program, *Le Notti dell'Angelo*, in 1997, we decided to devote an entire episode to the Venice Biennale and, in particular, to interviewing De Dominicis, who had a room of his own in the Padiglione Italia.[4] De Dominicis invited us not only to shoot the film, but also, quite unexpectedly, he involved us in installing his work, which, as usual, was untitled—a small transparent polyhedron elevated as though by magic inside a display case. Though he did allow us to film the work as we wished, I remember he started getting nervous and railing against the public when they went too close to the work and made comments about it, thinking they had discovered the "trick" he had used. He demanded that the gallery be closed, and with us he traced out a sort of borderline on the floor using black adhesive tape to create a distance for the au-

---

<table>
<tr><td>3</td><td>See Duccio Trombadori, "A Memo at the End of the Century," in this volume, 90.</td></tr>
<tr><td>4</td><td>*Le Notti dell'Angelo* followed on from *L'Angelo*, once again thanks to the intelligence and experimental drive of Gregorio Paolini. The group of authors consisted of the present writer with Francesca Tomasin, Anton Giulio Onofri, Alessandra Galletta, Michele De Mieri, and Maddalena Bregani. It was broadcast weekly on Canale 5, and then on Italia 1 for its 1995–96, 1996–97, and 1997–98 seasons.</td></tr>
</table>

dience. However, the eye of the video camera was clearly exempt from this boundary, possibly because De Dominicis infallibly sensed that, by its very nature, the camera's mechanical inhumanity was anti-interpretational, unlike the human eye, capturing the phenomenon in its apparent timelessness. Later on, he allowed himself to be interviewed, for what was to be the last time. In this interview, De Dominicis appeared lying on a four-poster bed in his palatial apartment frescoed by Tiepolo in Venice. After making it clear that he would answer the questions half-concealed by the bed's cushions, he demanded that he should be accompanied on the bed by someone who would remain unseen. We also agreed on the conversation we would have, of which I remember only one brilliant fragment. When asked, "Why are your works at the Biennale?" he replied, "Oh, they went there by themselves …"

In other words, here too, as in the interview-artwork of 1995, the situation was reversed, and the interviewer ended up with nothing in his hands. One always gets the impression that De Dominicis was doing something not behind our backs, but in front of us—although it was right before our very eyes, we still could not see it. It is not some mystery or deliberately hidden secret but eternally deviated evidence, a manifestation that is always impossible. A phenomenon displayed in the negative, an appearance shown in reverse—often by turning his back, suspending his works, as well as hiding behind permanent sunglasses, etc.—basically constitutes the truth of video technology because, behind its superficially documentary vocation, video creates the strange paradox of an unmoving, Zeno-like time that may be repeated, but never ended. It was this metaphysical secret that De Dominicis had captured on video and in the very soul of television.

<u>GDD TV (LAST)</u>

Of course, it is true that these are intuitions found in the work of many leading artists, from Dan Graham to Jan Dibbets, as well as in some video installations by Studio Azzurro. These artists have also worked on concepts that are inherent in video, such as delays or time shifts; one need only think of Graham's *Past Continuous Present* of 1976, a video installation in which the spectator sees himself on two different monitors, one live and the other with a slight delay, or the possibility of suspending the stream of images such as in Dibbets's famous *Fireplace* video, which is simply the film of a fire in a fireplace, to be shown uninterrupted throughout the whole day on a television broadcast, or the use of the monitor as a fragment of a continuum, as in Studio Azzurro's *Nuotatore* (Swimmer), which shows a man "swimming" from one monitor to another. However, in all these cases, and in many others, the artistic endeavor consists mainly in extracting and laying bare the intrinsic truth of video or television as independent technological media. Whereas, in the case of De Dominicis, there is an original, primeval truth that video and television do no more than reveal.

To understand this truth, one need only read the close confrontation between the famous "Letter on Immortality" (1971) and the words of *The Essence of Nihilism* (1972) by Emanuele Severino: where the former states, "To truly exist, we should halt time," the latter responds, "Man is the eternal appearing of the truth of Being." And yet, despite any nostalgia to "return to Parmenides" or another type of refusal to become part of modernity, one needs to reread these phrases from a radically contemporary viewpoint. "The tree," says Severino, almost paraphrasing De Dominicis, "is eternal … and its becoming, then, *cannot* mar its Being." This would appear to be an absurd phrase and an intentional insult to common sense, but, possibly, its absurdity lessens if we think of a tree captured on video or if we think of the possibility of cloning the tree through its DNA …

Are these technologies not living proof and almost the incarnation of this desperately essentialist metaphysics that has been perceived and taken up as much by modern "Parmenideans" such as Severino, as they have been revealed in De Dominicis's art?

Translated by Simon Turner

A version of this essay was originally published in Italian, French, and English in a special issue of *Flash Art International* (June 2007): 112–19. This issue served as the catalogue for De Dominicis's solo exhibition curated by Andrea Bellini and Laura Cherubini at the Centre National d'Art Contemporain de la Villa Arson, Nice (June 29–October 7, 2007), Fondazione Merz, Turin (November 8, 2007–January 6, 2008), and MoMA PS1, New York (October 19, 2008–February 9, 2009).

Ecstasy Between the Silhouettes

Jean-Christophe Ammann

Gino De Dominicis was possessed, illuminated by the immortal world of ideas, and found their embodiment in life. One might call this a kind of Platonism; did De Dominicis's drive not contain within it an obsession to feel and understand the self, the artist's self—foregrounding not the individual person but his function as a medium—as an eternal idea and this idea's embodiment? De Dominicis went so far as to write, "By fixing himself in time at an age he chooses and by interrupting the process of aging, man would break the spell cast by the most mysterious dimension prevailing in the universe; and this would be the first step toward the possibility of a greater understanding of life."[1]

In the end, even his death remained a mystery; although he died a peaceful, natural death on November 29, 1998, in his well-known dandyish clothes, it was as if he had summoned death on his own terms. De Dominicis understood art as an investigation into the origins of things, using the means of his generation and his moment to reflect his own present. His approach is noteworthy in that an anthropologically based conception of the immortal—for an origin beyond origins—fascinated him.

For a closer examination of *Senza Titolo (Urvasi e Gilgamesh)* (Untitled [Urvasi and Gilgamesh]) [IT 200] (1979–80), it is worth taking a look at the work's protagonists. The story of the Sumerian king of Uruk, Gilgamesh, has survived in numerous forms, the oldest of which, from approximately 1200 BCE, exists on twelve clay tablets. I would argue that the heart of the hero's conflict was always whether Gilgamesh, two parts god and one part human, could achieve immortality. Unable to return from the underworld with the plant promised to grant him eternal life, Gilgamesh returns to Uruk resigned to his fate. The second figure, Urvasi, is a Hindu *apsara* or nymph of divine origin and extraordinary beauty. She aroused the wrath of Mitra and Varuna, who then damned her to live on earth. Her husband is Pururavas, who embodies the sun, the imperishable light of knowledge. Urvasi, in contrast, symbolizes the foggy patches of twilight and night that, when drawn toward the sun, turn into clouds.

De Dominicis selected these two protagonists very carefully. Not only does their selection bring together two entirely different cultures, it also connects binaries of mortal/immortal, order/chaos, and masculine/feminine as constitutive givens of universal nature. We see Gilgamesh on the right of the image, Urvasi on the left—highly stylized, razor-sharp profiles, silhouetted in all black. They face each other. Urvasi's majestic, challenging gaze is directed straight ahead, apparently asking something of Gilgamesh's secretive, somber visage—as if she could feel his slightly downcast

30

---

1   See Gino De Dominicis, "Letter on Immortality," in this volume, 61, 64.

eyes, emphasized in the tilt of his hat. It seems as if he is looking below her chin, toward the recess bound by the high curve of her breast that is portrayed in a ritualized abstraction. A narrow and deep wedge cuts into this recess, almost an allusion to female sex, the convexity of protruding, slightly parted labia.

In his insightful 1986 essay on Gino De Dominicis, "Art to the Power N," Germano Celant discusses the artist's variations of *Urvasi and Gilgamesh* that first began with an earlier, photographic version from 1979.[2] Though Celant rightly emphasizes the background beyond the figures, there is another aspect at play: what articulates this gaze onto the background is the frame's empty shape, which is the construction of the black shapes' incisiveness. In the lower part of the image, the part between Gilgamesh's garment and Urvasi's torso, we recognize a shape resembling both Africa and South America. Our view of the background is directed precisely here. With soft pencil strokes, the artist sketches, in a manner connecting the Italian Renaissance to Dutch painting, a water landscape in which a boat holds a ferryman on the shore in the foreground, and in the background an Egyptian pyramid rises up from the trees, behind which, in the sky, just under the rim of Gilgamesh's hat, a UFO is visible. The overall look of the drawing suggests the light of an early morning mist, as if the objects were formed from the fog, as if a gigantic spiritual and mental power had given these objects shape, or as if a power at the height of its ability becomes a pure vision that acquires its own figure and form.

We know that, at least in the Hittite version of the epic, Gilgamesh crossed the waters of death in his effort to reach the immortality he strove for. (It is an open question whether the ferryman at the shore is setting off or arriving.) We know that every pharaoh's dynasty created its own immortal cosmos, that the pyramids were tantamount to a "philosopher's stone." And we believe that the UFOs that arrive from distant galaxies project human time into a space-time continuum opposed to our own image of finitude.

In this small work, De Dominicis condenses Mesopotamia, the Indian subcontinent, Africa, and South America. If he does not touch on the dimension of Christianity, it is because it is already broached in the person of Gilgamesh. His complaint was heard by Anu, the supreme god of the sky who then adopted him as his son and vicar of eternal life. This paternal act foreshadows our own image of Christ and leads, eventually, to the Christian image of the world. In De Dominicis's version, Gilgamesh and Urvasi appear as magnetic poles in a dimension of anthropological depth. Whoever looks upon humanity must gain this form of knowledge through a cosmological key, that of *longing*.

Crime and punishment, guilt and atonement are markers along this path. A paradise lost is intolerable. And yet, De Dominicis proclaims no utopia. He does not displace this world into a beyond for the sake of the beyond, but rather, as an artist, he demarcates the area that confers meaning through his work's interpretation of the resonance field of a cosmic dimension. He conjures up, in his creation, the unspeakable and wonderful contingency of the artist-individual projected upon himself.

Translated by Damion Searles
This essay was originally written in German in a longer version titled "Ekstase im Scherenschnitt: Zu einem Werk von GDD." It was published in Italian as "I profili e l'estasi" in *De Dominicis. Raccolta di scritti sull'opera e l'artista*, ed. Gabriele Guercio (Turin: Umberto Allemandi, 2001), 15–21.

The Buddha of the Future

Norman Bryson

It is an image that has the power to haunt you, to make you want to return to it again and again: *Opera ubiqua (Delfina D. D. – Auronia D. D.)* (Ubiquitous Work [Delfina D. D. – Auronia D. D.]), [IT 548] (1996). At each encounter it resonates with a set of feelings that I, for one, find in no other work of his: a unique amalgam of dread and delight, of anxiety and peace. To begin on a personal note: since I first set eyes on Gino De Dominicis's *Opera ubiqua* it has not left me alone. The configuration of its eyes, mouth, nose, and eyebrows, with their strange elongations and compressions; the dreamy, melting features cut across by two great arcs sweeping in from the corners of the frame; the sense of a deep, world-renouncing inwardness that somehow coexists with a quality of caricature and the grotesque: the various elements combine to form a *singularity*, an object so unlike all others that it obliges you to stay with it, spend time with it, and try to understand why it has this special ability to take hold of you, and in a mild way to obsess your visual imagination. To be sure it is the product of obsession, part of De Dominicis's extraordinary series of faces where the nose is pulled—as though skin and flesh were elastic—into a weirdly pointed beak or proboscis. It is as though the artist were visualizing a species that is based on the human pattern but has undergone a different evolution; or is visualizing the human body as itself an anomalous work of evolution, whose sheer strangeness opens up the question of what, then, *is* the norm, the central condition, of the human being?

It is clear, too, what kind of historical image forms its basis: Buddhist art of the Far East, and specifically the great wave of sculpture that spread from China into Korea and Japan in the sixth and seventh centuries CE. Perhaps most European viewers will tend to sense this provenance in a general way, and let it go at that. Yet for viewers more familiar with the canon of Far Eastern art, a particular prototype is recognizable at once—Maitreya, the Buddha of the Future: for example, the wonderful gilt-bronze Maitreya from the Three Kingdoms period, now in the Korean National Museum in Seoul, or the Maitreya (Japanese, *Miroku bosatsu*) carved from camphor wood in Chūgū-ji Temple at Nara. As central to the pantheon of Far Eastern art as are the Winged Victory of Samothrace or the Venus de Milo in the West, they are figures whose depiction of meditative calm, of a withdrawal from the world that is concurrently an immersion in the harmony of mind and world, has rarely been equaled. How, we might ask, do such prototypes convey their feeling of serenity and charm? What set of visual conventions do they follow—and how did De Dominicis alter those conventions?

One way to answer this is to reflect on the way that Dominicis's Far Eastern prototypes involve a dramatic interplay between ascending and descending forms: between forms that travel upward, as though toward a superior dimension or level of consciousness, and forms that fall back down, toward the earthly existence that sustains them. At the center of this play of vectors is placed the moderating, harmonizing body—and face—of the Buddha. De Dominicis's drawing sums up the essentials of this double pull and its resolution in the ecstatic face of enlightenment. For the vertical or ascending register, Buddhist sculpture creates an array of body halos shaped like large flames, "mandorlas" whose surfaces are adorned with small, flickering fires. On the descending or gravity-bound side, the body is covered with drapery whose flattened pleats point over and over to the earth or cascade downward like water. Resolving and synthesizing these contrary directions—the weight of the material world, of karma and the cycle of birth and death, versus the lightness of the dharma, of release from suffering—the figure of Maitreya partakes of both worlds: a creature of gravity, he sits or leans forward, his body has mass and substance; yet, absorbed into the highest level of contemplation, he is also weightless, a being of light and air, a sheer radiance.

How does De Dominicis build his image on this foundation? Partly by accepting its way with directions and pushing it still further. In his drawing the nose and eyebrow join in majestic, sweeping lines that project outward and upward from the face, past the upper corners of the frame. Coming together in perfect symmetry at the bridge of the nose, they point down to this world, to the body and its earthly support. The eyes and mouth take the same curves and flatten them around the figure's full, gently curving cheeks. The whole face is structured, then, around a rise and fall: an ascent that projects beyond the boundary of the image into space, a descent that follows the downward vertical of the figure's strangely elongated nose. Then the artist adds some sfumato from the European repertoire, letting the facial features melt, as though the figure's inner absorption were so intense as to dissolve external features in the force field of its own inwardness, into a nondifferentiation that has overcome the duality of "outside" and "inside." Facial features—those markers of individuality or of *separate* existence—blur into a field of tenderness so subtle it reminds you of how it feels when your own face presses next to the face of the one you cherish—parent, child, lover: so close that you almost feel your mind, and their mind, touch and fuse.

But in modernity, can the kind of preestablished harmonies that come down to us in the ancient art of Asia really be sustained? Isn't De Dominicis's point exactly that, for us, while ideas of inner stillness and peace are still intelligible and real, they unfold against a much more turbulent psycho-social framework? In *Opera ubiqua*, the "upward" and "descending" registers of the image are still there, but in a condition of disalignment or disconnection; the relation between them is subject to new degrees of stress. Hence the strangeness of that nose, its sharpness and thinness; already it has about it a quality that is like a crest, or a blade; it *cleaves* the surface of the drawing; it introduces into the melting unity of the face a principle of conflict and division. The tip of the nose overhangs the mouth, as though the "downward" direction were now far more powerful than in the original image, plunging directly into suffering and egoic isolation. In sum, present in the drawing is the idea that becomes fully-fledged, and independently developed, in what one might call De Dominicis's beak-monsters.

These monsters are, in fact, complex beings. In one version, the face is reduced to a birdlike mask whose vestigial eyes are permanently closed, as though they had been sewn or sealed closed (*Senza Titolo* [Untitled] [IT 259] [1985]). Here the lineaments of perfection convert to radical imperfection and deformity: the aquiline nose becomes vulture-like, and what once was flesh has turned into cuttlebone. In a version of *Opera ubiqua* from 1989 (*Senza Titolo* [Untitled] [IT 327]), the face is both sinister and comical, like the mask of a plague doctor. The force that ruins De Dominicis's negative or corrupted face is evidently deathly: other works show the disfigured beak as a pointed blade, ludicrously projecting from the skull of a skeleton. And yet the "beak-monster" can also assume a presence that is more personal, even sympathetic; in another version, the face has the tormented character of a portrait study, and its eyes, too, are sunken and withdrawn—as are the eyes of Maitreya. The "beak-monster" is, then, in some sense a transformation of the Buddha of the Future. Yet it might be wrong to think of it as a distorted or degenerated version of the Maitreya: rather, both images seem coeval or simultaneous with one another, different aspects of a face which, in both of its avatars, mixes serenity and the grotesque in a singularly unsettling combination.

If De Dominicis is always a metaphysical artist, exploring the range of feeling that clusters around conceptions of mortality and eternity, transience and transcendence, it is clear that the expression he gives to such feeling is eminently idiosyncratic. His work accepts, almost as its opening move, that there exists no public, consensual visual language or vocabulary of symbols to enable communication between the artist and the wider social field. Though religious or quasi-religious symbols indeed abound in his work (deities, crosses, stars, pyramids, triangles), it is as if these recommended themselves to the artist precisely because the systems to which they originally belonged have long since passed away. They are, in fact, the relics of symbols, abandoned symbols, as distant from our world as the Vedas, or Sumer, or alchemy—or early Buddhist Asia. Collective symbols become parts of a private language, a cult with only one worshipper: the artist.

Or, perhaps, if we count the viewer, two. Yet the artist's mode of address is strangely oblique. Imagine a situation in which artist and viewer share a common store of symbols, markers of their imagined community: that is the situation that is absent in De Dominicis, and its unavailability is the precondition of the work. If his drawing summons early Buddhist visual forms, this is precisely because we do not belong to (and can barely imagine) the historical world of early Buddhist culture. In his hands, the whole notion of the symbol becomes vestigial, or comical: Sumerian divinities with trunk-like noses and elephant legs; world-heroes like Gilgamesh or Maitreya, handled like caricatures or cartoons. At stake is De Dominicis's refusal of anything except a private language as his preferred mode of activity—the only mode, in his view, possible for the kind of art he was destined to produce.

The idea of a private language, Wittgenstein argued, is logically incoherent: for something to be a language there must always exist the possibility of a second speaker, and a third, a community. And yet there may be such a thing as an *oblique* language, a language that deliberately renounces a common lexicon or shared cultural reference points. If it uses recognizable terms or elements, this is not because these are equally close to each speaker or because they establish a familiar kind of communication. Just the opposite: they are chosen because they are remote, equally remote from everyone. Sumerian deities, like the Buddhist Maitreya, are forms that are equidistant from all of us. De Dominicis's symbolic language is predicated on indirection. He does not seek to reproduce himself symbolically, and yet the obsessiveness that energizes his art is not solipsistic either. One can see that for this artist, certain deformations of the body were so charged with psychic meaning that they had to be repeated and varied, again and again. The repetition of certain key disfigurations (of the eyes, nose, mouth) produces a kind of emotional "hieroglyph" that resists any easy or certain decoding. I cannot know exactly what affect and psychic charge such distortions of form actually carried for their original maker. Yet perhaps I do not need to know with any precision for the hieroglyph to work its magic in me just the same.

I may not have access to the autobiographical or private dimension of the symbols that De Dominicis uses, but I can recognize that the symbols are obsessive, that their particular configuration of form—this configuration, and no other—is the marker of a set of feelings by which I can still be fascinated and moved. Perhaps that is what De Dominicis discovered: that in order to succeed, art need not aspire to be the transmission of an *x*, relayed to a viewer who receives the transmission intact, and opens and reads it like a letter. There may be no path of communication at all, no shared symbols; there can still be (oblique) reverberations. Somehow, Maitreya and the beak-monster are transformations of each other: that is all we can be sure of, and all we may need to know. De Dominicis realized that if the private language is strong enough and obsessive enough, it will still be able to captivate and disturb without needing any further translation into the mundane currency of public speech. The hermetic, intensely private symbolic language of De Dominicis radically refuses the uniformity and standardization of all ideological situations. As Germano Celant has put it, De Dominicis's work employs ways of thinking "for which we don't have much of a key."[1] but which still have the power to cast a spell over us with their elusive, indelible forms.

This text is an expanded version of an essay originally published as "Il Buddha del futuro" in De Dominicis. Raccolta di scritti sull'opera e l'artista, ed. Gabriele Guercio (Turin: Umberto Allemandi, 2001), 25–31.

1   Germano Celant, "Art to the Power N," in this volume, 28.

V

THE UNIVERSE IS IMMOBILE: IMMORTALITY AS MASTERPIECE

The Question of Immortality in the Gilgamesh Corpus

Giovanni Pettinato

Gino De Dominicis felt the weight of the human condition and was obsessed with the reality of aging. In his "Letter on Immortality," he writes about this very issue:

> *Aging is an internal illness, which, from around the age of twenty-six, begins to corrode body and mind. Then we think we have become used to the process and it seems inevitable to us; however, all man's actions have always been nothing but unconscious responses to this dramatic problem.*[1]

In his art De Dominicis found in Gilgamesh, the Sumerian hero who had first attempted to overcome death, the model and ideal to embody his inner strife; indeed, the legendary king of Uruk is associated with the goddess Urvasi, Indian deity of beauty and life, and becomes the prototype of the man who battles death.

I do not know from which book De Dominicis drew his inspiration for such a choice, but it is clear that his source was very reliable. That he blended the different traditions of Mesopotamia and India should not surprise or shock us, since everything fits perfectly well into the artist's freedom to utilize any means available to convey his thinking.

As an expert on the Mesopotamian world and in particular of both the Sumerian and Assyro-Babylonian traditions of the figure of Gilgamesh, I can only congratulate De Dominicis a posteriori in regard to the choice he made, because he hit the mark, interpreting the figure of the Sumerian king and of his fight against death just as it is depicted in the various cuneiform texts.

To date there are seven well-known Sumerian poems and a work, "the classic epic," in Babylonian, that feature the legendary Sumerian king of Uruk as hero. The dominant theme of these works is the human condition, with all of its flaws and limitations imposed by the divine world. Gilgamesh himself is a peculiar being; he is two-thirds god and one-third man! This explains why he alone can confront the issue of death and carry out such an extreme attempt to ultimately overcome it. As we learn from the entire Mesopotamian corpus, Gilgamesh fails in his quest, and though this failure is tragic, it does not leave us disappointed, because the experience garnered by our hero is the source of the very wisdom that any human being must aspire to.

1 See Gino De Dominicis, "Letter on Immortality," in this volume, 62–63.

Death in the Sumerian Poems

The issue of death is treated in exemplary fashion in three of the Sumerian epic poems: "Bilgames and Huwawa," "Bilgames, Enkidu, and the Netherworld," and the shorter "The Death of Bilgames."[2] All three compositions deal with mortality from every possible perspective, and the answers we receive about it are always unequivocal.

At the very beginning of "Gilgamesh and Huwawa," the hero addresses the sun god, outlining the problem that troubles him and the pain he feels when his fellow citizens die:

> *"O Utu, let me speak a word to you, give ear to what I say!*
> *Let me tell you something, may you give thought to it!*
> *In my city a man dies, and the heart is stricken,*
> *a man perishes, and the heart feels pain.*
> *I raised my head on the rampart,*
> *my gaze fell on a corpse drifting down the river, afloat on*
>   *the water:*
> *I too shall become like that, just so shall I be!*
> *'No man can stretch to the sky, no matter how tall,*
> *no man can compass a mountain, no matter how broad!'*
> *Since no man can escape life's end,*
> *I will enter the mountain and set up my name.*
> *Where names are set up, I will set up my name,*
> *where names are not yet set up, I will set up gods' names."*[3]

Our hero most certainly suffers because of the fate others must endure, but he also suffers for himself: hence his decision to undertake the perilous journey toward the "mountain of life" to understand its secret. Perhaps aware that he cannot attain the impossible, Gilgamesh lays out his plan to the gods, in order to ensure that his life does not end—not in the physical sense, but morally, for himself, through fame and glory, which would allow his life to continue through the memories of others.

The extent to which Gilgamesh worries about death emerges clearly in the other epic poem, "Gilgamesh, Enkidu, and the Netherworld," where we find a description of conditions in the Afterlife. Obviously, it would be too much to cite the entire text; for this reason I will provide just a few lines, from which we can understand the negativity of "life" after death. While venturing into the netherworld to retrieve some of Gilgamesh's lost items, his friend Enkidu is taken prisoner. When he can momentarily return to earth, he describes the conditions of the Afterlife as follows:

> *He hugged him tight and kissed him,*
> *in asking and answering they made themselves weary:*
> *"Did you see the way things are ordered in the Netherworld?*
> *If only you could tell me, my friend, if only [you could tell] me!"*

2   Editor's note: Quotations from the epic of Gilgamesh are from *The Epic of Gilgamesh*, trans. Andrew George (London: Penguin, 1999). In the earlier Sumerian poem fragments, the name Gilgamesh is rendered as Bilgames.

3   "Bilgames and Huwawa: 'The lord to the Living One's Mountain,'" Version A, lines 21–34.

> *"If I am to [tell] you the way things are ordered in the*
> > *Netherworld,*
> *O sit you down and weep!" "Then let me sit down and weep!"*
> *"[The one] whom you touched with joy in your heart,*
> *he says, 'I am going to [ruin.]'*
> *Like an [old garment] he is infested with lice,*
> *like a crack [in the floor] he is filled with dust."*
> *"Ah, woe!" cried the lord, and he sat down in the dust.*[4]

The fate that met his friend's body was a horrible one, and it is clear why Gilgamesh resigns himself to turning into dust. However, for Gilgamesh, death is still the fate of others and not yet something that will happen to him. Gilgamesh's future, in fact, is foreshadowed in the third poem, "The Death of Gilgamesh." Then, in a dream, it is revealed to the king of Uruk that he has been predestined to regality but not to eternal life:

> *Great Mountain Enlil, the father of the gods,*
> *conversed in the dream with the lord Bilgames:*
> *"O Bilgames, I made your destiny a destiny of kingship, but I*
> > *did not make it [a destiny] of eternal life.*
> *For mankind, whatever life it has, be not sick at heart,*
> *be not in despair, be not heart-stricken!*
> *The bane of mankind is thus come, I have told you,*
> *what (was fixed) when your navel-cord was cut is thus come,*
> > *I have told you.*
> *The darkest day of mortal man has caught up with you,*
> *the solitary place of mortal man has caught up with you,*
> *the flood-wave that cannot be breasted has caught up*
> > *with you,*
> *the battle that cannot be fled has caught up with you,*
> *the combat that cannot be matched has caught up with you,*
> *the fight that shows no pity has caught up with you!*
> *But do not go down to the Great City with heart knotted*
> > *(in anger),*
> *let it be undone before Utu …"*[5]

Though our hero is bound to die just like any other man, the god Enlil sweetens the pill by emphasizing that the gods have been generous with him, granting him the very rare privilege of ruling over all others.

Death in the Classical Epic

When one reads the classical version of the "Epic of Gilgamesh" compiled by the Akkadian Sîn-lēqi-unninni (between 1300 and 1000 BCE) and retraces all of the adventures of our hero, the prologue can hardly be ignored: in the first eight lines with an insistent tone, Sîn-lēqi-unninni posits the equation that *knowledge = wisdom*. For him, the adven-

---

4   "Bilgames and the Netherworld: 'In those days, in those far-off days,'" lines 244–54.

5   "The Death of Bilgames: 'The great wild bull is lying down,'" Nippur Tablet 1, v, lines 12–26.

tures of Gilgamesh constitute important and necessary steps that progress toward the ending which our hero attains wisdom.

It is this interpretation that this same compiler advises, to see what other motivations and themes mean, as highlighted by Giorgio Buccellati,[6] and to consider the episodic steps and ways of getting closer to the ideal as ends within themselves. It is for this reason that I am convinced that the true reading of the poem cannot exclude the intrinsic motivations the author gives. The fact that the compiler mentions the unfaltering quest for eternal life as an integral part of our hero's spiritual journey and that Gilgamesh went through every possible kind of suffering in order to attain wisdom only confirms reading the composition through this wise lens.

All scholars agree on the epic's subdivision into two parts: the first part narrates the wondrous adventures of the two heroes Enkidu and Gilgamesh through their epic deeds, entailing the killings of the monster Huwawa and the Bull of Heaven; in the second part, beginning with Tablet VII, Gilgamesh, the hero who is two-thirds god and one-third man, is forced to confront the everlasting human problem of death.

Gilgamesh attempts to overcome death, hoping that a definitive solution might come from Utnapishtim, the hero of the great flood, but as we learn from Tablet XI, in which the flood myth is presented, even the semi-god fails, and in this failure the compiler Sîn-lēqi-unninni sees the logical conclusion to his composition. We may certainly be surprised that he praised Gilgamesh's wisdom at the beginning of the epic, but this praise means that what seems like a failure at the conclusion of the poem is, in fact, nothing of the sort.

The outline of Gilgamesh's figure, found in the entire epic, could not lead to such a miserable ending: the king of Uruk, besides being two-thirds god, is a true sovereign; actually, it is far from an overstatement to claim that he is the prototype and role model for the true sovereign. If my interpretation about the "life plan" is correct, it is, in fact, in his moment of "failure" that Gilgamesh shows himself to be this true sovereign.

But let us follow the most salient stages of his exhausting quest for eternal life. The moment that clearly marks the break between the first and second parts of the epic is the death of his friend Enkidu. This is not to say the theme of death does not surface in the first six tablets, only that this section presents an ancient understanding of death by linking Enkidu's death to the Sumerians' concept of death: according to this ancient view, death could only be countervailed by fame. (This will be addressed in detail later, in my discussion of the Sumerian poem "Gilgamesh and Huwawa.") This is something fully on display in the Paleo-Babylonian epoch, but I would argue that this conclusion cannot be securely reached in the Sîn-lēqi-unninni version due to the several lacunae in its relevant parts.

The centrality of death and the consequential fate of man in the Afterlife is outlined in Enkidu's dream found in Tablet VII, beginning in

---

6   Giorgio Buccellati, "Gilgamesh in chiave sapienziale," *Oriens Antiquus* 11 (1972): 2–36.

line 161. It is especially the description of the netherworld that makes it evident that this issue was also a major concern for Sîn-lēqi-unninni.

The harsh reality of death's meaning is fully found in the epic from Tablet IX onward, when Gilgamesh wonders about his ultimate fate, realizing that Enkidu's end cannot be dissimilar from his own. The question he asks himself, "I shall die, and shall I not then be as Enkidu?"[7] and the statement, "I grew fearful of death, and so wander the wild,"[8] fully bespeak the king of Uruk's deep sense of despair and dark bitterness when faced with his imminent fate.

The words repeated by Gilgamesh, first to the tavern keeper Siduri, then to the oarsman Urshanabi, and lastly to the hero of the flood, Utnapishtim, can only be read as the thread linking the whole second part of the epic:

> *["my friend Enkidu, whom I loved so dear,]*
> *[who with me] went through every danger:*
> *[the doom of mortals overtook him.]*
>
> *"[Six days] I wept for him [and seven nights:]*
> *[I did not surrender his body for] burial*
> *[until a maggot dropped from] his [nostril.]*
> *[Then I was afraid that I too would die,]*
> *[I grew] fearful of death, [and so wander the] wild.*
>
> *"What became of [my friend was too much] to [bear,]*
> *so on a far road [I wander the] wild;*
> *what became of my friend Enkidu [was too much to bear,]*
> *so on a far path [I wander the wild.]*
>
> *"How can I keep silent? How can I stay quiet?*
> *My friend, whom I loved, has turned to clay,*
> *my friend Enkidu, [whom I loved, has turned to clay.]*
> *[Shall] I not be like him and also lie down,*
> *never to rise again, through all [eternity?]"[9]*

Unlike the earlier version of the epic, in the classical epic, the tavern keeper Siduri does not respond to Gilgamesh's anguish concerning death. Siduri, herself a divine figure, invites Gilgamesh to embrace the healthiest kind of hedonism: that is, to make the most of the joys of his earthly existence, beginning with those that a family can offer, because the gods, in creating man, established death as each one's fate. Here in the classical epic, however, the compiler Sîn-lēqi-unninni cannot put such words in the tavern keeper's mouth because, in the ancient view, death is a consequence of the Great Flood. This change is perhaps one of the most significant innovations of the classical epic. The oarsman Urshanabi who leads Gilgamesh across the

7   Tablet IX, line 4.
8   Tablet X, line 62.
9   Tablet X, lines 233–48.

subterranean waters to where the hero of the flood resides does not solve our hero's problem either; instead, the burden of the answer is placed on the hero of the flood, Utnapishtim, who does not refuse to undertake such a difficult task. The hero of the flood reminds Gilgamesh of the inescapability of death, repeating it three times—at first by hinting at it, and then by stating it bluntly.

Perhaps we should follow these three answers to better understand the mental process of our ancient scribe. The first comes immediately after Gilgamesh discloses to the hero of the deluge the deep bitterness felt for his friend's death and explains all of his pilgrimages, which have reduced him to the poverty of a vagabond. It is precisely the shabbiness of his appearance that has rendered him unworthy as king, and this condemnation is also made in Tablet XI; after the failure of the sleep test, Utnapishtim makes his position clear:

> *Said Uta-napishti to him, to [Gilgamesh:]*
>   *"Why, Gilgamesh, do you ever [chase] sorrow?*
> *You, who are [built] from gods' flesh and human,*
>   *whom the [gods did fashion] like your father and mother!*
>
> *"[Did you] ever, Gilgamesh, [compare your lot] with the fool?*
>   *They placed a throne in the assembly, and [told you,] 'Sit!'*
> *The fool gets left-over yeast instead of [fresh] ghee,*
>   *bran and grist instead of [best flour.]*
>
> *"He is clad in a* rag, *instead of [fine garments,]*
>   *instead of a belt, he is girt [with old rope.]*
> *Because he has no advisers [to guide him,]*
>   *his affairs lack counsel ......*
>
> *"Have thought for him, Gilgamesh, ...,*
>   *[who is] their master, as many as ......?"*[10]

In this first answer, the hero of the deluge explains to Gilgamesh that his nature is fundamentally different from that of the vagabond. Gilgamesh is the king of Uruk, not only because he is made of the flesh of gods and humans, not only because he is similar to his father and mother, but because, as sovereign, he has a particular nature. According to Sîn-lēqi-unninni, one of the work's fundamental teachings is found in this difference between commoners and the sovereign.

Unfortunately, Gilgamesh's reply is full of lacunae, and as a result, we do not know exactly how he responded. In fact, when we do get past these missing parts, again Utnapishtim is the one speaking, and this time, his answer to Gilgamesh's main question about death's purpose is unambiguous:

---

10   Tablet X, lines 266–79.

"[But you,] you toiled away, and what did you achieve?
You exhaust yourself with ceaseless toil,
  you fill your sinews with sorrow,

"bringing forward the end of your days.
  Man is snapped off like a reed in a canebrake!
The comely young man, the pretty young woman—
  all [too soon in] their [prime] Death abducts them!

"No one at all sees Death,
  no one at all sees the face [of Death,]
no one at all [hears] the voice of Death,
  Death so savage, who hacks men down.

"Ever do we build our households,
  ever do we make our nests,
ever do brothers divide their inheritance,
  ever do feuds arise in the land.

"Ever the river has risen and brought us the flood,
  the mayfly floating on the water.
On the face of the sun its countenance gazes,
  then all of a sudden nothing is there!

"The abducted and the dead, how alike is their lot!
  But never was drawn the likeness of Death,
never in the land did the dead greet a man.

"The Anunnaki, the great gods, held an assembly,
  Mammitum, maker of destiny, fixed fates with them:
both Death and Life they have established,
  but the day of Death they do not disclose."[11]

From the hero's answer we learn what is above all an absolutely new concept in Mesopotamian culture: that death, as mentioned above, was decided as humanity's fate after the catastrophe of the deluge. As this essay is not the place for an in-depth examination of all the implications of Utnapishtim's speech, we are also far from understanding the entirety of what the hero of the flood states within it: what especially escapes our comprehension is the comparison between the abducted prisoner and the dead and what constitutes their similarity. It is no coincidence that some translators choose to amend the text and turn the "prisoner" into the "one who sleeps."

In these first two answers to Gilgamesh's question of death, the hero of the deluge presents him with the dialectical possibility of being left in doubt about his fate: earlier on, he was told he was a special being, and now he is being told that he, along with the whole of humankind, is bound

11   Tablet X, lines 297–322.

to die. As one can infer from Gilgamesh's subsequent speech, our hero is still deluded and believes that he can conquer death; the hero of the deluge, by asking a question that may look harmless at first glance, compels Gilgamesh to accept death's harsh reality:

> *"But you now, who'll convene for you the gods' assembly,*
> *so you can find the life you search for?"*[12]

In fact, only a decision of the divine assembly, summoned for this specific purpose, could have changed the outcome of the situation. But Utnapishtim's query is only a rhetorical question, and in an attempt to convince Gilgamesh once and for all that he cannot overcome death, he subjects Gilgamesh to a test to see if he can avoid sleep for a week. As we clearly remember, Gilgamesh does not pass, and Utnapishtim, recalling his critique of the sovereign's foolish demeanor, finds no better conclusion to all of Gilgamesh's pilgrimages than turning him back into a king, urging the ferryman Urshanabi to take Gilgamesh to the wash house. Therefore, it is once again the figure of the true sovereign, who is entirely different from all other human beings, that saves Gilgamesh from complete failure.

We should now take into consideration the so-called plant of life. Some have seen this final episode, which narrates Utnapishtim's last gift to King Gilgamesh, the gift and revelation of the existence of a peculiar plant, as the real solution to all of Gilgamesh's problems. This stems from an interpolation added by the majority of scholars and translators at the end of line 270 of Tablet XI: "you will obtain life." However, nothing in the text justifies such an interpolation; Utnapishtim's gift is defined as the "Plant of Heartbeat" and the very explanation that Gilgamesh provides for this plant—"Its name shall be 'Old Man Grown Young,' / I will eat it myself, and be again as I was in my youth!"—leads us to one conclusion only: by eating that plant, Gilgamesh would have remained at the stage of youth, with the restless heart and anxieties typical of that age.[13] Hence, some scholars interpret this plant wholly as an instrument to regain youth. If one wishes to explain it more accurately, by eating that plant, Gilgamesh would instead return to the stage found in the first part of the epic.

In fact, Gilgamesh's loss of the plant is also a sign of his greatness as sovereign. Gilgamesh hadn't forgotten that he was a king entrusted with the fate of his subjects and he loses the plant precisely in order to share it with his fellow citizens. In fact, his first thought after getting hold of it is to take it to Uruk to feed it to the city's elderly. However, Utnapishtim's gift could not be extended to the rest of humanity: the plant was meant solely for Gilgamesh, perhaps as a reward for all of his pilgrimages and for the perseverance he had shown in pursuing the unattainable ideal of eternal life. Nevertheless, Gilgamesh would have shared it with other men, which is why the snake that steals it from him becomes the only creature able to take advantage of it. As touched on above:

12   Tablet XI, lines 207–8.
13   Tablet XI, lines 299–300.

Then Gilgamesh sat down and wept,
down his cheeks the tears were coursing.[14]

The scribe expresses the manifold emotions the hero goes through, the first of which is surely his realization that he did not know how to fulfill his role as king. However, it is in this final acknowledgment of his failure that Gilgamesh's complete wisdom and maturity are attained—the qualities of a true sovereign of Mesopotamia.[15]

Translated by Allison Grimaldi Donahue
This essay, titled "Gilgamesh e l'immortalità," was originally published in *De Dominicis. Raccolta di scritti sull'opera e l'artista*, ed. Gabriele Guercio (Turin: Umberto Allemandi, 2001), 73–84.

14   Tablet XI, lines 308–9.
15   Giovanni Pettinato, "Gilgamesh e la pianta della vita," *Studi Orientali e Linguistici* V (Istituto di Glottologia, Università degli Studi di Bologna, 1994–95): 11–41.

Untitled: The Immortal

Achille Bonito Oliva

A taut thread ran through the thirty-year association between Gino De Dominicis and myself: discussion and debate regarding the link between art and criticism, two fields of activity that in those moments of dialogue were embodied in us two alone. As anyone who knows us might have imagined, this was a form of dueling predicated on playful audacity. Perhaps unconscious of his own Romantic stance, Gino De Dominicis identified with the artist/demiurge, the supreme artificer and alchemist of materials. With lucid and playful intent, I played with ironic detachment the inseparability of the gestures of creation and reflection. So the detached critic often clashed with the artist of pathos, producing the unavoidable drama of the long nights that accompanied our days.

De Dominicis violently championed the primacy of the artist. This was because he liked to position himself within an Edenic locus, where it was possible to obscure the excesses of reality—and thus the excesses of the system, of which the work of art was destined to become part. Hence his obstinate, pugnacious stance; his refusal to recognize all those figures who, in various ways, made up the warp and woof of art. If the artist is the custodian of an alchemical laboratory, a magus who generates the gold of form from base matter, then the critic is the figure who reflects (upon) that form, who asserts its cultural—and ultimately economic—significance.

The Romantic spirit has always been permeated by a nocturnal view of art, which has persisted right up to the neo-avant-gardes, who have espoused such views as a way of confirming that they exist outside of the perversion of "progress." The world thus becomes a locus to be transformed into the "non-instance" of the work of art. As for the work of art itself, it is an emblematic shield, used by an artist/acrobat who manages to present himself as "other" by revealing to us that thing which he has created. In De Dominicis's work, the form is always one of figuration. I would even say it is "violently egotistical"—a theater for acting out the conflicting roles of the work of art and those who can only look at that work. The artist feels the need to throw down a romantic challenge; by denying any further privilege to the gaze as such, he removes that gaze to a distance of archaic terror (*Terza soluzione d'immortalità (Gino De Dominicis vi guarda)* [Third Solution of Immortality (Gino De Dominicis Is Watching You)] [IT 122] [1972]). There is no allowance for expedients that might provide one with "another" point of view. Everyone stands there, struck dumb by the fascination of the work of art, by the power of its epiphany. Seized upon by the work of art, the spectators are like iconographical hostages of an image that, almost always, chooses to present itself as "untitled."

De Dominicis has no doubt that figurative art is superior to other artistic languages, which are contaminated by their associated metaphysics. The work of visual art shows only itself; a static and splendid black hole, it sucks in time past, present, and future, nullifying day and night. What shines is the reverberation of the work itself—a work that is often impregnated with gold and silver. Imbued with the chromatic inflections of the archetypically "precious," the work is thus made comparable to the incorruptibility of the metals themselves (the "world in balance" found in the black-and-gold *Senza titolo* [Untitled] [IT 453] [1994]). To the incorruptibility of art De Dominicis would then link the poetics of the body, in a public proclamation of the immortality incontrovertibly guaranteed by, and for, the artist alone (*Il pittore* [The Painter] [IT 497] [1996], depicted with a gold head).

The work of art is clearly the declaration of a desire; the lapsus revealing a need for extension in space, it nullifies time. The image is a sort of apnea within the surface around matter itself (*Io sono sicuro che voi siete [e sempre sarete] all'interno o all'esterno di questo triangolo* [I Am Sure That You Are (and Always Will Be) Inside or Outside This Triangle] [IT 110] [1970]). Art and criticism have always measured themselves (and each other) within the conflict and competition generated by this tension. Their roles complementary, they can never stand as victor and defeated. Instead, they are the confirmation of that "standstill" within the work which is its moment of movement par excellence. In the dynamic reflection of analysis, the clear gleam of the image is woven into the fabric of words.

The vitality of this conflict is emblematic of an association that has now lasted forty years, and which here deserves to be reflected upon in tranquility. The artist is someone who transforms matter into the symbolic gold of form; the critic is someone who changes contemplation into the ringing gold and currency of social communication.

The Gene of Art: An Apologia of Limits

Western art has, in general, adopted a method of allegorical representation that always tends toward abstraction. Allegory is always some sort of flight. A mimicking of meaning, it involves the establishment of a certain distance from the physicality of things. In effect, it favors a theatricality that serves to guarantee the reassuring spectacle of a two-level existence: the fiction of art and the reality of life.

Gino De Dominicis, however, opted for a method of metonymy. The form of the work as presented is elaborated in such a way that all the visual components serve to define each other/themselves through (in) their own function and presence. The principle of presentation here corresponds exactly with the principle of apparition, with the artist's ability to produce an image which, in his own words, is lovingly unprecedented in the history of art. And this unprecedented nature is maintained even if the artist generally deals with themes that do have a history: mythology, death, the immortality of the body, the invisible, the ambiguity of the feminine.

In recent decades art has generally pursued an Oedipal path; it has developed themes and languages within the protection of a well-trodden course that unfolds along a progressive line. And in doing so, it has used up the energy, the cultural and iconographical resources, of our history, leaving nothing but entropy. Hence, the artist faced the past, with his shoulders firmly blocking the future. De Dominicis's works instead occupy a circular temporal system where past, present, and future flow together in immediacy (*Senza titolo* [Untitled] [IT 244] [1982], with the monstrous three-headed figure). In a contrary way, art is freed from the bonds and pledges of the contemporary, opening up to wider and more original horizons.

De Dominicis always strove to achieve a nonfilial status in his art. Rather than adopting a particular iconographic "chromosome" of a particular artistic "gene" inherited from the past, he was someone who laid claim to the paternal authority necessary to found new families of images. The circular temporality in his work meant that it was neither archaeological nor invested in the future. His starting point was elsewhere: the recognition of the spatial limits of our culture that still paradoxically writes its own past. In generating his new families of images, De Dominicis would, through the course of his creative adventures, use the most disparate materials. Sometimes happening to fit in with the buzzwords of the moment, these works—irrespective of whether they were installation, performance, and video or painting, sculpture, and drawing—drew upon these resources in order to achieve better communication within the social body as a whole. De Dominicis made use of the dark sign of immortality, the hyper-iconic sign of the cross (plus the words "33 AD": *Immortalità dell'anima* [Immortality of the Spirit]) or even the swastika (plus "1919": *Immortalità della razza* [Immortality of the Race]). And he might even combine the two (plus "1971": *Immortalità del corpo* [Immortality of the Body]) in a sign that presents itself as the future (*Immortalità* [Immortality] [IT 137] [1971]). Furiously reiterated, these emblems of death (*Necrologio [Manifesto mortuario]* [Necrology (Mortuary Poster)] [IT 73] [1969]) were not exhibited as if drawn from some personal reserves of artistic language and themes. They are disquieting icons of immortality (*Calamita cosmica* [Cosmic Magnet] [IT 314] [1988–89]). The sign does not only bar the way to death, it also paralyzes movement. If the body is subject to the dissolution of time, this means that every modification it undergoes is a movement toward silence and death: immortality is achievable only with the suspension of the temporal dimension of existence. Immortality is a body that does not age, suspended instead in an instantaneous perception of reality. Art is the praxis which plumbs the black hole of death, highlighting the defeat of extinction. At the same time, it is the dimension that can reestablish the primacy of the anthropological over the generalized existence of the animal world. Man can lay claim to and exercise intellectual and cultural powers, and thus concentrate his efforts on overcoming this limit.

Science is viewed as a product of the Enlightenment, and hence its inquiries are already directed to the final solution of the ultimate problem: the overcoming of unhappiness is the overcoming of the defeat found in death. Depicted in the work *Senza titolo* (Untitled) [IT 206] (1986), which was briefly shown at the 53rd Venice Biennale, the cross and swastika, while being two signs that indicate the errors of history, at the same time, reveal in their fusion something about collective memory. The ideological import of the sign lies in the restoration of a project for existence in the world: the reduction of death to a permanent area within life. The use of the cross and the swastika serves to signify the abandonment of ideology as the expression of group interests, be they the interests of the dominant class of the Christian Middle Ages or the bourgeoisie of Nazi Germany, and the restoration of the pure value of ideology-as-project.

De Dominicis shifted the language of art from the space of *allegorical representation*, which always tends toward abstraction, to the metonymic space of *presentation* where all the components work together to concretely define themselves and each other by their own function and presence (*Senza titolo* [Untitled], known as "Sbarre violate" [Violated Bars] [IT 227] [1980]). On the other hand, the "solution of immortality" envisaged by De Dominicis in *Seconda soluzione di immortalità (l'universo è immobile)* (Second Solution of Immortality [The Universe Is Still]) [IT 150] (1972), through the *presentation* of an observer with Down syndrome actually indicated immortality "in act," for it played upon the total absence of a historical memory of time, upon an instant-by-instant perception of the world. The move beyond metaphor and the metonymic invasion of the space of the real thus nullify "fiction"; they impinge upon the spectator at specular levels.

In contrast, Duchamp's gesture of putting a moustache upon the *Mona Lisa*, apart from its reference to the androgyny of *Mona Lisa*, did not appear truly scandalous because the iconoclastic gesture stopped at the threshold of metaphor. Even more importantly, the "affront" was perpetrated not upon the original but upon a copy and thus further exalted the fetishism of the original "work of art." However, when László Tóth took a hammer to Michelangelo's *Pietà* itself, he truly threatened a monument to predictable wonders. His gesture was, however, in comparison obviously *not artistic*; it moved beyond the threshold of the gratification of obsessive imagination. A violent *appropriation* of the *Pietà*, his act was a violation that was also a real *expropriation* of the work. True, the history of art does contain the legendary "performance" of Michelangelo striking his own statue of Moses, but his gesture is not classified as pathological. The artist's awareness that he occupies the space of metaphor, of the superfluous, drives him to real gestures that embody unresolved conflicts, which "freeze" the work of art in the form of what appears to be sublimation.

In De Dominicis, the image puts itself forward as a model for behavior and action itself. The two men suspended in the air (*Senza titolo [Immortalità]* (Untitled [Immortality]) with "the young and the old man" [IT 124] [1971]) indicate that only by correcting—by intervening upon—the dimension of space and time is it possible to produce a world of immortality, as in *L'immortale invisibile e il luogo* (The Invisible Immortal and the Place) [IT 320] (1989). The physical suspension of figures resorts to a balancing act; it throws off the impositions of gravity. Breaking free of the ground means suspending the process of dissolution; it removes the negative conditions (of time and space) which cause that dissolution to occur. *Tentativo di volo* (Attempt to Fly) [IT 84] (1969) furthers the attempt to produce oneself in new forms. Thus art becomes the space that signals, that embraces and develops, a theme that is obsessively common to one and all: the overcoming of death. If all men directed their energies in this direction, there would be no loss and dispersal of mental energy. Instead, that energy would be concentrated, becoming an instrument for the preservation and salvation of the physical health of the body; *Il tempo lo sbaglio lo spazio* (Time, Mistake, Space) [IT 95] (1969) presents us with a human skeleton in a pair of roller skates and a canine skeleton.

De Dominicis takes the problem of art as a system of publicity one step further.

Art embraces and directs all social thoughts upon the same problem; it is the public demonstration of the reversal of our biological limits. The cocktail party held to celebrate the overcoming of the second law of thermodynamics was an apologia of limits themselves.

Art became shared praxis with didactic intent; drawing public attention to our anthropological "standard," it indicated (and overturned) the limit of life itself. In effect, during the period of Conceptualism, the great artist was Plato, who, as Nietzsche has commented in *Daybreak*, wanted to contemplate things only in the pale images of the mind. De Dominicis created three images belonging to the same family in the years immediately preceding this period (1968–69). The first was the balanced rod *Asta in bilico (Equilibrio 1)* (Suspended Rod [Equilibrium 1]) [IT 47] [1967]), then the bucket of water with a hook inside (*Secchio con acqua sospeso da terra con il gancio di una catena che fa presa sull'acqua* [Bucket with Water Suspended from the Ground, with the Hook of a Chain that Grips the Water] [IT 59] [1968]), and then the men suspended in midair. After these came the overcoming of the second law of thermodynamics and the work at the 1972 Venice Biennale in which a young man with Down syndrome was placed among such other works as the ball caught in the moment before rebounding (*Palla di gomma (caduta da due metri) nell'attimo immediatamente precedente il rimbalzo* [Rubber Ball [Falling from a Height of Two Meters] in the Moment Right Before Bouncing Back] [IT 70] [1968–69]); the invisible cube (*Cubo invisibile* [Invisible Cube] [IT 45] [1967]); and the rock awaiting spontaneous movement (*Attesa di un casuale movimento molecolare generale in una sola direzione tale da generare un movimento spontaneo del materiale* [Waiting for a Random One-Directional Molecular Movement that Could Generate a Spontaneous Movement of Material] [IT 85–89] [1969]). Continuous laughter provided the soundtrack for this arrangement, of a quality rather different to that joyous laughter of the statue *Madonna che ride* (Laughing Madonna) [IT 152] (1972). In these self-evidently paradoxical forms, De Dominicis reiterates the essential need for art to produce emotions that "involve" us, to do more than generate mental ideas and impressions (*Tentativo di far formare dei quadrati invece che dei cerchi attorno a un sasso che cade nell'acqua* [Attempt to Form Squares Instead of Circles Around a Stone Falling into Water] [IT 83] [1969]).

Art is no introduction to an inclined plane of knowledge—a knowledge that Plato envisaged as entirely separate from reality. It is, if anything, the possibility of resolving the antinomies between two diverse "planes" (reality/knowledge) through the solution of an image that really shifts the boundaries within which our vision, our iconography, are enclosed. This is confirmed in *Lo Zodiaco* (The Zodiac) [IT 105] (1970), which, for the first time, eschews the vitalistic conventions of performance art, with the immobile individuals being fixed in places imposed by the artist, just as a painter might do with an impasto of different colors. "Man believes the world itself to be overloaded with beauty—and he forgets himself as the cause of this" (Nietzsche).[1] The importance of this idea is striking in De Dominicis's work—so much so that we forget "by heart" the context and thus get to the essence of the work; formally rooted within an image that at first sight appears "above suspicion" is a source of disturbance—and it is that disturbance which art introduces (*Senza titolo* [1987/1991–92], also known as *Gioconda* [IT 301]).

If, in this family of images, De Dominicis marks out the limit of our present, other families of images appear on the horizon ahead of us. An iconography erupts upon us in the very matter and substance of paint, the manual handling of which is heralded in an early drawing of a woman (*Donna allo specchio* [Lady with Mirror] [IT 25] [1965–66]) and the exhibition of small colored figures (1973). "A boundary is not that at which something stops but, as the Greeks recognized, the boundary is that from which something begins its presencing" (Heidegger).

In his paintings, among his images were ones from Sumerian mythology; these flow forward from the past, from an esoteric culture that based its system of expression upon the centrality of the image. As a result, what emerges is an affinity that goes beyond a mere reprisal of iconography and imposes other presences upon our world and habitat (Con titolo [*In principio era l'immagine; No!*] [With Title (In the beginning was the image; No!)] [IT 238] [1981–82]). In their asymmetry, these images possess the troubling silence of a real presence. De Dominicis moves through time to create an iconography that presents itself before us with all the incisiveness of an apparition that flashes upon our gaze—a gaze run through by this sudden appearance of the different. Complete with eyes that listen and noses that see, these figures let themselves be held by the frame of the picture; enclosed and hieratic, they emerge from within the depths of spaces that are joyfully unbalanced, gently "lucid" (the black face of *Senza titolo* [Untitled] [IT 322] [1989]).

In the eighties and nineties, De Dominicis's life was inhabited by these figures. They live within ghostly architectural structures set against mysterious backgrounds; they are armed with rods; their furtive hands and ironic profiles become a mark of their enigmatic presence in the contemporary. With the blind skill of the artist, De Dominicis balances accounts with the temporality of a history distinct from our own. And the circularity of

---

1   Editor's note: In the original publication of this essay, the author deliberately omitted references for the quotations cited.

this link would become even more firmly established in later years, in a family of images exhibited in 1986. These figures seem to come from the future. With their protruding noses and single central eyes, they seem ready to occupy the space that had been occupied by reason and rationality (*Senza titolo* [Untitled] [IT 265] [1985] [1985–88], depicting a sacral one-eyed figure with a beak nose). Created in various sizes and in colors including blue, red, and black, these figures suddenly produced a new disturbance, an unforeseen short circuit in our vision, in a gaze that can "overcome the constrictions of culture and reemerge with all the innate rawness of savages delighting in grimaces" (Goethe). The dart of the gaze, the turgid eruption of those eyes and noses, seem to take in all the ridiculous accidents of our present, absorbing them in a sort of majestic silence. The eyes are held half-closed in order not to see *(Opera ubiqua (Delfina D. D. – Auronia D. D.)* (Ubiquitous Work [Delfina D. D. – Auronia D. D.]), [IT 548] [1996]). Are there perhaps other prehensile organs that the future will make known to us?

The Epiphany of the Image

All of De Dominicis's work bears the mark of a time that closes upon itself in a circle that lies outside the shifts and adjustments of "cultural events." It responds to the challenge posed by an art that does not want to reduce the past or the present to the same thing, nor does it want to unduly ennoble them. What it wants is to inhabit an unrestricted horizon.

De Dominicis's entire oeuvre reveals the praxis of an artist who requires more than simple set-piece strategies. The entire field of the imagination is brought into play, run through by a dual compulsion that refuses to respect "high" and "low," that, at one and the same time, emphasizes the movement of dissemination and of concentration, like in the cosmogonic landscape of *Senza titolo* (Untitled) [IT 570] (1997–98), which can be read in both ways. The hand and the head—the entire anatomy—of the artist participates in the moment of creation; and that creation involves the free flow of the imagination, the exercise of a fantasy that knows no boundaries and at the same time accepts being "inscribed" within a stylistics that is woven in and of conscious awareness and skill in handling the languages of art. Art is, in effect, both a bulimic overflowing and an exercise in measure; it systematically overcomes boundaries and safety limits. Working beyond these, it manages to produce a "system" of impossibilities, a project predicated upon inattention/distraction. All this arises from an attitude that is emblematic of the artist, a figure caught within the organized discomposure of the rigorous lines of an image both calibrated and automatic (the synthetic figure of *Senza titolo* [Untitled] [IT 337] [1986–89]).

Creative design and chance are simultaneously interwoven within De Dominicis's work, which is intended to balance out the inadequacy of a reality that has become schematic and reductive. Art produces bewilderment and knowledge, loss of sense and the extension of sense. It is a praxis that undermines the canons of communication and thus generates disorientation.

In De Dominicis's art the image is generated by a structural ambiguity; it eludes the innate pride of everyday language to reach a place of interwoven relations, wherein signs take their place within instantaneous fugues and chords. While the impulse that runs through the body of the artist may be uncontrollable, what is fully controllable is the manual skill and ability necessary to make the authority of the image both striking and explicit (*Senza titolo* [Untitled] [IT 256] [1985], also known as "Lady Diana").

One cannot struggle against that skill and ability; indeed, the artist organizes abandonment-by-design, a sort of inner discipline that is capable of duplicating the world because, as De Dominicis himself has commented, "art does not repeat visible things; it makes visible." The artist surrenders himself to the flow of imagination, adopting an oblique stance with regard to language; a loss of conscious awareness serves to make him receptive to the nomadic shifts of the signs he employs.

De Dominicis may know the nature of the language he is using, but he never tries to tame or dominate it. Instead, he backs up the action of that language through the adoption of procedures predicated upon both choice and design. The result itself, however, is free, totally unbound by expectations or foresight. Indeed, it is not the artist who possesses foresight, it is the language of art that contains within it unwonted images and results. The artist is always aware that the active *bullying of the language* of art results in a numbing of creative processes and an automatic impoverishment of the techniques of artistic composition. While the unconscious and the intelligent work of chance are values that are part of the work of art itself, which give art its character of complex necessity, the artist must go further. He must explore different cultures that are distant in both time and space—for example, the culture of the Sumerians. For this opens up new myths and a new state of spirituality; it heightens the discipline of surrender to the empathy of the image.

In this way, bewilderment becomes an achievement—as does the acquisition of a rudimentary, automatic manual skill; passing, paradoxically, through/beyond technical mastery, this protects the work via a sort of involuntary beauty. This involuntariness is that ability of abandonment/surrender, that feeling of indifference, which allows the artist never to anticipate results; to trust himself to the condensation operated by the language of art. Such clear-sighted abandonment/surrender is the necessary starting point.

A constant characteristic of De Dominicis's art is a praxis and language that explores the surface. Space has no depth; it is a pure two-dimensional pictorial support into which one never sinks or plunges (the goddess-queen of *Senza titolo* [Untitled] [IT 426] [1991]). Such plunging is, if anything, to be found in the operation of psyche and imagination prior to the work itself; it is the movement that supports the "setting in operation" of the image. Signs and marks are disseminated across the surface in a natural manner; and the tension inspiring that dissemination is the desire for expression. But expression is no mere naturalistic "copying" of the obscurities of the psyche. Nor is it the achievement of some unified/unifying locus of significance. It is the instinctive distribution of signs in accordance with fragmentary condensation and intensity. The system of such distribution/disposition is that of the constellation, thrown off by a center of irradiation which knows no hierarchies or points of gravitational attraction and has no periphery. Instead, as it spreads its rays, such a system of irradiation makes it possible to bring together both the abstract and figurative image (*Senza titolo [Pianeti]* [Untitled (Planets)] [IT 612] [1990]; the standing figure of *Senza titolo* [Untitled] [IT 434] [1992]).

In De Dominicis's work, color is part of the play of composition; it enhances hypnotic intensity. The language of color has its own internal biology, which allows for noteworthy exercises of free will. Thus an internal energy radiates from within the work. The artist attempts to create linear disorientation, a disorientation that throws one back upon the occult force within the things of this world; for example, a table contains within its impassive surface the ghostly density of a universe balanced between revelation and concealment (*Come io vedo questo tavolo, questi piatti, questa bottiglia, queste posate, questo bicchiere, e questa pianta* [As I see this table, these plates, this bottle, this cutlery, this glass, and this plant] [IT 114] [1970]).

Art works to penetrate the thick patina of things, to get beneath the false opulence of matter and materials; it aims to reveal the energy that runs through all bodies and governs the dynamism of the world (*Senza titolo [Guerriero]* [Untitled (Warrior)] [IT 404] [1990]). That is why the image has to be stripped of depth, in order to sustain the flux that relates things to each other along lines of flow and continuity. At times, signs thus achieve a lightness, a fluctuating emptiness of "import," which enables them to capture, contemporaneously, both the outer skin and inner core of things. Objects and figures are restored as if suspended, relieved of their weight; they are transcribed in a way that merely hints at visual nomination (the evanescent face, at the very limits of the visible, in *Senza titolo* [Untitled] [IT 322] [1989]).

De Dominicis is thoroughly aware of the specific character of visual language; of the fact that its constituent elements cannot pretend to be other than what they are. If anything, the character of visual language allows one to formulate certain consonances within existence—for example, an artist's ability to observe goes with his detachment from things as such. Hence, the unfailing lack of "depth" in visual language—its "superficial" nature—is highlighted; it is seen to be consonant with the type of relation that the artist aims for with things, his lack of preference for one object rather than another. The artist is not attracted by the sensual permeability of things, which would lead him to feel them as evocations. Instead, he is inclined to see the skeleton that holds them up, their own particular framework. He then "restores" those objects in a system of simultaneous relations that accentuates their individuality, their fluctuating nature: for they could disappear (the "invisible statues" [IT 195–98] [1979]). And language itself reveals the same fluctuation, the same interior shifting and mobility. The artist exists in an alarmed state; the gaze itself is precarious. For the artist is always amazed by the internal tension of things and by the fact that, at the same time, their being appears to be preordained. Art thus becomes the project of a sensibility that is naturally alarmed.

A drive toward disorder slips into the work, disarticulating the composition, pushing it toward an overturning of the order of the déjà vu (the "reversed perspective" of *Senza titolo* [Untitled] [IT 422] [1991]). An inextricable knot of signs tends to constitute a field of precarious relations, all resting upon an instability or stability that is only momentary. At times the work reveals an expressionism of palette and brushstroke, with the image being deformed, disconnected from everyday normality. The artist does not paint the world; if anything, he looks at it in order to forget it better.

Often in De Dominicis's painting, figure and background flow into each other inextricably, in a relation that enables one to identify routes of sensibility—routes made up of undulant passages, returns, points of intersection, vanishing points (the ziggurat/head in *Senza titolo* [Untitled] [IT 399] [1990]). The fluency of the visual components is a further sign of the stripping bare of sensibility, of De Dominicis's ability to look beyond appearances. The image is accompanied by a sense of minute observation, of analysis that both decelerates and accelerates to the maximum. The elementary line De Dominicis uses to describe his internal landscapes is often taken to the point of distortion, a distortion that is the fruit of an exaggerated description of details, a miniaturized rendering of the accidents and circumstances which accompany the formation of the image. Art makes the visible glaring and patent. And this means that the image is a locus of shifting coagulation, drawing into itself the vortices of signs which make it dense with relations, heavy with the unsayable. There is an indeterminacy here resulting from shifting trajectories, filiform consonances, and subtle dissonances (*Senza titolo* [Untitled] [IT 455] [1994], depicting the union of male and female; a work also known as "Totem").

On other occasions, the image De Dominicis creates is a tangled mass of brushstrokes; it oscillates between an anthropomorphic mask and the transmutation of that mask into something other than itself (the Leonardoesque self-portrait known as "Old Woman" [IT 395] [1989]). The traces on the surfaces are infinite and refuse to be pinned down; they run free, following their own logic, inexhaustible and obsessive. They are traced like the veins in a tablet of marble seen in childhood, where the hand cannot stop itself, given the smoothness of the surface and the temptation to follow through the networks of interlocking signs. Space is the pictorial support that becomes a single whole with the image itself; there is no interruption between them (the untitled "self-portrait" made with ink [IT 324] [1989]).

Sometimes the figures themselves might be packed together, next to each other, in anamorphic lines that follow a rhythm that is both internal and introverted (*Senza titolo* [Untitled] [IT 283] [1986], known as "The Last Supper"). There is no order that provides for a frontal view of the image, because the figures fill all the points of the picture or drawing. An almost comic quiet reigns within the composition. It is as if the gaze of the artist had calmly assumed within itself all the alterations of a language that naturally inclines toward anamorphosis, distortion, and nightmare.

De Dominicis pursues the phantasm that inhabits the language of art, which lies within its deepest ambiguities. Images are not substitutes for other images; they are the sole possible representations. Sometimes they pretend to animate or mimic characters to be found in the familiar traits of a face or an object. But in reality they take on the mask of purely linguistic entities, so much so that, like these linguistic entities, they have an irresistible ability to adapt, the power to refer to nothing other than their own inner trajectory. Landscapes, too, seem to precipitate along the slopes of the two-dimensional surface; they may be static but they are also hung in the balance along diagonals that bring together houses, natural features, and human figures (like the figure with the flag in *Figura a piazza del Popolo* [Figure in Piazza del Popolo] [IT 317] [1989]). Everything is seen by a gaze that "grazes the ground," swooping either to encounter or move far from things themselves. These landscapes seem imbued with a sort of animistic feeling and a use of line that is inspired by the subtle interior geometry of nature—that is, the invisible "dematerialized" structure of the world.

47

The gaze here is total, all-embracing; it can capture details as they flow incessantly by. These details are then held in an osmosis that does not aim for formal equilibrium; instead, it pursues the simultaneous copresence of both of any pair of possibilities. Depth and surface have the same visual presence, as if a single force had managed to seize both the visible and invisible and transport them to the locus of epiphanic revelation—a locus inhabited by the image. This is the locus wherein one can keep spatial elements in simultaneous relationship with each other (*L'appuntamento* [The Appointment] [IT 295] [1987]).

There is an energy field that saturates De Dominicis's images, that defines the spatial in terms that are both shifting and essential. Simultaneity arises from the desire to describe a universe in which space and time are dimensions whose entire potential is conjugated together at one and the same time—the potential of the above and below, of close and distant, of first and last, of present and imminent. The image is governed by a perfect circularity; it is contained entirely within the self-sufficient echoes of a language that is capable not only of anticipation but also of copresence. And these features contain within themselves the archaeology, the present and future, of the world—embracing abstraction and figuration, acceleration and deceleration (*Figura* [Figure] [IT 457] [1994]).

55

At other times, the point of view seems to emerge from within the image itself, to break through it into the outside. In each and every case, transparency and opacity are both qualities of the image (the transparent figure on the sea in *Senza titolo* [Untitled] [IT 315] [1988–90]). However, it is not a case of imitating the apparent freedom of nature in its untamed state. Instead, the artist takes upon himself the implicit ability of chaos to become structured in accordance with the potential underlying the cosmos, the potential for a system of relations in which the specific and the universal, order and disorder, the microcosm and macrocosm, openly co-exist. So he does not struggle against Nature, nor does he try to become integrated within it (*Opera viva che deforma il tempo* [A Living Work that Deforms Time] [IT 402] [1990]).

In the image, *formation* counts much more than form. The former covers the uninterrupted path along which the artist moves during the whole course of the work—a work that is his life itself. The second is the individual result, the delight of static narcissism as it dwells before the mirror elaborated within the work. The drive toward art arises in an origin that is ideal and "airy," an origin to which the artist must remain true if that primary original energy is to penetrate each part of the composition and the whole itself. In effect, the artist must exercise a sort of creative governance over the work.

Art is the ongoing despoliation of what already exists; it works toward one further step, within a dimension that runs between the indeterminacy of the point of departure and the calibrated economy of an end result. That result, in fact, slowly manifests itself to the eyes of the artist himself through a sort of "Annunciation of the Image," an apparition of that particular sign as the only one possible. It is the unveiling and epiphany of an image that has all the *terribilità* of essence, of indivisible substance. What was divided and separated is now reunited in a shifting relationship with a whole that condenses time and space, life and death.

The Trompe l'Oeil of Immortality

A picture is always the locus of immersion, of trespass into the territory of an imagination without drama. The work of art defuses the drama of that moment of Vision; it captures the gaze of the spectator within the world of art, and it does so using a "plot" that, at first sight, does not seem to undermine the usual codes of perception. However, the work of art transports the spectator to a silent place of no return, where diversity takes on the cordial aspects of both the descriptive and the analytical. The image presents itself in a state of grace; it is disguised as a process in which a sense of displacement prevails. The image appears to eschew all reduction to and all integration with the landscape of things that surround it (*Ubiquità* [Ubiquity] [IT 90–94] [1970]).

The work of art invites one to participate in the *ostranenie* that is part of the very normality of the real: to explore this condition in depth, to see it with eyes that remain wide open. There is no point in indulging in reverie, in closing oneself away in one's own world of fantasy; it is reality itself that acquires that sense of *ostranenie*. As we gradually open an amazed gaze upon the world around us, it is reality itself that appears to be displaced. In effect, the more we free our gaze of our personal fantasies and phantasms, the more we enter into contact with the surprising and epiphanic substance of the world. What is essential is that our vision should be stripped clean, freed of all previous reveries, prejudice, or impetuosity.

De Dominicis draws upon the universe of the everyday—a world that is made up of small presences, which have none of the heroic and unrepeatable character of the world of *mythology*. However, his images still achieve a specificity and displacement that generate *ostranenie* (the Sumerian with a tie and coat in *Con titolo* [With Title] [IT 258] [1985]; the owl-man with hat in *Senza titolo* [Untitled] [IT 311] [1990]). Displacement here means shifting the object well outside its usual context. The artist understands that to paint a banal object means to transfer it into a different reality, the reality of the language of art where all identities are threatened with crisis because they exist on the other side of a boundary beyond which the object is given as a mere possibility and can only be "recognized" within that place of no return. At the end of the peripatetic wanderings that the eye pursues through all the pathways of the image, it is no longer possible to turn back; too much time has passed and any possible means of retreat have been closed off. After an initial process of courting, the spectator's gaze is now a prisoner; held and crystallized within the image, the eye surrenders itself to the power of the familiar iconography, which has swiftly managed to transform itself into the de-familiar, to undergo metamorphosis. The work of art puts itself at the service of such mutations, happily following the rules of displacement, de-familiarization, and condensation to create "traps" for the gaze (*Immagine della dea sumera Warka* [Image of the Sumerian Goddess Warka]) [IT 189] [1977–83], with which De Dominicis won the 13th Paris Biennale in 1985).

Trompe l'oeil is par excellence such a trap. It is the visual bait that captures the attention of the spectator; that obliges the eye to plunge into the scene of the picture and submit to the subtle modifications of the real. This "scene," however, never takes on the premonitory tones of tragedy, of the unveiling of some silent monstrosity. In fact, it is constructed with all the perspectival clarity of a de Chirico painting; physiognomies are as shaded and umbral as those found in da Vinci, while there is a sort of descriptive clarity, the clarity of someone who intends to hide nothing, not even the desire for immortality. The eye enters this scene and, from the very beginning, is capable of judging each and every distance, glimpsing each and every detail. Ultimately, however, there is another level of visual reality, within which hatches a "small monstrosity." That diversity never takes on the Romantic and visionary *terribilità* of the nocturnal image; instead, it passes itself off in understatement, maintaining the character of a diversity which is wryly domestic and ironic.

In De Dominicis's art, monstrosity is never truly abnormal. It is cordial and meek, ready to engage with the spectator, to permit the gaze to witness the birth/discovery of a diversity that does not allow us to howl out in reaction (*Lady Diana*). Rather than a howl or scream there is a murmur, which is in keeping with an image that takes on a lucidly comic character. It is our visual culture, our world of the visible, which contains the possibilities of metamorphosis. The artist may, for example, work via the procedure of the "readymade," surgically transplanting the image to endow it with "monstrous" new life. De Dominicis indicates one of the ways in which language proliferates; he points out the birth of a language constantly ready to generate monsters, images made visible outside the modes of everyday Vision. The language of art is polymorphous and perverse; it is ever-changing, unstable and unpredictable. It is, ultimately, totally amoral. Such amorality makes possible the production of metamorphosis from and into the monstrous, the presentation of image mutations that encounter no obstacle in presenting themselves in an entirely new manner via juxtapositions that are both terrible and cordial (from the series of the "Devils" (1985–86) to the informal "Monster" [IT 564] [1997]).

Exploiting the moral inertia of art, the artist first "constructs" the title of the work as such. And the work then becomes the application of a rule; it is the visual realization of the distinction between end result and the expectations raised by its title. Painting is, in effect, the distance existing between the *signifié* of the title and the *signifiant* of the image, which tends to liquefy the semantic coagulation implicit in "giving a title." Things again become fluid because the amoral willingness of the language of art backs up the movement of the image. In De Dominicis, the comic tends to redirect the artist's anxiety away from the peremptory, authoritarian, and paternal self-affirmation of the title; it serves to shift recognition of the paternity of an image away from what is semantically "fixed" by tradition. The work of art exploits the irresponsibility of language in order to achieve a different process of fecundity, a different process of birth. For the language of art is neither male nor female; it has no connotations that can constrain it within one stable identity, make it recognizable in accordance with established schema, schema that, in their very nature, are always paternal.

For De Dominicis, art is the praxis of "de-responsibilization"; it is a technique for undercutting and holding at a distance any form of easily recognizable paternity. The peremptory nature of the image reveals the essential shamelessness of the work of art, which parries all attempts at categorization by reality (*Senza titolo* [Untitled] [IT 252] [1984]; the maternity in *Con titolo* [With Title] [IT 501] [1992]).

The image is contagious; there is a price to pay for its concession of itself to the gaze.

And it strives to act upon the whole cerebral cortex. The image thus tends to draw in the spectator as an accomplice, as someone jointly responsible for the atrocity of an anomaly committed by others, elsewhere. In art there are no punishable crimes because there is no code of professional conduct to be applied. The hypocrisy of the image consists in presenting as entirely normal situations that, elsewhere, would be unbearable and abnormal. The hypocrisy of the spectator lies in not even batting an eyelid.

The Sidereal Unconscious of Art

In De Dominicis's art, painting, by pure internal necessity, ceases to be any sort of elegiac illustration; it strives toward images whose identity is based upon the double process of displacement and condensation. The picture becomes a frame that contains the presence of *images in dreams*, which take form with all the oneiric lightness of apparitions that occur outside all the norms of naturalistic representation. Art no longer illustrates the self-evidence of things but rather their internal distraction, to the point where it actually breaks down the geometrical coordinates underlying the code of figurative depiction. In De Dominicis's paintings there is no background as such. Instead, a sort of impermeable wall contains duels between signs that explode upon the surface of the painting, a surface covered with colors that are reminiscent of the heights of the heavens or the vertiginous depths of the oceans. The picture becomes a stage for the acting-out of the archaic belligerence between forces that are destined never to be quelled, between energies that can be called up but never held back. This is why the artist uses a language that is both organic and figural, lying between the *informale* and a sort of "suspect" figuration.

The urgent hand pursues the flow of shifting phantasms whose own implacable tension finds the strength to declare itself in the very indeterminacy of the images themselves. The implacability of the phantasm is the fruit of a consciousness that derides the logocentrism of our predominantly Western culture. It is the result of an anthropological condition which preserves the memories of archaic mysteries and cruel rituals linked to a culture whose roots lie in the very substance of the primitive imagination. The space of the picture becomes the astral, sidereal locus within which the various elements engage in combat. The paradox is that the profound, indefinite space of the unconscious seems to be equated with the space of the other universes that stand so high above us. In effect, the unconscious of art is sidereal (the "Triptych of the Planets" [IT 439] [1992–93], exhibited at the 45th Venice Biennale).

For De Dominicis this conflict is the effect of the will-to-power of an unconscious that is ungovernable, that is the origin of antisocial behavior. This is why the image is always cynical and at the same time full of pathos. The artist is aware that he is showing us a state of permanent ambivalence. While his anthropoid figures maintain all the energy of the human condition, while they are governed by instinct and the forces of the unconscious, they also have all the geometric *terribilità* of automatic robot warriors whose inclination to conflict and combat cannot be defused. Conflict and struggle seem to be the sole mode of encounter and social engagement open to these creatures. They seem to be elemental parts of a single great Being, of the structural sidereal Substance that embraces both the greatest depths and the farthest-flung distances.

The surface is dotted by islands of signs, by filiform sinuous figures that inevitably lead on to other loci of conflict. The artist traces out the visual coordinates of an existence born "under the sign" of struggle. Sometimes, the forms close upon themselves. Tending toward the circularity of possible planets, they follow their own elliptical orbit or perhaps enter upon a course that leads to a collision which does not destroy them but, rather, increases their power to expand over space. In fact, they rupture into fragments that are happily scattered across the picture, leaving traces as they go.

54

The heights of the heavens become a fertile terrain, like a garden where other forms proliferate (the planets of *Senza titolo* [Untitled] [IT 478] [1995]).

The ambivalence of these wars is given precisely by the fact that the image describes the terrible "uncontainability" of life, which may let itself be threatened but never destroyed. The artist De Dominicis is aware that the "death drive" contains within itself another drive—the drive toward unrestrainable regeneration, which is implicit in the genetic memory that opposes the geometric neatness of entropy. Art is, in fact, the instrument of representation that reiterates the indecision of an existent oscillating between the nullification and affirmation of life. In this sense, catastrophe and eroticism go together in the same work at the same time; they are the alternating and often interwoven movements that delimit the sense of the image.

Catastrophe is an entropic movement; it is that toward which the conflicts between signs tend, signs which, paradoxically, regain the energy to engage in new clashes/encounters precisely through their clashes with each other. The artist's paint and color are applied without form, in a rough, improvised manner; nervous energy and speed deliberately deny any material thickness to the painted forms.

Within the field of the painting electricity is generated, resulting in a luminous diagram of shifting flashes and gleams that are always ready to move elsewhere, to illuminate other areas of conflict. Both line and color are subject to continual shifts, which deny them the possibility of full reciprocal integration with each other—a *décollement* that is a further symptom of conflict. In some works the conflict is intentional; precise trajectories mark out the hostile exchanges between the various parts. At other times, the conflict arises from the very nature of things, which are caught up inextricably within a sort of magma, which are ineluctably carried toward the shifting, uncertain terrain of "de-semination." There are no separate or isolated parts; everything is linked by the thread of ongoing fragmentation, open to new combinations and aggregation, and thence to further possibilities of rupture.

The universe of images is thus made up of gaseous bodies and mechanical components, of fragmentary solid states and other non-rigid moments of unity. Everything is predicated upon indeterminacy; everything moves toward the precarious existence of galaxies of forms that are constantly ready to break up into a thousand segments, bound by no center of gravity. In effect, there is no specific center, no spatial hierarchy ("Clouds" [IT 360] [1994]). De Dominicis's linguistic universe is made up of the turbulence of systems of signs imbued with desire. In his work, these wander within the second dimension of the canvas in search of ever-new collisions, open to ever-new possibilities; they are driven both toward life and toward death. The artist manages to bring together the organic and the automata (Ninsun in *Ninsun [La mamma di Gilgamesh]* [Ninsun (The Mother of Gilgamesh)] [IT 631] [1996–97]), both competing in a conflict whose uncertain outcome could be the extermination of life or the proliferation of other life. Caught between the two poles that have always marked out the philosophical boundaries for any kind of artistic representation, this conflict is the only threshold that offers us even the suspicion of immortality. Here, as De Dominicis urged, it is possible to be contemplated by the work of art. The artist has given body to an unrepeatable canon of work, something that is also a stimulus for others to remain at the avant-garde of the classical.

Translated by Jeremy Scott
A longer version of this essay, titled "Senza titolo: l'immortale," was originally published in *Gino De Dominicis: The Immortal*, ed. Achille Bonito Oliva (Milan: Electa; Rome: Fondazione MAXXI, 2010), 13–27.

Dimensionless

Richard Shiff

Car and hen

Gino De Dominicis's "Letter on Immortality" opens with an assertive thud.[1] His reference to "things" pertains to *all* things, not merely some. The Italian word is *cose*, which is as general and generic as the corresponding English—a linguistic placeholder available when a writer either fails to, or does not wish to, narrow the field of reference.

When, without exception, the things of the macrocosm lack existence, existence would seem to lose its value as an identifying property or attribute. Analogously, if every object were entirely red, the attribute of color would convey no differential meaning. Nonexistence implies its antithesis, its other; it is the differential that secures value for existence, a green for the red. Somewhere existence exists. And when nonexistence pertains to all *things*, whatever exists cannot belong to the class of "things" in the sense of De Dominicis's initial proposition, which is in retrospect less dumbfounding. He explains: "In order to really exist, things would have to be eternal, immortal; only in this way would they be not merely the verification of certain possibilities, but truly things."[2] Familiar things, like the human bodies and mentalities with which we identify, are neither immortal nor, therefore, "truly things." Our existence seems at best derivative and limited. Our identities, we ourselves, amount to a panoply of transient historical possibilities.

With this sense of a "thing"—whether regarded as an expansion or a reduction of the general concept—the attribute of existence would presume an unchanging state with respect to the history of the "thing" in all its aspects (theological, cosmological, geological, biological, psychological, ideological, and so on). All secondary attributes—in a person, for example, their stage of life—would be as unchanging as the primary one of existence. A history evolves, whereas whatever exists does not. To take De Dominicis at his word, all things—the common things we encounter in daily life—because they lack existence, must be regarded as no more than pseudo-things that spuriously claim some greater status. Pseudo-things leave a historical record (dates of birth and death, for example) but no trace of an essence. These pseudo-things adopt the forms that an evolving history induces in them.

Art, however, is an exceptional "thing." Despite what art historians, preoccupied with context, usually claim, the "things" we know as art resist historical pressures and influences. De Dominicis demonstrated his understanding of the plight of "things" through the curious objects that populated his exhibitions. He also invoked the conceptual irony of anachro-

1   Gino De Dominicis, "Letter on Immortality," in this volume, 59, 62.
2   Ibid.

nism. "All works of art are contemporary," he claimed: "Otherwise, it would be as if, seeing a 1920s car come down the road, you decided to cross the street regardless, thinking that you couldn't be run over [by a 'thing' from] a different period in history."[3]

De Dominicis's metaphor is apt. He wittily confuses the potential of an automobile to move from here to there (a function in three dimensions) with the fixed chronological location associated with the production of a specific type of vehicle (a historical identity in four dimensions, restricted to a context). By imposing the limitation of time—adding this fourth dimension to the three of space—the constructions of our historical discourse counteract the potential longevity of a thing. De Dominicis recognized that he had inherited a culture of modernity that privileged change and entertained the possibility of obsolescence. He also experienced a postmodern culture that regarded identities as fluid, whether in the sense of being transitory or in the sense of being recurrent. From either perspective, modernist or postmodernist, events will seem historically relative and dependent on the conditions of perception. As entities affected by, if not created by, human interpretation, the things that history identifies—societies of people, environments of objects, events of political significance—will have no essence. Their existential value will change in relation to their position in whatever sociocultural hierarchy prevails, establishing a context. To De Dominicis, context is irrelevant. He implies that art—forever contemporary—is like an automobile of no specific vintage. It has no historical identity and encounters no historical constraints. De Dominicis's notion of an art beyond history entails an immortal art, which exists in any present time as well as in any past time with which art historians might associate it.

Another metaphor—or rather, an allegory. A common hen appears among the pseudo-things of De Dominicis's reasoning: "At the moment in which a hen fulfills its 'natural duty' to lay an egg, it ceases to be a hen in order to become nothing other than the means by which nature verifies the possibility of an egg, and thereby of the world of birds." The hen serves its historically sanctioned biological function. De Dominicis concludes his "Letter" in the redeeming hope of "tak[ing] a hen for a walk."[4] He would relieve the creature of its assigned position in the lawful, natural order of things (pseudo-things). The hen would assert its immutability as a truth, an existent thing beyond the demands of history and the evolving culture of animal husbandry. It would do as it wished. What it might wish, presumably, is to amble aimlessly. Removed from its identity in nature, the hen becomes at once immortal and without direction, no longer a placeholder in the evolutionary game of chicken and egg.

3   Gino De Dominicis, statement of 1997, repr. in Francesca Franco, "Godi Cinsi Domine—Godi Cinsi Demoni: Writings, Interviews, Comments of G. D. D.," in *Gino De Dominicis: The Immortal*, ed. Achille Bonito Oliva (Milan: Electa; Rome: Fondazione MAXXI, 2010), 100. See Gino De Dominicis, "Maxims, 1969–1996," in this volume, 95. See also Gino De Dominicis, statement published at the time of the 1993 Venice Biennale, in Franco, "Godi Cinsi Domine," 95.

4   De Dominicis, "Letter on Immortality," 61, 64.

<u>Permanence</u>

Aware of De Dominicis's aesthetic experimentation (reference to specific cases follows), and in the spirit of his philosophical speculations, I venture some related propositions. My focus is the shape a human life assumes under the normative conditions that limit it. Or rather, what we might attain were we released from these longstanding restraints. To exist in De Dominicis's strict sense of the term, a thing—a human person, for example—must escape the limitation of mortality. Existence has no life span.

By my reckoning, the dimensional boundaries that limit the life of a thing to its historical conditions must number at least four: durational time, material space or substance, projective image (sensory representation), and vocative name (linguistic sign or concept). Think of time as the most physical of dimensions and of language as the most conceptual. Associating time with a fourth dimension and space or substance with a third adheres to convention—the foundation for De Dominicis's example of the 1920s car that moves along in years (time) as readily as along the streets (space). Pictures and other graphic images occupy a second dimension, which leaves the verbal name or linguistic identity to inhabit a first. The referent of a name, a first-dimension entity, finds no fully adequate representation in the parallel dimensions: the second of graphic sign, the third of spatial location, the fourth of temporal moment. The four dimensions interact as much in interference as in correspondence. Each presents its own historical perspective.

What dimensional number might we assign to the putative immortality, the eternal contemporaneity, of De Dominicis and his art? Immortality exists beneath the first dimension and beyond the fourth; it lies outside the events, designations, and identities to which history shackles all things. The categorical number or dimension of immortality must be either zero or infinity, for each of these options resists being equated to a single value or quantity. Nor do the words that indicate these numbers express the nature of their reality, their existence. We can select one-dimensional words or symbols to signify zero (0) and infinity (∞) and can position these signs within two-dimensional diagrams; in turn, such diagrams might generate topographic models in three dimensions and their configuration might conform to the period style of a decade or a century in four-dimensional temporality. These uncountable "numbers" nevertheless remain indeterminate and undecidable—homeless ciphers that join no history, whether generative or degenerative.

Like De Dominicis, Donald Judd believed in the transformative potential of art; the existence of a work was a property or attribute to be acknowledged, not merely taken for granted. In 1964 he remarked: "Things that exist exist, and everything is on their side."[5] It was reason enough to pursue his project for a permanent installation of works of unusually large scale in Far West Texas. Into an unforeseeable future, Judd's objects would

<hr>

5   Donald Judd, "Black, White, and Gray," in *Complete Writings 1959–1975* (Halifax: Press of the Nova Scotia College of Art and Design, 1975), 117.

exist just as they were, conveying the sense that they had existed, like Stone-henge, well into an irretrievable past. De Dominicis expressed the same con-cern for escaping spatial displacement, material modification, or any other form of change that would constitute a history for a work: "The major arts … stay put in one place and are not nomadic … [But] my own works … have been [physically] transported from Rome to Venice"—a regrettable histor-ical fact.[6] "This is a period that does not like the visual arts; it prefers the 'nomadism' of languages that unfold in space and time: writing, music, cin-ema, television, etc. … Everything is 'dematerialized' and abstracted; the only things that resist this are works of art in drawing, painting, and sculp-ture."[7] The various "preferred" media were occupying the four dimensions yet were "dematerialized" by their "nomadism" or mobility—their materi-ality being compromised by the mutability resulting from dimensional deg-radation, loss of energy, entropy. History fades the traces of things that be-come obscured within it. Rather than establishing permanent existences, history evolves. Existence does not.

"Each language," De Dominicis wrote, "originates in a press-ing need. Physical immediacy is the pressing need behind the major arts."[8] History establishes the need, but by satisfying it, the work of art removes it-self from the demands of history. A "major" work of art is perpetually phys-ically immediate—or, as De Dominicis would say, "contemporary"—despite the empirical evidence of historical change in its reception. Language, a first dimension that threatens to distance the immediacy of the zero dimension of art, answers the "pressing need" with concepts and strategies. De Domi-nicis's linguistic titles and subtitles provide clues to the motivations of his works, as with his 1972 conceit directed at the second law of thermodynam-ics, *Seconda soluzione d'immortalità (l'universo è immobile)* (Second Solu-tion of Immortality [The Universe Is Still]) [IT 150].[9] Nevertheless, under the ideal condition of existing under no condition, a work of art resists one-dimensional verbal translation, which would subject it to historical interpre-tation. Accordingly, many of De Dominicis's works never bore titles.

Nor did Judd's. As a philosophical point, his desire for per-manence equated to eternal existence, not eternal significance. Meaning changes in history; existence remains. In this respect, Judd's thought aligned with Ludwig Wittgenstein's musings (Friedrich Nietzsche's, too) on factors of time extending beyond human comprehension. By a cruel trick, language facilitates the formulation of questions that yield no proper, fully satisfying responses: "At some point one has to pass from explanation [significance] to

25

6   De Dominicis, statement published at the time of the 1993 Venice Biennale, in Franco, "Godi Cinsi Domine," 95. See also Gino De Dominicis, "Some Impressions, Venice, June 15, 1993," in this volume, 70.

7   Gino De Dominicis, statement of 1996, in Franco, "Godi Cinsi Domine," 101.

8   Gino De Dominicis, text for La Nuova Pesa Gallery, Rome, 1986, in ibid., 98. See also Gino de Dominicis, "Maxims, 1969–1996," in this volume, 96.

9   The second law proposes that a closed system either maintains its degree of order or suffers an increase in disorder; it cannot increase the existing order, or the energy asso-ciated with it. For De Dominicis, art demonstrated otherwise. During his lifetime, ad-vanced research in the theoretical sciences, such as that of Ilya Prigogine, lent indirect support to his position.

mere description [existence]. What we call historical evidence points to the existence of the earth a long time before my birth—the opposite hypothesis has nothing on its side."[10] At times, we must believe or have faith in the truth of a condition that lacks existential or phenomenological standing.[11] Wittgenstein, Judd, and De Dominicis may not have agreed as to which things possess true, lasting existence; but they concurred in perceiving existence, strong or weak, as a central issue for aesthetics. The "things that exist exist," but to what end? Perhaps they meet a "pressing need."

Wittgenstein's statement opposing description to explanation alludes to the antiquity of the planet as a factual condition independent of any direct observation on the part of a human subject. We can say what we know with reasonable certainty without being more than hypothetical as to *how* we know it. Quentin Meillassoux, whose philosophical support Gabriele Guercio enlists as he interprets De Dominicis's art, would refer to such a "fact" of description as a case of "ancestrality."[12] Ancestral states are material facts without conditions, as unconditional as the works of art that De Dominicis sought to create ex nihilo. Such art would lack discursive, ideological, material, expressive, or psychological assurances of its origin, along with all other imaginable conditions, at once generative and restraining. Art ex nihilo finds no place in history. The timing of absolute beginning, origin ex nihilo, the zero-point, has no influence on the shape or extent of a historical timeline. Zero predetermines nothing.

With his example of the hen, De Dominicis implies that things already occupying dimensions and functioning within them—whether animate bodies or inanimate objects, and perhaps even events—are the "things" that do not exist in any permanent sense, things subject to the second law of thermodynamics (existence as stasis or eventual loss of energy, entropic decay). But the dimensions themselves exist, or rather act, as if to reduce the existential value of physical bodies, restricting the freedom of those bodies by imposing historically determined conditions. A body performing an action lacks self-sufficiency because temporalized; an object occupying a position lacks self-sufficiency because spatialized; an image represented lacks self-sufficiency because abstracted and projected; a reference or name lacks self-sufficiency because conceptualized and systematized. In their dimensional guises, limited by the terms of from one dimension (names, linguistic markers) to four (historical time, entailing precedents,

10 Ludwig Wittgenstein, *On Certainty*, ed. G. E. M. Anscombe and G. H. von Wright, trans. Denis Paul and G. E. M. Anscombe (New York: Harper and Row, 1972), 26e (emphasis eliminated). Compare Friedrich Nietzsche, *The Gay Science*, trans. Walter Kaufmann (New York: Vintage Books, 1974), 172: "'Explanation' is what we call it, but it is 'description' that distinguishes us from older stages of knowledge and science. Our descriptions are better—we do not explain any more than our predecessors."

11 "To 'postulate' a proposition is no more than to hope it is true." Charles Sanders Peirce, "The Doctrine of Necessity Examined," in *Collected Papers*, ed. Charles Hartshorne, Paul Weiss, and Arthur W. Burks, vol. 6, *Scientific Metaphysics* (Cambridge, MA: Harvard University Press, 1958), 30.

12 Quentin Meillassoux, *After Finitude: An Essay on the Necessity of Contingency*, trans. Ray Brassier (London: Continuum, 2008), 1–27. Compare Gabriele Guercio, "Repositories of the Unconditional: Gino De Dominicis' *Mirror* and the Work of Art as Model of Immortality," *Res: Anthropology and Aesthetics* 55–56 (Spring–Autumn 2009): 309–10.

conventions, ideologies), "things," as De Dominicis asserts, do not *exist*. Existence is absolute, unconditional. Humans, objects, representations, and linguistically ordered signs of all kinds assume their dimensional positions only relative to each other, that is, as correlatives. When asked whether time, space, or history (recorded as image and name) "exist," De Dominicis answers "no" to each question.[13]

My reference to human existence as "correlative" nods not only to Meillassoux but also to Guercio. As he proceeds to analyze De Dominicis's work of 1988, *Specchio che tutto riflette tranne gli esseri viventi* (Mirror That Reflects Everything Except Living Beings) [IT 302], Guercio invokes the terminology of both Meillassoux and Alain Badiou, one of Meillassoux's former professors. De Dominicis's art lends itself to their line of French philosophical thought, characterized by theorization of the unconditional. An unconditional work of art acquires existence in a state outside normative structures and communicative systems of signs. As I have suggested, its position must lie beneath or beyond culture, language, and all sources of identity. Badiou theorizes the subtraction of unnamable singularities from a system established in history; Meillassoux, as we know, features ancestrality (factual existence independent of any correlative link to the subjectivity of a life-form in time and space).[14] A body engaged with art is not winding down as an aspect of its organic, entropic decay but is winding up like a timeless timer, gaining in energy rather than in disorder: "Once it is finished," De Dominicis stated in 1997, "the work must surprise me, give me back more energy than I invested in the making of it. In this way a work is 'anti-entropic' and contradicts the second law of thermodynamics. One thus reappropriates the problem of death and the immortality of the body."[15] The art-body drops out of (subtracts itself from) its place in the historical order constituted by time (dimension four), space (three), and the sign, whether pictorial (two) or linguistic-conceptual (one). By severing art from its origin in human creation and its perception in human sensibility, De Dominicis takes leave of the old social humanism, the newer romantic modernism, and current forms of cultural relativism.[16]

13   Gino De Dominicis, interview by Achille Bonito Oliva, 1992, in Franco, "Godi Cinsi Domine," 94–95.

14   Guercio, "Repositories of the Unconditional," 8–23; Alain Badiou, "On Subtraction," in *Theoretical Writings*, ed. and trans. Ray Brassier and Alberto Toscano (London: Continuum, 2004), 103–17; Meillassoux, *After Finitude*, 26–27.

15   De Dominicis, statement of 1997, in Franco, "Godi Cinsi Domine," 100. See also Guercio, "Repositories of the Unconditional," 319n27; Gino De Dominicis, "Maxims, 1969–1996," in this volume, 95.

16   Because De Dominicis regards "major" art as (ideally) operating in a zero dimension, he would seem to resolve, or at least dodge, the problem articulated by Marion Milner, who argued from a late modernist perspective that a "false picture is only avoided if we think about art in terms of its capacity for fusing, or con-fusing subject and object, seer and seen and then making a new division of these.... Clearly the great difficulty in thinking logically about this problem is due to the fact that we are trying to talk about a process which stops being that process as soon as we talk about it, trying to talk about a state in which the 'me-not-me' distinction is not important, but to do so at all we have to make the distinction." Marion Milner, *On Not Being Able to Paint* (London: Heinemann, 1957), 161. Circumventing the concerns of Milner, De Dominicis might accept the proposal of Gilles Deleuze and Félix Guattari: "The organism is that which life sets against itself in order to limit itself, and there is a life all the more intense, all the more power-

Spontaneity

Badiou and Meillassoux notwithstanding, art of no dimension directs me to their unacknowledged predecessor C. S. Peirce. Art that lacks dimension should not be linked to the one-dimensional, language-based practices of the 1960s known as Conceptual Art, nor to the conceptual gestures of the historically situated Marcel Duchamp, whose practice in four dimensions inspired speculation that many others confined to one dimension (discourse about concepts of art). Striking parallels appear when I juxtapose Peirce's cosmology to De Dominicis's notion of an "anti-entropic" art. With such art, the formulaic relation of order to disorder, expense of energy to its ultimate loss, no longer applies. "We must not confuse art with culture," De Dominicis writes, implying that culture must follow the vicissitudes of human history even as it advances historical change.[17] Culture is entropic and bears the seeds of degeneration within it. Its nature is neither free nor permanent.

De Dominicis adds two corollary notions to his statement about art and culture. First: "The visual artwork is a living thing that does not need to be seen to exist and relate to the world."[18] Contrary to Duchamp and a slew of modern theorists, no communicative interaction with human subjects is required of art, which justifies its existence through its being, not its historical significance. A work that De Dominicis conceived in 1967, *Cubo invisibile* (Invisible Cube) [IT 45], consists of a square laid out on the floor of an exhibition area. The demarcation assumes the force of a barrier, inhibiting viewers from transgressing the boundary. Because no one steps within the delineated square, this two-dimensional sign projects a three-dimensional volume, otherwise unoccupied by matter—a cubic solid, inaccessible to vision, permanently materialized (rendered physical) even in its lack of material. What may seem initially to be a pseudo-thing becomes truly a thing in the strong sense of existence. It demonstrates that its presence in the world requires no human observer; no correlative subjectivity need sense it.

De Dominicis's first corollary entails his second: "The artistic masterpiece is anti-entropic."[19] Art, "major" art, escapes the systemic degeneration into disorder that ordinarily befalls instances of order. Faithful to my immersion in De Dominicis, here I do no more than describe his position rather than explain its origin, evolution, or validity. My commentary would otherwise revert to correlation by presenting my subjective view, from within *my* history, as an understanding of *his* art. Historical interpretation causes true art to become untrue (not truly existing). It becomes dependent on the interpreter. Quotations from the artist contribute linguistic documentation, a one-dimensional slice of *world* history. They amount to no more than testimony, not proof of any proposition, whether empirically based or theoretical.

ful for being anorganic." Gilles Deleuze and Félix Guattari, *A Thousand Plateaus: Capitalism and Schizophrenia*, trans. Brian Massumi (Minneapolis, MN: University of Minnesota Press, 1987), 503.

17   De Dominicis, statement published December 9, 1996, in Franco, "Godi Cinsi Domine," 99. See also Ela Caroli, "Get Thee Behind Me, Dear Creative!" in this volume, 92.

18   Caroli, "Get Thee Behind Me," 92.

19   Ibid. See also Duccio Trombadori, "A Memo at the End of the Century," in this volume, 90.

Back to Peirce: he establishes two polar forces—chance or spontaneity and habit or law. To articulate his cosmology, he imagines a line of evolutionary transformation in both natural and human development. At one extreme is the absolute origin, which responds to spontaneity; at the other extreme is the absolute end, which responds to law. These ultimate limits are demarcations in time, space, and all dimensions that would factor into any historical account. The extremes are not elements of something otherwise less extreme; they are instead outside or apart from what they limit, as if at once continuous and discontinuous with the totality. Peirce identifies the absolute origin as "completely undetermined and dimensionless potentiality."[20] His word: *dimensionless*. The origin is "nothing, pure zero ... prior to every first.... There is no individual thing, no compulsion, outward nor inward, no law."[21] Peirce's two extremes, origin and end, correspond to the infinite past and the infinite future: "The state of things in the infinite past is chaos, tohu bohu, the nothingness of which consists in the total absence of regularity. The state of things in the infinite future is death, the nothingness of which consists in the complete triumph of law and absence of all spontaneity."[22]

As positions at infinity, the extremes cannot be reached by causal links to the past or by causal projections to the future. Such movements back or ahead would have to exceed the quantifiable limits of our four familiar dimensions. Like an infinite future, an infinite past endures forever, which is to say that it encompasses no time because it involves no change (nothing happens). This would be a past *before* any chance instance of similitude or regularity marked it with an element of form. Peirce's sense of spontaneity involves the chance convergence of some likeness within an undifferentiated, chaotic "powder of feelings," or, to invoke more of his terminology, a situation of interminable Firstness lacking the compelling consciousness of differentiation that characterizes Secondness. The likelihood of the spontaneous convergence of similar "feelings" is extremely low, but the frame for such an event to occur, a "first" event when Firstness morphs into Secondness, is infinite in extent. Statistical improbability encounters indefinite opportunity—a conceptual standoff of a type that would have appealed to De Dominicis.

The existence of a point of transition to a world measured in dimensions—temporal, spatial, representational, nominal—would seem to present a paradox. "Now you must not ask me what happened first," Peirce writes, as a logical mind retreating from the inconceivable: "But springing away from the infinitely distant past to a very, very distant past, we find al-

---

20   Charles Sanders Peirce, "The Logic of Continuity," in *Collected Papers*, vol. 6, 135.

21   Charles Sanders Peirce, "Objective Logic," in ibid., 148.

22   Charles Sanders Pers Peirce, "To Christine Ladd-Franklin, on Cosmology," in *Collected Papers*, vol. 8, *Reviews, Correspondence, and Bibliography* (Cambridge, MA: Harvard University Press, 1958), 214. Compare Peirce, "A Guess at the Riddle," in *Collected Papers*, vol. 1, *Principles of Philosophy* (Cambridge, MA: Harvard University Press, 1960), 225: "Not only substances, but events, too, are constituted by regularities. The flow of time, for example, in itself is a regularity. The original chaos, therefore, where there was no regularity, was in effect a state of mere indeterminacy, in which nothing existed or really happened." See also Peirce, "A Neglected Argument for the Reality of God," in *Collected Papers*, vol. 6, 336–37.

ready evolution had been going on for an infinitely long time.... Like had begun to produce like [and] a passable approximation to a real time was established."[23] Life or organicism as we understand it had begun, an ancestral fact that we fail to understand by the same internalization that lets us recognize that we feel alive. Here, in some philosophical dream world, Peirce meets Meillassoux, and De Dominicis encounters both.

Once inaugurated, the evolutionary history that Peirce imagined continues, despite, as he writes, "occasional lacunae and derailments." His phrasing may or may not strike a reader as facetious understatement, depending on one's attitude toward statistical improbabilities within unfathomable stretches of opportunity. Organic life evolves in the direction of regularity. Conscious minds perceive the laws of nature as they reason through these same laws in operation within themselves: "The tendency to form habits or tendency to generalize, is something which grows by its own action, by the habit of taking habits itself growing." With increasing adherence to habit, with increasing regularity, sentient life becomes ever more fixed in its form—ironically approaching the condition of brute matter, so stable as to seem perpetually immobile. Peirce writes: "I suppose matter is merely mind deadened by the development of habit."[24] The extreme sluggishness of the mentality of a stone entails that the spontaneity of an intuition would be correspondingly less likely to occur in mineral life than within the incomparably more sentient life of humans. Yet no stone known to us, present in time and space, will have reached its infinite end as pure lifeless matter; no mass of rock will be entirely lacking in some glimmer of sentient consciousness. Granite, basalt, and sandstone appear devoid of organic life only because their spontaneous stirrings occur at such improbably long intervals, "occasional lacunae" in the natural order. "We have no reason to think," Peirce argues, "that even now [after eons of evolution] time is quite perfectly continuous and uniform in its flow."[25] Nor would a habit-bound "thing," its qualities and actions as predictable as the regular passage of time, be entirely lacking in the potential for spontaneity, an aspect of its primordial being.

Mineral life, mineral existence: enter De Dominicis's stone, exhibited in 1972. Peirce might have been fascinated to have such art to consider. Entitled *Attesa di un casuale movimento molecolare generale in una sola direzione, tale da generare un movimento spontaneo della pietra* (Waiting for a Random One-Directional Molecular Movement that Could Generate a Spontaneous Movement of Material) [IT 85–89] (1969), this was one of several elements comprising the controversial *Second Solution of Immortality (The Universe Is Still)*, notably including an observer with Down syndrome (a person devoid of most theoretical preconceptions). I previously mentioned this work with respect to De Dominicis's interest in the second law of thermodynamics. The artist, his designated observer, or anyone else waiting for the stone to move would have, as the cliché puts it, "all the time in the world." The given condition of the stone from which an infinitely improbable stirring might spring is itself of infinite, immovable duration. De Dominicis created a Peircean case of statistical improbability within an unfathomable stretch of opportunity.

De Dominicis's stone is of "this world," the historical one, ordered and classified according to the dimensions that history articulates: time (four), space (three), representational image (two), identifying name (one). If the block of stone were to move in the way that De Dominicis fantasizes—but this is no fantasy, for the movement has at least *some* statistical probability—then it would violate the laws of nature, demonstrating their imperfection. No laws are perfect; the spontaneous happens. Because the type of exception that De Dominicis imagines is so rare, none occurring within a typical lifetime, the laws of nature will remain in force even if violated. Each exception nevertheless recalls those primordial instances of chance from which, paradoxically, the habits of association and regularity arise (Peirce: "like had begun to produce like").[26] What animate being would be positioned to recollect such spontaneity, ever so infrequent? A thousand-year-old man would hardly be old enough. The state of a stone lies already so far toward the extreme of deathlike regularity on the linear scale of evolution that any unanticipated movement would represent a radical reorientation of the direction of time. Could such movement register in belief, even if observed? If we were to experience something analogous, even far less of an exception to natural law, we would likely surmise that we were dreaming.

Waiting for signs of lithic animation, De Dominicis anticipates the unanticipated—or rather, the unanticipatible (we can't anticipate what never happens). Yet, the movement he awaits is no more improbable than his own immortality, which he actively seeks, proposing a pragmatic means of achieving it: "We should direct all our efforts and all our capacities (particularly scientific and technological capacities) toward this single aim.... The fear of death and aging ... was never faced with the necessary sangfroid."[27] Like spontaneous movement in brute matter, De Dominicis's immortality would reorder the dimension of time. Historical time accommodates neither a willfully autonomous stone nor an organically suspended human body that halts its aging process. Either of these potentialities would introduce an improper factor to chronological sequence—perhaps a reversal or a sideways redirection—forcing time to renegotiate its relation to substances that occupy three dimensions and to redefine the two- and one-dimensional signs that refer to both animate and inanimate being.

The projects that De Dominicis devised around the time of his "Letter" share an interest in awaiting events infinitely unlikely to occur.

26   Peirce, "To Christine Ladd-Franklin, on Cosmology," 215.
27   De Dominicis, "Letter on Immortality," 63.

His 1969 *Tentativo di far formare dei quadrati invece che dei cerchi attorno ad un sasso che cade nell'acqua* (Attempt to Form Squares Instead of Circles Around a Stone Falling Into Water) [IT 83] is comparable to his *Waiting for a Random One-Directional Molecular Movement that Could Generate a Spontaneous Movement of Material*; in both cases, success would demand that molecules of matter defy the statistical odds against their configuration in a manner opposed to the habits or laws of nature. Because the potential exists for a square ripple to appear instead of a circular one, a sufficient number of stone-throws ought to produce the desired effect, just as a sufficient number of courses of organic life, restricted to four dimensions and ending in death, ought to produce *one* that instead passes outside to become dimensionless and immortal.[28]

The laws of nature are habits to be broken. If infallible and immune to spontaneity, they would bear no differential significance, like redness never broken by greenness. In the wake of innumerable stone throws, testing the law, De Dominicis's square ripple would occur only with infinite infrequency.[29] The average number of occurrences over a block of infinite time—hard to imagine as countable because of the infinitely long intervals separating such events—might be so minute an infinitesimal quantity that its one-dimensional linguistic approximation would have to be "none" or (as I've already suggested) "never." We wait and wait, but it never happens. Yet "never" is absolute. The desired occurrence, statistically possible, might be better described as "occasional"—here I recall Peirce's phrasing, "occasional lacunae," of which a square ripple would surely be one. Ever so slightly, this anomaly would retard the chronological advance of the laws of nature, "never" to be completely realized so long as life as Peirce conceived of it continued, whether within the dimensions of cumulative history or subtracting itself out. What is an occasion other than a chance occurrence? De Dominicis was playing with chance.

In 1968–69, De Dominicis projected his *Palla di gomma (caduta da 2 metri) nell'attimo immediatamente precedente il rimbalzo* (Rubber Ball [Falling from a Height of Two Meters] in the Moment Right Before Bouncing Back) [IT 70]. His one-dimensional title suits the two-dimensional photographic propagation of this conceptual project, which removes or subtracts the object from its history within three-dimensional space and four-dimensional time. The titled ball can be depicted as two-dimensional or materialized as three-dimensional. A material ball in the environment of a gallery possesses physicality analogous to that of a stone. An exhibition visitor might await the chance redistribution of the molecules of the ball, anticipating that the object would rise, as if completing a bounce. Given time and space, it could happen. Conceived as a bouncing ball, the object subtracts

---

28   If Jesus of Nazareth was the one—or the One—De Dominicis's art would have generated a scientific account of the theological construct.

29   Note the reference to "infinite infrequency" in Peirce, "The Doctrine of Necessity Examined," 41: "By thus admitting pure spontaneity or life as a character of the universe … producing infinitesimal departures from law continually, and great ones with infinite infrequency, I account for all the variety and diversity of the universe."

itself from time by moving infinitely slowly. Released from correlation with history—its bounce invisible within the course of a mortal human life—the ball, this thing, "exists."

Peirce reasoned that the evolution of life entailed not only that chance or spontaneity continue to affect the course of events, but also that habit assert dominance over chance occurrence. The logic of De Dominicis followed a deviant path. He expected—or acted on the faith—that spontaneity would regain dominance over habit and natural law, arresting the hyperbolic inversion of the two forces as Peirce imagined their interaction (nearly all spontaneity in the infinite past, nearly all habit in the infinite future). Under a De Dominicis regime, material objects would acquire existence as things that truly existed. The hen could take a walk. And all aspects of the human (body, mind, soul) would regain any energy lost to entropy—all toward achieving immortality.

This essay was commissioned for the present volume. The author thanks Donato Loia, John Semlitsch, and Todd Bradway for essential aid in research.

Between Eternity
and Impermanence

Gabriele Guercio

One of Gino De Dominicis's earliest works, *Il tempo lo sbaglio lo spazio* (Time, Mistake, Space) [IT 95] (1969), consists of a human skeleton wearing roller skates and holding onto the leash of a canine skeleton. If an academically trained art historian were tempted to connect this work to the Robert Rauschenberg performance *Pelican* (1963), in which the artist skates while donning a pair of wings, then De Dominicis could be interpreted as mocking the invasive ascendancy of American art in his native country.[1] However, if asked, De Dominicis would tell a different story: that the titular "mistake" refers to humanity's compulsive attempts to extend the limited time we have on this planet by accelerating our traversal of space.[2] The mistake is, quite simply, living according to teleological narratives of progress and civilizing expansion aided by supplementary tools that augment bodies and minds. The roller skates are prosthetics that distinguish us from animals by interweaving nature and technology. Yet as the artwork mercilessly shows, it makes no difference; mortality spares neither dog nor man.

Although *Time, Mistake, Space* is motivated by defiance, it is not necessarily just in defiance of contemporary art. Its defiance is aimed at the overall mentality of modernity, in which time is regarded as a resource that must be mastered, exploited, and capitalized.[3] While the roots of the idea that time itself is a historically active force can be traced to the seventeenth century, it becomes increasingly widespread after the Second World War when economic growth was unanimously deemed the chief source of

1   *Pelican* was first performed at Concert of Dance Number Five, an evening of performances by Judson Dance Theater at the Pop Festival, Washington, DC, May 9, 1963. See, among others, Steve Paxton, "Rauschenberg for Cunningham and Three of His Own," in *Robert Rauschenberg: A Retrospective*, ed. Walter Hopps and Susan Davidson (New York: Solomon R. Guggenheim Museum, 1997), 260–67. In 1964 the artist was awarded an honorary Golden Lion for painting at the 32nd Venice Biennale. American critics supportive of neo-avant-garde trends explained the victory in terms of artistic preeminence, but Europeans felt quite differently. Pierre Cabanne, for instance, took the episode as evidence of America's attempt to colonize Europe. In Italy, the liberal magazine *ABC* complained that, "Everything is lost. Even a sense of shame." See Laurie J. Monahan, "Cultural Cartography: American Designs at the 1964 Venice Biennale," in *Reconstructing Modernism: Art in New York, Paris, and Montreal 1945–1964*, ed. Serge Guilbaut (Cambridge, MA: MIT Press, 1990), 369–416.

2   Gino De Dominicis, conversation with the author, March 1996.

3   As Reinhart Koselleck has observed, in the second half of the seventeenth century time ceased to act as a neutral container of the stories and began to acquire a historical value itself: human adventure was no longer accomplished *in* time but *thanks to* time, whose dynamic character showed itself as a historically active force. See Reinhart Koselleck, *Vergangene Zukunft: Zur Semantik geschichtlicher Zeiten* (Frankfurt am Main: Suhrkamp Verlag, 1979). Recently Koselleck's view has been reconsidered among historians, who have indicated the coexistence of various regimes of historicity in modern and contemporary time. See, for example, François Hartog, *Régimes d'historicité. Présentisme et expériences* (Paris: Points, 2015). The risk of acceleration (anathema to De Dominicis) remains a key issue among these historians; see Hartmut Rosa, *Beschleunigung: Die Veränderung der Zeitstrukturen in der Moderne* (Frankfurt am Main: Suhrkamp Verlag, 2012).

global change, and consumerism, marketing, and financial gain were taken as the key means of furthering modernization. In the West, a trust in unlimited productivity galvanized politicians, radical artists, and businesspeople alike as they repeatedly broadcast their conviction that the world was being peaceably knit together by capitalism and technology.

Time, Mistake, Space was subsequently altered in its composition; the skeleton balances a golden rod mysteriously on its index finger. Rods are discrete and recurring artworks in their own right,[4] but the addition of a rod to the skeleton extends the work's original meaning. While the first version objected to the prominence given to changeability and becoming, the addition of the rod connects the image of death to art. It is as if death itself were actually the outcome of the mistake—as if our mistaken attempts to manipulate time and have it at our disposal have turned us into mortal beings. Conversely, art stands apart. Epitomized by the golden rod, it points to a perfection with no referent in nature—no laws of physics can explain why the rod stands as it does, nor could the sculptural artifice have been predicted in advance, since the nascence of its form coincides with its creation. Equally revealing, the rod outlasts the man and the dog: juxtaposed with their remains, it embodies a vector of time that belongs solely to itself, a way of being that challenges finitude and dispenses with becoming.

The arrangement of the rod and two skeletons raises the question of whether art should be understood as that which could amend the titular mistake. At that time, death and immortality were on De Dominicis's mind. His "Letter on Immortality" (1970) argues that, "for things to truly exist, they must be eternal, immortal" rather than "mere occurrences of certain possibilities." The same goes for human beings; they must stop in time and thus finally begin to live. As for the topic of death, for his first solo show at L'Attico, Rome, De Dominicis crafted a funerary poster announcing both the exhibition and his own demise, made to resemble those customarily used in Italy, especially the South, to alert people of someone's passing and to provide the date of their funeral (*Manifesto mortuario* [Necrology (Mortuary Poster)] [IT 73] [1969]). Although in this announcement there is no direct allusion to the works on view, it suggests that the inaugural moment of De Dominicis's career coincides with his departure from worldly affairs. It would seem to imply that the making of the artworks went hand-in-hand with their author's initiatory death and transference to another realm. In fact, some of those works achieve in the artistic domain what the "Letter" auspicates: the possibility of stopping in time and breaking "the spell cast by the most mysterious dimension prevailing in the universe."

Art and Immortality

It was not until 1972 that De Dominicis explicitly linked art to the idea of conquering death. In his paradigmatic work made for the 36th Venice Biennale, *Seconda soluzione d'immortalità (l'universo è immo-*

---

4 See, for example, *Asta in bilico (Equilibrio 1)* (Suspended Rod) [Equilibrium 1] [IT 47] (1967), in this volume, no. 2, 223.

bile) (Second Solution of Immortality [The Universe Is Still]) [IT 150], the participation of a youth affected by Down syndrome, Paolo Rosa, provoked a scandal and subsequent censorship, but it was precisely because of the unfathomable nature of Rosa's lived experiences that the three works in front of him, which had previously been exhibited at L'Attico, created a sense of absolute stillness.[5] These works were the stone (*Attesa di un casuale movimento molecolare generale in una sola direzione, tale da generare un movimento spontaneo della pietra* [Waiting for a Random One-Directional Molecular Movement that Could Generate a Spontaneous Movement of Material] [IT 85–89] [1969]), the ball (*Palla di gomma (caduta da 2 metri) nell'attimo immediatamente precedente il rimbalzo* [Rubber Ball [Falling from a Height of Two Meters] in the Moment Right Before Bouncing Back] [IT 70] [1968–69]), and the square (*Cubo invisibile* [Invisible Cube] [IT 45] [1967]). Together the works conjure a time outside evolution and irreversibility, a space immune to movement determined by causation or by the will of human or divine agents. The whole setting evinced what would become the central belief of De Dominicis's oeuvre—namely, that artworks are models for achieving immortality of the body.

Such a belief does not pertain to art in general, or to any generic creative output, but instead to a precise understanding of the visual arts. Years later, in 1995, De Dominicis cogently summarized this point when he claimed that "every artistic expression springs from a unique outlook and desire," and that painting, sculpture, and architecture "are immobile, material, and mute, arising from a refusal to accept decay and death. They create forms that do not submit to time, and therefore institute and perpetuate the yearning for immortality."[6] Across remote civilizations and cultures, image-making has been tied to transience, death, and the enigma of afterlife. It suffices to recall that, in two accounts of the origin of art found in *Natural History* (35.15 and 35.43), Pliny the Elder connects the birth of artistic representation to the desire to create everlasting likenesses, which can overcome spatial and temporal gaps and defy the caducity of human existence.[7] De Dominicis's statement goes further; it raises the prospect of yet another kind of understanding, one in which images themselves can be thought of as conveying a protocol for human immortality.

5   In these 1960 works, De Dominicis's practice partly corroborates a key insight of art critic and historian Cesare Brandi, according to whom art is pure "presentness" or *astanza*: whether the artist is Giotto or Alberto Burri, through a work of art's very emergence, it is something extremely real and yet withdrawn, isolated, and bracketed with regard to this or that determined empirical realm. Brandi's writings are quite numerous; see, among others, *Carmine o della Pittura* (Rome: Scialoja, 1945), *Segno e Immagine* (Milan: Il Saggiatore, 1960), and *Le due vie* (Bari: Laterza, 1966).

6   Gino De Dominicis, "Maxims, 1969–1996," in this volume, 95.

7   Pliny reports that Butades, a potter of Sicyon, invented clay portraiture because his daughter, in love with a young man who was going abroad, drew in outline on a wall the shadow of his face thrown by a lamp. Butades pressed clay on the outline and made a relief, which he hardened by exposure to fire, thus creating a lasting semblance of the youth. Previously Pliny had noted that the art of painting was said to have begun with tracing someone's shadow, thus positively ascribing to images the peculiar ability to compensate for absence, if not death, by preserving someone's effigy. See Pliny, *Natural History*, trans. H. Rackham (Cambridge, MA: Harvard University Press, 2003), vol. IX, Books 33–35, 271–73, and 371–73.

From Leonardo to Lessing and after, artistic culture in Europe has seen a number of claims about the primacy of vision, variously aimed at establishing the merits of painting, sculpture, and architecture, and of images in general, both autonomously as well as in comparison to literature and poetry. With De Dominicis, however, the claim takes an unusual turn. What is at stake is not the aesthetic appeal of a medium per se, or the equation of artistic expressivity with certain materials, and it is even less concerned with the advocacy of an overarching notion of "visual culture" versus any reductive definition of art or artistry.

While he shares Giorgio de Chirico's belief that "all existing things and phenomena seen by man left their mark on his spirit in the form of images, before words were found to name them,"[8] De Dominicis maintains that the visual arts should be understood as hinting at a precise, human aspiration. By virtue of their being still, extant, and silent, the visual arts can intimate the urge to become immortal. Although the elixir of life was not disclosed in the Venice exhibition, its "solution" not being definitively inferred, De Dominicis's works do inspire fresh insights into the nature of artistic phenomena. They demonstrate that artworks may introduce the concept of timelessness in a world that does not know of it. In their own right, artworks can engender the new beginning described in the "Letter," the event that allows humanity to "stop in time" and "begin to live." By holding so firmly to this central thought, De Dominicis's poetics of immortality offers an opportunity to explore how and why the visual arts may claim the primacy of eternity over impermanence even if we cannot learn about bodily immortality itself from the artist.[9] No longer relegated to the realm of religion and mysticism, the "eternal" can be experienced as a localized, immanent quality that defines being both in human and nonhuman forms. This experience is intimately related to art; it fosters the intuition that immortality is not necessarily a privilege reserved for deities, a promise to be fulfilled at the end of time, or an achievement possible only for the wealthy elite. Rather, immortality may be something that can happen to anyone who becomes aware of the freedom to start something anew, in ways reminiscent of the leap that, at some point, made us "human," "thinking," and "mortal."

---

8   See Giorgio de Chirico, *Il meccanismo del pensiero: Critica, polemica, autobiografia 1911–1943*, ed. Maurizio Fagiolo (Turin: Einaudi, 1985), 408–12.

9   There are three fairly widespread meanings of the term *eternity*, namely: a time without beginning or end, or everlasting; a dimension that transcends time entirely and is separate from it; and a state that includes time but precedes and exceeds it. Eternity is therefore described either in terms of infinite duration in both directions, or in terms of complete absence of time: it comes into conflict with infinity, especially in its implication of an estrangement from the becoming of things. See Carlos Eire, *A Very Brief History of Eternity* (Princeton, NJ: Princeton University Press, 2010); Charles J. Caes, *Beyond Time: Ideas of the Great Philosophers on Eternal Existence and Immortality* (Lanham, MD: University Press of America, 1985); J. M. Bering and D. F. Bjorklund, "The Natural Emergence of Reasoning About the Afterlife as a Developmental Regularity," in *Developmental Psychology* 40, no. 2 (March 2004): 217–33; Pierre Chaunu, *La mémoire de l'éternité* (Paris: Éditions Robert Laffont, 1975); and Julian Barbour, *The End of Time: The Next Revolution in Physics* (London: Phoenix, 2000). See also Yitzhak Y. Melamed, ed., *Eternity* (Oxford: Oxford University Press, 2016).

<u>Universal Stillness</u>

Announced first in *Time, Mistake, Space*, eternity and impermanence became even more present in the *Second Solution* which distinguished itself by the novel juxtaposition of objects and a person. For however short a time before his presence sparked a scandal, Rosa gazed at the three works on the ground and at the Biennale's visitors, prompting them to meet his eyes and look toward where he was looking. In this exchange of glances, something shifts out of place, some communication is cut off; it is a seeing that never translates into knowing but is, rather, the discovery of a radical divide. Looking at Rosa, one is thrust into a space-time that neither contains nor envisions us. Our experience of him is undefinable, as is his inscrutable figure; we are not able to discern any particular mood, attitude, or familiar perceptual characteristic; we do not know precisely what it is we have in common with him in our "response" to the artwork. There does not seem to be any shared notion of the world, or common ground; we are plunged into the same void that we encounter when we try to engage his mesmerizing gaze.

Rosa introduces the possibility of seeing without seeing ourselves, that is, without depending on any given historical accounts, cultural frames, or narcissistic complacencies that may be entailed in the recognition of a specific visible "object." Arguably, this mode of seeing is congenial to the three artworks in front of him. Their titles identify them as independent entities: they suggest that the stone will move of its own accord, that the ball is there in order to bounce, and that an invisible cube rests on the ground. Each of these three works upsets the divisions between immobility and duration, causation and chance, being and nonbeing. The cube is invisible, yet occupies the space and volume outlined by the white paint; the ball is clearly on the ground, yet once we read the title of the piece, it is as if it were already in the air; the stone is subject to gravity, yet random molecular fluxes could make it shift position. Not only are the works presented as being capable of inner animation, but, also, each refers to a space-time of its own. It is difficult to reduce them or compare them to anything that came before.

Rosa is their warden in that, while granting their invisible, nontemporal, and miraculous aspects, he vouches for the fact that the stone, ball, and cube are pure "singularities" and irreducibly themselves.[10] By maintaining stillness and impeding the arbitrary projections of exterior meanings, the *Seconda soluzione* indicates that, in the visual arts, the time in which the work comes into existence or is contemplated by a viewer may be as unimportant as the date on which a mathematical or geometrical theorem is discovered. Thus, at the specific juncture when an artwork makes its appearance, every tie between cumulative time and the work vanishes or buckles.

10   I am taking the term "singularity" from Gilles Deleuze, "Fifteenth Series of Singularities," in *Logic of Sense* (New York: Columbia University Press, 1990), 100–108; and "À quoi reconnaît-on le structuralisme?," in *Histoire de la philosophie*, vol. 8, *Le XXe siècle*, ed. François Châtelet (Paris: Hachette, 1973), 299–335. For a more in-depth analysis of singularity in the works of Gino De Dominicis, see my *L'arte non evolve. L'universo immobile di Gino De Dominicis* (Monza: Johan & Levi, 2015).

However, rather than denying the historicity of existence, art-making may instead disclose the eternal inside the boundaries of the human condition. It is not so much that past, present, and future ought to be seen as if bracketed within eternity, but that eternity can trespass into time. A work of art is an example of this trespass because it marks a beginning, a radically unprecedented novelty, and therefore epitomizes, in the here and now, what is timeless. The two concurrent operations the *Second Solution* announced in the year 1972 are the withdrawal of itself from the realm of impermanence and the allowing of eternity to slip into time and persist within it. By offering glimpses of a universe sealed in stillness, it suggests that creating a work, lingering before it, and recognizing that it is looking back at us, are experiences that can prepare us for the revolution of bodies and minds that the human species has imagined as immortality.

Subtraction, Parallax, Resurrection

Individually and as a whole, Rosa and the three works appear "subtracted" and in parallax from any point of view anchored to a predefined world. This is key in De Dominicis's oeuvre. It corroborates the belief that, as it brings about a rift in space-time that makes the dimensions of viewer and viewed seem disconnected from each other, an artwork not only appears "objective" and unaltered over time but also fosters and perpetuates the desire to exist now and forever.

A culmination of this modus operandi is marked by *Specchio che tutto riflette tranne gli esseri viventi* (Mirror That Reflects Everything Except Living Beings) [IT 302], a work conceived in 1969 but built and then destroyed in 1988 at Galleria Lia Rumma in Naples.[11] However, there is a second paradigmatic work, realized in 1977 and first exhibited in 1983 at Paolo Sprovieri's gallery in Rome, where subtraction and parallax are connected to concepts of resurrection (*Immagine della dea sumera Warka* [Image of the Sumerian Goddess Warka] [IT 189] [1977–83]).[12] The work consists of an enlarged color photograph which the artist modified using oil paint, depicting the so-called *Mask of Warka*, a female head sculpted out of alabaster (currently in the National Museum of Iraq in Baghdad) that represents the Lady of Uruk. Scholars tend to believe that the Lady of Uruk is Inanna, the Sumerian goddess of fertility, love, and war. The sculpture was discovered in 1938–39 in the Eanna temple district of Uruk and is dated to the late fourth millennium BCE.[13]

32

28

11   See Gabriele Guercio, "The Ancestral Objection," in this volume, 128–39.

12   This work is also known by the phrase which appeared on the invitation card for De Dominicis's 1983 exhibition at Galleria Sprovieri: "*Era estate, una notte mia figlia disse: 'L'arte moderna fa ridere i polli, l'arte antica li rattrista, l'Arte li fa piangere' poi ci baciammo a lungo in bocca*" ("It was summer, one night my daughter said to me: 'Modern art could make the chickens laugh, ancient art could make them sad, Art could make them weep' then we shared a long, passionate kiss"). The title itself gestures to interesting parallels between art-making, the search for immortality, and incest. For the full discussion of this point, see Guercio, *L'arte non evolve*.

13   Archaeologist André Parrot describes the *Mask of Warka* as "one of those masterworks of sculpture that, defying explanation, stand supreme on their own merits." See André Parrot, *Sumer: The Dawn of Art*, ed. André Malraux and Georges Salles, trans. Stuart Gilbert and James Emmons (New York: Golden Press, 1961), 86. There was nothing nostalgic about De

Since the *Mask of Warka*'s eyes have been lost, the artist performs an act of restitution by painting two huge, bloodshot blue irises and giving form and life back to the Lady's gaze. Where the photo made the particular and unrepeatable likeness of the *Mask of Warka* repeatable indefinitely, De Dominicis's pictorial intervention breaks the link between the photographed object and the photograph of the object. It brings the ancient effigy back to a state of pure reality, inviolate and unique.

Assuming that the Lady does come back to life, the new painted image interweaves the living and the dead, the animate eyes and stony head. It is as if the work exists on two planes at once, or perhaps nowhere at all, raising a number of questions: Is life more intense in the here and now, in front of the painting, or in a "then" that, through the painting of the photograph, mysteriously returns in spite of death? Should its beginning be sought in the era of the Sumerians, or in the moment ushered in by the introduction of the two bloodshot eyes? Do those eyes mean that the ancient head has come back to life? Or, on the contrary, has it always been alive, and do those eyes revealed by the artist attest to its immortality?

Arguably, the *Mask of Warka* emerges on different dimensional planes because of a gap created by the work itself. It is noteworthy that when it was first exhibited, the repainted Sumerian effigy was placed in an inaccessible room and visible through a peephole which forced viewers to see the work using only one eye.[14] This perceptual mode enacts a parallax, where an object changes position depending on the location from which it is observed, which is what happens when one looks at the same thing while alternating opened and closed eyes.[15] De Dominicis's staging meant that, through an angular shift, the painted photo and the woman could be captured from two coplanar viewpoints. But is the original body or likeness returning to presence, or must this origin be regarded as omnipresent, just as the woman is immortal?

It would seem that she can achieve a second life either as a repetition (an infinite resurfacing of identity or returning to presence) or as a parallactic emergence (an eternal, omnipresent identity). With the former option, if one accepts transmigration as an infinite repetition of the same,

Dominicis's growing interest in Sumerian civilization during the 1970s, which was fueled by more personal considerations linked to the figure of Gilgamesh. De Dominicis was impressed by the inventiveness of the Sumerians, who were a step ahead of later civilizations in many fields, from the organization of cities to education, trade, and the transmission of knowledge. On the Sumerians, see, among others, Giovanni Pettinato, *La saga di Gilgamesh* (Milan: Rusconi, 1992); Giovanni Pettinato, *I Sumeri* (Milan: Rusconi, 1994); and Harriet Crawford, ed., *The Sumerian World* (New York: Routledge, 2013). It is worth noting, on the other hand, that De Dominicis was also fascinated by the pseudo-archaeological theories of Zecharia Sitchin (1920–2010), a scholar of Semitic and Sumerian languages who developed the theory of the "ancient astronaut," which attributes the creation of the Sumerian civilization to an alien race which supposedly came to Earth from a hypothetical twelfth planet found in Babylonian mythology. See, by Sitchin, the *Earth Chronicles* series, especially *The Twelfth Planet* (Rochester, VT: Bear & Company, 1991) and *The King Who Refused to Die: The Anunnaki and the Search for Immortality* (Santa Fe, NM: Bear & Company, 2013).

14   One is reminded of Marcel Duchamp's *Étant donnés* (1946–66); however, viewers are able to look at Duchamp's final work with both eyes simultaneously.

15   On the notion of the "parallactic gap," see Kojin Karatani, *Transcritique: On Kant and Marx*, trans. Sabu Kohso (Cambridge, MA: MIT Press, 2003). See also Slavoj Žižek, *The Parallax View* (Cambridge, MA: MIT Press, 2006).

then it follows that the ancient likeness has (re)arisen in another segment of time. Its postmortem replica, crafted and staged by the artist, proves its incipient bodily resurrection.[16] But it could also be that the Lady never died and has always remained immobile and impervious to becoming because, if seen in parallax, from an alternative perspective, she inhabits another perennial present that intersects with our own.

The Lady of Uruk may belong to infinite time and so is resurrected after her long withdrawal from secular time, or she may be eternal and so represent the prototype of an immortal life that allows her to be there as well as in a multiplicity of coextensive presents. But rather than antagonizing or contrasting the infinite and the eternal (the resurrection and the parallax), De Dominicis's work positions them side by side. The transformed likeness of the Lady of Uruk suggests that both the infinite and the eternal, each in its own way, are ideas that respond to the need to detect realms unaffected by the impermanence of the here and now, a discovery that can galvanize the desire to reconstitute oneself after death.

This reconstitution may be seen as both the theme and aim of the work. There is an analogy between the sculpted head, the Sumerian goddess, the repainted photo, and the work itself. It inspires the thought that, by means of subtraction, parallax view, and the resurrection of original forms, certain artworks could reclaim the right to emerge in a given context—historical, art historical, etc.—without establishing any contiguity, continuity, or reflection and without fulfilling expectations or following predetermined criteria of intelligibility. They could instead generate breaks and unbridgeable gulfs between themselves and everything else. A work of visual art embodying an image that aspires to remain as it is, in a realm parallel yet asymmetrical to our own, be it a painting, drawing, sculpture, or piece of architecture, manifests a time that cannot be calculated in relation to bodily change or measured through the cycles of nature, or an organism's birth, growth, deterioration, and death. Identifying an artwork implies seeing and understanding an entity that has an independent psychic reality, and whose values, truths, and meanings are made by and for humans in ways such that they stand in this moment as they stood in the beginning and will forever. An important corollary to the view that the artworks, in some sense, re-evoke and actualize the enigma of the beginning of all things is that there is no reason to classify or conceive of past artistic phenomena as something remote and separate from us. In the view of De Dominicis:

16   This hypothesis reiterates problems faced in the ancient Jewish and Christian traditions, where scholars debate the possible continuity between the body that dies and that which rises, or, on the contrary, whether the latter is of a different nature from the former and its (re)appearance at the end of time is conditional on divine intervention. On the dichotomy between the immortality of the soul (for the Greeks) and the resurrection of the dead (for Christians and Jews), see the still valuable collection of texts *Immortality and Resurrection: Four Essays by Oscar Cullmann, H. A. Wolfson, Werner Jaeger and Henry J. Cadbury*, ed. Krister Stendhal (New York: Macmillan, 1965). On resurrection, see Caroline Walker Bynum, *The Resurrection of the Body in Western Christianity, 200–1336* (New York: Columbia University Press, 1993); James H. Charlesworth, *Resurrection: The Origin and Future of a Biblical Doctrine* (New York: T & T Clark, 2006); and Charles S. Duthie, ed., *Resurrection and Immortality: A Selection from the Drew Lectures on Immortality* (London: Samuel Bagster, 1979).

All works of art are contemporary. Otherwise, it would be like seeing a car from the 1920s approaching and deciding to cross the street anyway, thinking that you couldn't be run over because the car is from another era. But that's not how things are. And for the work of art it is the same thing: it is always "live."[17]

No longer bound to an art historical progression of styles, techniques, and concerns, let alone to the discourses of their eras, artworks partake in the millenary epic of humanity, expressing its hope for the absolute and serving as possible sites of subtraction, parallax, and resurrection with respect to the time and evolution of specific cultures and histories.[18]

Advocating the contemporaneity of artworks is hardly tantamount to faith in the possibility of a sort of artistic transcendence from the burdens of the human condition. De Dominicis's practice does not aim for the end of history or attempt to revive a worldview based on the intuition of abiding and sacred principles. His works tend to veer away from the orbit of Western modernity, with its materialistic, scientific, and technological tenets and confidence in the unending augmentation and subjugation of resources. At the same time, his works seem to endorse an optimistic belief in a "new era," in the freedom to invent a new way for the species to dwell on Earth and beyond. An artwork exemplifies this engendering whenever it entails both the creation and safeguarding of images, meanings, truths, and values, which open the historical dimension and inspire the species to reorient itself away from the transient and toward the permanent.

The Living Artwork

As implied by the poster that announced De Dominicis's death, the biography of an artist may be irrelevant. It is another life that truly matters, one that is embedded in the artworks. De Dominicis claims that "a perfect living object, a work of art can have an influence upon biological processes."[19] His understanding of the visual arts corroborates an arcane concept, traceable to the civilization from which he drew part of his inspiration. Sumerians attributed to images and artifacts a multidimensional capacity for action, considering them far from inanimate things—entities full

17   De Dominicis, "Maxims, 1969–1996," 95.

18   De Dominicis's separation of artworks from their historical dimensions needs further clarification. Notions of artistic progress and contextuality were challenged in two influential books published in the 1980s, Arthur C. Danto's *The Transfiguration of the Commonplace* (1981) and Hans Belting's *The End of the History of Art?* (1983). A split occurs between art, history, and art history because, according to Danto, the collapse of aesthetic ideals after Duchamp made it impossible to distinguish art from everyday objects and, according to Belting, because artworks are not amenable to historical description and contemporary artists refuse to be part of a unified history of art. In terms of the poetics of immortality, however, there are other reasons to defy a link between art and history. Rather than indicating, as in Belting and Danto, a saturation point or epilogue soon to be followed by a new stage of development, the rift between art and history suggests that there is no artistic evolution. Moreover, De Dominicis's anti-evolutionary position is far removed from avant-garde ideology. His aversion to the mythos of modernity makes it comparable, if anything, to the thesis of a prophetic essay by Cesare Brandi, *La fine dell'avanguardia* (The End of the Avant-Garde, 1949), which proclaimed the inevitable exhaustion of an artistic outlook bent on glorifying progress to the extent that anyone not at the cutting edge is charged with being reactionary or outside of history.

19   De Dominicis, "Maxims, 1969–1996," 96.

of life and therefore capable of acting in reality.[20] For De Dominicis, the art-work is "anti-entropic" and contradicts the second law of thermodynamics, which postulates the irreversibility of many phenomena, such as the passage of heat from a warm body to a cold one.[21] If entropy provides evidence to support the perception of time, artworks inspire experiences and cognitions that seem to contradict, if not halt, this perception. They are pure excess, exceeding the means employed and supplying more energy than was needed to make them. Not only are they endowed with lifelike qualities of their own, but they can also give life to things that might not have been, or might have been different from what they are now. In their presence, one may receive the neat impression that what was not there, now is. Lacking any specific precedent, a work may constitute or touch upon something unknown, surprising, yet incomprehensible in the discourse predominant in the realm where the work emerges, thereby affecting the situation so that it can never be the same. The work's ubiquitous, multidimensional character introduces timeless themes and questions into a domain habituated by transience and irreversibility.

Artistic practice can therefore aim at the creation and transmigration of perennial identities. Paolo Rosa and the Lady of Uruk are two instances of this: the former because of his inscrutability and the stillness he sanctions, and the latter because of her spatiotemporal pervasiveness. But there is more. During the 1980s, De Dominicis's oeuvre is populated with half-human and half-divine figures, harbingers of possible biological mutations and simultaneously the custodians of ancient knowledge. Their likenesses sometimes have a deformed, fanciful appearance and sometimes blend Eastern and Western facial features or gender characteristics. In any case, they are "monstrous" icons, prodigiously composed of anthropomorphic and artificial elements. For instance, the purple and yellow figure on the black background of *Senza titolo* (Untitled) [IT 265] (1985) has for a nose a three-dimensional cone (modeled from painted clay) half as long as its entire body; flattened out by a yellow garment, the figure itself would lack any thickness or solidity were it not for the angle of its right arm, which reaches into its garment toward its breast, suggesting some kind of depth, and perhaps even

40

20   Irene J. Winter has indicated that, in the early Sumerian texts, the construal agent/patient supplants that of subject/object so that language can accord agency to a temple or a statue and suggest the outward effects of an object projected into the world. See Irene J. Winter, "Agency Marked, Agency Ascribed: The Affective Object in Ancient Mesopotamia," in *Art's Agency and Art History*, ed. Robin Osborne and Jeremy Tanner (Oxford: Blackwell, 2007), 42–69. The ascription of agency to images and artifacts, characteristic of cultures that predate Western modernity, is also pivotal for a radical rethinking of the anthropology of art; see Alfred Gell, *Art and Agency: An Anthropological Theory* (Oxford: Oxford University Press, 1998).

21   On more than one occasion, De Dominicis took this law to task. In 1972 he organized a cocktail party at Palazzo Taverna in Rome to celebrate the overthrow of entropy. His hypothesis, as presented in a text on that occasion, was as follows: "If everyone could imagine and desire their own salvation, the preservation of their body for eternity, that would mean that finally there would be no mental dispersion (entropy). Therefore, the 'second principle of thermodynamics' would no longer be valid, because it would be contradicted by the behavior of an organism that can project, without distraction (entropy), its own eternal condition as an 'isolated system.'" See Miriam Mirolla, "Immortality," in this volume, 74.

the extraordinary power to touch its own heart with its hand. Its looming snout points toward the ground, while a single big eye stares out from the center of a head topped by a crown, thus making the entire figure reminiscent of the likeness of Queen Puabi found in the Royal Cemetery at Ur. The regal ornament and extraordinary nature of the figure adds to its aura. Balanced between ancestral pasts and suspended futures, generative roots and uncharted routes ahead, the effigy in *Untitled* appears to recapitulate, catalyze, and project the image of a species that is not entirely of this world but doesn't completely transcend it either.

Are these specimens of unidentified forms of life summoned into existence by way of the artworks? Can an artist endeavor to turn inanimate materials into something alive? De Dominicis is not alone in this grand pursuit. From the Sumerian belief in the agency of objects and pictures to the myth of Pygmalion in classical antiquity, from Petrarch and Michelangelo to Picasso, from the Pacific art that inspired Paul Gauguin and Henri Matisse to the masks of native Alaskans, the making and the appraisal of drawing, painting, and sculpture have intermittently stirred the desire to value a work for its degree of aliveness, for its capacity to stand out as a living entity, even if by means other than those proper to organic life. This tendency has not been exclusively concerned with commending artistic powers of depiction, naturalism, or imagination, but rather with establishing a symmetrical relationship between art and life, human and natural agencies, whereby, just as the characteristics and values of life are ascribed to the work or recognizable in it, the properties and meanings of art can be interchangeably ascribed to life or recognizable in it.

De Dominicis's stance contributes to both the unraveling and furthering of some of the implications of that symmetrical relationship by inviting us to look afresh at the penchant for a "living art." Admittedly, the study and individuation of bodily postures, attitudes, and emotions were not always intended to improve artistry per se. They reflect a need to reclaim the freedom to (re)invent the corporeal domain according to its organic, anthropocentric, and supernatural components alike. That artworks may carry and irradiate life depends not so much upon their faithful representations of external data as on their provision of models able to enhance common psychic processes and increase the qualitative awareness with which one usually understands oneself, others, and the world. The transfiguration of data by a surplus of physical and mental energies also dignifies the human species, even if only implicitly. This transfiguration indicates a self-determination to initiate unexpected turns in the course of its planetary existence. Whether represented as if in motion or in stasis, the body presented by an artwork is in itself a meaningful carrier of volitions, thoughts, and emotions. With De Dominicis, the possibility of a human transubstantiation made viable by art registers a new twist. It is the creative act, the very predilection for images versus other means of expression, such as words or sounds, which takes unprecedented significance with regard to the corporeal domain.

Whose Immortality?

The Epic of Gilgamesh (ca. 2600 BCE) may be the prototypical text narrating a quest for bodily immortality, but in subsequent cultures and religions immortality assumes another cluster of meanings.[22] While ancient Greek philosophers believed solely in the survival of the soul, the three major monotheistic religions—Judaism, Christianity, and Islam—surmise that immortality is achieved through the resurrection of the body at the end of time. Eastern doctrines such as Hinduism and Buddhism maintain that immortal souls depart from the body, linger momentarily in an incorporeal state, and may eventually adhere to a new body at the time of birth, thus undergoing cycles of reincarnation.

De Dominicis fully advocated Gilgamesh's rebellion against the doom of bodily mortality. He was convinced that the hero was not only a king who stubbornly searched for the plant of life, but an artist.[23] Along with thinking of immortality in a corporeal sense, De Dominicis imagines it as an event that ought to affect individuals as well as the species as a whole. His universalizing intent is explicit in the "Letter" and in his *Biglietto d'auguri* (Greeting Card for the Immortality of the Body [1971]) [IT 140] that wishes "everyone" immortality. Just as Gilgamesh eventually loses the miraculous plant that erases death—a snake steals it—De Dominicis produces no unequivocal formula that would allow one to live forever. Nonetheless, the association he draws between immortality and the visual arts in the *Second Solution* is unique in that, through the figure of Paolo Rosa, it cogently speaks of both human nature and artistic creation. Supposing, however, that works of visual art can intimate that human beings are not meant to suffer death or entropy, do they also make it possible to imagine the emergence of a new immortal human species?

For answers, one must return to Paolo Rosa. Today, as in 1972, Rosa's otherness is unsettling because, despite apparent differences, there is something of him in us and vice versa. Though we do not share a correlative present, we do belong to the same species: an impersonal resemblance ties us to this seemingly other figure. We also realize that Rosa's anomalies are not something to be corrected, adjusted, or eliminated in the name of some presumed normalcy. Indeed, De Dominicis held the protagonist of his most controversial work in esteem, considering him the harbinger of a still unaccountable vision. For his 1990 solo exhibition at the Centre National d'Art Contemporain Le Magasin in Grenoble, the artist reconstructed the setting from the Venice Biennale with just a few variations. While the stone, ball, and cube are once again on the floor, Rosa's chair is now made of wood and aluminum, painted black, with a semicircular backrest and pointed legs (*L'immortale invisibile e il luogo* [The Invisible Immortal

22 *The Epic of Gilgamesh* was discovered in 1872 by George Smith, who, studying fragments of clay cylinders and tablets in the British Museum's storage rooms, succeeded in producing a translation of the Chaldean account of the Great Flood, now known as the eleventh tablet of *The Epic of Gilgamesh*.

23 A belief confirmed by recent archaeological studies that discovered Gilgamesh's designs for Ur's city walls. I am grateful to the late Giovanni Pettinato for this observation.

and the Place] [IT 320] [1989]). It is again placed in the corner of the room, but hangs sixteen feet off the ground. Italo Tomassoni recalls how De Dominicis told him that the "invisible immortal" sat there in that levitating seat.[24] The new chair represents a sort of ex post facto beatification of Rosa; it announces that his destiny has been fulfilled and that, like saints or enlightened souls, he has ascended to heaven. And yet despite his extraterrestrial quality Rosa remains one of us, if only because he was alive and shared the hallmarks of our species when he became part of the *Second Solution* in 1972. Like many of the prodigious icons in De Dominicis's later works, Rosa conjures up the likelihood of a form of life that exists both within and beyond the world as we know it. As a result, the new chair of the "invisible immortal" suggests that immortality could be an inherent part of human life, even something that we harbor within us and have in common.

<u>What Are Masterpieces For?</u>

While the prospect of immortality concerns the entire species, De Dominicis was always highly selective artistically. In him, there is no compliance with the belief that anything has the potential to pass as a work of art—one of the chief assumptions that sustains the unregulated, market-driven apparatus of institutions and business that for some time now has fueled the globalized industry of contemporary art. Against this leveling, he not only asserts the metaphysical nature of the visual arts but, further, claims also that immortality finds "its own paradigm in the masterpiece." Since the medieval guilds, where the term gained currency to single out a qualitatively superior artwork whose making would guarantee the title of "master" to an apprentice, the masterpiece has shifted in its overtones and has undergone varying fortunes.[25] However, when De Dominicis uses the word, he is not necessarily thinking of the works most admired in museums around the globe, nor is he envisioning a supreme artistic ideal that artists must be compelled to achieve in concrete form.[26]

Arguably, there are other reasons why a masterpiece may point the way to immortal life. First, insofar as it comes to be commended over a variety of periods and cultures for its proof of outstanding skill or its overarching content or both, a masterpiece is a perfect instance of an artwork "broadcasting live"; it corroborates De Dominicis's belief that artworks are all contemporary. The masterpiece's timeless status sees to it that it will appear subtracted and/or in parallax whenever approached from the

24   Italo Tomassoni, ed., *Gino De Dominicis. Catalogo ragionato* (Milan: Skira, 2011), 356–58.

25   See Walter Cahn, *Masterpieces: Chapters on the History of an Idea* (Princeton, NJ: Princeton University Press, 1979), and Jean Galard et al., *Qu'est-ce qu'un chef d'œuvre?* (Paris: Gallimard, 2000).

26   This ideal became almost an obsession during the modern era. Hans Belting has argued that, in the early nineteenth century, as artistic practice achieved its autonomous status in society, not only did artworks begin to be regarded as the sites where art must find its raison d'être but art itself was conceived as an absolute. Taking inspiration from Balzac's tale "The Unknown Masterpiece," Belting coins the term "invisible masterpiece" to designate and describe the quest for this unattainable ideal that continues throughout the twentieth century. See Hans Belting, *The Invisible Masterpiece*, trans. Helen Atkins (London: Reaktion Books, 2001).

viewpoints of given historical contexts, starting with the very context within which it emerges. The act of deeming a work a masterpiece could, instead of depending upon predetermined parameters of judgment, entail as its guideline the adoption of the sense of quality. "Quality" alludes to what is exclusively proper to a work of art at its innermost core, which resists quantitative analysis and cannot be measured, translated, or reduced to a term other than itself. Thus perceived, masterpieces signal a specific difference from other works or objects. They lack ascertainable genealogies and overrule the chain of causation, distorting time and space while galvanizing the intuition that the origin is hardly a remote event. Masterpieces signal that a beginning is a breakthrough which, in variable scales and intensities, may happen in every present moment. Whatever the time and place of its provenance, a masterpiece can be seen as attesting to the human ability to shape its own presence on the planet. The making of a masterpiece regenerates life by opening up the possibility of reconfiguring the limits between being and nonbeing, existence and nonexistence. The definitions normally assigned to these polarities change or become objects of reexamination in view of the masterpiece's inception. Within its orbit, the delusional attempt to extend time by hastening our traversal of space can be amended. The ideology of frenzied progress and novelty for its own sake is overpowered by the longing to get closer to being and attain its maximum perfection.

De Dominicis's stance may be further explored by recalling Gertrude Stein's speculations on masterpieces. In a lecture delivered at Oxford in 1936 titled, "What Are Master-pieces and Why Are There So Few of Them," Stein indicated that the making and appreciation of a masterpiece entails not only a relinquishment of received knowledge but also a flight out of time: human nature and identity, as conceived in their worldly intercourse, must be transcended. As she put it, "The second you are you because your little dog knows you you cannot make a master-piece and that is all of that."[27] Though puzzling, Stein's words conjure up a situation where art reveals its profound connection to both death and immortality.[28] Something resembling a loss of the self must occur in the midst of daily life—your dog no longer acknowledges who you are on the basis of who you were and will be. This "death" is paralleled by a dawning awareness that another form of existence is possible; an existence that is attested to by the masterpiece itself, as well as by the lived experiences of its maker and users. Accordingly, De Dominicis's claim that a masterpiece is a model of immortality suggests that a masterpiece casts humans in the sphere of a never-ending life by as-

27   Gertrude Stein, "What Are Master-pieces and Why Are There So Few of Them," in *Writings 1932–1946* (New York: Library of America, 1998), 360. On Stein's view of the masterpiece, see Belting, *The Invisible Masterpiece*, 364. Donald Judd alluded to Stein's lecture in a 1983 essay, in which he argued that contemporary art is "only a cut above being ordinary commodity and close to being manipulated as any compliant commodity should be"; see Donald Judd, "A Long Discussion Not About Master-pieces but Why There Are So Few of Them," in *Donald Judd Writings*, ed. Flavin Judd and Caitlin Murray (Marfa, TX: Judd Foundation; New York: David Zwirner Books, 2016), 355.

28   The analogy between immortality and death has also been discussed—albeit from a very different viewpoint—by Jean Baudrillard; see *The Vital Illusion*, ed. Julia Witwer (New York: Columbia University Press, 2000).

serting its own eternal status: it uncovers the dimensionless realm that Stein evokes in her lecture.

Faith in masterpieces ultimately suggests that there is no indeterminacy or relativism but only essences, ideas, sentiments, and agencies that acquire significant forms through art. These forms are the habitat of meanings, truths, and values that may both engender and perpetuate awareness among artists and nonartists, so that a tradition may establish itself and operate as the token of a localized eternity that disrupts the impermanence and entropy.

History Without Death

The closing line of De Dominicis's "Letter" reads, "I hope one day to take a glass, fill it with wine and drink it, to take a hen for a walk, and for it to be really me who is doing it."[29] As he imagines it, the life of an immortal is no longer attached to the ongoing verification of transitory possibilities in time and space. The moment the divide between being and becoming is surmounted, there are no longer any reasons why Dominicis's hen (or Stein's little dog) ought to recognize the person walking it as someone changing in time. He imagines immortality as a unity between doer and deed, a mindful handling of objects; it is a harmonious alliance among living and nonliving realms. De Dominicis's "Letter" speaks of the prospect of overcoming alienation and appropriating human agency in ways that would allow individuals to truly live, no longer confined within fractional and perishable states, by availing themselves of an unprecedented consciousness of being whole.

It cannot be predicted whether this development will ever happen in the future. However, even if unwittingly, by aiming at being absolute in their stillness, silence, and tangible presence, artworks can spark the intuition that the coincidence of existence and essence is not a chimera. Albeit in a limited way, they operate so that the sense of a never-ending life can be experienced on this side of impermanence. In proximity to artworks, artists and nonartists have the opportunity to prepare themselves for the leap, or new start, that could plunge them into another form of life. This is probably why Rosa, the signifier of the unknown and the warden of three artworks in 1972, acquires immortal status in 1990 and, although no longer visible, still occupies a space of his own. Originality and radical discontinuity can teach us about the void from which new beginnings arise and even encourage us to imagine ancestral pasts and the primeval emergence of matter and life itself. This implies that art could help both artists and nonartists recognize that disembodied attributes of mortals (such as values, truths, knowledge, ethics, etc.) have not simply been transmigrating in time alongside them. These attributes have gone beyond the here and now, rising to the immortal permanence of dignified human features and aspirations so they may be revitalized, shared, and integrated in an overall attempt to defeat death. In fact, the permanence of these attributes does not belong to the

29   De Dominicis, "Letter on Immortality," 61, 64.

horizon of measurable time and visible space, but lives on precisely through the kind of embodiment that art-making performs. Art-making is truly one of the most enduring ways to banish finitude while rescuing being from the oblivion of becoming.

As bearers of anti-entropic qualities, artworks are valuable means of conserving against the accidental loss of any genetic or cultural heritage but they are also multi-scalar; they integrate pasts and futures and can reconfigure the relation between becoming and being. Not only can artworks deform or cut through time and bring into reality quanta of eternity, but they can also dissolve the dichotomy between the ancient and modern that has afflicted artistic practice in the West. This is probably one of the reasons why De Dominicis could candidly say that he preferred antediluvian art to modern and ancient art, and that modern artists should know that, in fact, "they are the most ancient."[30] The acquisition of this knowledge may offer a way toward amending the "mistake." At the very least, it would surely yield an awareness that death is no longer part of our understanding of history.

This essay was written for the present volume.

30   De Dominicis, "Maxims, 1969–1996," 96.

ALL WORKS OF ART ARE CONTEMPORARY

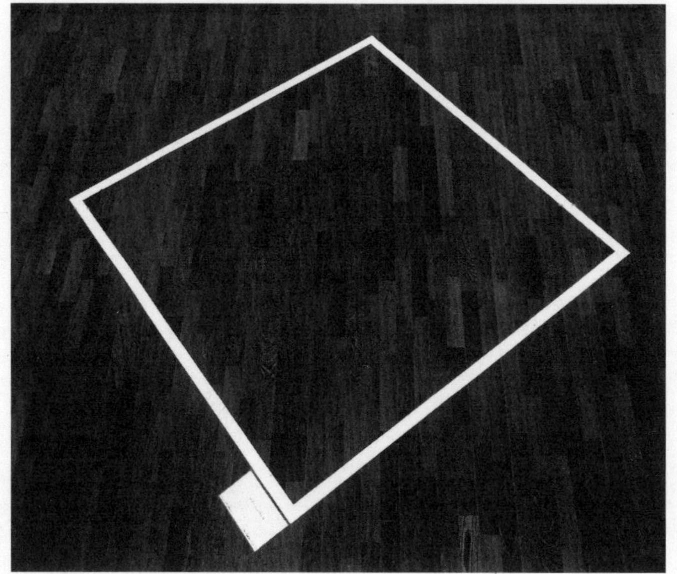

1   *Cubo invisibile* (Invisible Cube), 1967. Acrylic on floor, 47⅝ × 47⅝ inches (121 × 121 cm). De Donno Collection, Foligno [IT 45]

→   21, 26, 27, 38, 41, 44, 48, 117, 132, 178, 197, 205, 207

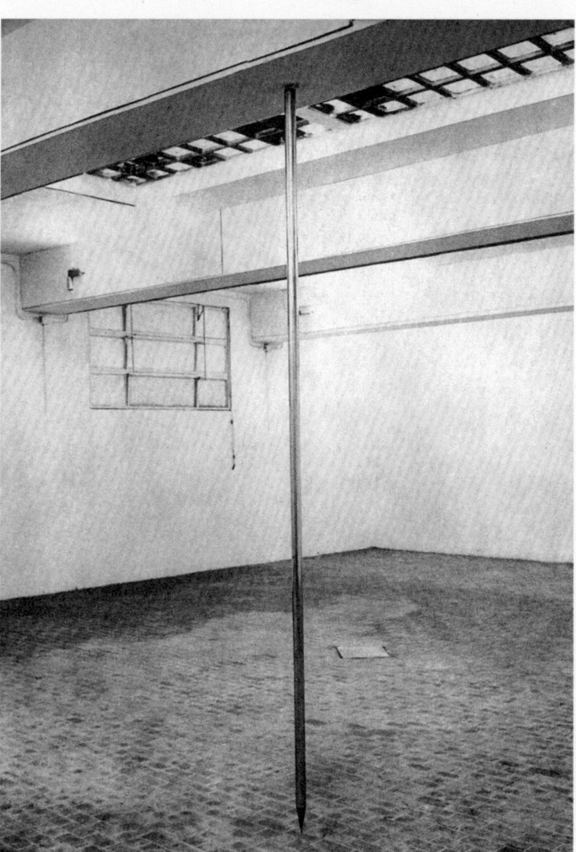

2   *Asta in bilico (Equilibrio 1)*
(Suspended Rod [Equili-
brium 1]), 1967. Brass, gold
leaf, 13⅛ feet, diameter
1⅝ inches (4 m, diameter
4 cm) [IT 47]
→   40, 178

3   *Secchio con acqua sospeso da
terra con il gancio di una
catena che fa presa sull'acqua*
(Bucket with Water Suspended
from the Ground, with the
Hook of a Chain that Grips
the Water), 1968. Assembled
objects. Private collection,
Como [IT 59]
→   36, 178

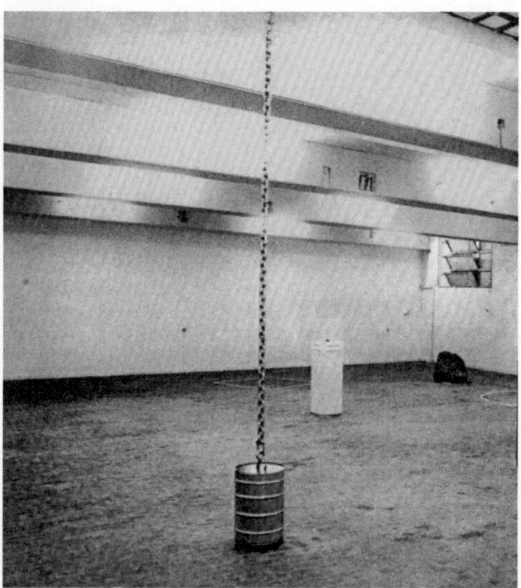

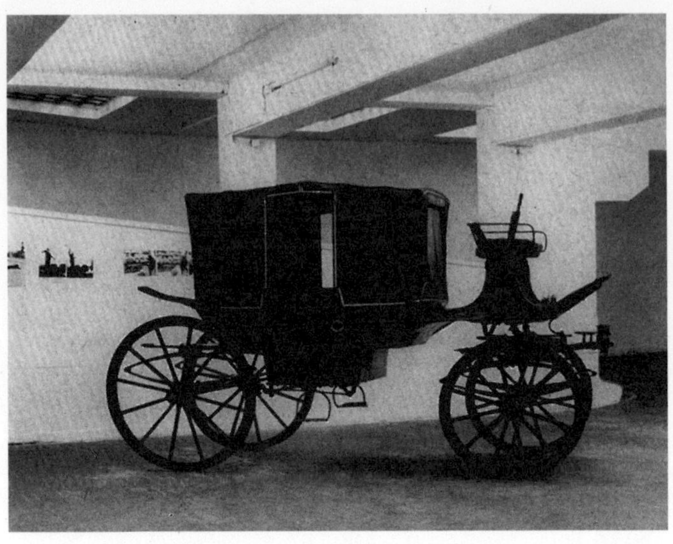

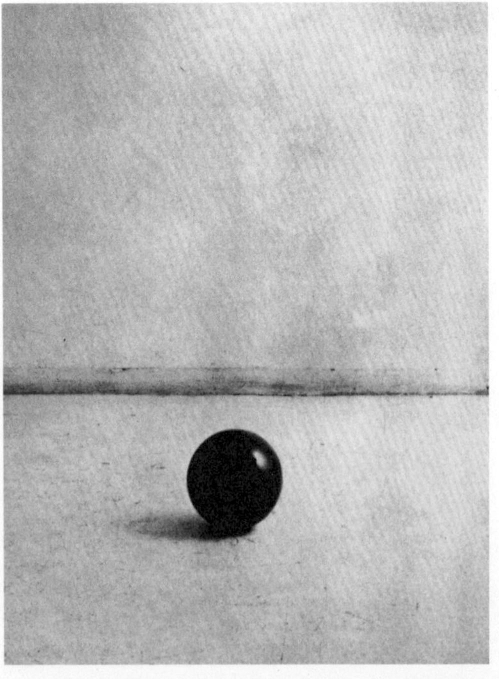

4   *Mozzarella in carrozza*
(Mozzarella in a Carriage),
1970. Vintage carriage,
mozzarella, 82⅝ × 68½ ×
141¾ inches (210 × 174 ×
360 cm). Private collection,
Modena [IT 69]
→   22, 22n6, 27, 38, 41, 42, 106,
117n6

5   *Palla di gomma (caduta da
2 metri) nell'attimo immediatamente precedente il rimbalzo* (Rubber Ball [Falling
from a Height of Two Meters]
in the Moment Right Before
Bouncing Back), 1968–69.
Red rubber, diameter
5⅞ inches (15 cm). Marilena
and Lorenzo Bonomo Collection, Bari [IT 70]
→   37, 41, 122, 132, 178, 201, 205

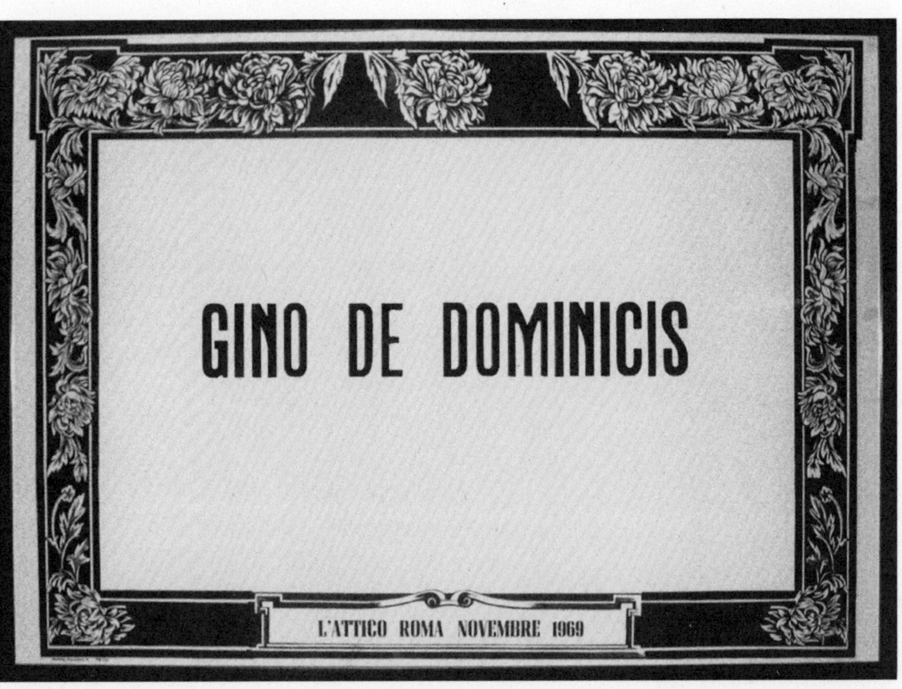

GINO DE DOMINICIS
L'ATTICO ROMA NOVEMBRE 1969

7
Cilindro invisibile (Invisible Cylinder), 1969. Acrylic on floor, 5½ × 106⅜ inches (70 × 270 cm) [IT 74]

→ 41, 118

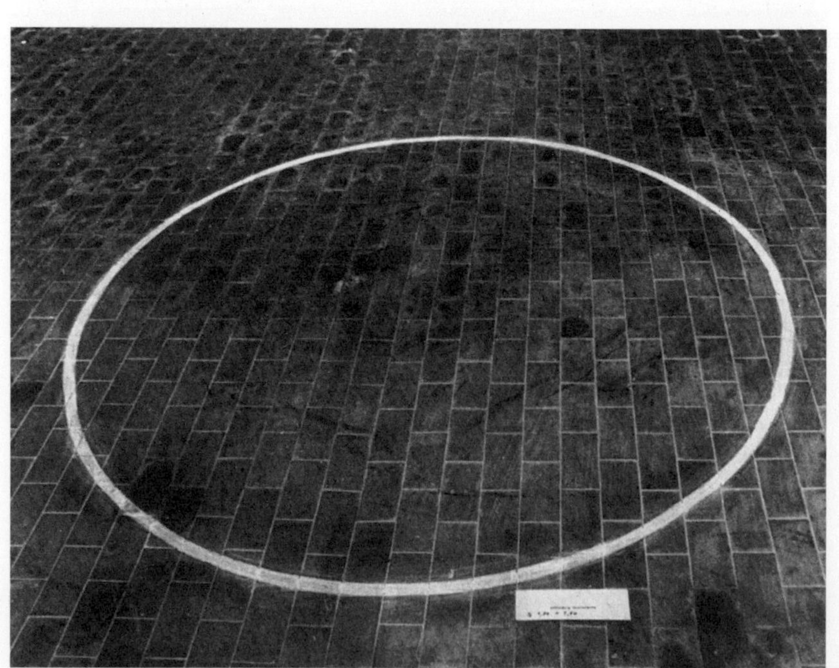

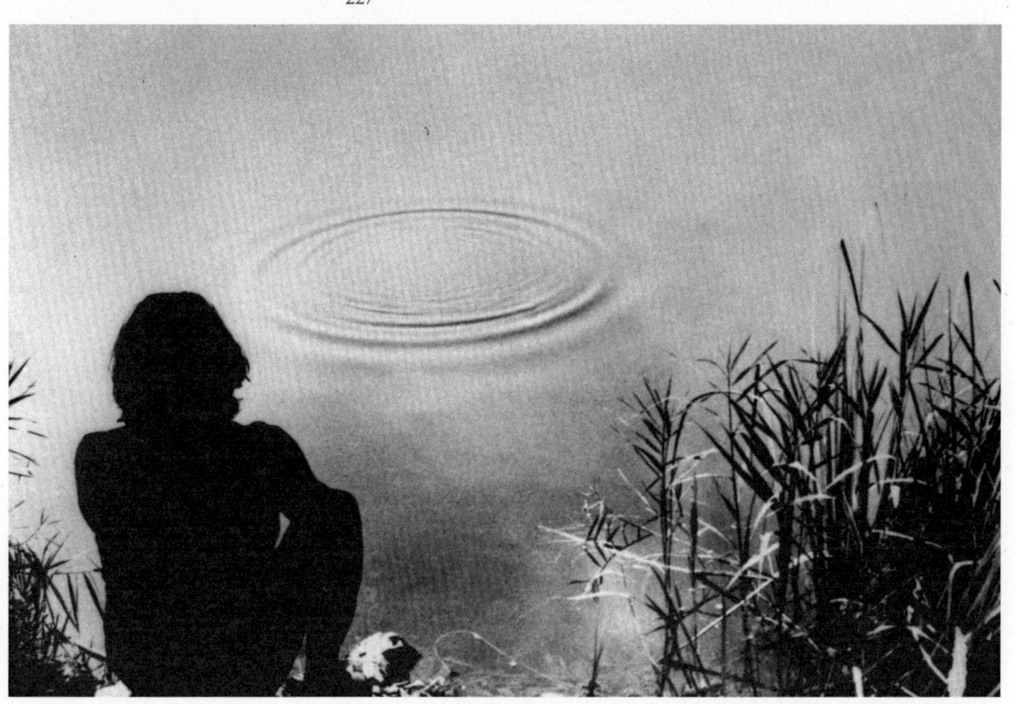

8

Tentativo di far formare dei quadrati invece che dei cerchi intorno ad un sasso che cade Nell'acqua (Attempt to Form Squares Instead of Circles Around a Stone Falling into Water), 1969. Black-and-white photograph, 18⅞ × 26⅝ inches (48 × 67 cm). Silvio Sansone Collection, Salerno [IT 83]

→ 20–21, 36, 41, 149, 178, 201

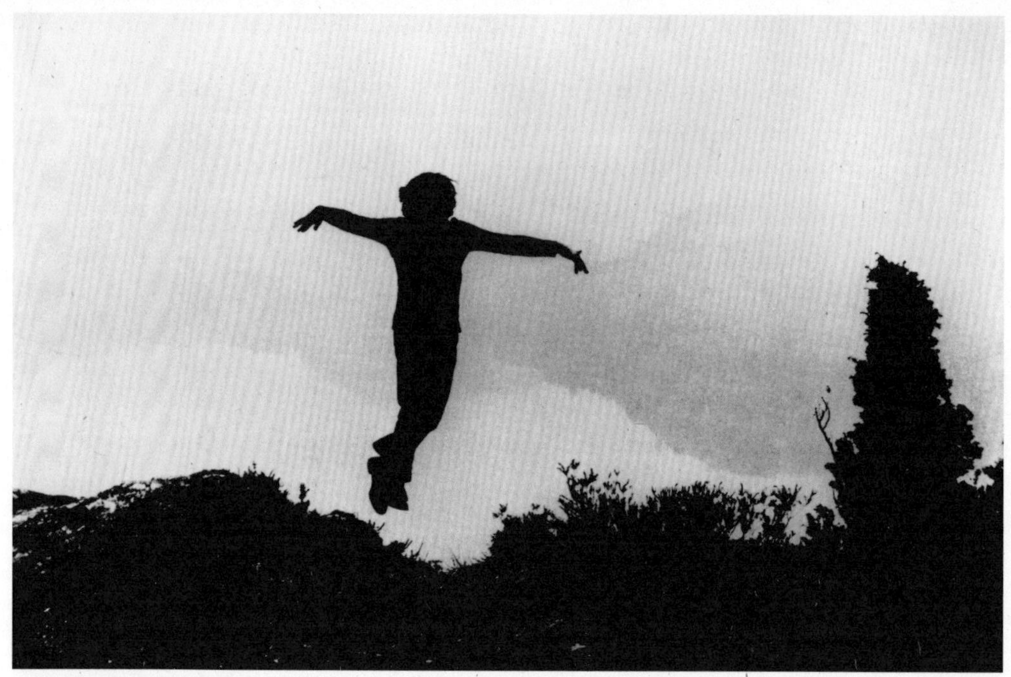

9   *Tentativo di volo* (Attempt to
Fly), 1969. Black-and-white
photograph, 18⅞ × 26⅜ inches
(46 × 67 cm). Silvio Sansone
Collection, Salerno [IT 84]

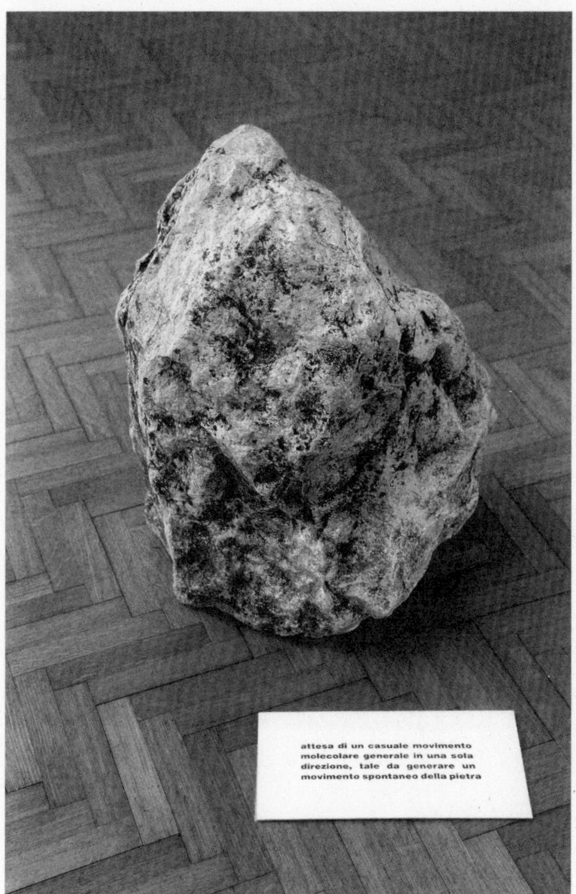

10 *Attesa di un casuale movimento molecolare generale in una sola direzione, tale da generare un movimento spontaneo della pietra* (Waiting for a Random One-Directional Molecular Movement that Could Generate a Spontaneous Movement of Material), 1969. Stone, card bearing signature and title. Perezzani Collection, Sanguinetto [IT 87]

→ 27, 37, 41, 116, 132, 178, 199, 201, 205

11 *Ubiquità* [Ubiquity], 1969. Opal, each 8¼ × 6½ inches (21 × 16.7 cm) [IT 92]

→ 185

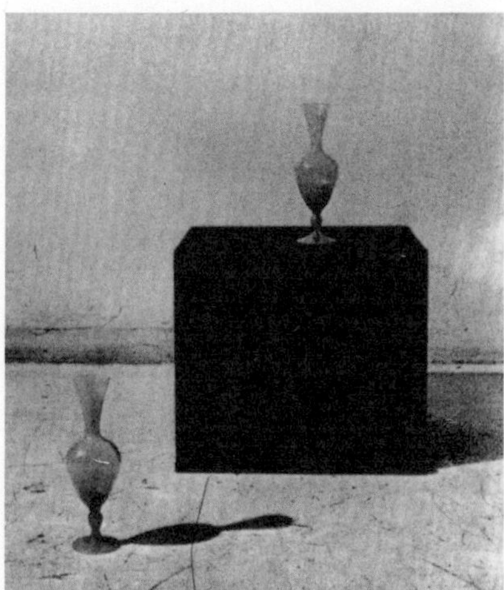

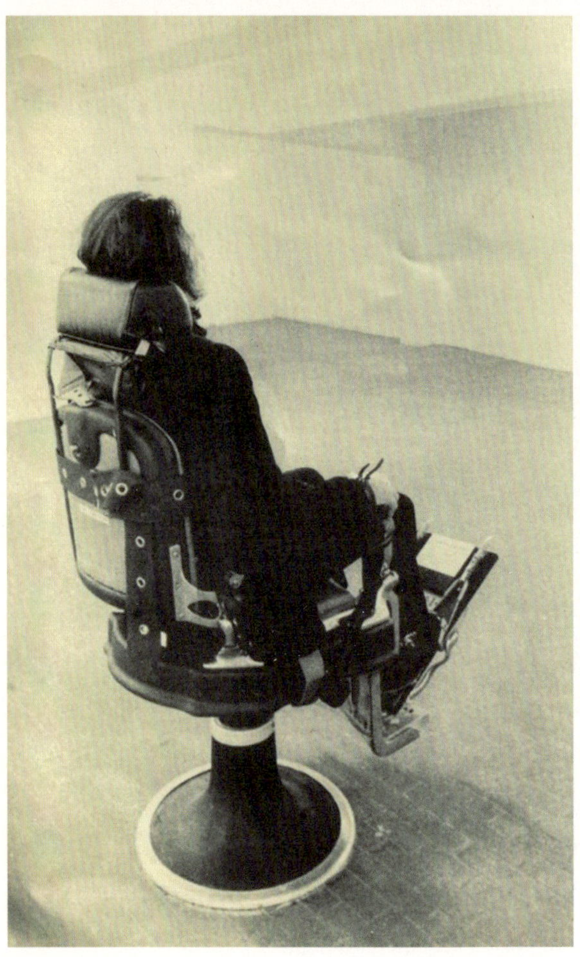

12 *Poltrona per un viaggio nello spazio* (Armchair for Space Travel), 1969. Barber's chair, card. Dimensions and whereabouts unknown [IT 81]. The photograph, taken on November 5, 1969, at L'Attico, Rome, shows the artist strapped into the chair. A mathematical formula and a card are placed on the gallery walls. A facsimile of the card was possibly placed on the chair to be read by the traveler. The text provides detailed specifications for space travel as well as the rotation and speed of the earth and sun, indicating that the chair's occupant, while sitting, is also traveling through space.

→ 36–37, 45

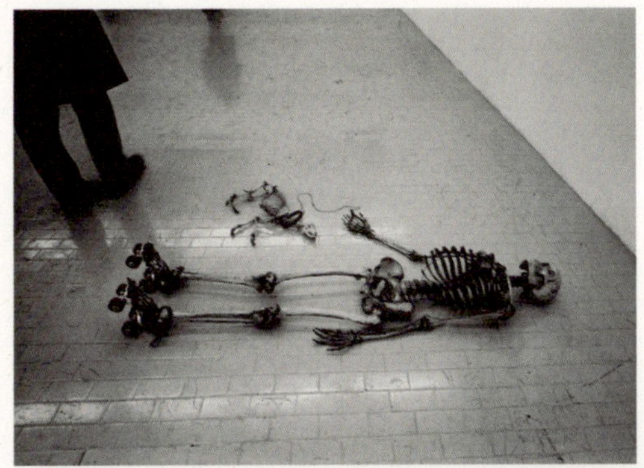

13 Lower left: *Il tempo lo sbaglio
lo spazio* (Time, Mistake,
Space), 1969. Human skeleton,
dog skeleton, roller skates,
leash, and painted metal rod,
157½ × ca. 86⅝ × 66⅞ inches
(400 × ca. 220 × 170 cm).
Lia Rumma Collection, Naples
[IT 95]
Upper left: The work in its
first state

→ 21, 36, 44n14, 45, 115, 126–27,
178, 203–4, 207

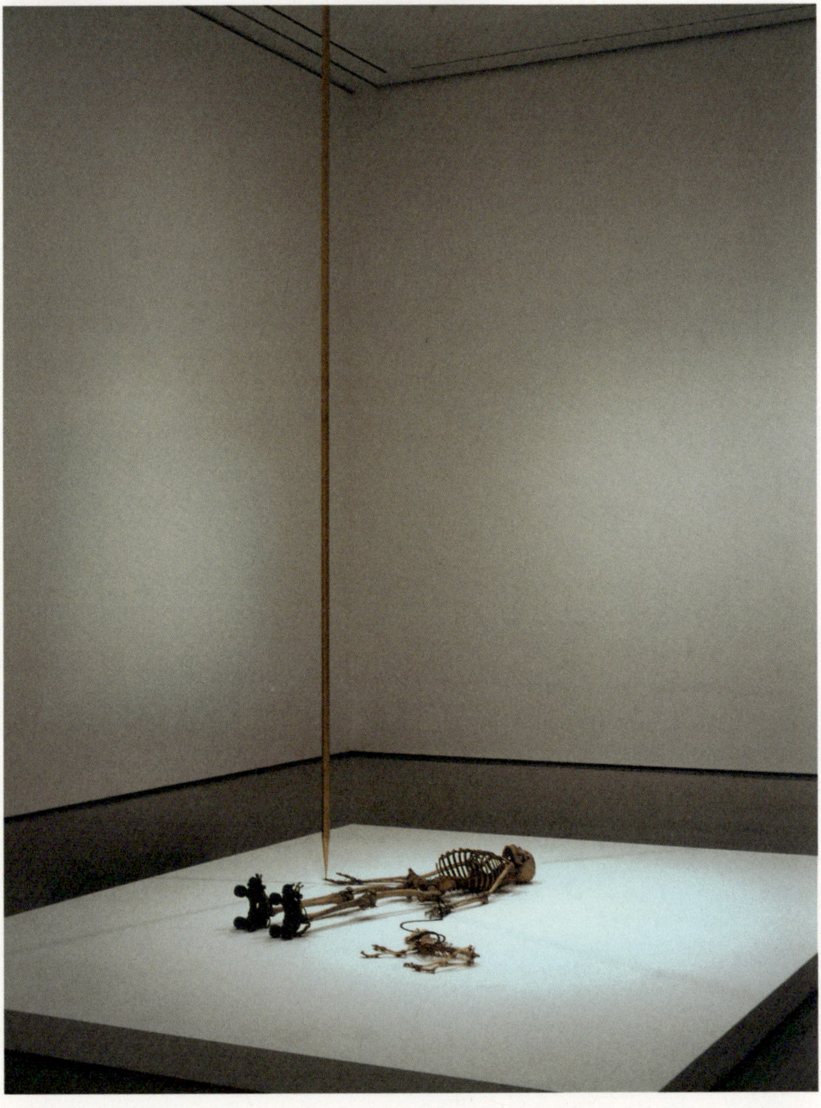

14 *Senza titolo (Il giovane e il vecchio)* (Untitled [The Young and the Old]), 1969. Black-and-white photographs, 15⅜ × 19¾ inches (39 × 50 cm). Silvio Sansone Collection, Salerno [IT 101]

→ 37

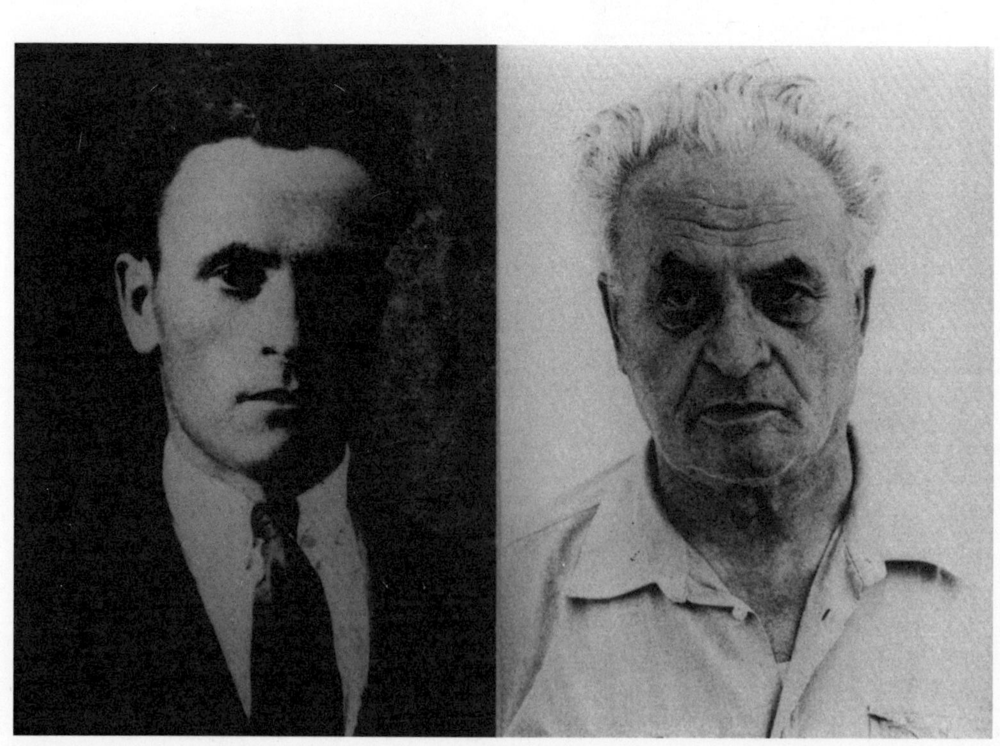

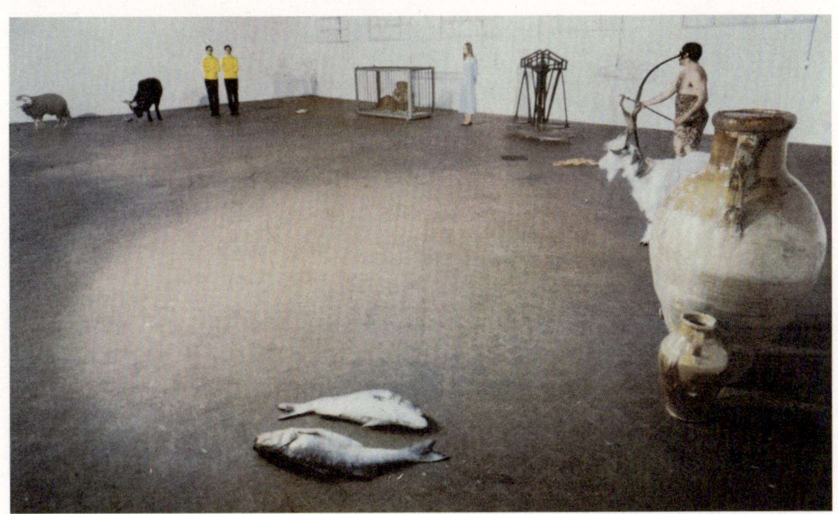

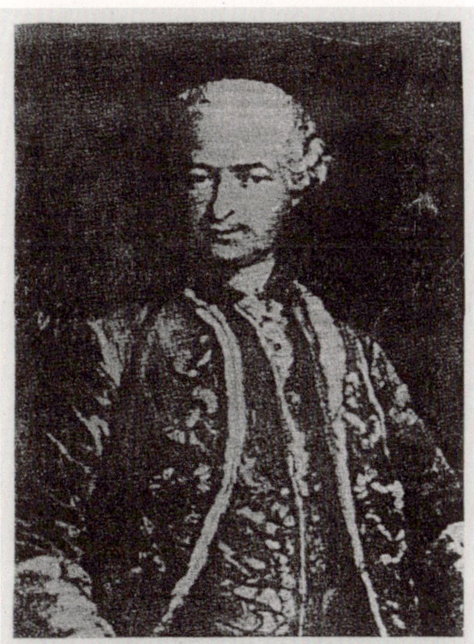

(Gino De Dominicis)

15 *Lo Zodiaco* (The Zodiac), 1970. Living figures, objects [IT 105]

→ 21, 32, 42, 47, 73, 148, 179

16 *Io non sono il conte di Saint Germain* (I am not the Count of St. Germain), 1970. Printed cardboard on Masonite, 11⅞ × 8¼ inches (30 × 21 cm). Dei Campiani Collection, Brescia [IT 112]

→ 33, 37

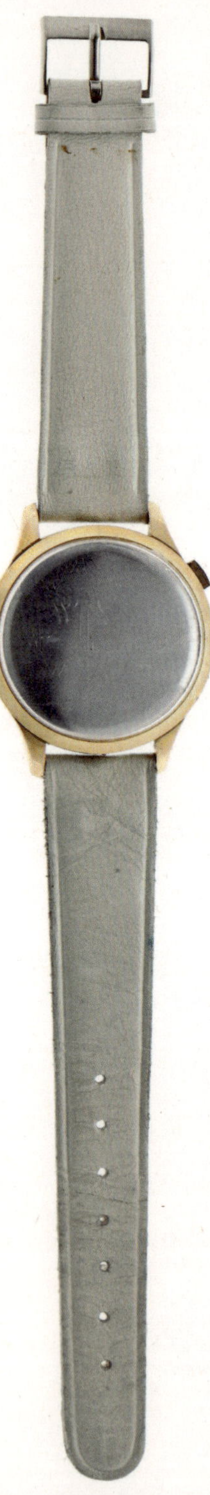

17 *Orologio* (Watch), 1970.
Leather, mirror, and metal,
9⅞ × 1⅜ × ⅛ inches (25.5 ×
3.5 × 0.5 cm). Lia Rumma
Collection, Naples [IT 113]
→ 24, 39, 115, 147

18 *Come io vedo questo tavolo, questi piatti, questa bottiglia, queste posate, questo bicchiere e questa pianta* (As I see this table, these plates, this bottle, this cutlery, this glass, and this plant), 1970. Wooden table, ceramic plates, fork, knife, glass goblet, glass bottle, and succulent, 31½ × 35⅝ × 30⅞ inches (80 × 90.5 × 78.5 cm). Private collection, Bari [IT 114]

→
182

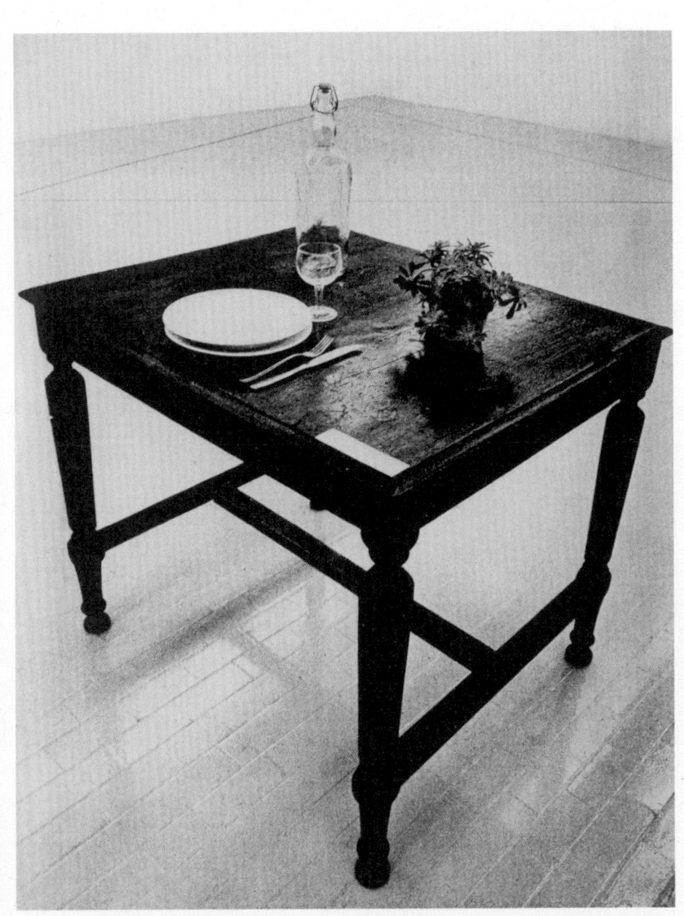

19 *Senza titolo* (Untitled), 1970.
Black-and-white photographs,
each 11⅝ × 8½ inches (29.5 ×
21.5 cm). Private collection,
Rome [IT 115]
44n14, 141

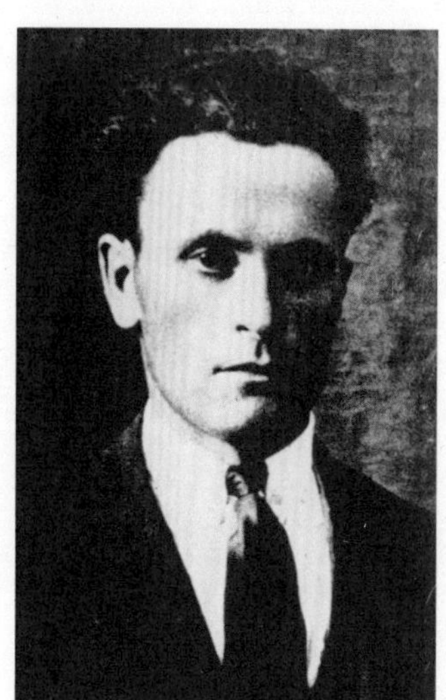
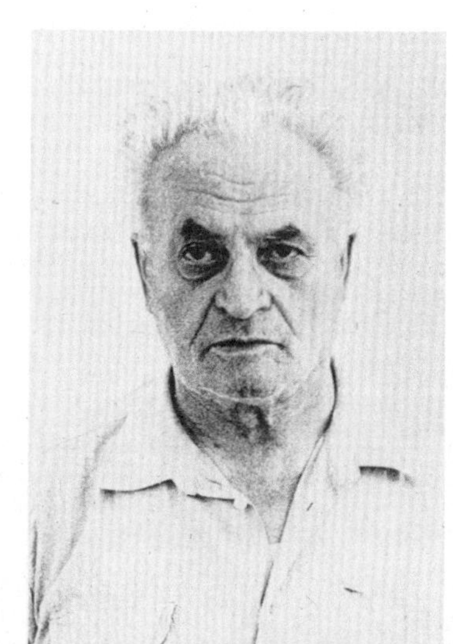
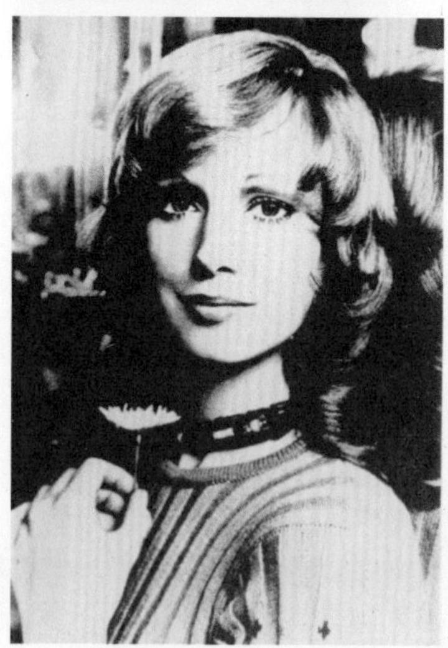
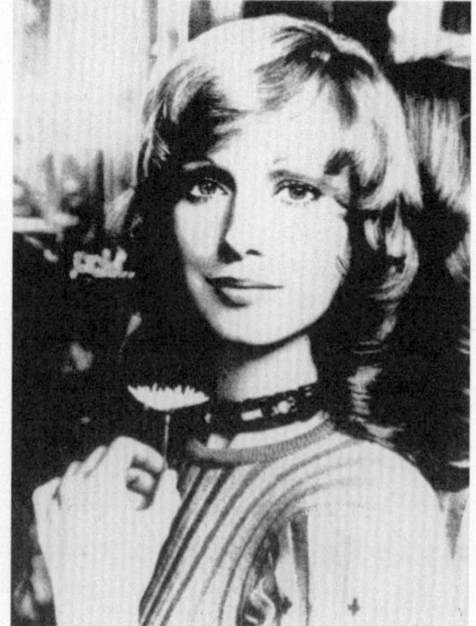

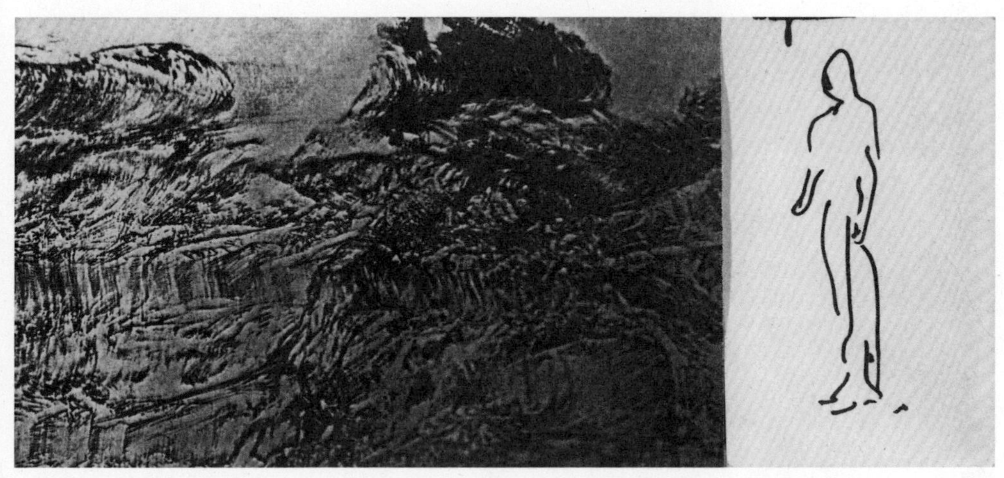

20   *Senza titolo* (Untitled), 1970.
Photocopied sheet and felt-tip
pen on paper, mounted on
glass, 7 × 9 inches (18 × 23 cm).
Paul Maenz Collection, Berlin
[IT 121]
→   35

21 *Terza soluzione d'immortalità (Gino De Dominicis vi vede)* (Third Solution of Immortality [Gino De Dominicis Is Watching You]), 1970. Black-and-white photograph, 15 ⅜ × 20 ½ inches (39 × 52 cm). Paliotto-Incutti Collection, Naples [IT 122]
120n19, 174

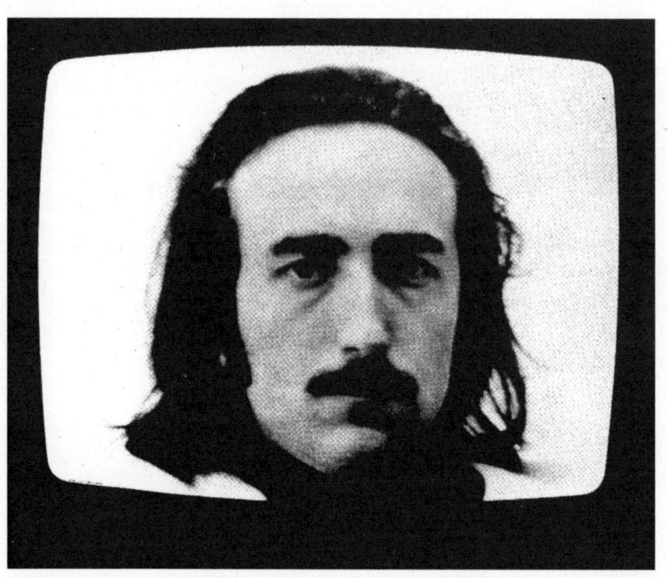

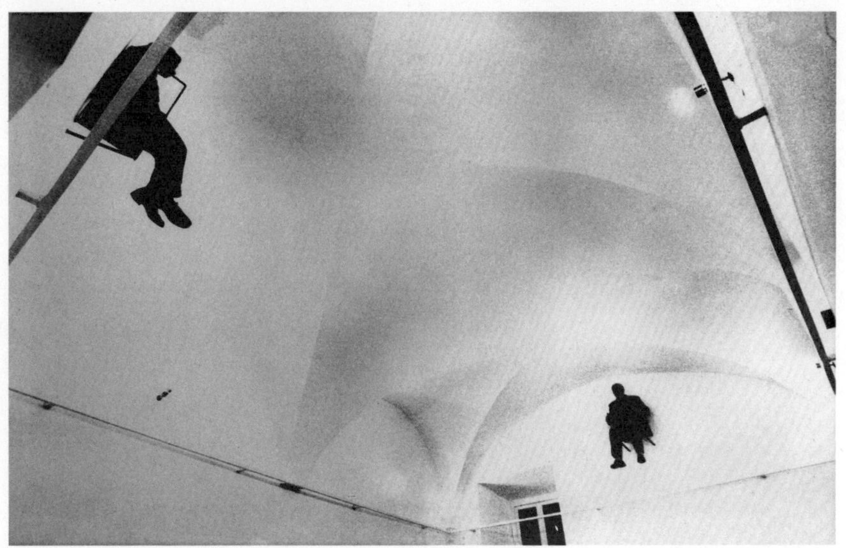

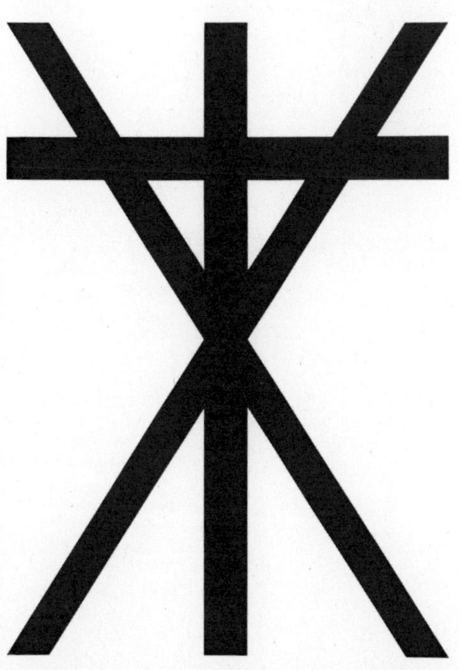

22   *Senza titolo (Immortalità)*
      (Untitled [Immortality]), 1971.
      Black-and-white photograph
      mounted on plywood, 18½ ×
      27½ inches (47 × 70 cm).
      Private collection [IT 124]
→   35, 37, 43–44, 177

23   *Immortalità* (Immortality),
      1971. Black ink on card, 12⅛ ×
      8¼ inches (30.8 × 21 cm).
      Bruno Corà Collection, Rome
      [IT 137]
→   176

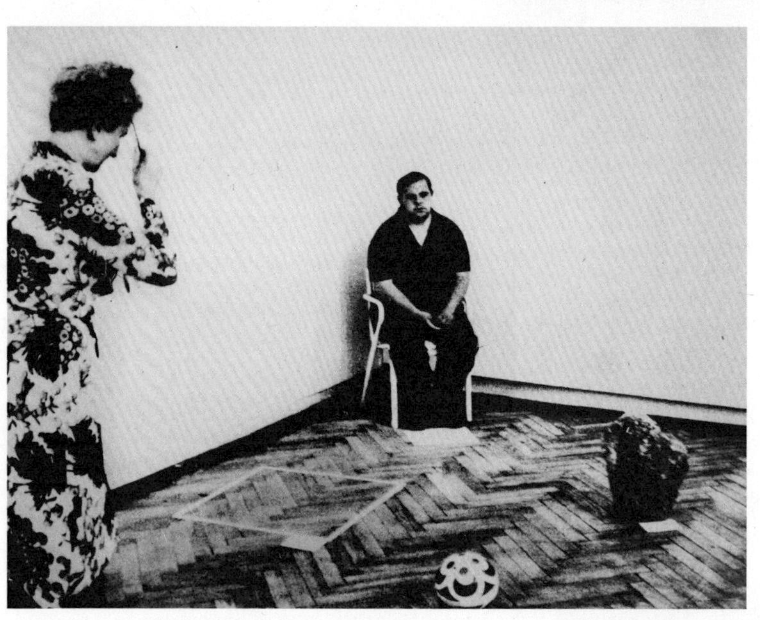

24 *Biglietto d'auguri* (Greeting
    Card for the Immortality
    of the Body), 1971. Print, 9⅛ ×
    8¾ inches (23.2 × 22.4 cm).
    [IT 140]
→   37, 214

25 *(foto ricordo) Seconda soluzione
    d'immortalità (l'universo è
    immobile)* ([souvenir photo]
    Second Solution of Immortal-
    ity [The Universe Is Still]),
    1972. Black-and-white photo-
    graph, 20 × 24¾ inches (51 ×
    63 cm). Lia Rumma Collection,
    Naples [IT 150]
→   15, 21, 27–28, 31, 38, 42–43,
    73–74, 78, 83, 116, 129, 129n5,
    147, 177, 194, 199, 204–5, 207,
    215

26 *Madonna che ride* (Laughing
Madonna), 1972. Colored plaster statue, 78¾ × 23⅝ inches
(200 × 60 cm). Destroyed by
the artist [IT 152]
→ 22, 28, 35, 120, 148, 178

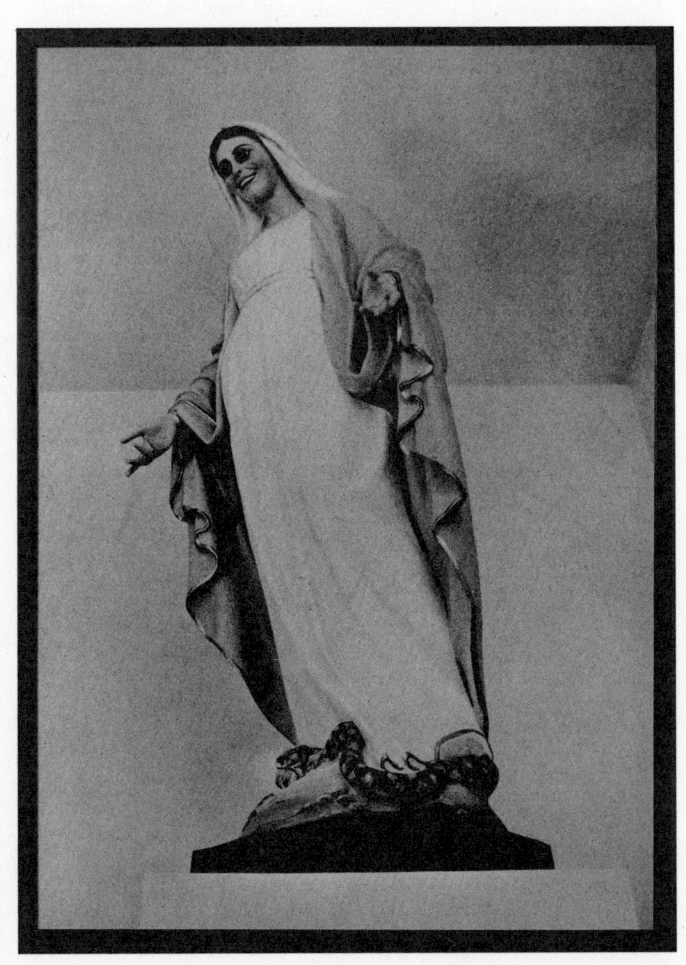

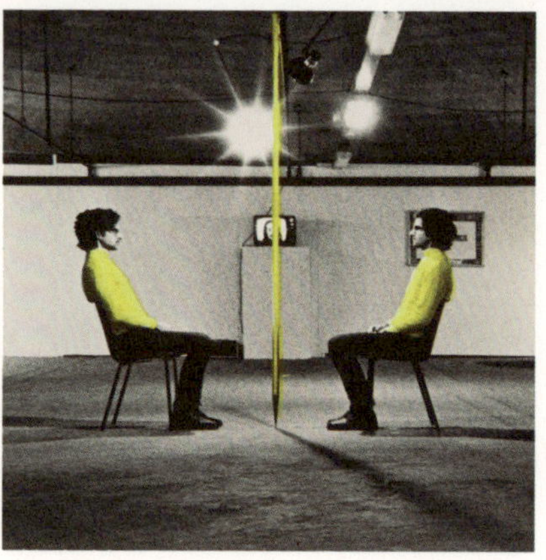

27   *Senza titolo (I gemelli)*
(Untitled [The Twins]), 1973.
Color photograph, 5½ ×
5½ inches (14 × 14 cm). Silvio
Sansone Collection, Salerno
[IT 173]
→   35, 38

28   *'Era estate, una notte mia
figlia disse: "L'arte moderna fa
ridere i polli, l'arte antica li
rattrista, l'Arte li fa piangere"
poi ci baciammo a lungo
in bocca' (Immagine della dea
sumera Warka)* ("It was summer, one night my daughter
said to me: 'Modern art could
make the chickens laugh,
ancient art could make them
sad, Art could make them
weep,' then we shared a long,
passionate kiss" [Image of the
Sumerian Goddess Warka]),
1977–83. Oil on color photograph, 49¼ × 37⅜ inches
(125 × 95 cm). Private collection, Sassuolo [IT 189]
→   29, 39, 144, 186, 208

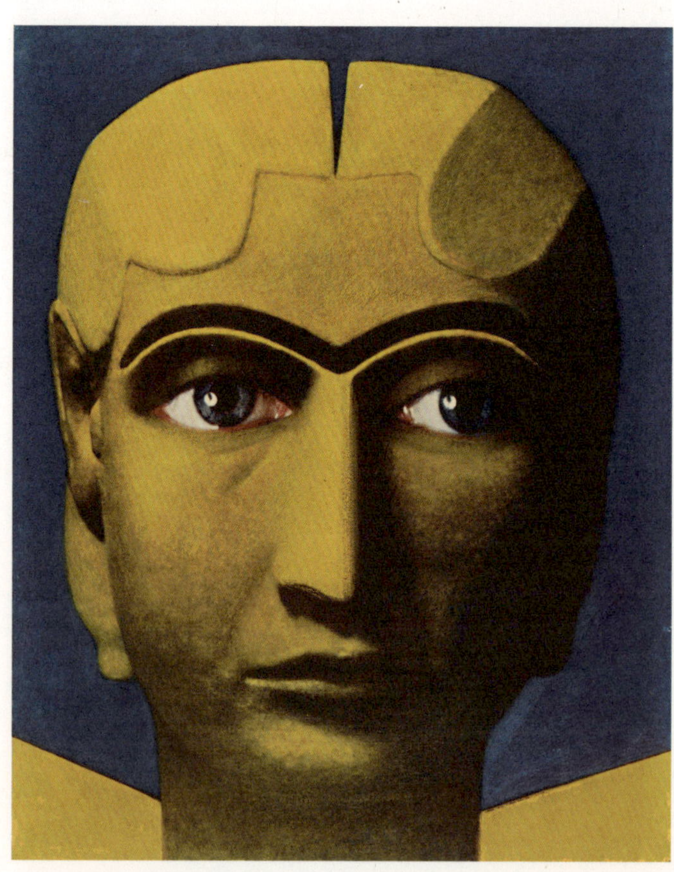

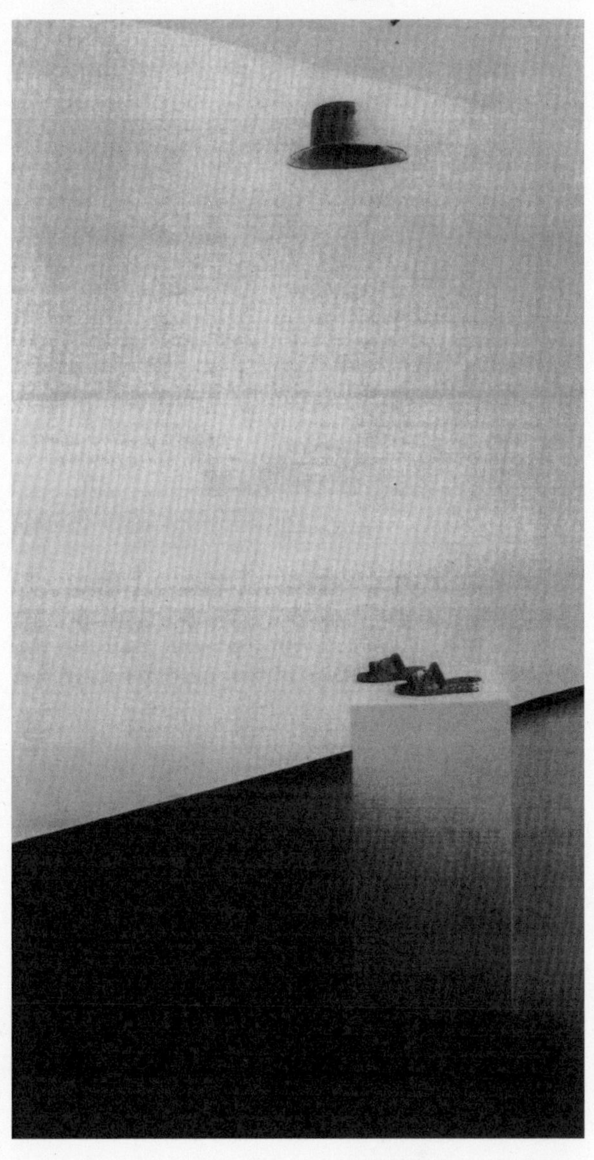

29 *Senza titolo (Statua invisibile)*
(Untitled [Invisible Statue]),
1979. Straw hat, slippers,
and pedestal, dimensions variable [IT 198]
→ 146–47

→

30 *Senza titolo (Urvasi e Gilgamesh)* (Untitled [Urvasi and Gilgamesh]), 1979–80. Pen and pencil on photographic paper, 6¼ × 5 inches (15.8 × 12.8 cm). Giorgio Franchetti Collection, Rome [IT 200] 25, 154–55

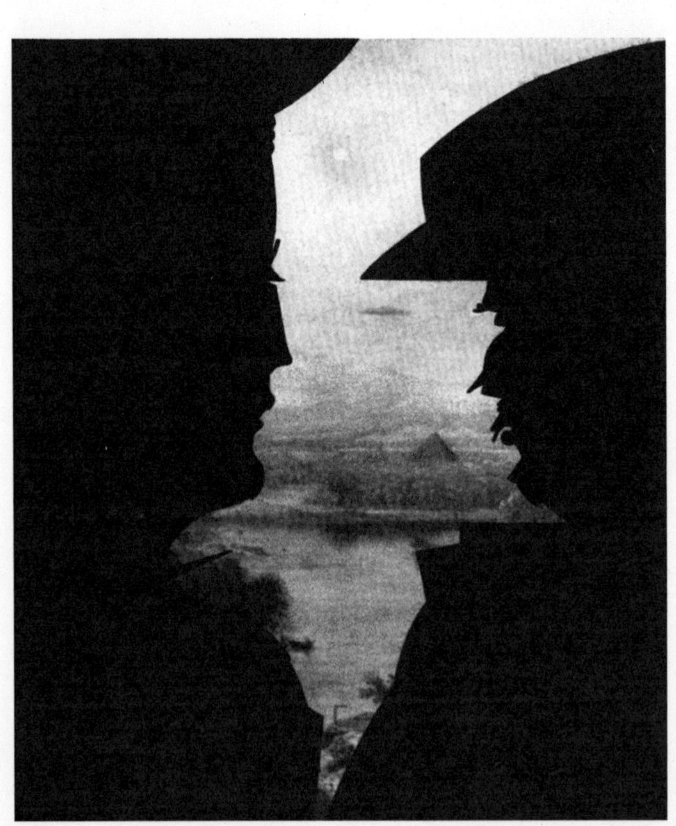

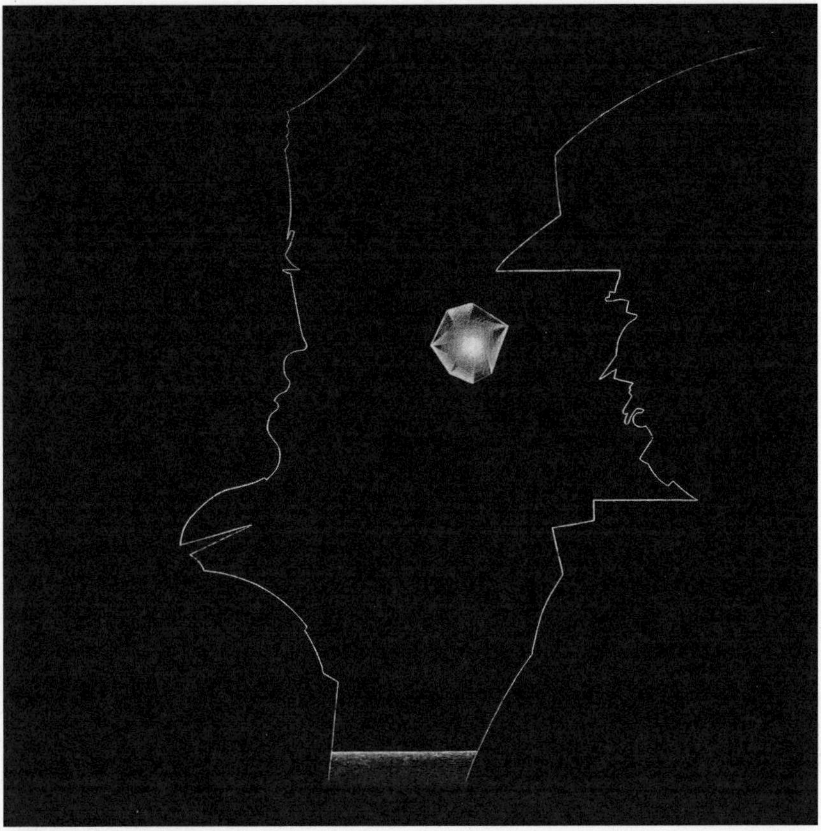

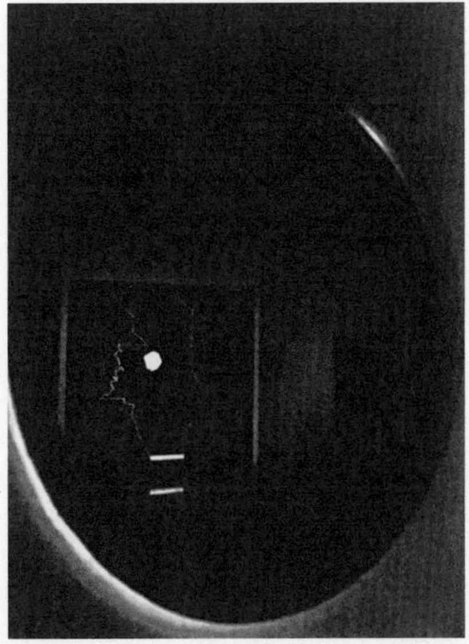

31   *Senza titolo (Urvasi e Gilgamesh) – il notturno* (Untitled
[Urvasi and Gilgamesh] –
the Nocturnal), 1987. Tempera
and graphite on wood, 94 ½ ×
94 ½ inches (240 × 240 cm).
Castello di Rivoli, Museo
d'Arte Contemporanea, Turin
[IT 207]
→   39

32   *Senza titolo (Specchio che tutto
riflette tranne gli esseri viventi)*
(Untitled [Mirror that Reflects
Everything Except Living
Beings]), 1988. Oval frame with
glass, two coextensive asymmetrical settings. The mirroring
work to No. 31, as featured
in the photograph, was subsequently destroyed [IT 302]
→   39, 46, 122, 128–39, 196, 208

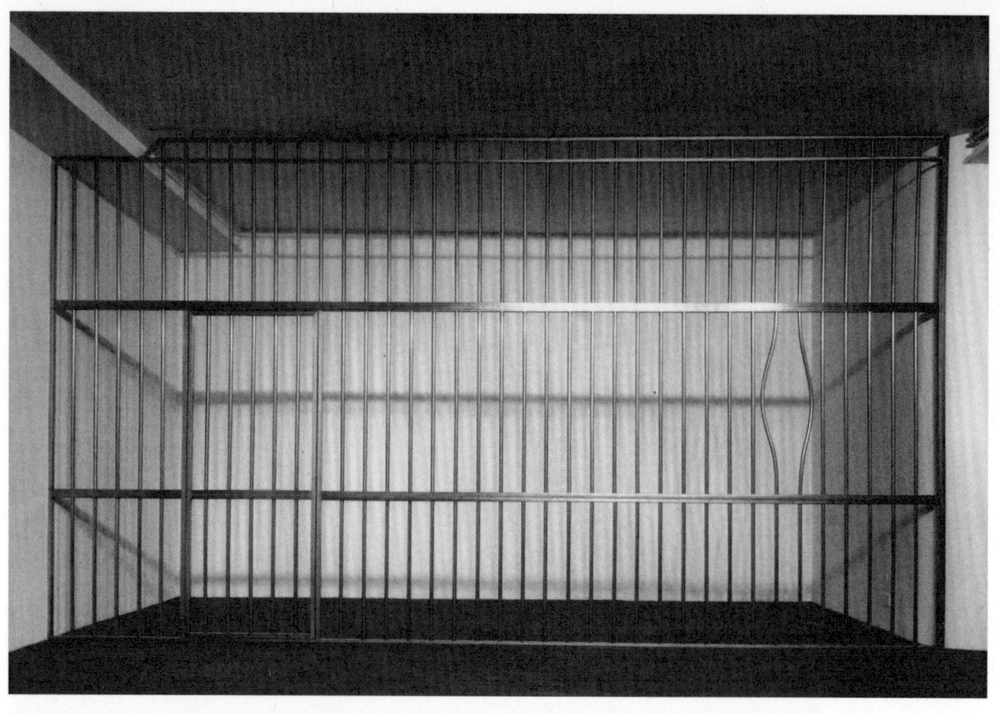

33   *Senza titolo* (Untitled), 1980. Steel, 118⅛ × 236¼ inches (300 × 600 cm). Lia Rumma Collection, Naples [IT 227]

→   38, 45, 177

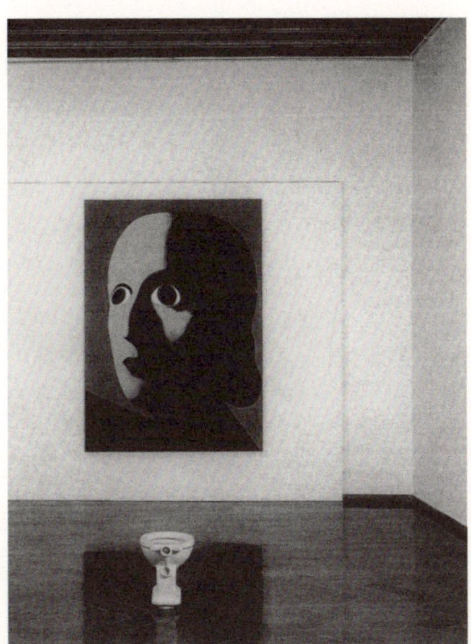

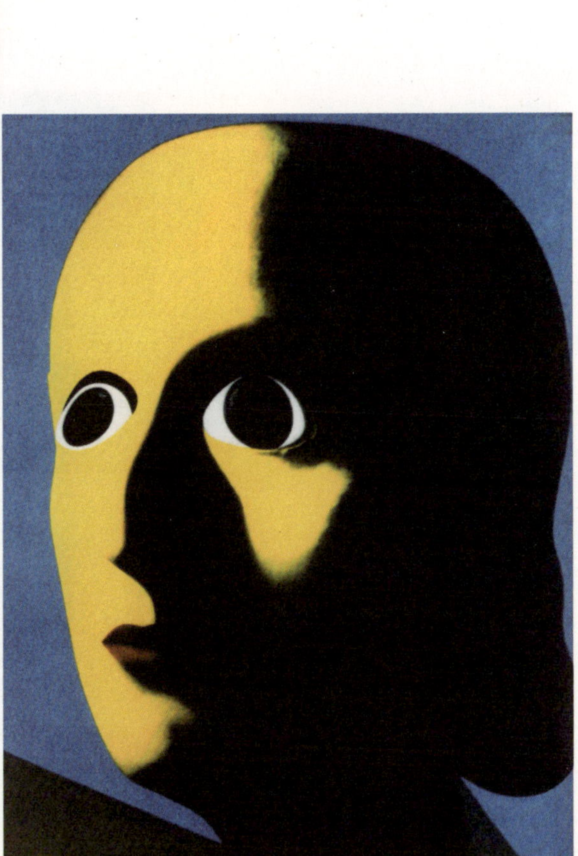

34 Lower right: *Con titolo (In principio era l'immagine; No!* (With Title [In the beginning was the image; No!]), 1981–82. Oil stick and pastel on paper mounted on aluminum panels, in two parts, 109 × 77⅛ inches (276.8 × 196 cm) overall. The Museum of Modern Art, New York [IT 238]
Upper left: View of the work as shown in 1982 at Galleria Gian Enzo Sperone, Rome
36, 41n6, 179

→

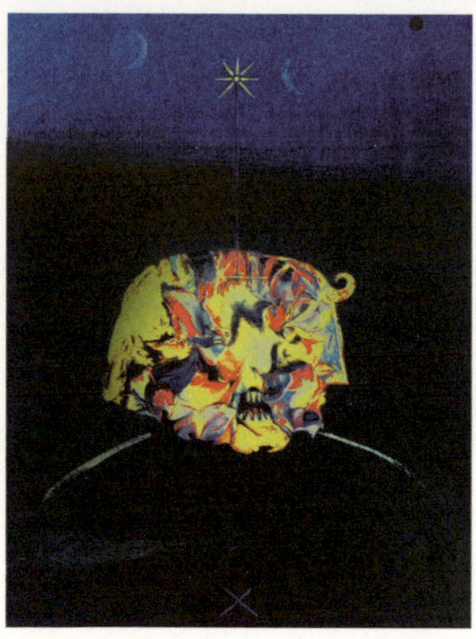

35   *Senza titolo* (Untitled), 1982.
Tempera and colored chalk
on cardboard and canvas,
5½ × 11⅜ inches (39.5 × 29 cm).
Private collection [IT 244]
→ 176

36   *Senza titolo (Guerriero con
lancia)* (Untitled [Warrior with
Spear]), 1982. Tempera and
pastel on panel, 98½ ×
82⅝ inches (250 × 210 cm).
Private collection, Zurich
[IT 245]
→ 29

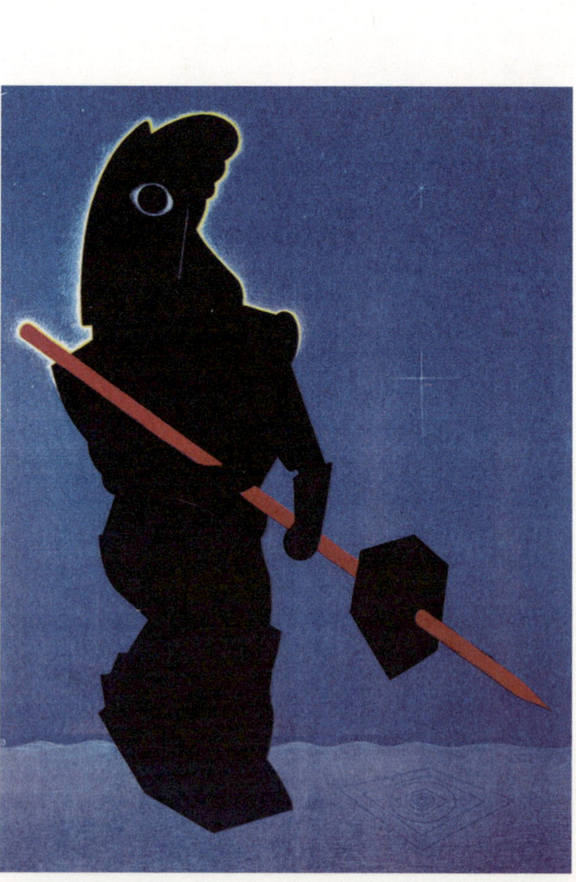

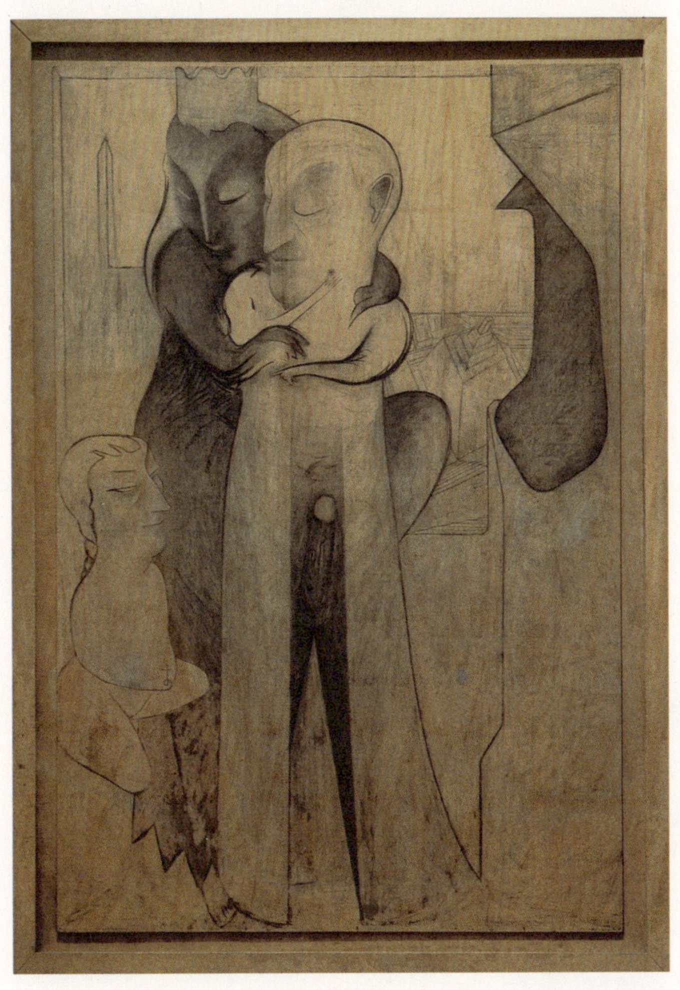

37 *Con titolo* (With Title), 1984. Charcoal and pastel on panel, 95¼ × 63¾ inches (242 × 162 cm). Galleria Nazionale d'Arte Moderna e Contemporanea, Rome [IT 252]
→ 39, 187

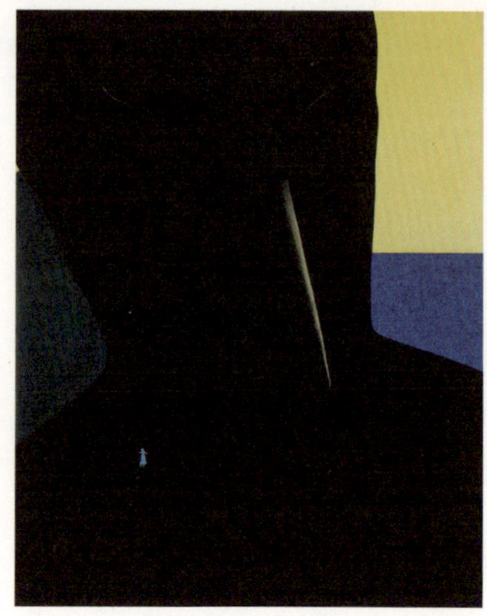

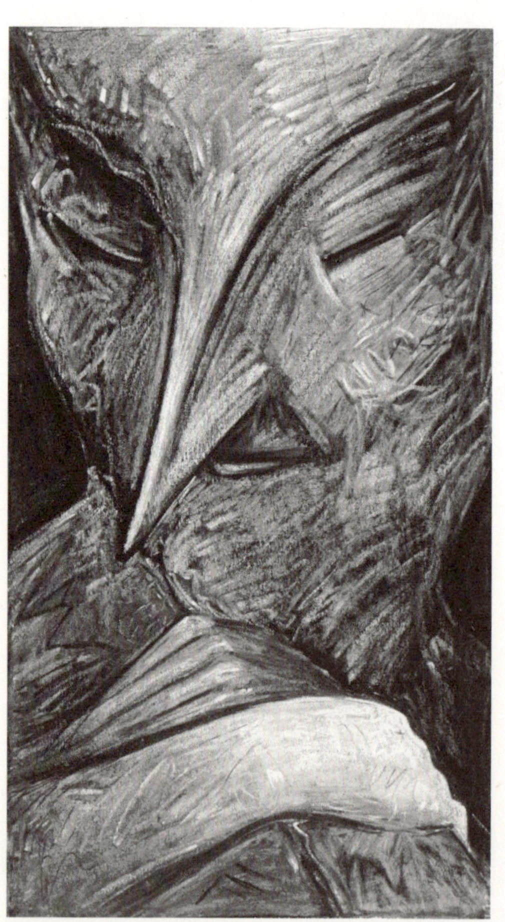

38   *Senza titolo (Lady Diana)*
(Untitled [Lady Diana]), 1985.
Mixed media on wood, 86⅝ ×
82⅝ × 23⅝ inches (220 ×
210 × 60 cm). Private collection, Lugano [IT 256]
→   181, 186

39   *Senza titolo* (Untitled), 1985.
Chalk on wood, 28¾ ×
14⅛ inches (73 × 36 cm). Silvio
Sansone Collection, Salerno
[IT 259]
→   159

40 *Senza titolo* (Untitled), 1985.
Tempera and clay on panel,
94½ × 65 inches (240 ×
165 cm). Chiara and Francesco
Carraro Collection, Venice
[IT 265]
→
39, 49, 180, 212

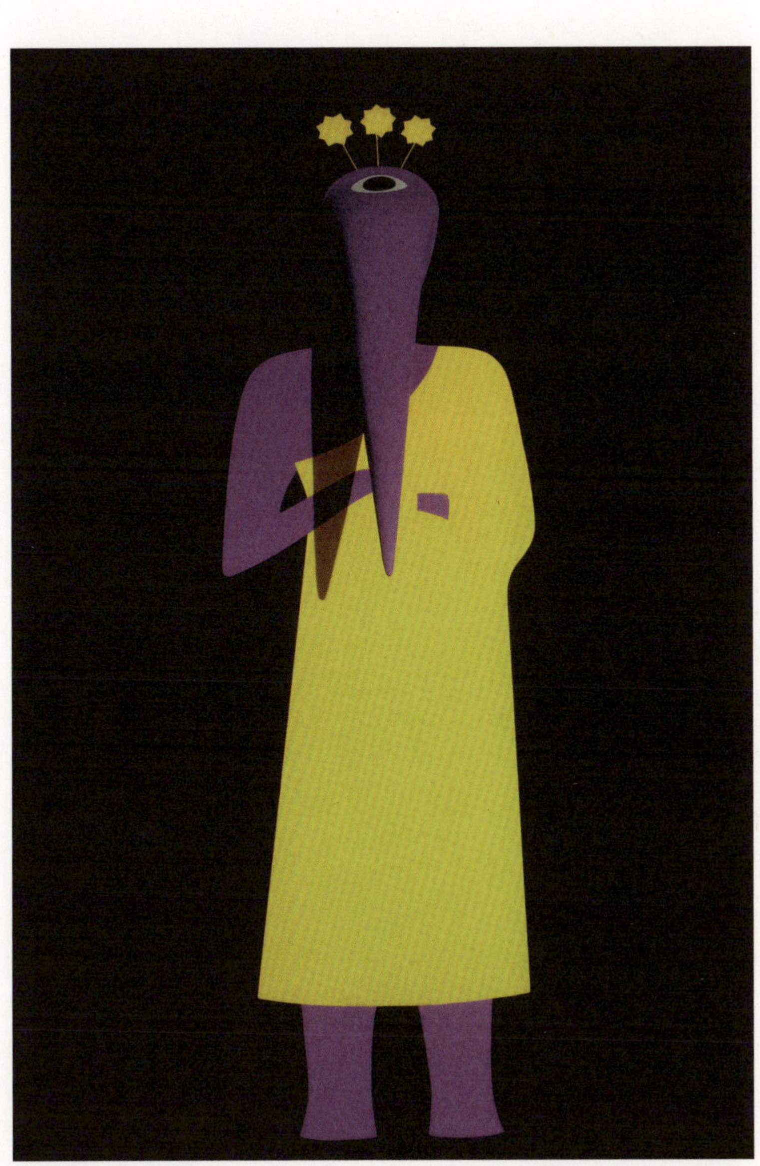

41 *Senza titolo (Coppia con asta)*
(Untitled [Couple with Rod]),
1985. Pencil and charcoal
on panel with painted wooden
rod, 94½ × 63 inches (240 ×
160 cm). Galleria Nazionale
d'Arte Moderna e Contemporanea, Rome [IT 267]

→ 142

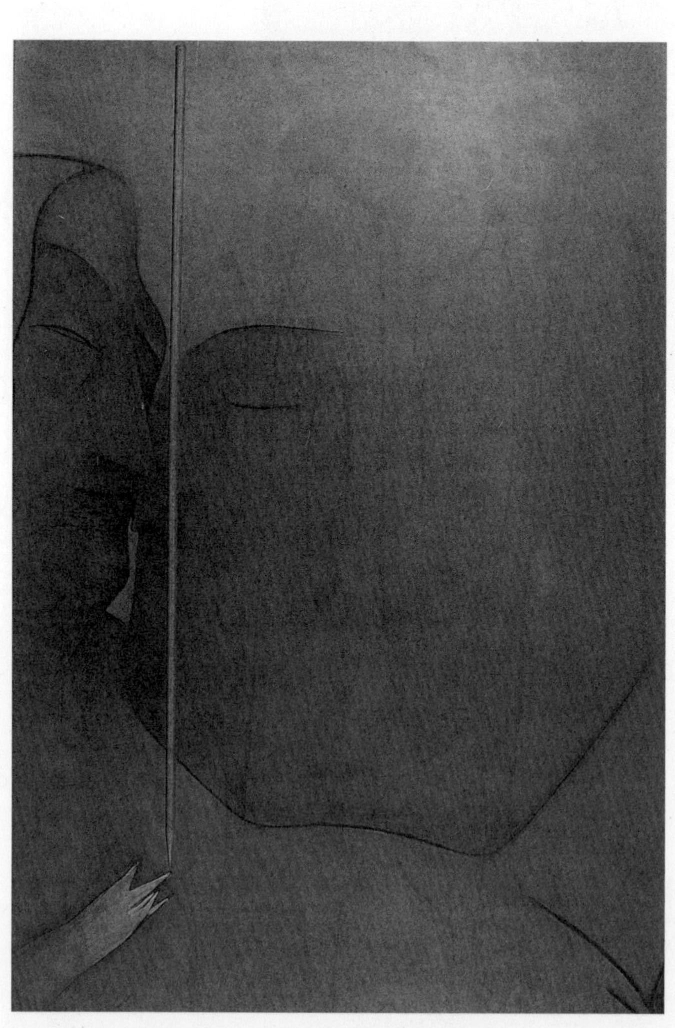

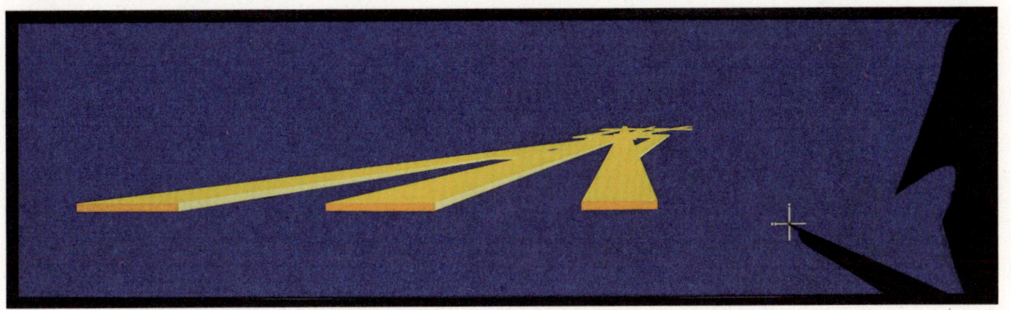

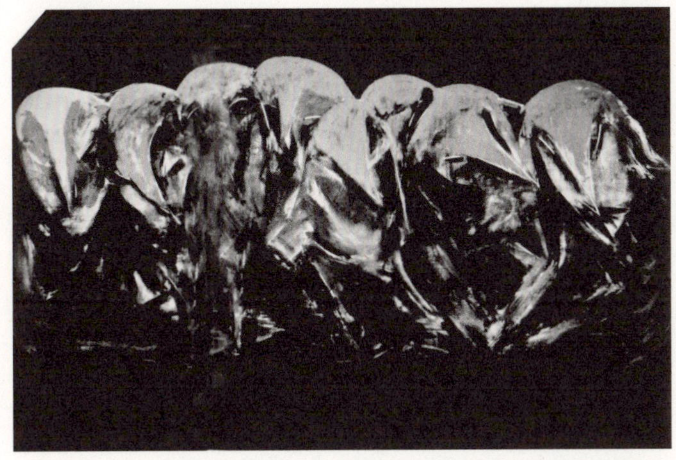

42   *Senza titolo* (Untitled), 1985. Tempera and acrylic on wood, 41⅜ × 131⅞ inches (105 × 335 cm). Lia Rumma Collection, Naples [IT 268]
→ 39

43   *Senza titolo* (Untitled), 1986. Mixed media on wood, 82¼ × 105⅞ inches (209 × 269 cm). Private collection, Carpi [IT 283]
→ 183

44 *Senza titolo (Gioconda)* (Untitled [Gioconda]), 1987/ 1991–92. Graphite on panel, 19¾ × 19¾ inches (50 × 50 cm). Calabresi Collection, Rome [IT 301]
→ 179

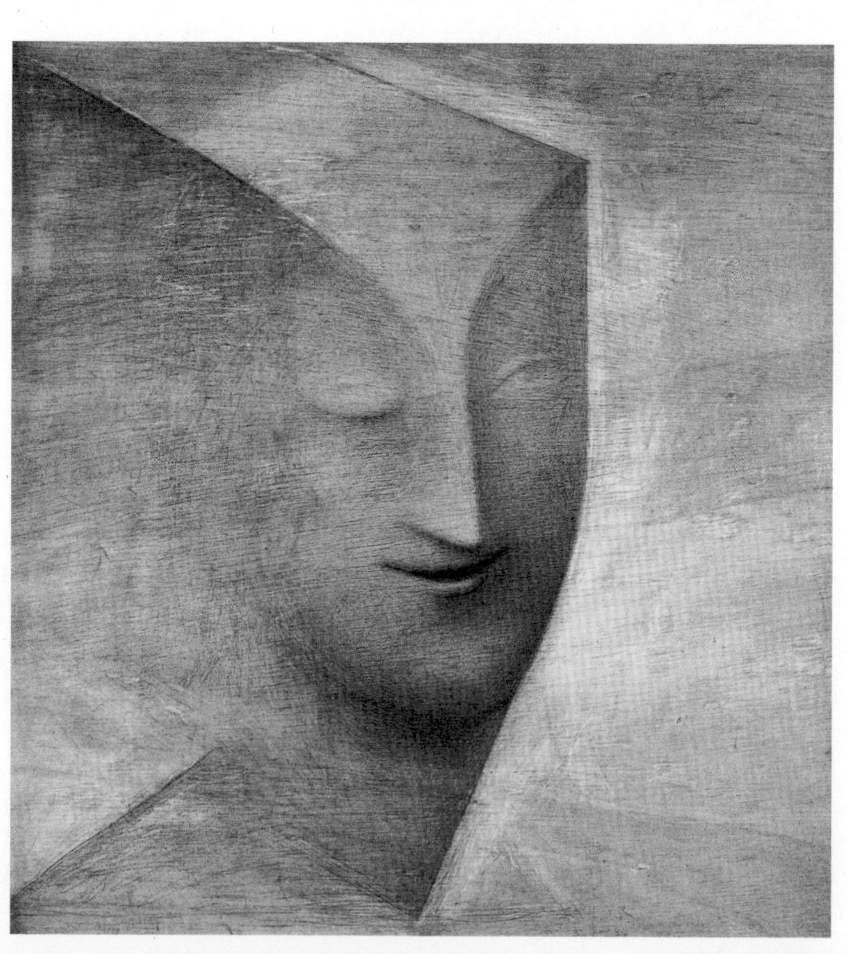

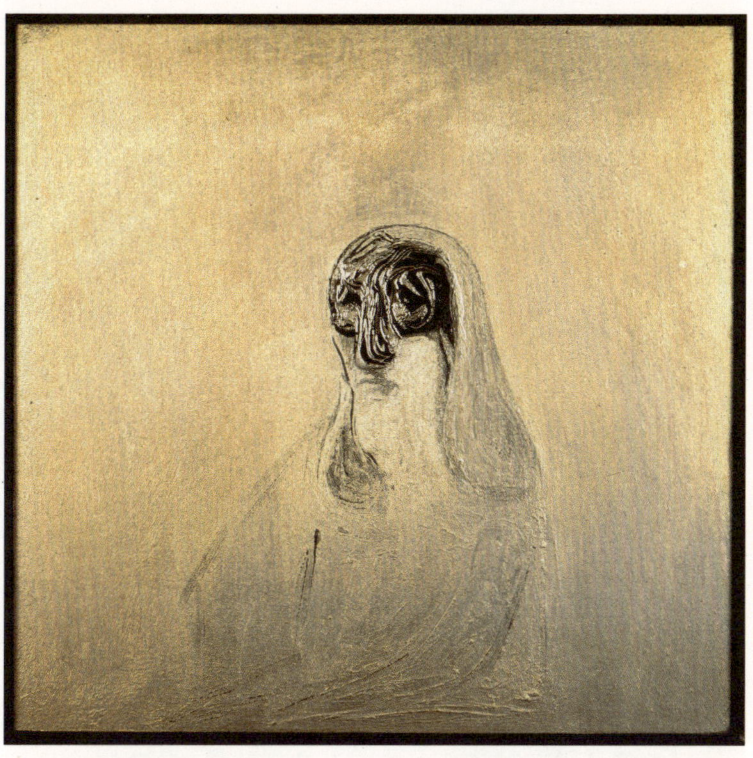

45 *Senza titolo* (Untitled), 1988.
Tempera and gold paint
on wood, 15¾ × 15¾ inches
(40 × 40 cm). Lia Rumma Collection, Naples [IT 313]

→ 119

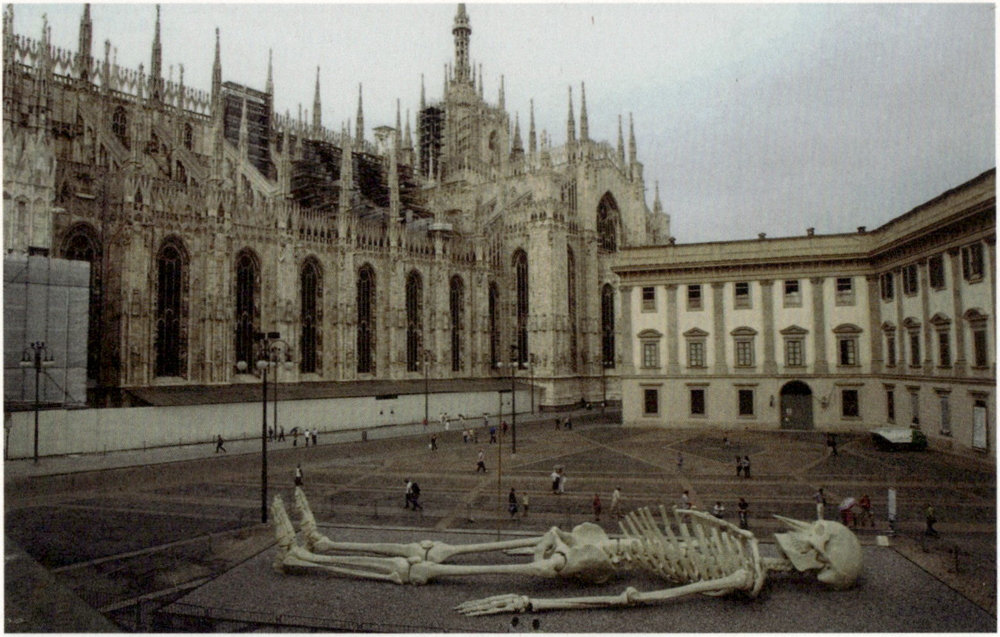

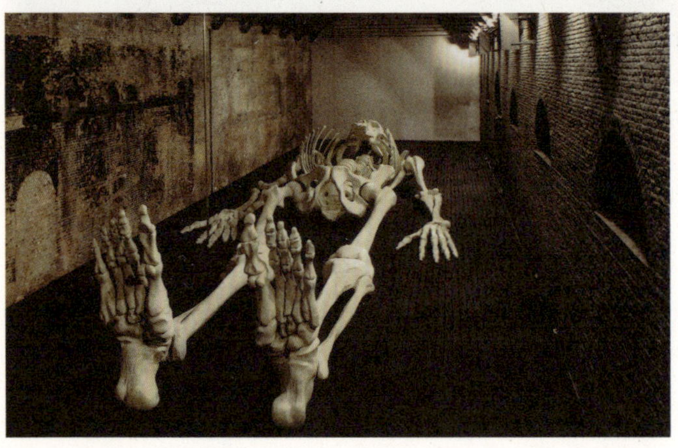

46   *Calamita cosmica* (Cosmic
Magnet), 1988–89. Plaster,
polystyrene, synthetic
resin, iron core, and vinyl glue,
342½ × 944⅞ × 248 inches
(870 × 2400 × 630 cm).
Fondazione Cassa di Rispar-
mio di Foligno Collection,
Foligno [IT 314]

→   176

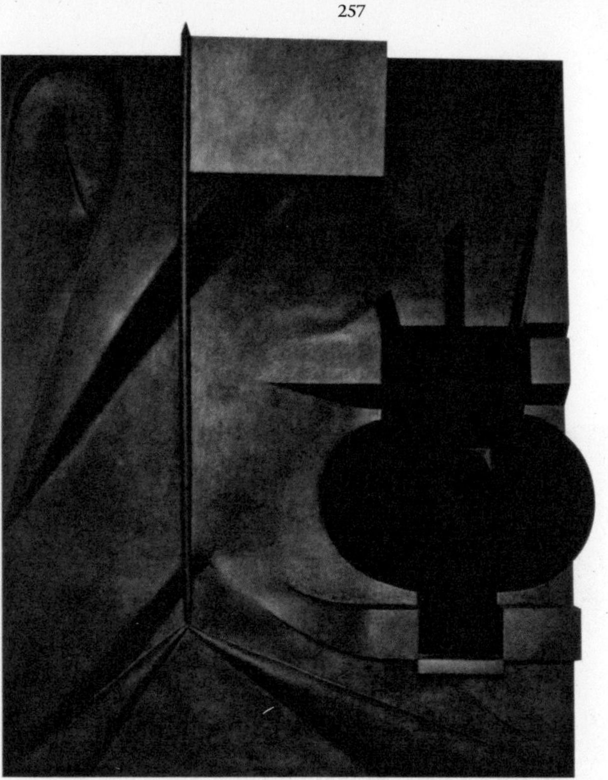

47 *Senza titolo (Figura a piazza del Popolo)* (Untitled [Figure in Piazza del Popolo]), 1989. Acrylic and assembled elements on panel, 109½ × 84¼ × 31½ inches (278 × 214 × 80 cm). Lia Rumma Collection, Naples [IT 317]
→ 184

48 *L'immortale invisibile e il luogo* (The Invisible Immortal and the Place), 1989. Metal chair painted black, 39⅜ × 19¾ × 19¾ inches (100 × 50 × 50 cm). Private collection, Lugano [IT 320]
→ 177–78, 214–15

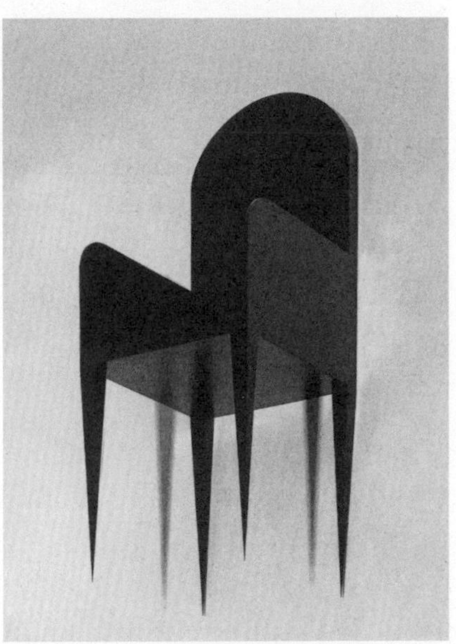

49 *Senza titolo* (Untitled), 1989. Mixed media on wood, 106¼ × 106¼ inches (270 × 270 cm). Lia Rumma Collection, Naples [IT 322]

→ 179, 182

50 *L'artista e il suo doppio* (The Artist and His Double), ca. 1980s. Mixed media on photograph, 9¼ × 14⅛ inches (23.5 × 36 cm). Private collection, Tezze di Arzignano [IT 370]

→ 142

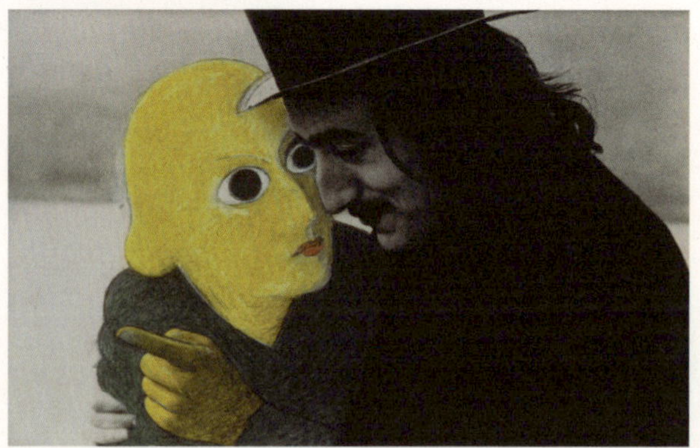

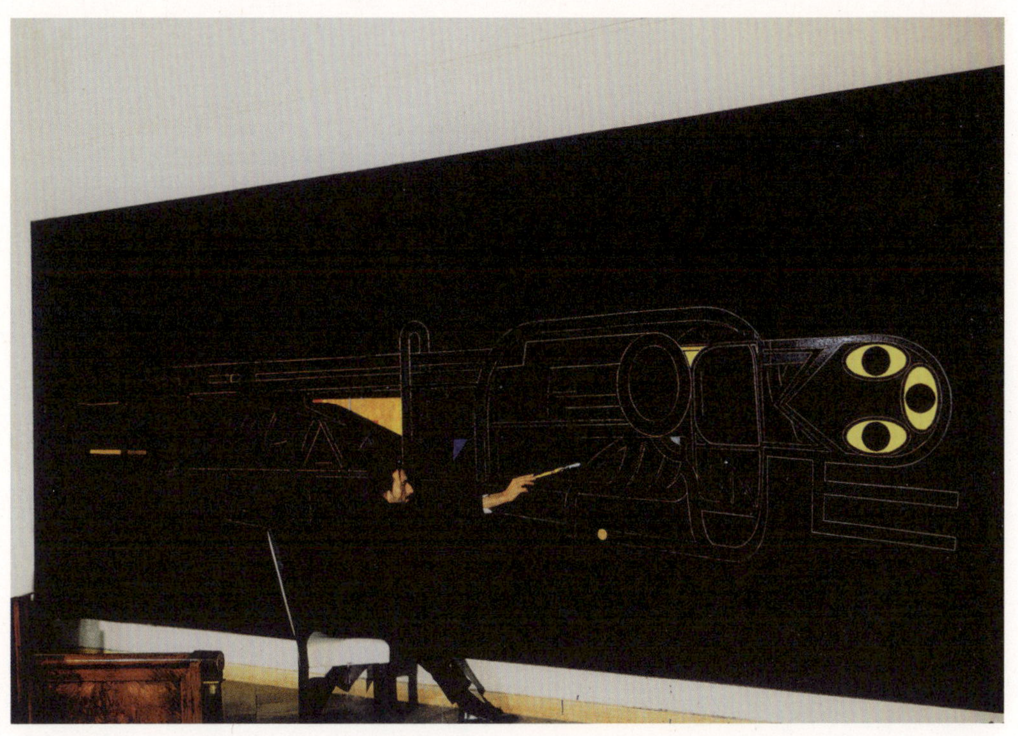

51 *La fondazione sumera di Roma* (The Sumerian Foundation of Rome), 1990. Tempera and gold on wood, 255⅞ × 106¼ inches (650 × 270 cm). Probably destroyed by the artist [IT 401]

→ 46n18, 72, 78

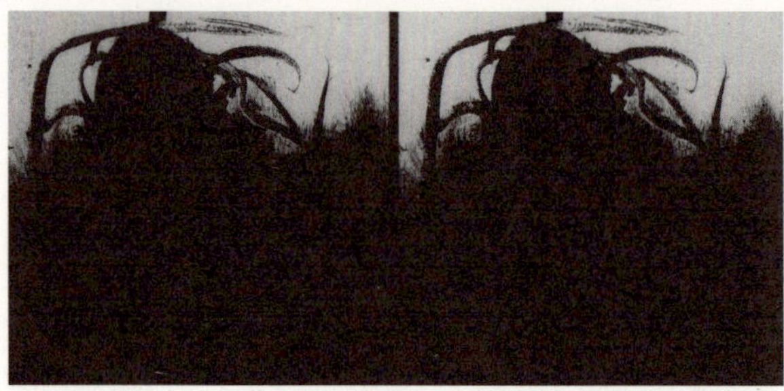

52   *Opera viva che deforma il tempo* (A Living Work that Deforms Time), 1990. Tempera and acrylic on wood, diptych, each 19¾ × 19¾ inches (50 × 50 cm). Bianca Attolico Collection, Rome [IT 402]

→   185

53   *Senza titolo (Prospettiva rovesciante)* (Untitled [Reversed Perspective]), 1991. Graphite on poplar board, 78¾ × 78¾ inches (200 × 200 cm). Giorgio Franchetti Collection, Rome [IT 422]

→   183

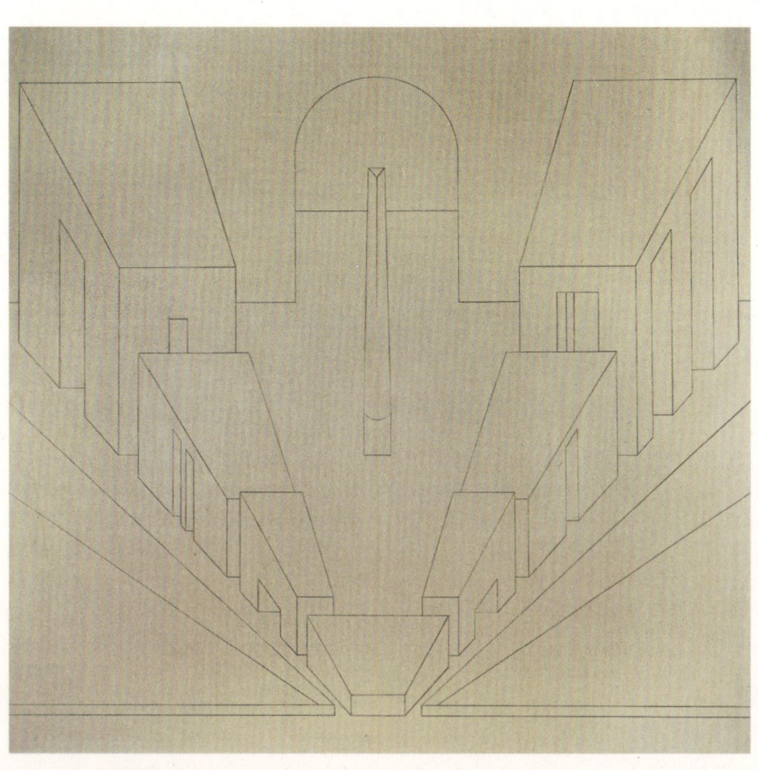

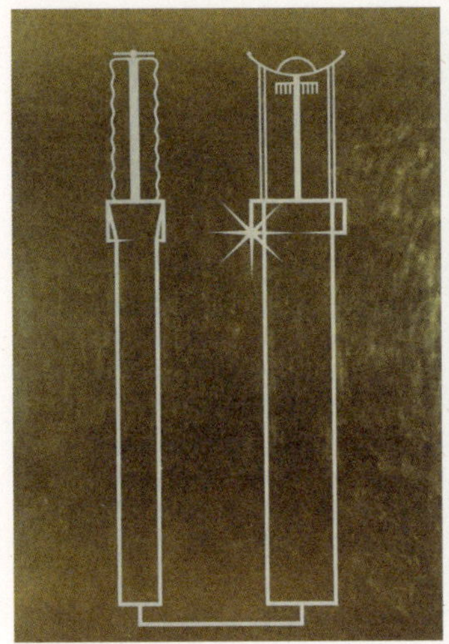

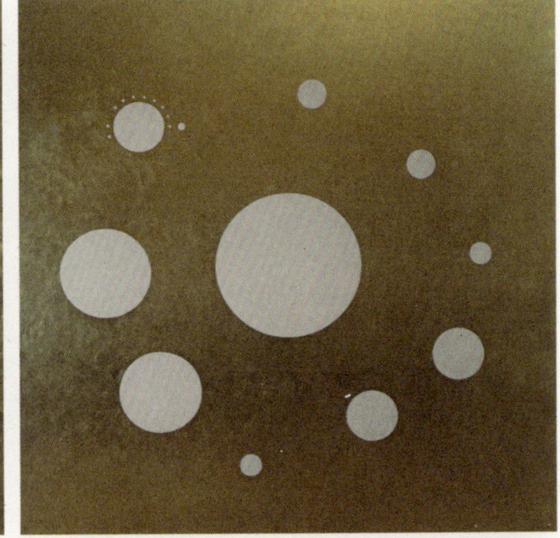

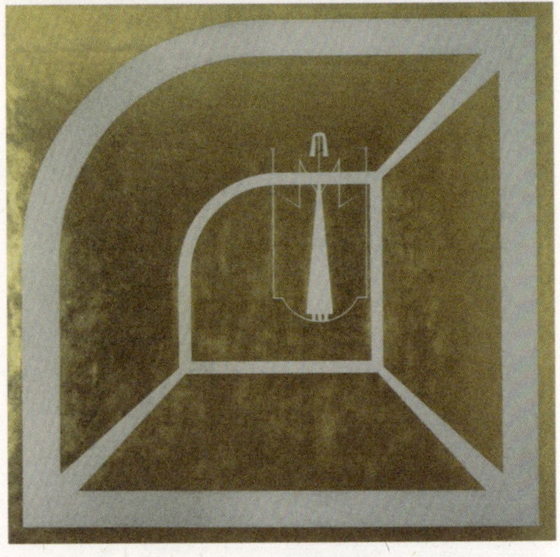

54 *Senza titolo* (Untitled), 1992–93. Mixed media on crystal and honeycomb panel, triptych, 110¾ × 71¾ inches (281 × 181 cm), 110¾ × 110¾ inches (281 × 281 cm). Rosa and Gilberto Sandretto Collection [IT 439]

→ 188

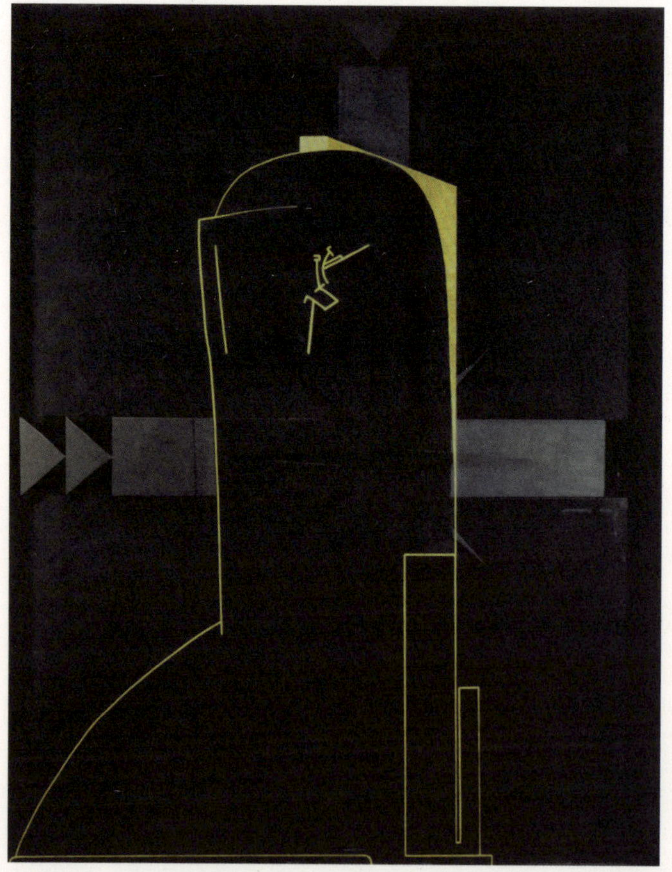

55 *Figura* (Figure), 1994.
Tempera and gold on wood
and crystal, 104⅜ ×
80⅜ inches (265 × 204 cm).
Lia Rumma Collection,
Naples [IT 457]
184

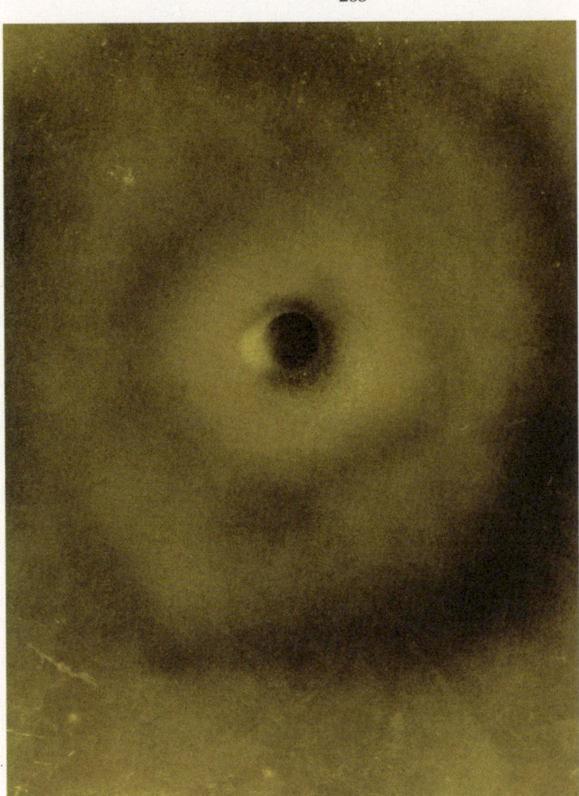

56   *Senza titolo (Autoritratto)* (Untitled [Self-Portrait]), 1995. Tempera on Masonite, 27½ × 19⅝ inches (70 × 50 cm). Consolandi Collection, Milan [IT 471]
→   123

57   *Senza titolo* (Untitled), 1995. Acrylic, airbrush, and collage on canvas, 21¼ × 21¼ inches (54 × 54 cm). Gabriele Guercio Collection, Milan [IT 478]
→   189

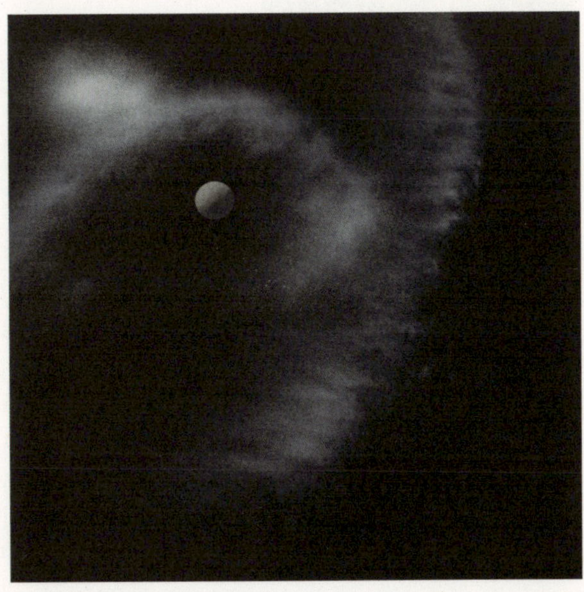

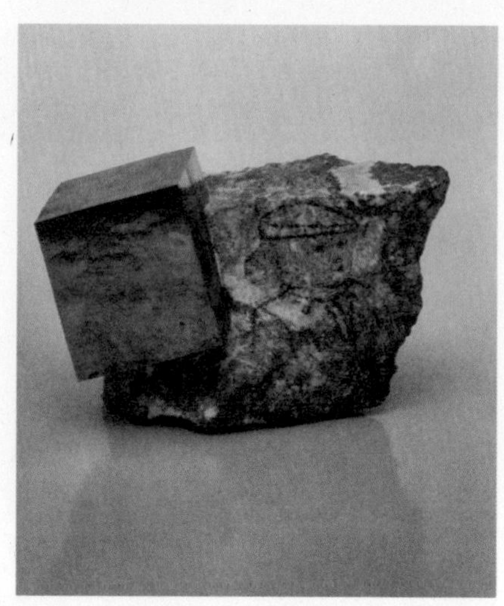

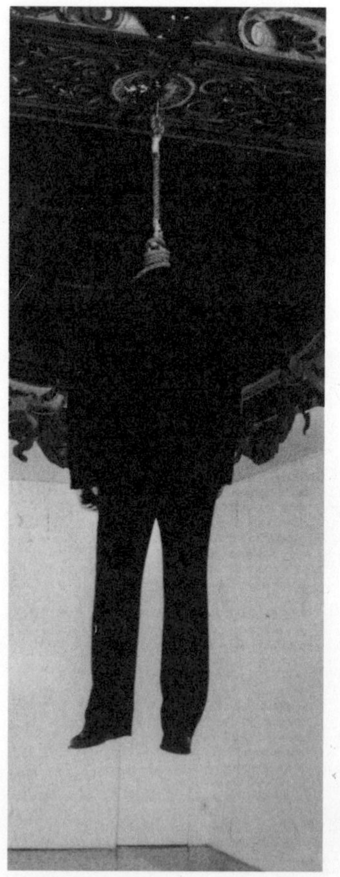

58   *Opera non titolata* (Work without a Title), 1995–96. Drawing
on vermentino stone and pyrite, 2 × 3 × 3⅜ inches (5 × 8 ×
8.5 cm). Giovanni Michelagnoli
Collection, Venice [IT 480]
→   115

59   *L'impiccato (Il pittore impic-
cato)* (The Hanged Man
[The Hanged Painter]), 1996.
Photo of the event held on
April 11, 1996, at Galleria
La Nuova Pesa, Rome, featur-
ing a living person, hanging
from the ceiling for 27 minutes
[IT 482]
→   118

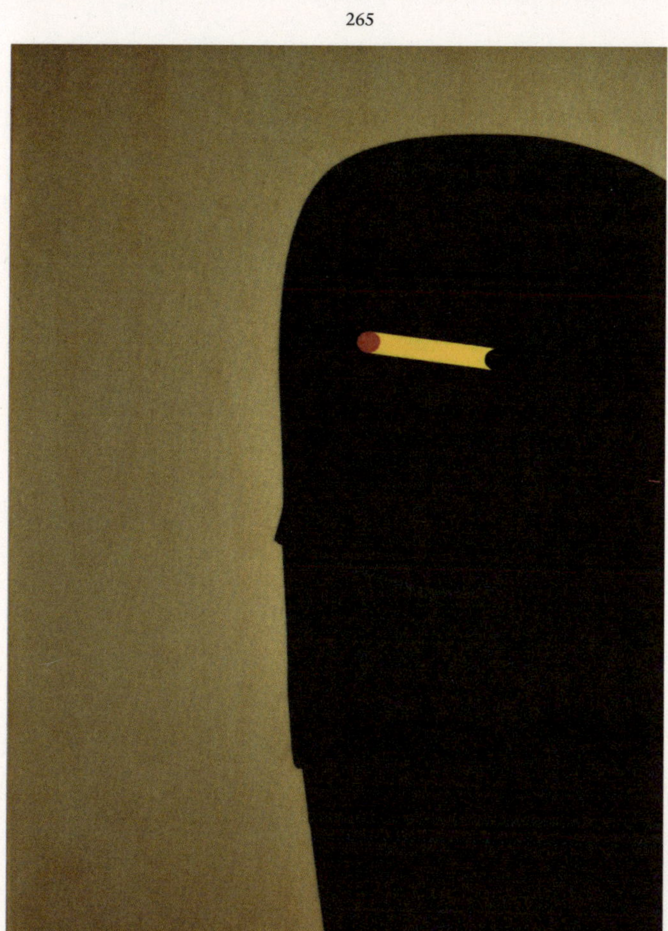

60 *Opera non titolata* (Work without a Title), 1996. Tempera on wood, 96⅞ × 56¼ × 2¾ inches (246 × 143 × 7 cm). Private collection, Rome [IT 483]

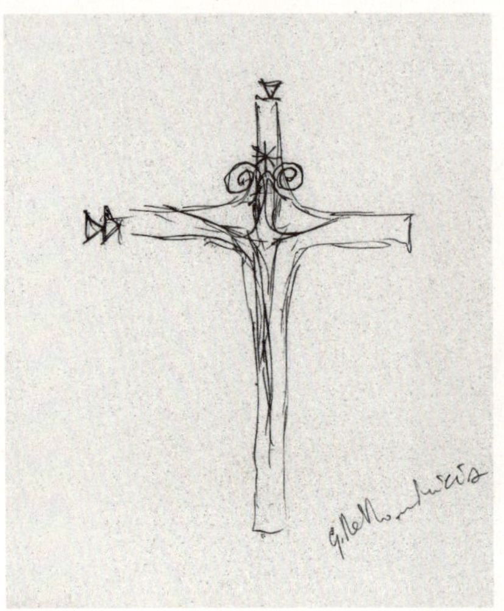

61 *Senza titolo (Schizzo per Gilgamesh)* (Untitled [Sketch for Gilgamesh]), 1997. Ink on paper, 5⅞ × 4¾ inches (15 × 12 cm). Private collection, Lugano [IT 525]

62 *Opera non titolata* (Work without a Title), 1997. Tempera on wood, 96⅞ × 96⅞ × 2¾ inches (246 × 246 × 7 cm). Private collection, Rome [IT 540]

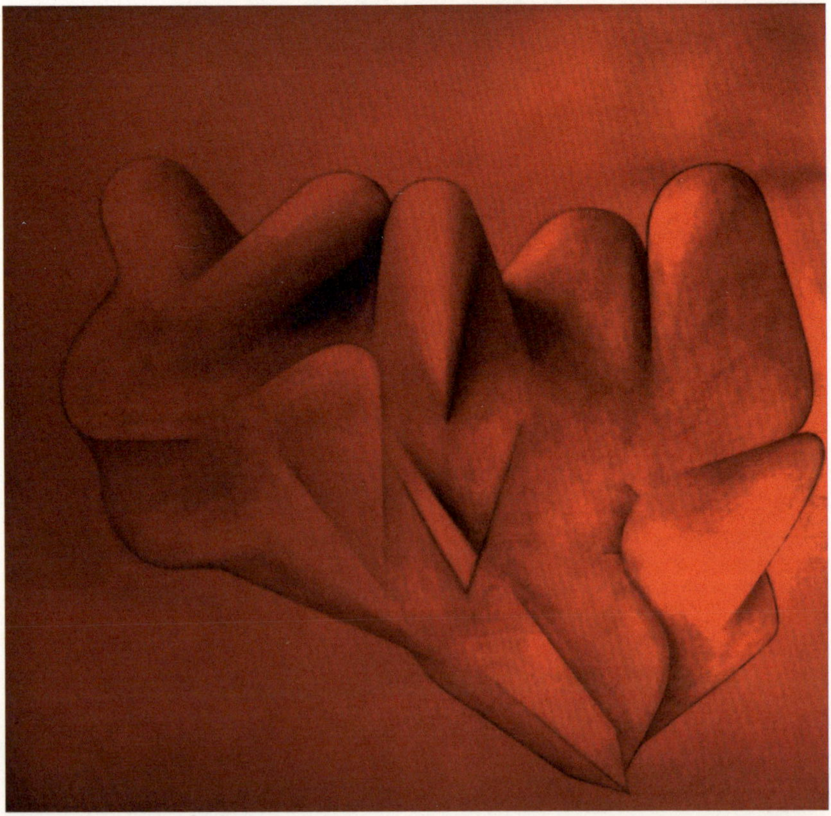

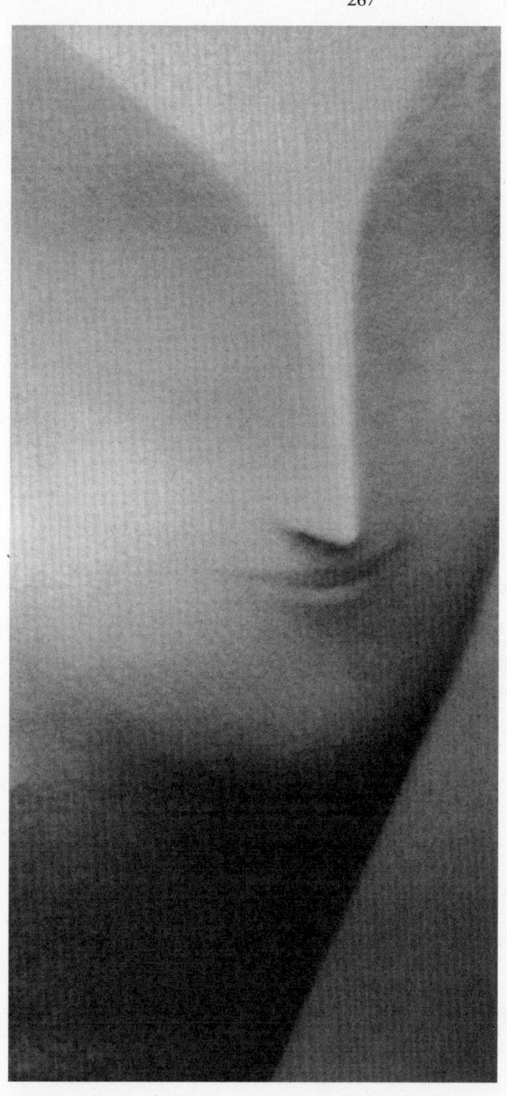

63   *Opera ubiqua (Delfina D. D. –
      Auronia D. D.)* (Ubiquitous
      Work [Delfina D. D. – Auronia
      D. D.]), 1996. Screenprint on
      Masonite retouched in pencil,
      33 × 15 inches (84 × 38 cm).
      Uneditioned proof. Private
      collection [IT 548]
→   143, 157–59, 180

64

*Auronia D. D., uscita dal paral-
lelepipedo di vetro, volteggia
invisibile nella bacheca. Auronia D. D. a 99 anni in 99 luoghi*
(Auronia D. D. leaves the glass
parallelepiped, spins invisibly
on a board. Auronia D. D.
in 99 places for 99 years), 1997.
Glass, crystal, and pencil
on wood, 22 ⅝ × 41⅞ inches
(57.5 × 106.2 cm) [IT 542]
143–44

→

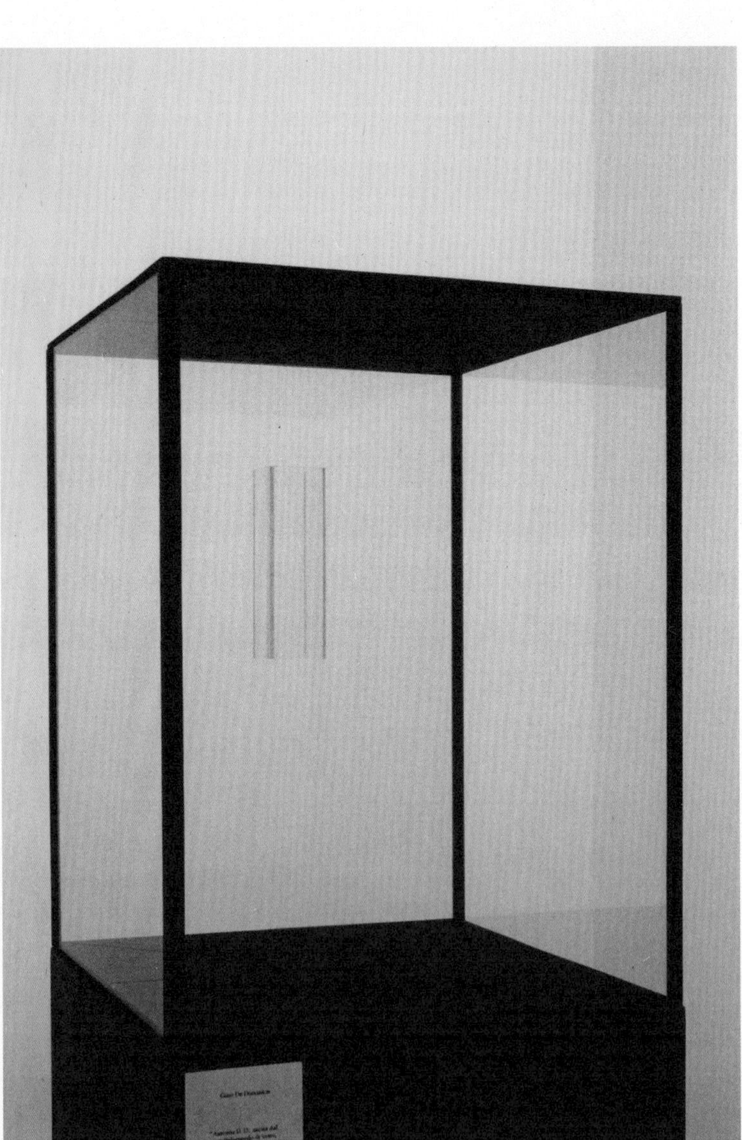

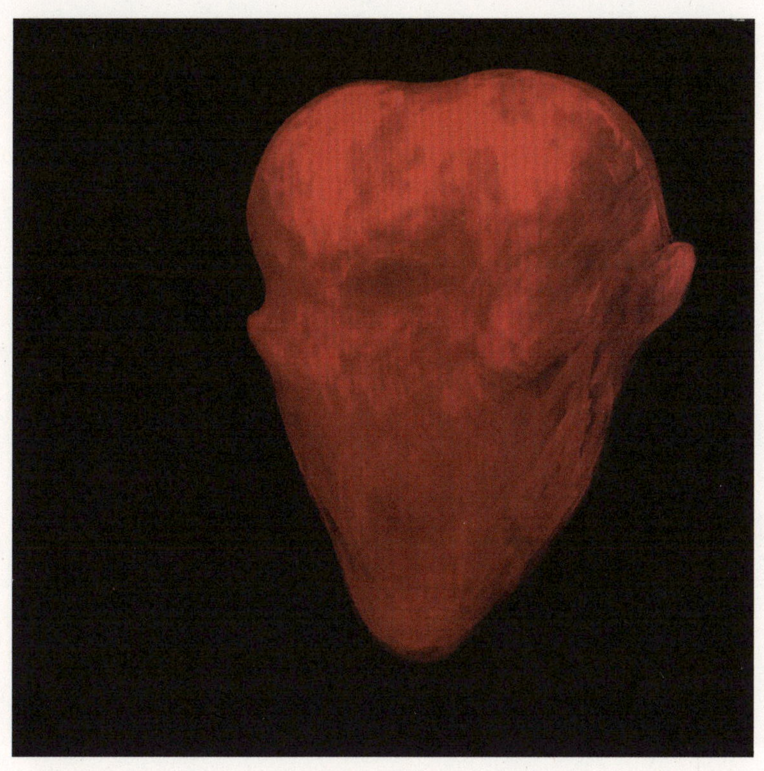

65   *Autoritratto (Cuore rosso)*
(Self-Portrait [Red Heart]),
1998. Enamel on canvas,
39⅜ × 39⅜ inches (100 ×
100 cm). Private collection
[IT 581]

→   123

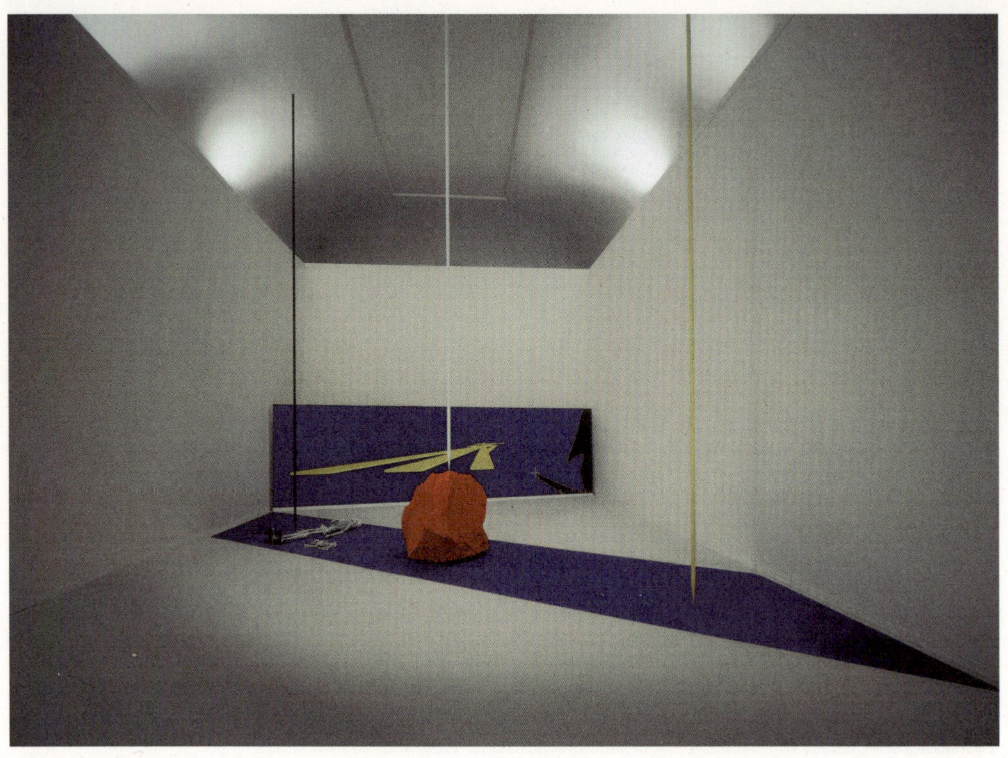

For his exhibition in the Sala dei Camuccini at Capodimonte in July 1986, curated by Lia Rumma, Gino De Dominicis showed a painting previously exhibited at Galleria Emilio Mazzoli in Modena. He later destroyed it and made a smaller version, reproduced in this volume, 253, no. 42. The artist repainted some of his major works for the exhibition, including the skeleton (painted white) and a larger version of the stone (painted red), and placed rods among them. A white wall surrounds the works, isolating them, while, beyond the frame of this photograph, to the right, stands another work (reproduced in this volume, no. 39, 250), as if isolated from the whole setting De Dominicis created.

SELECTED BIBLIOGRAPHY

1967

Barilli, Renato. "L'Arte Povera." In *L'Arte Moderna*, edited by Franco Russoli, 90–91. Milan: Fabbri Editori, 1967.

Dorfles, Gillo. "La Body Art." In *L'Arte Moderna*, 233.

Farroni, Giovanni M. "I miti d'oggi nella pittura del giovane De Dominicis." Exhibition review, Ancona. *La voce Adriatica*, May 10, 1967.

1970

Barilli, Renato. "Le persuasioni." *NAC*, no. 37 (May 1970): 12–13.

Barilli, Renato, Maurizio Calvesi, and Tommaso Trini, eds. *3a biennale internazionale della giovane pittura. Gennaio '70. Comportamenti progetti mediazioni*. Exh. cat. Bologna: Alfa, 1970. Published in conjunction with an exhibition of the same title, organized by and presented at the Museo Civico, Bologna, January 31–February 28, 1970.

Rubiu, Vittorio. "Una poltrona per lo spazio." *Il Corriere della Sera*, January 11, 1970.

1971

Bonito Oliva, Achille, ed. *7a Biennale di Parigi. Italia / 7e Biennale de Paris. Italie / 7th Paris Biennale. Italy*. Exh. cat. Florence: Edizioni Centro Di, 1971. Published in conjunction with the VII Biennale de Paris, held at the Parc Floral de Paris, Bois de Vincennes, Paris, September 24–November 1, 1971.

———. "Biennale di Parigi." Review of the VII Biennale de Paris. *Flash Art*, no. 27 (October/November 1971): 2–3.

———, ed. *Pèrsona. bitef, International Theater Festival, Beograd, September 10*. Exh. cat. Florence: Edizioni Centro Di, 1971. Published in conjunction with the International Theater Festival, Beograd, September 10–26, 1971.

Calvesi, Maurizio. "Contributo alla crisi." In *Album (9–68, 2–71)*, edited by Fabio Sargentini, n.p. Rome: L'Attico, 1971.

Celant, Germano. "Sorella morte." *Domus*, no. 497 (April 1971): 52–54.

———, ed. *Arte Povera: 13 italianische Kunstler: Dokumentation und Werke*. Exh. cat. Munich: Kunstverein München, 1971. Published in conjunction with an exhibition of the same title, organized by and presented at the Kunstverein München, Munich, May 26–June 27, 1971.

De Dominicis, Gino. "De Dominicis." *Flash Art*, no. 25/26 (June/July 1971): 8–9.

Di Castro, Federica. "Identifications." *NAC*, no. 4 (April 1971): 32–33.

Fischer, Konrad, Junger Harten, and Hans Strelow, eds. *Prospect 71 – Projection*. Exh. cat. Düsseldorf: Art Press, 1971. Published in conjunction with an exhibition of the same title, organized by and presented at the Städtischen Kunsthalle, Düsseldorf, October 8–17, 1971.

Galerie nächst St. Stephan, ed. *Situation Concepts*. Exh. cat. Vienna: Galerie nächst St. Stephan, 1971. Published in conjunction with an exhibition of the same title, organized by and presented at the Galerie nächst St. Stephan, Vienna, March 15–April 10, 1971.

Menna, Filiberto. "Gli artisti italiani alla Biennale di Parigi." Review of the VII Biennale de Paris. *Il Mattino*, November 10, 1971.

Rasy, Elisabetta. "Gino De Dominicis." In *Pèrsona. bitef, International Theater Festival, Beograd, September 10*, edited by Achille Bonito Oliva, 16–21. Exh. cat. Florence: Edizioni Centro Di, 1971.

Rustichelli, Franco. "Una formulazione matematica del problema dell'immortalità." In *Album (9–68, 2–71)*, edited by Fabio Sargentini, n.p. Rome: L'Attico, 1971.

Tomassoni, Italo. "Dall'oggetto al concetto all'elogio della tautologia – Considerazioni provvisorie." *Flash Art*, no. 28/29 (December 1971/January 1972): 14–15.

Vincitorio, Francesco. "Gino De Dominicis." *NAC*, no. 1 (January 1971): 27–28.

1972

Arbasino, Alberto, Eugenio Caddini, Fabio Mauri, Geno Pampaloni, Mario Penelope, and Luigi Preti. "Boomerang per la Biennale." *La Fiera Letteraria*, no. 29 (July 1972): 5.

Arcangeli, Francesco. "Italia." In *36. Biennale di Venezia. Esposizione Internazionale d'Arte*, edited by La Biennale di Venezia, 91–93. Exh. cat. Venice: La Biennale di Venezia, 1972. Published in conjunction with the XXXVI Esposizione internazionale d'arte, held at the Giardini della Biennale, Venice, June 11–October 1, 1972.

Barilli, Renato. "Dall'oggetto al comportamento." *Le Arti*, no. 3 (March 1972): 34–38.

———. "Italia." In *36. Biennale di Venezia. Esposizione Internazionale d'Arte*, edited by La Biennale di Venezia, 96–99. Exh. cat. Venice: La Biennale di Venezia, 1972.

Barilli, Renato, Alberto Boatto, Achille Bonito Oliva, Filiberto Menna, Gianni E. Simonetti, and Tommaso Trini. "Autodafé Autodasé." *DATA*, no. 5/6 (July 1972): 16–19.

Barilli, Renato, Rossella Bossaglia, and Luciano Caramel. "La Biennale come paradigma." *NAC*, no. 8/9 (August/September 1972): 3–6.

Biason, Renzo. "La mostra degli orrori." Review of the XXXVI Esposizione internazionale d'arte, Venice. *Oggi*, June 24, 1972.

Bonito Oliva, Achille. *Il territorio magico. Comportamenti alternativi dell'arte*. Florence: Edizioni Centro Di, 1972.

Borghese, Giulia. "Oggi dal magistrato i genitori del mongoloide." Review of the XXXVI Esposizione internazionale d'arte, Venice. *Il Corriere della Sera*, June 12, 1972.

———. "Sdegno degli artisti alla Biennale." Review of the XXXVI Esposizione internazionale d'arte, Venice. *Il Corriere della Sera*, June 10, 1972.

———. "Un povero minorato esposto alla Biennale di Venezia." Review of the XXXVI Esposizione internazionale d'arte, Venice. *Il Corriere della Sera*, June 9, 1972.

Calvesi, Maurizio. "De Dominicis segnalato da Maurizio Calvesi." In *Catalogo Nazionale Bolaffi d'arte moderna no. 7*, edited by Carluccio Bolaffi, 52–53. Milan: Giulio Bolaffi Editore, 1972.

———. "La farfalla è un volatile di sinistra." Review

of the XXXVI Esposizione internazionale d'arte, Venice. *L'Espresso*, June 18, 1972.

Del Pesco, Daniela, and Mariantonietta Picone. "Note sull'arte concettuale." *Op. cit*, no. 25 (September 1972): 5–34.

"Flashback su Kassel." Review of Documenta 5. *Befragung der Realität – Bildwelten heute*, Kassel. *Flash Art*, no. 35/36 (September/October 1972): 18.

Guarini, Ruggero. "Cuore e Quore." Review of the XXXVI Esposizione internazionale d'arte, Venice. *Il Messaggero*, June 11, 1972.

Guttuso, Renato. "C'è un limite anche all'ignobile." Review of the XXXVI Esposizione internazionale d'arte, Venice. *Il Giorno*, June 25, 1972.

———. "Gli occhi chiusi di Venezia." Review of the XXXVI Esposizione internazionale d'arte, Venice. *Il Giorno*, June 25, 1972.

———. "La Biennale in coabitazione." Review of the XXXVI Esposizione internazionale d'arte, Venice. *La Stampa*, November 12, 1972.

"Kassel. Documenta 5." Review of Documenta 5. *Befragung der Realität – Bildwelten heute*, Kassel. *NAC*, no. 8/9 (August/September 1972): 39–40.

Liguori, Alfonso Maria. "Non raggiungeremo l'immortalità." *Il Corriere della Sera*, November 4, 1972.

Longo, Filippo. "Biennale di Venezia. Gino De Dominicis: ovvero della pietà cristiana." Review of the XXXVI Esposizione internazionale d'arte, Venice. *Flash Art 5*, no. 35–36 (September/October 1972): 21.

Manganelli, Giorgio. "Un santino senza aureola." *L'Espresso*, June 18, 1972.

Pasolini, Pier Paolo. "Il mongoloide alla Biennale è il prodotto della sottocultura italiana." *Il Tempo*, June 25, 1972.

Preti, Luigi. "Offesa volgare all'arte e al senso morale." *La Fiera Letteraria*, no. 25 (June 1972): 6.

Riva, Vittorio. "Vecchi scandali per nuovi ricchi." *L'Espresso*, June 18, 1972.

Schum, Gerry. "Videogalerie Gerry Schum." *Flash Art*, no. 28/29 (December 1971/January 1972): 15.

———. "Video-nastri." In *36. Biennale di Venezia. Esposizione Internazionale d'Arte*, edited by La Biennale di Venezia, 3–33. Exh. cat. Venice: La Biennale di Venezia, 1972.

———. "Video tappa Gerry Schum." *DATA*, no. 4 (May 1972): 70–73.

Szeemann, Harald, ed. *1972 Documenta 5*. Exh. cat. Kassel: Documenta and C. Bertelsmann Verlag, 1972. Published in conjunction with Documenta 5. *Befragung der Realität – Bildwelten heute*, held at the Museum Fridericianum, Friedrichsplatz, and Neue Galerie, Kassel, June 30–October 8, 1972.

———. "Scandalo a Venezia." Review of Documenta 5. *Befragung der Realität – Bildwelten heute*, Kassel. *L'Osservatore Romano*, June 10, 1972.

Tortora, Enzo. "Cinico trampolino." Review of the XXXVI Esposizione internazionale d'arte, Venice. *La Nazione*, June 10, 1972.

———. "E sarebbe un artista?" Review of the XXXVI Esposizione internazionale d'arte, Venice. *Il Resto del Carlino*, June 1, 1972.

Trini, Tommaso. "Kassel sana in Monaco sano." Review of Documenta 5. *Befragung der Realität – Bildwelten heute*, Kassel. *DATA*, no. 5/6 (Summer 1972): 66–67.

Valsecchi, Marco. "La bimba esposta alla 36a Biennale." Review of the XXXVI Esposizione internazionale d'arte, Venice. *Il Giorno*, June 13, 1972.

———. "Una stupida bravata." Review of the XXXVI Esposizione internazionale d'arte, Venice. *Il Giorno*, June 11, 1972.

Weiermair, Peter. "Anmerkungen zur Emanzipation der Kunst." *Alte und Moderne Kunst*, no. 121 (1972): 30–36.

1973

"Assolto l'artista che 'espose' un giovane minorato a Venezia." *Il Corriere della Sera*, April 12, 1973.

Barilli, Renato. "Le due anime del concettuale." *Op. cit*, no. 26 (January 1973): 63–88.

Bonito Oliva, Achille, ed. *8e Biennale de Paris. Italia*. Exh. cat. Florence: Edizioni Centro Di, 1973. Published in conjunction with the 8th Paris Biennale, organized by and presented at the Musée d'Art Moderne de la Ville de Paris, Paris, September 14–October 21, 1973.

———. "Comportamenti alternativi dell'arte a Roma." *Capitolinum*, no. 4/5 (April/May 1973): 29–38.

———, ed. *Contemporanea*. Exh. cat. Florence: Edizioni Centro Di, 1973. Published in conjunction with an exhibition of the same title, organized by and presented at the parking garage of Villa Borghese, Rome, November 1973–February 1974.

———. "La citazione deviata." In *Critica in atto: 6–30 marzo 1972*, edited by Achille Bonito Oliva, 156–63. Rome: Incontri Internazionali d'Arte, 1973.

Cossato, Vittorio. "Espose alle Biennale il mongoloide: assolto." *Il Giorno*, April 12, 1973.

Marchesin, Giuliano. "Assolto (non costituisce reato) il giovane artista che espose un minorato alla Biennale di Venezia." *La Stampa*, April 12, 1973.

Menna, Filiberto. "De Dominicis o della immortalità." Exhibition review, Modern Art Agency, Naples. *Il Mattino*, April 10, 1973.

Querel, Vittore. "Alla ricerca estetica dal 1960 al 1970." *La settimana a Roma*, June 1, 1973.

Toselli, Franco, and Germano Celant, eds. *An Exhibition of New Italian Art*. Exh. cat. Belfast: Arts Council of Northern Ireland; Dublin: David Hendriks Gallery, 1973. Published in conjunction with an exhibition of the same title, organized by and presented at the Arts Council of Northern Ireland Gallery, Belfast.

Utimpergher, Delfo. "Assolto il pittore che espose il minorato." *Il Messaggero*, April 12, 1973.

1975

Barilli, Renato, Gillo Dorfles, and Filiberto Menna, "L'Arte Povera." In *Al di là della pittura. Arte povera, Comportamento, Body art, Concettualismo*, 65–96. Milan: Fabbri Editori, 1975.

1976

Bonito Oliva, Achille. "L'arte degli anni Settanta." In *B76. La Biennale di Venezia. Settore arti vi-*

277

sive e architettura. Catalogo generale, edited by La Biennale di Venezia, 10, 17. Exh. cat. Venice: La Biennale di Venezia, 1976. Published in conjunction with the XXXVII Esposizione internazionale d'arte, held at the Giardini della Biennale, Venice, July 14–October 10, 1976.

Montale, Eugenio. "È ancora possibile la poesia?" Lecture given at the Accademia di Svezia, Rome, December 12, 1973. Reprinted in *Sulla Poesia*, edited by Giorgio Zampa and Eugenio Montale, 5–14. Milan: Mondadori, 1976.

1977

Barilli, Renato. "Dall'opera al coinvolgimento." In *1960–1977 / Arte in Italia*, edited by Renato Barilli, Antonio Del Guercio, Filiberto Menna, and Leonardo Mosso, 9–21, 58. Exh. cat. Turin: Galleria Civica d'Arte Moderna, 1977. Published in conjunction with an exhibition of the same title, organized by and presented at the Galleria Civica d'Arte Moderna, Turin, May–September 1977.

Bonito Oliva, Achille. *Autocritico automobile. Attraverso le avanguardie*. Milan: Il Formichiere Editore, 1977.

1978

Bonito Oliva, Achille. "Apologia del limite (1972/73)." In *Passo dello strabismo. Sulle arti*, edited by Achille Bonito Oliva, 217–19. Milan: Feltrinelli, 1978.

———. "Natura morte." In *Artenatura*, edited by La Biennale di Venezia, 16–19. Venice: Edizioni La Biennale di Venezia, 1978.

———. "Pèrsona (1971/72)." In *Passo dello strabismo*, 83–87.

———. "Sei stazioni per artenatura. La natura dell'arte." In *B78. Dalla natura all'arte, dall'arte alla natura*, edited by La Biennale di Venezia, 50. Exh. cat. Milan: Electa, 1978. Published in conjunction with the XXXVIII Esposizione internazionale d'arte 1978, held at the Giardini della Biennale, Venice, July 2–October 15, 1978.

Calvesi, Maurizio. *Avanguardia di massa*. Milan: Feltrinelli, 1978.

1979

"Assenze e allusioni." Galleria Mario Pieroni, Rome. *Paese Sera*, May 11, 1979.

Tomassoni, Italo. "Del classico." *Flash Art*, no. 92/93 (October/November 1979): 32.

1980

Salerno, Giovan B. "Nella stanza vuota dell'arte. I fantasmi di Borges." Exhibition review, Galleria Pio Monti, Rome. *Il Manifesto*, June 10, 1980.

Tomassoni, Italo. "De Dominicis, Prini, Pisani." *Flash Art*, no. 98/99 (Summer 1980): 42.

———. "Gino De Dominicis." *Flash Art*, no. 100 (November 1980): 46.

1981

Ammann, Jean-Christophe. "Identité italienne." Exhibition review, Centre Georges Pompidou, Paris. *Domus*, no. 621 (October 1981): 57–64.

Calvesi, Maurizio. "Les vicissitudes de l'art italienne. L'Art en Italie depuis 1959." In *Identité italienne*, edited by Germano Celant, 29–30. Exh. cat. Paris: Centre Georges Pompidou, 1981. Published in conjunction with an exhibition of the same title, organized by and presented at the Centre Georges Pompidou, Paris, June 25–September 7, 1981.

Celant, Germano. "Pour une identité italienne." In *Identité italienne*, 5–23.

Ciardi, Nives. "Pinocchio." *Domus*, no. 617 (May 1981): 66–67.

Panicelli, Ida. "Gino De Dominicis." Exhibition review, Galleria Pio Monti, Rome. *Artforum* 19, no. 6 (February 1981): 88–89.

Ponente, Nello, ed. *Linee della ricerca artistica in Italia 1960/1980*. Exh cat. Rome: De Luca, 1981. Published in conjunction with an exhibition of the same title, organized by and presented at the Palazzo delle Esposizioni, Rome, February 14–April 15, 1981.

1982

Barilli, Renato. "Arte povera, conceptual art, multimedia." In *Arte Italiana 1960/82*, edited by Flavio Caroli, Renato Barilli, and Roberto Sanesi, 27–30. Exh. cat. Milan: Electa, 1982. Published in conjunction with an exhibition of the same title, organized by and presented at the Hayward Gallery, London, October 1982–January 1983.

Farci, Maria Silvia. "Si ricomincia dall'immagine." Exhibition review, Galleria Sperone, Rome. *L'Unità*, April 13, 1982.

Fuchs, Rudi, ed. *Documenta 7*. Exh. cat. Kassel: Weber U. Weidemeyer, 1982. Published in conjunction with Documenta 7, held in Kassel, June 15–September 28, 1982.

Tisdall, Caroline. "From the Spirit of Inquiry to the Pleasure Principle." In *Arte Italiana 1960/82*, 13–14.

Tosi, Barbara. "Gino De Dominicis." Exhibition review, Galleria Sperone, Rome. *Segno*, no. 26 (May/June 1982): 2, 9–30.

1983

De Fusco, Renato. *Storia dell'arte contemporanea*. Rome-Bari: Laterza, 1983.

"Ironia e archeologia in Gino De Dominicis." Exhibition review, Galleria Sprovieri, Rome. *Il Corriere della Sera*, July 4, 1983.

Menna, Filiberto. *La linea analitica dell'arte moderna. Le figure e le icone*. Turin: Giulio Einaudi Editore, 1983.

1984

Barilli, Renato. *L'arte contemporanea. Da Cézanne alle ultime tendenze*. Milan: Feltrinelli, 1984.

Dorfles, Gillo. *Le ultime tendenze nell'arte d'oggi. Dall'Informale al Postmoderno* (1978). Milan: Feltrinelli, 1984.

1985

Bonito Oliva, Achille, ed. *XIII Biennale di Parigi*. Exh. cat. Berlin: Viceversa, 1985. Published in conjunction with the XIII Biennale de Paris, organized by and presented at La Grande Halle de La Villette, Paris, October 2–November 10, 1985.

Fuchs, Rudi, ed. *Ouverture / Arte Contemporanea*. Exh. cat. Turin: Umberto Allemandi, 1985. Published in conjunction with an exhibition of the same title, organized by and presented at the Castello di Rivoli, Turin, December 1984–June 1985.

1986

Barilli, Renato. "Con un palmo di naso." Exhibition review, Galleria Emilio Mazzoli, Modena, and Museo di Capodimonte, Naples. *L'Espresso*, September 14, 1986.

Bonito Oliva, Achille. *Arte Santa*. Exh. cat. Ravenna: Edizioni Essegi Ravenna, 1986. Published in conjunction with an exhibition of the same title, held at the Loggetta Lombardesca, Ravenna, May 11–August 31, 1986.

———. "Artisti. Gino De Dominicis." *Il Giornale dell'Arte Vernissage*, no. 40 (December 1986): 87–89.

Bonuomo, Michele. "Una scena senza attori e senza trama." Exhibition review, Museo di Capodimonte, Naples. *Il Mattino*, August 3, 1986.

Celant, Germano. "Art to the Power N: Gino De Dominicis." *Artforum* 25, no. 4 (December 1986): 100–106.

Christov-Bakargiev, Carolyn. "Gino De Dominicis." *Flash Art International* 20, no. 131 (December 1986/January 1987): 58–63.

Tazzi, Pier Luigi. "Modena: Gino De Dominicis. Galleria Emilio Mazzoli." Exhibition review, Galleria Emilio Mazzoli, Modena. *Artforum* 25, no. 3 (November 1986): 146–47.

Testori, Giovanni. "Fiamme degli inferi per l'uomogufo." Exhibition review, Galleria Emilio Mazzoli, Modena. *Il Corriere della Sera*, July 23, 1986.

1987

Barilli, Renato. *Il ciclo del postmoderno. La ricerca artistica degli anni '80*. Milan: Feltrinelli, 1987.

———. "Una galleria inimitabile: testimonianze." In *L'Attico 1957–1987. 30 anni di pittura, scultura, musica, danza, performance, video*, edited by Fabio Sargentini, Roberto Lambardelli, and Lucia Masina, 69–70. Exh. cat. Milan: Arnoldo Mondadori Editore, 1987.

Bonito Oliva, Achille. "A futura memoria." In *L'Attico 1957–1987*, 71–73.

———. "Il gene dell'arte." In *Antipatia. L'arte contemporanea*, edited by Achille Bonito Oliva, 120–23. Milan: Feltrinelli, 1987.

Calvesi, Maurizio. "Galleria L'Attico: una storia che attraversa le nuove avanguardie." In *L'Attico 1957–1987*, 73–74.

Carandente, Giovanni. "Storia di una galleria." In *L'Attico 1957–1987*, 9–18.

Christov-Bakargiev, Carolyn. "Bebé, yuppies e maturi, tre generazioni in fiera." *Il Sole 24 Ore*, May 31, 1987.

Rubiu, Vittorio. "Un gallerista precursore." In *L'Attico 1957–1987*, 75–76.

Rumma, Lia. "De Dominicis. Immortalità in attesa di accettazione." *Il Giornale dell'Arte*, no. 42 (February 1987): 14.

Sargentini, Fabio, Roberto Lambardelli, and Lucia Masina. *L'Attico 1957–1987. 30 anni di pittura, scultura, musica, danza, performance, video*.

Exh. cat. Milan: Arnoldo Mondadori Editore, 1987. Published in conjunction with an exhibition of the same title, held at the Chiesa di San Nicolò, Spoleto, July 1–August 30, 1987.

1988

Alfano Miglietti, Francesca. "Arte Concettuale e Arte Povera." In *Arte in Italia 1960–1985*, edited by Francesca Alfano Miglietti, 67–103. Milan: Giancarlo Politi Editore, 1988.

Bonito Oliva, Achille. "La pittura italiana." In *Il Tallone di Achille*, edited by Achille Bonito Oliva, 56. Milan: Feltrinelli, 1988.

Celant, Germano. "Gino De Dominicis." In *Arte dall'Italia*, edited by Germano Celant, 219–27. Milan: Feltrinelli, 1988. (First published in *Artforum* 25, no. 4 [December 1986]: 100–105, as "Art to the Power N: Gino De Dominicis.")

Christov-Bakargiev, Carolyn. "Arte e ideologia." In *Arte in Italia 1960–1985*, 105–22.

Gatt, Giuseppe. "L'oggi non esiste parola d'artista." Exhibition review, Galleria Lia Rumma, Naples. *Avanti*, September 18, 1988.

Grazioli, Elio. "Protagonisti e influenze." In *Arte in Italia 1960–1985*, 205–18.

Sgarbi, Vittorio. "Come in uno specchio." Exhibition review, Galleria Lia Rumma, Naples. *L'Europeo*, July 1988.

Tomassoni, Italo. "Il caso Gino De Dominicis…" *Flash Art*, no. 144 (June 1988): 38–41.

Trimarco, Angelo. "Specchio inquietante delle nostre brame." Exhibition review, Galleria Lia Rumma, Naples. *Il Mattino*, July 10, 1988.

Verzotti, Giorgio. "Le scuole romane." In *Arte in Italia 1960–1985*, 41–59.

Vettese, Angela. "Al di là del tempo la vera esistenza." Exhibition review, Galleria Lia Rumma, Naples. *Il Sole 24 Ore*, September 4, 1988.

1989

Braun, Emily. "Gino De Dominicis." In *Italian Art in the 20th Century*, edited by Emily Braun, 432. Exh. cat. Munich: Prestel, 1989. Published in conjunction with an exhibition of the same title, organized by and presented at the Royal Academy, London, January 14–April 9, 1989.

Celant, Germano, ed. *Arte Povera*. Turin: Umberto Allemandi, 1989. Reprint of the exhibition catalogue *Identité italienne. L'art en Italie depuis 1959*.

Tisdall, Caroline. "Materia: The context of Arte Povera." In *Italian Art in the 20th Century*, 363–68.

Trimarco, Angelo. "Elogio della purezza e dell'immortalità in opere senza tempo." Exhibition review, The Murray and Isabella Rayburn Foundation, New York. *Il Mattino*, December 19, 1989.

Vettese, Angela. "De Dominicis negli Usa." Exhibition review, The Murray and Isabella Rayburn Foundation, New York. *Il Sole 24 Ore*, November 12, 1989.

1990

Apa, Mariano. "Gino De Dominicis ovvero: il luogo dell'immortalità reticente." *Artetra*, no. 2 (May 1990): 36.

Besacier, Hubert. "Gino De Dominicis, Magasin." Exhibition review, Centre National d'Art Contemporain Le Magasin, Grenoble. *Artscribe International*, no. 82 (Summer 1990): 91.

Blase, C. "Der Mensch/ein weisser Riese." Exhibition review, Centre National d'Art Contemporain Le Magasin, Grenoble. *Frankfurter Allgemeine*, April 23, 1990.

Bonami, Francesco. "Gino De Dominicis Intimation of Immortality." *The Journal of Art*, no. 4 (January 1990): 13–15.

Bouisset, Maïten. "À Grenoble, l'homme masqué et le promeneur." Exhibition review, Centre National d'Art Contemporain Le Magasin, Grenoble. *Beaux Arts Magazine*, no. 78 (April 1990): 152.

Bourriaud, Nicolas. "Lo spettacolo tragico della nostra impossibilità di afferrare i segni dell'eterno." Exhibition review, Centre National d'Art Contemporain Le Magasin, Grenoble. *Flash Art*, no. 156 (June/July 1990): 115–17.

Brenson, Michael. "Death, Myth and a Resistance to Conventions." Exhibition review, The Murray and Isabella Rayburn Foundation, New York. *New York Times*, January 5, 1990.

Calvesi, Maurizio. "Cronache e coordinate di un'avventura." In *Roma anni '60: al di là della pittura*, 34.

Calvesi, Maurizio, and Rosella Siligato, eds. *Roma anni '60: al di là della pittura*. Exh. cat. Rome: Carte Segrete, 1990. Published in conjunction with an exhibition of the same title, organized by and presented at the Palazzo delle Esposizioni, Rome, December 20, 1990–February 15, 1991.

Cherubini, Laura. "Intervista ad Alberto Boatto." In *Roma anni '60: al di là della pittura*, 318.

———. "Le divergenze dell'arte." In *Dimensione futuro: L'artista e lo spazio. XLIV Esposizione internazionale d'arte*, edited by La Biennale di Venezia, 21–34. Exh. cat. Venice: La Biennale di Venezia, 1990. Published in conjunction with the XLIV Esposizione internazionale d'arte, held at the Giardini della Biennale, Venice, June 27–September 30, 1990.

Christov-Bakargiev, Carolyn. "Alla ricerca di simboli perduti e immortali." Exhibition review, Centre National d'Art Contemporain Le Magasin, Grenoble. *Il Sole 24 Ore*, March 11, 1990.

Di Stefano, Anna Maria, and Cinzia Salvi. "Cronologia delle mostre e antologia critica 1959/1969/ Gino De Dominicis." In *Roma anni '60: al di là della pittura*, 456–57.

Drateln, Doris von. "Gino De Dominicis." Exhibition review, Centre National d'Art Contemporain Le Magasin, Grenoble. *Kunstforum International*, no. 107 (April/May 1990): 9–10.

Ferrari, Corinna. "De Dominicis a Grenoble. Uno scheletro lungo 24 metri." Exhibition review, Centre National d'Art Contemporain Le Magasin, Grenoble. *Il Giornale dell'Arte*, no. 76 (March 1990): 16.

"Gino De Dominicis: autoportrait en sumérien." Exhibition review, Centre National d'Art Contemporain Le Magasin, Grenoble. *Le Monde*, April 20, 1990.

"Gino De Dominicis, le silencieux." Exhibition review, Centre National d'Art Contemporain Le Magasin, Grenoble. *Le Figaro*, March 13, 1990.

Giroud, Michel. "Gino De Dominicis une épopée primordiale." Exhibition review, Centre National d'Art Contemporain Le Magasin, Grenoble. *Kanal Magazine*, no. 7 (April 1990): 41.

"Grenoble: stock nouveau au Magasin." Exhibition review, Centre National d'Art Contemporain Le Magasin, Grenoble. *Le Quotidien de Paris*, April 18, 1990.

Kohlmeyer, Agnes. "Vedere e non sapere." *Contemporanea*, no. 19 (Summer 1990): 64–69.

McEvilley, Thomas. "Gino De Dominicis." Exhibition review, The Murray and Isabella Rayburn Foundation, New York. *Artforum* 28, no. 6 (February 1990): 136–37.

Nickas, Robert. "Una sgradevole sensazione." Exhibition review, XLIV Esposizione internazionale d'arte, Venice. *Flash Art*, no. 157 (Summer 1990): 118–19.

Pirani, Federica. "Intervista a Renato Barilli." In *Roma anni '60: al di là della pittura*, 315.

Salerno, Giovan B. "Prodigi di De Dominicis a Grenoble." Exhibition review, Centre National d'Art Contemporain Le Magasin, Grenoble. *Il Manifesto*, April 12, 1990.

Siligato, Rosella. "Intervista a Fabio Sargentini." In *Roma anni '60: al di là della pittura*, 370–75.

———. "Intervista a Maurizio Calvesi." In *Roma anni '60: al di là della pittura*, 319–23.

Zahm, Olivier. "Gino De Dominicis: le sourire crépusculaire." Exhibition review, Centre National d'Art Contemporain Le Magasin, Grenoble. *Art Press*, no. 147 (May 1990): 33–35.

1991

Antolini, Adriano. "Le Neoavanguardie." In *Arte nel tempo. Dall'Illuminismo al Postmoderno*, edited by Pierluigi de Vecchi and Elda Cerchiari, vol. 3, 639. Milan: Bompiani, 1991.

Bonito Oliva, Achille. "Contemporanea. Rome." In *Die Kunst der Ausstellung*, edited by Berndt Kluser, 237. Frankfurt am Main: Insel Verlag, 1991.

———. *L'arte fino al 2000*. Florence: Sansoni, 1991.

Delfino, Domitilla S. "Breve intervista di Domitilla S. Delfino a Gino De Dominicis." *Il Giornale dell'Arte*, no. 91 (July/August 1991): 32.

Di Pietrantonio, Giacinto. "Roma anni '60. Al di là della pittura." Exhibition review, Palazzo delle Esposizioni, Rome. *Flash Art*, no. 161 (April/May 1991): 175–76.

Keeper, Angela. "Ricordo e foto/ricordo di una visita allo studio di Gino De Dominicis a Roma 1986." *Il Giornale dell'Arte*, no. 95 (December 1991): 48–49.

1992

Bonito Oliva, Achille. "Italiana." In *XII Quadriennale Italia 1950–1990*, 19–27.

———. *Paolo Uccello: battaglia nell'arte del xx secolo*. Exh. cat. Milan: Mondadori Electa, 1992. Published in conjunction with an exhibition of the same title, held at the Ex Convento San Carlo, Erice, July 25–October 10, 1992.

280

Quadriennale Nazionale d'Arte, ed. *XII Quadriennale Italia 1950-1990. Profili Dialettica Situazioni.* Exh. cat. Rome: Carte Segrete, 1992. Published in conjunction with an exhibition of the same title, organized by and presented at the Palazzo delle Esposizioni, Rome, July–September 1992.

1993
Bonito Oliva, Achille, ed. "Punti cardinali dell'arte." In *La Biennale di Venezia. XLV Esposizione Internazionale d'Arte. Punti cardinali dell'arte,* edited by La Biennale di Venezia. Exh. cat. Venice: La Biennale di Venezia, 1993. Published in conjunction with the XLV Esposizione Internazionale d'Arte, held at the Giardini della Biennale, Venice, June 14–October 10, 1993.
———, ed. *Tutte le strade portano a Roma?* Exh. cat. Rome: Edizioni Carte Segrete. 1993. Published in conjunction with an exhibition of the same title, organized by and presented at the Palazzo delle Esposizioni, Rome, March 11–April 26, 1993.
Capano, Leonardo. "De Dominicis, Gino." In *La pittura in Italia. Il Novecento, 1945-1990,* edited by Carlo Pirovano, vol. 2, 668. Milan: Electa, 1993.
Cherubini, Laura. "Da via Sallustiana a via del Lavatore. Per luoghi con gli artisti." In *Tutte le strade portano a Roma?,* 21–39, 236–37.
Crescentini, Marco. "L'ambiente romano." In *La pittura in Italia,* 505–35.
De Marco, Gabriella. "Il disegno tra utopia e progetto nell'arte povera e concettuale." In *Disegno italiano del Novecento,* edited by Giovanni Anzani, 309. Milan: Electa, 1993.
Fürstenberg, Adelina von. "Trésor de voyage." In *La Biennale di Venezia. Punti cardinali dell'arte,* vol. 2, 992, 995.
Gianelli, Ida, ed. *Un'avventura internazionale. Torino e le arti 1950-1970.* Exh. cat. Milan: Charta, 1993. Published in conjunction with an exhibition of the same title, organized by and presented at the Castello di Rivoli, Turin, February 5–April 25, 1993.
Mattei, Elena. "Travisamenti su Gino De Dominicis." *Segno,* no. 126 (Summer 1993): 32–33.
Trini, Tommaso. "Bussola. Verso il centro delle quattro direzioni comuni." In *La Biennale di Venezia. Punti cardinali dell'arte,* vol. 1, 370, 390–91.

1995
Calvesi, Maurizio. "Le Biennali dell'avanguardia." In *Venezia e la Biennale: I percorsi del gusto,* edited by Flavia Scotton, Marino Barovier, and Rosa Mentasti Barovier, 95–102, 316–17. Exh. cat. Milan: Fabbri Editori, 1995. Published in conjunction with an exhibition of the same title, organized by and presented at the Galleria d'Arte Moderna Ca'Pesaro, Venice, June 10–October 15, 1995.
Clair, Jean, ed. *La Biennale di Venezia 46. Esposizione Internazionale d'Arte. Centenario.* Exh. cat. Milan: Mondadori, 1995. Published in conjunction with the XLVI Esposizione Internazionale d'Arte, held at the Giardini della Biennale, Venice, July 11–October 15, 1995.

Di Martino, Enzo. "La Biennale di Venezia: 1895–1995, cento anni di arte e cultura." *Arte,* no. 263 (June 1995): 28, 30.
Fanelli, Franco. "GDD. Si prega di non disturbare gli artisti. Il più appartato tra i contemporanei parla del suo conflittuale rapporto con la biennale e Quadriennale." *Il Giornale dell'Arte,* no. 136 (September 1995): 6–7.
Negroni Manzini, Federica. "Breve intervista di Federica Negroni Manzini a Gino De Dominicis." In *La Biennale di Venezia 46. Esposizione Internazionale d'Arte,* 363–64.
Poli, Francesco. *Minimalismo, Arte Povera, Arte Concettuale.* Rome-Bari: Laterza, 1995.

1996
Barilli, Renato. "Il pennello in corpo." *L'Espresso,* May 10, 1996.
Cherubini, Laura. "Gino De Dominicis." Exhibition review, Galleria La Nuova Pesa, Rome. *Flash Art* 29, no. 199 (Summer 1996): 76–77.
Gianelli, Ida, ed. *Collezionismo a Torino: le opere di sei collezionisti d'arte contemporanea.* Exh. cat. Milan: Charta, 1996. Published in conjunction with an exhibition of the same title, organized by and presented at the Castello di Rivoli, Turin, February 15–April 21, 1996.
Vettese, Angela. *Capire l'arte contemporanea dal 1945 ad oggi.* Turin: Umberto Allemandi, 1996.

1997
Celant, Germano. "Future, Past, Present: A Labyrinth." In *XLVII Esposizione Internazionale d'Arte La Biennale di Venezia,* edited by La Biennale di Venezia, vol. 1, 11–12. Exh. cat. Milan: Electa; Venice: La Biennale di Venezia, 1997. Published in conjunction with the XLVII Esposizione Internazionale d'Arte, held at the Giardini della Biennale, Venice, June 15–November 9, 1997.
Fanelli, Franco. "La Biennale di Venezia 1997 dal vivo." *Il Giornale dell'Arte,* no. 157 (July/August 1997): 46–47.
Torrealta, Cecilia. "Frasi di Gino De Dominicis, 1969–96." In *XLVII Esposizione Internazionale d'Arte La Biennale di Venezia,* vol. 1, 66–67.

1998
Arcangeli, Gabriele. "De Dominicis artista 'fuori.'" *Il Giornale,* December 1, 1998.
Bossaglia, Rossana. "Fuori dal sistema." *Il Corriere della Sera,* November 30, 1998.
De Dominicis, Gino. "L'Arte e la Biennale." *Quadri & sculture,* no. 33 (November/December 1998): 21.
"De Dominicis, mistero sulle cause della morte." *Il Messaggero,* December 1, 1998.
Deho, Valerio. "Gino De Dominicis." *Flash Art* 31, no. 212 (October/November 1998): 134.
Di Genova, Arianna. "Il volto invisibile dell'arte." *Il Manifesto,* December 1, 1998.
"È morto Gino De Dominicis: espose un mongoloide alla Biennale." *Il Messaggero,* November 30, 1998.
Kohlmeyer, Agnes. "È morto Gino De Dominicis artista misterioso e provocatore." *Il Mattino di Padova,* November 30, 1998.
Neirotti, Marco. "De Dominicis ribelle e spietato." *La Stampa,* December 1, 1998.

"Ritratto dell'artista da giovane." *Il Giornale dell'Arte*, no. 163 (February 1998): 2.

Simongini, Gabriele. "Nella trasgressione anticonformista la cifra del suo rigore." *Il Tempo*, December 1, 1998.

Tadini, Emilio. "Il bello in diciassette punti. Secondo De Dominicis." *Il Corriere della Sera*, December 2, 1998.

Trombadori, Duccio. "De Dominicis, l'immobile." *Quadri & sculture*, no. 32 (August/September 1998): 76–77.

Vagheggi, Paolo. "L'artista che scandalizzò l'Italia." *La Repubblica*, November 30, 1998.

Valensise, Marina. "Contro i ciarlatani dell'arte. L'ultima intervista di Gino De Dominicis." *Panorama*, December 10, 1998.

Vettese, Angela. "Una vita incorruttibile." *Il Sole 24 Ore*, December 6, 1998.

1999

Brugiamolini, Fabiola, ed. *Sulle tracce di un'assenza. Esordi anconetani e altro di Gino De Dominicis*. Exh. cat. Ancona: Tipografia Emmepiesse, 1999. Published in conjunction with an exhibition of the same title, organized by and presented at the Atelier dell'Arco Amoroso, Ancona, April 24–May 23, 1999.

Caldirola, Maurizio, ed. *Alighiero Boetti, Francesco Clemente, Gino De Dominicis, Nicola de Maria, Mimmo Paladino, Richard Tuttle*. Exh. cat. Milan: Galleria Cardi, 1999. Published in conjunction with an exhibition of the same title, organized by and presented at the Galleria Cardi, Milan, July 1–September 30, 1999.

Coen, Ester. "Fu il mago degli atti irriverenti." Exhibition review, Galleria Nazionale d'Arte Moderna, Rome. *La Repubblica*, July 12, 1999.

Cortenova, Giorgio, ed. *Collezione Giorgio Franchetti-Premio Koiné SEAT per l'arte*. Exh. cat. Milan: Electa, 1999. Published in conjunction with an exhibition of the same title, organized by and presented at the Palazzo Forti, Verona, June 12–August 22, 1999.

De Dominicis, Gino. "Lettera sull'immortalità." *Flash Art* 32, no. 215 (April/May 1999): 82–84.

Detheridge, Anna. "Gino De Dominicis. Teatro dell'immortale e futura memoria." Exhibition review, Galleria Nazionale d'Arte Moderna, Rome. *Il Sole 24 Ore*, July 18, 1999.

Fanelli, Franco. "Mazzoli: 'Attenti, ora ai finti vedovi.'" *Il Giornale dell'Arte*, no. 173 (January 1999): 8.

———. "Un dandy di nome Gilgamesh." *Il Giornale dell'Arte*, no. 173 (January 1999): 8.

Gerace, Federica. *Gino De Dominicis*. Milan: Edizioni Charta, 1999.

Giuliani, Francesca. "Un viaggio in sette sale." Exhibition review, Galleria Nazionale d'Arte Moderna, Rome. *La Repubblica*, June 28, 1999.

Grasso, Sebastiano. "Vendo e trasmetto idee, come un commesso viaggiatore." Review of the XLVIII Esposizione internazionale d'Arte, Venice. *Il Corriere della Sera*, June 12, 1999.

Keeper, Angela. "Lo studio di De Dominicis." *Quadri & sculture*, no. 34 (January/February 1998): 21.

Kosuth, Joseph. "Gino De Dominicis e le mie notti romane." *La Repubblica*, July 1, 1999.

Marucci, Luciano. "Gino De Dominicis. La parabola artistica di un figlio delle avanguardie del '900." *Arti*, July 1, 1999.

Mirolla, Miriam. "L'immortalità." Interview with Gino De Dominicis. *Flash Art* 32, no. 214 (July/August 1999): 85–96.

———. "Ricordo di De Dominicis." Exhibition review, Galleria Nazionale d'Arte Moderna, Rome. *Flash Art* 32, no. 218 (October/November 1999): 64.

Pacifico, Maya. "GDD. I sumeri e il conte di Saint Germain." Exhibition review, Galleria Nazionale d'Arte Moderna, Rome. *Flash Art* 32, no. 216 (June/July 1999): 92–97.

Paparoni, Demetrio. "Abolire per legge il business delle autentiche di un'opera d'arte." *Tema Celeste*, no. 75 (July 1999).

Perretta, Gabriele. "Gino De Dominicis." Exhibition review, Galleria Nazionale d'Arte Moderna, Rome. *Flash Art* 32, no. 218 (October/November 1999): 127.

Pratesi, Ludovico. "Quel Down esposto al museo." Exhibition review, Galleria Nazionale d'Arte Moderna, Rome. *La Repubblica*, June 28, 1999.

Romana Morelli, Francesca. "Più grande, più bella per un futuro fatto di soli doni." Exhibition review, Galleria Nazionale d'Arte Moderna, Rome. *Il Giornale dell'Arte*, no. 179 (July/August 1999): 20.

Salaris, Claudia. "Gli anni intensi." In *La Roma delle avanguardie. Dal futurismo all'underground*, edited by Claudia Salaris, 223. Roma: Editori Riuniti, 1999.

Senaldi, Marco. "Lo spirito a Punxsutawney. Arti e misteri di Gino De Dominicis." *Flash Art* 32, no. 214 (February/March 1999): 78–84.

Sgarbi, Vittorio. "Il vero De Dominicis." *Quadri & Sculture*, no. 34 (January/February 1999): 74–75.

Tansini, Laura. "(Londra) Un successo la prima vendita internazionale tutta italiana." *Il Giornale dell'Arte*, no. 182 (November 1999): 93.

Tomassoni, Italo. "Gino De Dominicis 1947/1998." In *La Biennale di Venezia 48. Esposizione Internazionale d'Arte*, 363–64.

———, ed. *Gino De Dominicis. Giornata di Studi*. Rome: Edizioni Per Mari e Monti, 1999.

———. "Gino De Dominicis. Sulle tracce di un universo immobile." *Flash Art* 32, no. 214 (February/March 1999): 70–77.

Tomassoni, Italo, and Duccio Trombadori, eds. *In ricordo di Gino De Dominicis*. Macerata: Edizioni Per Mari e Monti, 1999.

Zevi, Adachiara. "Il tempo: uno scheletro che pattina." *Il Corriere della Sera*, July 5, 1999.

2000

Beatrice, Luca, ed. *Stefano Della Porta, da Giotto a Gino De Dominicis. archivio dell'immaginario*. Fano: Galleria Austuni, 2000.

Boatto, Alberto, and Maurizio Calvesi. "Per De Dominicis." *L'Espresso*, March 23, 2000, 13–14.

Celant, Germano. "Giù le mani da De Dominicis." *L'Espresso*, March 2, 2000, 161.

Codognato, Mario, Ester Coen, and Agnes Kohlmeyer. *(E così via) (And so on). 99 Artists from the Marzona Collection. Arte Povera__Minimal Art__Concept Art__Land Art*. Exh. cat. Berlin: Berlin Press, 2000. Published in conjunction with an exhibition of the same title, organized by and presented at the Galleria Comunale d'Arte Moderna e Contemporanea, Rome, June 20–September 17, 2000.

Gualdoni, Flaminio. *Arte in Italia 1943/1999.* Vicenza: Neri Pozza, 2000.

Lambardelli, Roberto, ed. *Gli amici del cuore. A Giorgio Franchetti.* Exh. cat. Spoleto: Del Gallo Editore, 2000. Published in conjunction with an exhibition of the same title, organized by and presented at the Palazzo Arroni, Spoleto, June 30–July 16, 2000.

Marrone, Maurizio, and Arianna Vennarucci. *Anima.* Exh. cat. Rome: Edizioni Opera Paese, 2000. Published in conjunction with an exhibition of the same title, held at the Convento delle Lucrezie, Todi, July 21–August 21, 2000.

Marucci, Luciano. "Ancona in ricordo di GDD (lettera a Giancarlo Politi)." *Flash Art* 33, no. 220 (February/March 2000): 61.

Minola, Anna, Maria Cristina Mundici, and Francesco Poli. *Gian Enzo Sperone. Torino, Roma, New York. 35 anni di mostre tra Europa e America.* Turin: Hopefulmonster, 2000.

Montesano, Giammarco. "L'immortalità di Gino De Dominicis." *Flash Art* 33, no. 224 (October/November 2000): 75.

"(Napoli) Fuochi di Sant'Elmo." *Il Giornale dell'Arte,* no. 187 (April 2000): 16.

Pirani, Federica, and Lorenzo Canova, eds. *Novecento. Arte e Storia in Italia.* Exh. cat. Milan: Skira, 2000. Published in conjunction with an exhibition of the same title, held at the Scuderie Papali del Quirinale and at the Mercati di Traiano, Rome, December 29, 2000–May 6, 2001.

Politi, Gianni. "Gino De Dominicis: Il re è nudo?" *Flash Art* 33, no. 221 (April/May 2000): 75–76.

Storr, Robert. "Fences Down." In *Modern Art Despite Modernism,* edited by Robert Storr, 95, 212. Exh. cat. New York: Museum of Modern Art, 2000. Published in conjunction with an exhibition of the same title, organized by and presented at the Museum of Modern Art, New York, March 15–July 26, 2000.

Tomassoni, Italo. "Il rispetto dell'identità. Ricordo di Gino De Dominicis." *Flash Art* 33, no. 221 (April/May 2000): 74.

"Una cornice antica per il moderno." *AD,* no. 227 (April 2000): 240–43.

2001

Ammann, Jean-Christophe. "I profili e l'estasi." In *De Dominicis. Raccolta di scritti sull'opera e l'artista,* edited by Gabriele Guercio, 15–21. Turin: Umberto Allemandi, 2001.

Bonito Oliva, Achille. "Senza titolo." In *De Dominicis. Raccolta,* 22–24.

Bryson, Norman. "Il Buddha del futuro." In *De Dominicis. Raccolta,* 25–31.

Buren, Daniel. "Gino De Dominicis." In *De Dominicis. Raccolta,* 32.

Calvesi, Maurizio, and Paolo Portoghesi. *Artisti Italiani del xx secolo alla Farnesina.* Catalogue of the collection. Rome: Edizioni dell'Elefante, 2001.

Cherubini, Laura. "La pittura come macchina del tempo." In *De Dominicis. Raccolta,* 33–34.

Detheridge, Anna. "Gino De Dominicis. Di me non avrete immagini." Review of *De Dominicis. Raccolta di scritti su l'opera e l'artista,* edited by Gabriele Guercio. *Il Sole 24 Ore,* December 16, 2001.

Di Pietrantonio, Giacinto, ed. *Camera Italia.* Bergamo: Lubrina Editore, 2001.

Gilbert, Creighton. "Un possibile rapporto tra Gino De Dominicis e la filosofia." In *De Dominicis. Raccolta,* 45–50.

Giorello, Giulio. "Una cosmica immobilità." In *De Dominicis. Raccolta,* 51–53.

Guercio, Gabriele. "Arte visiva e immortalità del corpo." In *De Dominicis. Raccolta,* 163–99.

Jarrard, Alice. "Vedere, credere?" In *De Dominicis. Raccolta,* 54–59.

Kiefer, Anselm. "Richiamo." In *De Dominicis. Raccolta,* 60–62.

Kosuth, Joseph. "Chiarezza." In *De Dominicis. Raccolta,* 63–66.

Kounellis, Jannis. "Due o tre frasi acritiche." In *De Dominicis. Raccolta,* 67.

Lauf, Cornelia. "La roulette e la storia dell'arte." In *De Dominicis. Raccolta,* 68–72.

Mammì, Alessandra. "Ho spiato l'avanguardia." *L'Espresso,* December 6, 2001.

Pettinato, Giovanni. "Gilgamesh e l'immortalità." In *De Dominicis. Raccolta,* 73–84.

Prini, Emilio. "… lato di vita." In *De Dominicis. Raccolta,* 85.

Rosenthal, Norman. "Lux in tenebris." In *De Dominicis. Raccolta,* 86–88.

Rubiu, Vittorio, ed. *Cannonata De Dominicis / Pascali.* Exh. cat. Rome: Associazione Culturale L'Attico, 2000. Published in conjunction with an exhibition of the same title, organized by and presented at the Associazione Culturale L'Attico, February 9, 2001.

———. "Donare è scrivere la propria vita." In *La Collezione Brandi Rubiu,* edited by Sandra Pinto and Marcella Cossu, 15. Exh. cat. Rome: Galleria Nazionale d'Arte Moderna, 2001. Published in conjunction with an exhibition of the same title, organized by and presented at the Galleria Nazionale d'Arte Moderna, Rome, November 2001.

Scalco, Luca. "Gino De Dominicis/Antologica 1970/1995." Accessed July 30, 2020. https://www.exibart.com/milano-bis/fino-al-31-xii-2001-gino-de-dominicis-antologica-1970-1995-milano-poleschi-arte/.

Sgarbi, Vittorio. "La Biennale Mutilata." Review of the XLIX Esposizione Internazionale d'Arte, curated by Harald Szeemann, Giardini della Biennale, Venice. *Panorama,* no. 25 (June 2001): 174–75.

Spinosa, Nicola. "Una sera nei cortili di Capodimonte." In *De Dominicis. Raccolta,* 89–92.

Stiles, Kristine. "Il mostro, la maschera e la coscienza allargata." In *De Dominicis. Raccolta,* 93–99.

2002

Ammann, Jean-Christophe, ed. *Continuità. Arte e Toscana 1990/2000 e collezionismo contemporaneo in Toscana.* Exh. cat. Florence: Maschietto Editore, 2002. Published in conjunction with an exhibition of the same title, organized by and presented at the Centro per l'arte contemporanea Luigi Pecci, Prato, February 24–June 10, 2002.

Bonito Oliva, Achille, and Sergio Risaliti. *De Gustibus. Collezione privata Italia*. Exh. cat. Florence: Maschietto Editore, 2002. Published in conjunction with an exhibition of the same title, organized by and presented at the Palazzo delle Papesse, Siena, March 3–May 12, 2002.

Caragliano, Renata. "Gino De Dominicis." In *Museo Nazionale di Capodimonte. Arte contemporanea*, edited by Nicola Spinosa, Achille Bonito Oliva, and Angela Tecce, 113–14. Naples: Electa, 2002.

Corà, Bruno, ed. *Exempla 2. Arte italiana nella vicenda europea 1960/2000*. Pistoia: Gli Ori Editori, 2002.

Guzzi, Domenico. *L'anello mancante. Figurazione in Italia negli anni '60 e '70*. Rome-Bari: Laterza, 2002.

Marmorini, Francesco. "De Dominicis tra scienza e metafisica." *Arte e Critica*, no. 32 (October/December 2002): 42–43.

Sossai, Maria R. *Artevideo. Storie e culture del video d'artista in Italia*. Cinisello Balsamo (Milan): Silvana Editoriale, 2002.

2003

"Associazione Gino De Dominicis." *Il Giornale dell'Arte*, no. 219 (March 2003): 45.

Bicocchi, Maria Gloria, "Tra Firenze e Santa Teresa dentro le quinte dell'arte ('73/'87)." *Art/tapes/22* (Venice: Edizioni del Cavallino, 2003), 28–31.

Canova, Lorenzo, ed. *Futuro Italiano*. Exh. cat. Rome: Ministero degli affari esteri, 2003. Published in conjunction with an exhibition of the same title, held at the European Parliament, Brussels, November 13–December 13, 2003.

Capasso, Angelo, ed. *Numeri. Mario Merz, Sol LeWitt, Alighiero Boetti, Gino De Dominicis, Emilio Prini*. Exh. cat. Rome: Pio Monti, 2003. Published in conjunction with an exhibition of the same title, organized by and presented at the Galleria Pio Monti, Rome, December 2003.

Celant, Germano. "Enigma da difendere." *L'Espresso*, October 2, 2003.

Ligabue, Simone. *L'ultima mostra di De Dominicis*. Reggio Emilia: Pari e Dispari, 2003.

Monti, Pio, ed. *When I was young. Segni depositati e moltiplicati dal 1970*, 18–19. Exh. cat. Rome: Pio Monti, 2003. Published in conjunction with an exhibition of the same title, organized by and presented at Pio Monti, Rome, May 2003.

Tomassoni, Italo. "Cronologia dell'immortalità (Gino De Dominicis)." *Storia dell'Arte*, no. 104/105 (2003): 161–80.

———. "Gino De Dominicis." In *Iconostasi, Stagioni e Territori dell'Arte*, edited by Mariano Apa, 9. Loreto: Assessorato alla cultura, 2003.

Tonti, Stefano, ed. *De Te Fabula. L'autoritratto contemporaneo*. Exh. cat. Jesi: Artemisia, 2003. Published in conjunction with an exhibition of the same title, held at the Palazzo dei Congressi, Jesi, February 8–March 2, 2003.

Vinca Masini, Lara. "Gino De Dominicis (Arte povera e arte processuale)." In *L'Arte del Novecento*, vol V: *dall'espressionismo al multimediale*, edited by Lara Vinca Masini, 952–55. Florence: Giunti, 2003.

2004

Barilli, Renato, ed. *W Lo Spac*. Exh. cat. Milan: Mazzotta, 2004. Published in conjunction with an exhibition of the same title, held at the Chiesa della Maddalena, Pesaro, April 17–May 16, 2004.

Bucci, Carlo A. "La prima consistente personale romana allestita dopo la morte dell'artista sei anni fa: quattordici lavori, metà degli anni '70." Exhibition review, Galleria Erica Fiorentini, Rome. *La Repubblica*, May 13, 2004.

Costantini, Costanzo. "A Gino De Dominicis è dedicata la mostra fino al 5 luglio alla Galleria Fiorentini." Exhibition review, Galleria Erica Fiorentini, Rome. *Il Messaggero*, May 19, 2004.

De Candia, Mario. "De Dominicis e la vita: misteri dell' invisibile." *TrovaRoma – La Repubblica*, n.d.

Fiorentini, Erica, ed. *Gino De Dominicis*. Exh cat. Rome: Galleria Erica Fiorentini, 2004. Published in conjunction with an exhibition of the same title, organized by and presented at the Galleria Erica Fiorentini, Rome, May 5–July 5, 2004.

Gramiccia, Roberto. "De Dominicis l'immortale." Exhibition review, Galleria Erica Fiorentini, Rome. *Liberazione*, May 19, 2004.

Lambardelli, Giuseppe R. "Un contraddittorio per Gino De Dominicis." *Arte e Critica*, no. 40 (October/December 2004): 42.

Lucariello, Saverio. "Gino De Dominicis. Comment ouvrir dans l'irrationnel, l'atemporel et la non-communication du sublime et du parfait." *Trouble*, no. 4 (April 2004): 81–90.

Magrelli, Valerio. "L'uomo 'vuoto' di De Dominicis." Exhibition review, Galleria Erica Fiorentini, Rome. *Il Corriere della Sera*, June 2, 2004.

Pratesi, Ludovico. "L'enigma De Dominicis." In *W Lo Spac*, edited by Renato Barilli, 34–35. Exh. cat. Milan: Mazzotta, 2004.

Rubiu, Vittorio. *Pascali uno e due*. Rome: Edizioni della Cometa, 2004.

2005

Borgna, Eugenio. "Trincea dell'esistenza." In *War is Over 1945–2005*, edited by Giacinto Di Pietrantonio and Maria Cristina Rodeschini Galati, 140–41. Exh. cat. Cinisello Balsamo (Milan): Silvana Editoriale, 2005. Published in conjunction with an exhibition of the same title, organized by and presented at the GAMEC – Galleria d'Arte Moderna e Contemporanea, Bergamo, October 15, 2005–February 26, 2006.

Bruciati, Andrea, and Elena Volpato, eds. *U_MOVE: utopia e imagine in movimento*. Exh. cat. Milan: Postmedia Books, 2005. Published in conjunction with an exhibition of the same title, organized by and presented at the Galleria d'Arte Contemporanea di Monfalcone, Monfalcone, May 21–June 5, 2005.

Calvesi, Maurizio, and Luigi Canova. *Segnali italiani della collezione d'Arte Contemporanea alla Farnesina*. Exh. cat. Rome: Arti Graf. La Moderna, 2005. Published in conjunction with an exhibition of the same title, organized by and presented at the Galleria dell'Accademia Serba delle Scienze e delle Arti, Beograd, September–October 2005.

Calvesi, Maurizio, Luigi Canova, and Renato Miracco, eds. *Italian Art 1950/1970. Masterpieces from the Farnesina Collection.* Exh. cat. Rome: Gangemi, 2005. Published in conjunction with an exhibition of the same title, organized by and presented at the National Gallery of Modern Art, New Delhi, February–March 2005.

Di Pietrantonio, Giacinto. "Ground is Over." In *War is Over 1945–2005*, 24.

Ferrara, Giorgio, and Duccio Trombadori, eds. *Fratelli d'Italia (Voyage dans l'Italie contemporaine).* Exh. cat. Paris: Institut Culturel Italien de Paris 2005. Published in conjunction with an exhibition of the same title, organized by and presented at the Italian Institute of Culture, Paris, April 8–July 8, 2005.

"Installazioni. Lo scheletro alieno di De Dominicis esposto ad Ancona." Exhibition review, Mole Vanvitelliana, Ancona. *Il Messaggero*, June 15, 2005.

"La scultura dello scandalo: uno scheletro lungo 24 metri." Exhibition review, Mole Vanvitelliana, Ancona. *Il Corriere della Sera*, July 14, 2005.

Masoero, Ada, ed. *Nello spazio nel cosmo.* Milan: Edizioni Gabriele Mazzotta, 2005.

Mézil, Eric, and Giorgi Verzotti. *Theorema, une collection privée en Italie: la collection d'Enea Righi.* Catalogue of the collection. Paris: Collection Lambert en Avignon, 2005.

Rodeschini Galati, Maria C. "Give peace a chance." In *War is Over 1945–2005*, 52.

Rorro, Angelandreina, ed. *20×20. Artisti dalla Galleria Nazionale d'Arte Moderna 1980–2000.* Exh. cat. Formello: Edigraf, 2005. Published in conjunction with an exhibition of the same title, organized by and presented at the Castello Colonna, Genazzano, July 2–October 2, 2005.

Tegelaers, Theo, and Rene Daalder. *The Gravity in Art.* Exh. cat. Amsterdam: De Appel, 2005. Published in conjunction with an exhibition of the same title, organized by and presented at De Appel, Amsterdam, December 2, 2005–January 22, 2006.

Tomassoni, Italo, ed. *Gino De Dominicis. Calamita Cosmica.* Exh. cat. San Marino: Maretti Editore, 2005. Published in conjunction with an exhibition of the same title, organized by and presented at the Mole Vanvitelliana, Ancona, June 26–October 2, 2005.

Vescovo, Marisa, ed. *L'opera al nero, tra astrazione e costruzione dell'immagine.* Exh. cat. Macerata: Artemisia, 2005. Published in conjunction with an exhibition of the same title, organized by and presented at the Mole Vanvitelliana, Ancona, July 22–October 2, 2005.

2006

Apa, Mariano. "De Dominicis. Reticente eternità." In *Accademia '05 un album di esercizi*, edited by Mariano Apa, 269–75. Perugia: Morlacchi Editore, 2006.

Bosoni, Gianpiero, ed. *Il modo italiano. Italian Design and Avant-garde in the 20th Century.* Exh. cat. Milan: Skira, 2006. Published in conjunction with an exhibition of the same title, organized by and presented at the Montreal Museum of Fine Arts, Montreal, May 4–August 27, 2006.

Cattelan, Maurizio, Massimiliano Gioni, and Ali Subotnick, eds. *Of Mice and Men: 4th Berlin Biennial for Contemporary Art.* Exh. cat. Berlin: Hatje Cantz, 2006. Published in conjunction with the 4th Berlin Biennial of Contemporary Art, Berlin, March 25–June 26, 2006.

Christov-Bakargiev, Carolyn. "Gino De Dominicis. Making mind and matter proceed together." *Flash Art International* 39, no. 248 (May/June 2006): 114–19.

Cicelyn, Eduardo, and Mario Codognato, eds. *Kounellis: Madre, Museo d'arte contemporanea Donnaregina.* Exh. cat. Milan: Electa, 2006. Published in conjunction with an exhibition of the same title, organized by and presented at Museo Madre, Naples, April 22–September 4, 2006.

Corà, Bruno, ed. *XII Biennale Internazionale di Scultura di Carrara. Una Biennale per il museo. La contemporaneità dell'arte.* Rome: Logos, 2006.

Cunaccia, Cesare. "Twin souls: De Dominicis & Viola." *L'Uomo Vogue*, no. 374 (October 2006): 38.

Dehò, Valerio, and Elena Pontiggia. *Ironica. La leggerezza dell'ironia.* Exh. cat. Verona: Edizioni dell'Aurora, 2006. Published in conjunction with an exhibition of the same title, organized by and presented at the Gruppo Credito Valtellinese, Milan, November 29, 2005–January 31, 2006.

Franciolli, Marco, and Bettina Della Casa, eds. *L'immagine del vuoto. Una linea di ricerca nell'arte in Italia.* Exh. cat. Milan: Skira, 2006. Published in conjunction with an exhibition of the same title, organized by and presented at the Museo Cantonale d'Arte, Lugano, October 7, 2005–January 7, 2006.

Fusi, Lorenzo. "The dark side of the moon." In *D'Ombra*, edited by Lea Vergine, 107–8. Exh. cat. Cinisello Balsamo (Milan): Silvana Editoriale, 2006. Published in conjunction with an exhibition of the same title, organized by and presented at the Palazzo delle Papesse, Siena, October 14, 2006–January 7, 2007.

Gigliotti, Guglielmo. "Renato Barilli: 'Solo una prova?' Fabio Segantini: 'Addio Gino.' Di Genova: 'Evviva Cattelan.'" *Il Giornale dell'Arte*, no. 76 (November 2006): 19.

Jeanspierre, Laurent. "Faire de sa mort une œuvre d'art une pedagogie cynique?" *Art press* 2, no. 3 (November 2006–January 2007): 16–17.

Kihm, Christophe. "Cynisme et art contemporain." *Art press* 2, no. 3 (November 2006–January 2007): 97.

Mirolla, Miriam. *L'art c'est moi. Quindici interviste sull'arte contemporanea.* Rome: Avagliano Editore, 2006.

Pallotti, Silvia. "La fisica del Novecento nell'opera di Gino De Dominicis" and "Una proposta per Gino De Dominicis. 'Sì, un sasso gettato nell'acqua potrebbe formare dei quadrati … se l'acqua fosse un mezzo discreto!'" In *Accademia '05 un album di esercizi*, edited by Mariano Apa, 257–68. Perugia: Morlacchi Editore, 2006.

Peraglie, Sandra. "L'eternità in Gino De Dominicis." In *Accademia '05 un album di esercizi*, 276–81.

Somers Cocks, Anna. "Knock/Down." *Il Giornale dell'Arte*, no. 248 (November 2006): 19.

Tomassoni, Italo. "Indefinibile ineffabile innominabile irriducibile." In *La Bellezza*, edited by Ivan Rizzi, 70–71. Exh. cat. Milan: Associazione Etica Europa, 2006. Published in conjunction with an exhibition of the same title, organized by and presented at the Museo della Permanente, Milan, May 6–June 4, 2006.

———. "Mongoloide d'artista, quando Gino De Dominicis scandalizzò la biennale con il signor Paolo Rosa." *Il Foglio*, January 25, 2006.

2007

Abramović, Marina. "Pack of Cigarettes." "Gino De Dominicis," ed. Laura Cherubini and Andrea Bellini, special issue, *Flash Art International* (June 2007): 98–101.

Barletta, Riccardo. "Scheletri e mozzarelle del Dalì italiano." Exhibition review, Fondazione Merz, Turin. *Il Corriere della Sera*, November 10, 2007.

Beatrice, Luca, ed. *Viaggio in Italia*. Exh. cat. Pietrasanta: Edizioni Galleria Astuni. Published in conjunction with an exhibition of the same title, organized by and presented at the Galleria Astuni, Bologna, January 9–16, 2007.

Bellini, Andrea. "A futura memoria." Special issue, *Flash Art International* (June 2007): 14–31.

Bertoldi, Cesare. "Calamità Cosmica a Versailles. Lo scheletro gigante andrà a Parigi." *Corriere dell'Umbria*, September 30, 2007.

Bonazzoli, Francesca. "Tutti pazzi per lo scheletrone." Exhibition review, Palazzo Reale, Milan. *Il Corriere della Sera*, April 1, 2007.

Bourriaud, Nicolas. "On the trail of Gilgamesh." Special issue, *Flash Art International* (June 2007): 130–33.

Celant, Germano. "Realtà invisibili." *L'Espresso*, September 27, 2007.

Cherubini, Laura. "Perfect living object. The work of Gino De Dominicis." Special issue, *Flash Art International* (June 2007): 32–85.

Cherubini, Laura, and Andrea Bellini, eds. "Gino De Dominicis." Special issue, *Flash Art International* (June 2007).

Christov-Bakargiev, Carolyn. "Making mind and matter proceed together." Special issue, *Flash Art International* (June 2007): 122–29.

Cortenova, Giorgio. "Gli enigmi dell'anima." In *Il settimo splendore: la modernità della malinconia*, edited by Giorgio Cortenova, 56–57, 90–91, 380. Exh. cat. Venice: Marsilio, 2007. Published in conjunction with an exhibition of the same title, organized by and presented at the Palazzo della Ragione, Verona, March 25–July 27, 2007.

Dalla Chiesa, Giovanna. "Che cosa c'entra la morte?" *Arte e Critica*, no. 51 (June/August 2007): 68–69.

D'Amico, Paola. "Uno scheletrone gigante al duomo. Milano si mette in coda." Exhibition review, Palazzo Reale, Milan. *Il Corriere della Sera*, March 30, 2007.

Di Genova, Giorgio, ed. *Storia dell'arte italiana del '900 per generazioni: generazione anni Quaranta*, vol. 1, 32, 53–63, 100. Bologna: Edizioni Bora, 2007.

"Folla e polemiche per lo scheletrone." Exhibition review, Palazzo Reale, Milan. *Il Corriere della Sera*, April 2, 2007.

Ginesi, Armando, ed. *Le Marche e il XX secolo. Atlante degli artisti*. Milan: 24 Ore Cultura, 2007.

Gualdoni, Flaminio. "Un dandy che giocava a scacchi con l'arte." Exhibition review, Palazzo Reale, Milan. *Il Corriere della Sera*, August 25, 2007.

Guercio, Gabriele. "Apropos of Paolo Rosa." Special issue, *Flash Art International* (June 2007): 86–97.

"Il grande scheletro conquista Milano." Exhibition review, Palazzo Reale, Milan. *Il Corriere della Sera*, May 15, 2007.

Kosuth, Joseph. "Dining out." Special issue, *Flash Art International* (June 2007): 102–5.

Lani, Giovanni. "Tour europeo per lo scheletrone." *La Nazione*, May 31, 2007.

———. "Un milione di persone per lo scheletrone cosmico di Gino De Dominicis." Exhibition review, Palazzo Reale, Milan. *Il Resto del Carlino*, June 7, 2007.

———. "Uno scheletrone nel parco del Re Sole." Exhibition review, Chateau de Versailles, Paris. *La Nazione*, October 10, 2007.

"Lo scheletrone e Kandinsky. Doppio sberleffo all'ignoto." Exhibition review, Palazzo Reale, Milan. *Libero*, April 18, 2007.

Masoero, Ada. "Quel sumero di De Dominicis." Exhibition review, Villa Arson, Nice. *La Nazione*, September 30, 2007.

Obrist, Hans Ulrich, and Laura Cherubini. "Gino De Dominicis." Special issue, *Flash Art International* (June 2007): 107–11.

Pontiggia, Elena. "Gino De Dominicis classico d'avanguardia." *Il Giornale*, August 27, 2007.

Sargentini, Fabio, ed. *L'attico anni lunari*. Exh. cat. Rome: Edizioni della Cometa, 2007. Published in conjunction with an exhibition of the same title, held at the Associazione culturale l'Attico, Rome, November 25, 2007–January 25, 2008, and MUSMA – Museo della Scultura Contemporanea, Matera, January 27–March 2, 2008.

Senaldi, Marco. "GGD TV." Special issue, *Flash Art International* (June 2007): 112–20.

Sgarbi, Vittorio, ed. *Arte italiana 1968/2007. Pittura*. Milan: Skira, 2007.

———. "La calamita della Madonnina." In *Camera con vista. Arte e interni in Italia 1900–2000*, edited by Luigi Settembrini and Claudia Gian Ferrari, 272–73. Exh cat. Milan: Skira, 2007. Published in conjunction with an exhibition of the same title, organized by and presented at the Piazzetta Reale, Milan, April 18–July 1, 2007.

Tomassoni, Italo. *Anni settanta. Artisti italiani fra cronaca e mito*. Rome-Bari: Laterza, 2007.

"Un'ora sola ti vorrei. Ritratto corale di Gino De Dominicis." *Mousse Magazine*, no. 6 (January 2007): 38–42.

Vallora, Marco. "L'uomo che inventò lo scheletro con i pattini." Exhibition review, Château de Versailles, Paris. *La Stampa*, November 9, 2007.

Verzotti, Giorgio. "Gino De Dominicis." Special issue, *Flash Art International* (June 2007): 134–39.

Vettese, Angela, and Claudia Fini, eds. *Lo Spirito dell'Arte. Opere della collezione Carlo Cattelani*. Cinisello Balsamo (Milan): Silvana Editoriale, 2007.

2008

Alizart, Marc, ed. *Traces du Sacré*. Exh. cat. Paris: Centre Georges Pompidou, 2008. Published in conjunction with an exhibition of the same title, organized by and presented at the Centre Pompidou, Paris, May 7–August 11, 2008.

Blain, Françoise-Aline. "Un Versailles Contemporain." *Beaux Arts Magazine*, no. 283 (January 2008): 14.

Bonami, Francesco, ed. *Italics, Arte Italiana fra tradizione e rivoluzione 1968–2008*. Exh. cat. Milan: Electa, 2008. Published in conjunction with an exhibition of the same title, organized by and presented at Palazzo Grassi, Venice, September 26–March 22, 2008, and the Museum of Contemporary Art, Chicago, July 18–October 25, 2009.

Bonito Oliva, Achille. "Gino De Dominicis. Ancona, 1947–Roma, 1998." In *Enciclopedia della Parola. Dialoghi d'artista 1968–2008*, edited by Achille Bonito Oliva, 266–69. Milan: Skira, 2008.

———, ed. *I fuochi dell'arte e le sue reliquie*. Exh. cat. Milan: Skira, 2008. Published in conjunction with an exhibition of the same title, organized by and presented at the Auditorium Parco della Musica, Rome, November 12, 2008–January 10, 2009.

Busine, Laurent, Italo Tomassoni, and Jean de Loisy, eds. *Gino De Dominicis. Calamita Cosmica*. Exh. cat. Brussels: MAC's, 2008. Published in conjunction with an exhibition of the same title, presented at the Musée des Arts Contemporains de la Fédération Wallonie-Bruxelles, Brussels, July 6–September 14, 2008.

Caroli, Flavio, and Ludovico Festa. *Tutti i volti dell'arte da Leonardo a Basquiat*. Milan: Mondadori, 2008.

Cherubini, Laura. "Oggetto vivente perfetto." *Flash Art*, no. 40 (June/July 2008): 270.

Hermann, Gauthier, Fabrice Reymond, and Fabien Vallos, eds. *Art conceptuel, une entologie*. Paris: Edition Mix, 2008.

Luccarini, Antonio. "De Dominicis genio da riscoprire." *Il Corriere Adriatico*, n.d.

Maffei, Giorgio, and Emanuele De Donno, eds. *In principium erat. Genesi di una collezione di opere e libri d'artista*. Exh. cat. Foligno: Viaindustriae, 2008. Published in conjunction with an exhibition organized by and presented at the Palazzo Trinci, Foligno, and Galleria Civica d'Arte Moderna, Biblioteca Giovanni Carandente, and Museo Archeologico Statale, Spoleto, April 27–May 25, 2008.

Mazzonis, Emanuela. "Gino De Dominicis." In *Italics*, 82–95, 170, 290.

Milzi, Gianpaolo. "Ancona. L'arte di dimenticare i suoi grandi." *Il Messaggero*, November 28, 2008.

Minini, Massimo, ed. *United Artists of Italy*. Exh. cat. Milan: Photology, 2008. Published in conjunction with an exhibition of the same title, organized by and presented at the Musée d'art moderne et contemporain de Saint-Étienne Métropole, Saint-Priest-en-Jarez, May 7–September 21, 2008.

Paparoni, Demetrio. *Metalgrafie. Viaggio nell'arte contemporanea italiana*. Milan: Skira, 2008.

Parlavecchio, Ida. "New York scopre l'arte radicale di De Dominicis." *Arte*, no. 423 (November 2008): 67–68.

Pozzati, Concetto, and Maura Pozzati. *L'Arte come amante. Da una collezione privata contemporanea*. Mantova: Casa del Mantegna, 2008.

Tomassoni, Italo. "Il caso Gino De Dominicis." *Flash Art*, no. 271 (August/September 2008): 102–5. Reprinted from *Flash Art*, no. 144 (June 1988): 38.

2009

Bellini, Andrea, and Laura Cherubini, ed. *Gino De Dominicis alla Fondazione Merz*. Turin: Fondazione Merz, 2009.

Birnbaum, Daniel, and Jurgen Volz. "Gino De Dominicis." In *La Biennale di Venezia. 53a Esposizione Internazionale d'Arte. Fare Mondi. Making worlds*, edited by La Biennale di Venezia, 38–39. Exh. cat. Venice: La Biennale di Venezia, 2009. Published in conjunction with the LIII Esposizione internazionale d'arte, held at the Giardini di Castello, Venice, June 5–November 22, 2009.

Désanges, Guillaume. "Gino De Dominicis." *Exit Express*, no. 41 (2009): 58.

———, ed. *Planet of Signs / Planète des signes*. Exh. cat. Paris: Le Plateau, 2008. Published in conjunction with an exhibition of the same title, organized by and presented at Le Plateau, Paris, September 10–November 15, 2009.

Di Groppello, Giulio. "Un Ginotauro nel labirinto." *Il Giornale dell'Arte*, no. 103 (April 2009): 4.

Guercio, Gabriele. "Repositories of the Unconditional: Gino De Dominicis' 'Mirror' and the Work of Art as Model of Immortality." *RES: Anthropology and Aesthetics*, no. 55/56 (Spring/Summer 2009): 308–23.

Tomassoni, Italo. "Lo spazio e l'immagine. Arte italiana degli anni sessanta." In *Lo spazio dell'immagine e il suo tempo*, edited by Italo Tomassoni, 73, 132, 148. Exh. cat. Milan: Skira, 2009. Published in conjunction with an exhibition of the same title, organized by and presented at the Centro Italiano Arte Contemporanea, Foligno, November 14, 2009–January 31, 2010.

Tran, Mai. "Petite cosmogonié estuarienne (Avec les œuvres de Gino De Dominicis, Roman Signer, Stéphane Thidet, Jimmie Durham, Ange Leccia et Anne de Sterk; rire, pendule, loups, serpent, nymphe et déluge inventent le mythe Estuaire)." In *Estuaire 2009. Le paysage, l'art et le fleuve*, edited by Jean Blaise, 36–45. Exh. cat. Nantes: Association

303, 2009. Published in conjunction with an exhibition of the same title, organized by and presented at the Estuaire Nantes Saint-Nazaire, Nantes, June 5–August 16, 2009.

Ventroni, Desdemona. "La galleria Schema a Firenze. Azioni e Comunicazioni (1972/1976)." *Ricerche di Storia dell'Arte*, no. 98 (November 2009): 37–48.

Viliani, Andrea, ed. *Civica 1989–2009. Celebration, Institution, Critique*. Exh. cat. Trento: Galleria Civica, 2009. Published in conjunction with an exhibition of the same title, organized by and presented at the Galleria Civica, Trento, October 9, 2009–January 31, 2010.

2010

Arbasino, Alberto. "Le curve del MAXXI. Il fascino del museo mattatore." Exhibition review, MAXXI, Rome. *La Repubblica*, June 28, 2010.

Baffoni, Andrea. "Gino De Dominicis o la logica di senso e di non-senso." *Contemporart*, no. 63 (June 2010): 26–28.

Barina, Antonella. "De Dominicis e i suoi scheletri scagliati contro la morte." Exhibition review, MAXXI, Rome. *Il Venerdì di Repubblica*, March 5, 2010.

Bartocci, Claudio. "La dimensione più misteriosa." In *Gino De Dominicis. L'immortale*, edited by Achille Bonito Oliva, 63–68. Exh. cat. Milan: Mondadori Electa, 2010.

Bonazzoli, Francesca. "Gino De Dominicis, un mistero cosmico." *Il Corriere della Sera*, May 29, 2010.

Bonito Oliva, Achille, ed. *De Dominicis a Saint Moritz*. Milan: Electa, 2010.

————, ed. *Gino De Dominicis. L'immortale*. Exh. cat. Milan: Mondadori Electa, 2010. Published in conjunction with an exhibition of the same title, organized by Achille Bonito Oliva and presented at the MAXXI – Museo nazionale delle arti del XXI secolo, Rome, May 30–November 7, 2010.

————. "Senza titolo: L'immortale." In *Gino De Dominicis. L'immortale*, 13–30.

Celant, Germano. "L'antiartista." *L'Espresso*, May 20, 2010.

Cherubini, Laura. "Gino De Dominicis. L'immortale." Exhibition review, MAXXI, Rome. *Flash Art*, no. 285 (July 2010): 79.

Dantini, Michele. "Ytalya subjecta. Narrazioni identitarie e critica d'arte 1937/2009." In *Il confine evanescente. Arte Italiana 1960–2010*, edited by Gabriele Guercio and Anna Mattirolo, 262–307. Exh. cat. Milan: Electa, 2010.

Diehl, Ute. "Die Sphinx von Rom." Exhibition review, MAXXI, Rome. *Monopol* (May 2010): 71.

Donà, Massimo. "Poiesis e Immortalità. Gino De Dominicis, l'antiplatonico." In *Gino De Dominicis. L'immortale*, 51–62.

D'Orazio, Costantino. "Claudio Abate. Giniamoci." *Flash Art*, no. 285 (July 2010): 36–39.

Franco, Francesca. "Godi Cindi Domine – Godi Cinsi Demoni. Scritti, interviste, testimonianze di G. D. D." In *Gino De Dominicis. L'immortale*, 87–104.

Guercio, Gabriele. "Gino De Dominicis." In *Enciclopedia delle Arti Contemporanee*, edited by Achille Bonito Oliva, 181–82. Milan: Electa, 2010.

————. "L'obiezione ancestrale. Considerazioni preliminari sullo Specchio che tutto riflette tranne gli esseri viventi." In *Gino De Dominicis. L'immortale*, 39–50.

————. "L'opera d'arte e il divenire generico del creativo. Cinque momenti 'italiani'?" In *Il confine evanescente. Arte italiana 1960–2010*, 343–90.

Guercio, Gabriele, and Anna Mattirolo, eds. *Il confine evanescente. Arte italiana 1960–2010*. Exh. cat. Milan: Electa, 2010. Published in conjunction with an exhibition of the same title, organized by and presented at the MAXXI – Museo nazionale delle arti del XXI secolo, Rome, February 25–October 10, 2010.

Magrelli, Valerio. "Viaggio nell'astronave museo troppo bello per servire agli artisti." Exhibition review, MAXXI, Rome. *La Repubblica*, May 26, 2010.

Mattarella, Lea. "Gino De Dominicis." Exhibition review, MAXXI, Rome. *La Repubblica*, May 29, 2010.

Mattirolo, Anna. "Introduzione." In *Gino De Dominicis. L'immortale*, 11–12.

Monti, Pio. *P'io&Gino*. Milan: Giancarlo Politi Editore, 2010.

Panza, Pierluigi. "Apre il MAXXI. È già polemica." Exhibition review, MAXXI, Rome. *Il Corriere della Sera*, May 14, 2010.

Pasini, Francesca, and Angela Vettese, eds. *Cosa fa la mia anima mentre sto lavorando? Opere d 'Arte Contemporanea della collezione Consolandi*. Exh. cat. Milan: Electa, 2010. Published in conjunction with an exhibition of the same title, organized by and presented at the Museo MAGA, Gallarate, November 13, 2010–February 13, 2011.

Pettinato, Giovanni, and Silvia Chiodi. "I segni dell' Antica Mesopotamia in Gino De Dominicis." In *Gino De Dominicis. L'immortale*, 69–81.

Sargentini, Fabio. "Gino De Dominicis. Il gusto della scandalo." In *Gino De Dominicis. L'immortale*, 83–86.

Sassi, Edoardo. "'È un'idea vecchia' Sgarbi torna all'attacco del MAXXI di Roma." Exhibition review, MAXXI, Rome. *Il Corriere della Sera*, May 29, 2010.

Tomassoni, Italo. "Epopea di Gino De Dominicis." In *Gino De Dominicis. L'immortale*, 31–38.

Trombadori, Duccio. "Gino De Dominicis, anarchico in cerca dell'immortalità." Exhibition review, MAXXI, Rome. *Il Foglio*, May 29, 2010.

Vallora, Marco. "De Dominicis accende il MAXXI." Exhibition review, MAXXI, Rome. *La Stampa*, May 31, 2010.

2011

Aita, Paolo. "Camere XIV. Gino de Dominicis, Ettore Spalletti, Joseph Kosuth." Exhibition review, RAM Radio Arte Mobile, Rome. *Rivista Segno*, no. 235 (March/April 2011): 38–39.

Beatrice, Luca. "Il mistero di De Dominicis resuscitato dal business dell'arte." *Il Giornale*, July 4, 2011.

Dantini, Michele. "Pattini a rotelle. Gino De Dominicis laicizzato." *Doppiozero*, October 17,

2011. https://www.doppiozero.com/materiali/fuori-busta/pattini-rotelle-gino-de-dominicis-laicizzato.

Giacomelli, Marco E. "De Dominicis. Niente o tutto." *Artribune*, October 30, 2011. https://www.artribune.com/attualita/2011/10/de-dominicis-niente-o-tutto/.

Gualdoni, Flaminio. "De Dominicis in 632 numeri." *Il Giornale dell'Arte*, no. 312 (September 2011): 46.

Guercio, Gabriele. *The Great Subtraction*. Brussels: ASA Publishers, 2011.

Larcan, Laura. "Ecco il De Dominicis segreto, un libro sull'artista che si nascose." Review of *Gino De Dominicis. Catalogo ragionato*, by Italo Tomassoni. *La Repubblica*, July 16, 2011.

Moliterni, Rocco. "Italia 150. Non ci resta che ridere." Exhibition review, Castello di Rivoli, Turin. *La Stampa*, March 6, 2011.

Tomassoni, Italo. *Gino De Dominicis. Catalogo ragionato*. Milan: Skira, 2011.

2012

Charans, Eleonora. *Gino De Dominicis. 2a Soluzione di immortalità (L'universo è immobile)*. Milan: Scalpendi Editore, 2012.

Clerici, Stefano. "De Dominicis, l'immortale viaggio al centro dell'artista." *La Repubblica*, January 23, 2012.

Dantini, Michele. *Geopolitiche dell'arte. Arte e critica d'arte italiana nel contesto internazionale, dalle neoavanguardie a oggi*. Milan: Christian Marinotti Edizioni, 2012.

Di Pietrantonio, Giacinto, and Umberto Palestrini. *Visioni. La fortezza plurale dell'arte*. Exh. cat. Cinisello Balsamo (Milan): Silvana Editoriale, 2012. Published in conjunction with an exhibition of the same title, organized by and presented at the Fortezza Borbonica, Civitella del Tronto, July 1–October 31, 2012.

Filardo, Daria, and Aldo Iori. *Arte torna Arte*. Florence: Giunti, 2012. Exh. cat. Published in conjunction with an exhibition of the same title, organized by and presented at the Galleria dell'Accademia, Florence, May 7–November 4, 2012.

Sassi, Edoardo. "I suoni dell'arte." *Il Corriere della Sera*, May 7, 2012.

Sgarbi, Vittorio. "Gino De Dominicis." In *La Stanza Dipinta. Scritti sull'arte contemporanea*, edited by Vittorio Sgarbi, 321–22. Milan: Bompiani, 2012.

———. *L'arte è contemporanea. Ovvero l'arte di vedere l'arte*. Milan: Bompiani, 2012.

Trombadori, Duccio. *De Dominicis amico pittore: storia e cronistoria di un sodalizio*. San Marino: Maretti Editore, 2012.

2013

Bucci, Stefano. "De Dominicis e i favolosi 70." Exhibition review, Palazzo delle Esposizioni, Rome. *Il Corriere della Sera*, December 19, 2013.

De Sanctis, Linda. "Irripetibili anni '70, quando l'arte era tutto." Exhibition review, Palazzo delle Esposizioni, Rome. *La Repubblica*, December 17, 2013.

Gigliotti, Guglielmo. "Tre associazioni e due cataloghi per l'artista che non voleva apparire." *Il Giornale dell'Arte*, no. 327 (January 2013): 5.

Lancioni, Daniela, ed. *Anni 70. Arte a Roma*. Guidonia: Iacobelli Editore, 2013. Exh. cat. Published in conjunction with an exhibition of the same title, organized by and presented at the Palazzo delle Esposizioni, Rome, December 17, 2013–March 2, 2014.

Meloni, Lucilla. *Arte guarda arte. Pratiche della citazione nell'arte contemporanea*. Milan: Postmedia books, 2013.

Meneguzzo, Marco, Bruno Di Marino, and Andrea La Porta, eds. *Artisti nello spazio: da Lucio Fontana a oggi: gli ambienti nell'arte italiana*. Exh. cat. Cinisello Balsamo (Milan): Silvana Editoriale, 2013. Published in conjunction with an exhibition of the same title, organized by and presented at the Complesso monumentale del San Giovanni, Catanzaro, October 11–December 29, 2013.

Perna, Raffaella. "Natura e problematiche della fotografia di opere effimere: lo Zodiaco di Gino De Dominicis nelle foto di Claudio Abate e Fausto Giaccone." In *Contemporanea. Scritti di storia dell'arte per Jolanda Nigro Covre*, edited by Ilaria Schiaffini and Claudio Zambianchi, 267–73. Rome: Campisano Editore, 2013.

Sassi, Edoardo. "Ribelle, classica, underground. La Roma artistica anni 70." *Il Corriere della Sera*, December 11, 2013.

2014

Bozzini, Didi. *Salviamo la pelle*. Exh. cat. Lucca: Claudio Poleschi Arte Contemporanea, 2014. Published in conjunction with an exhibition of the same title, organized by and presented at the Galleria Claudio Poleschi, Lucca, December 13, 2014–February 13, 2015.

Cachia, Amanda. "From Outsider to Participant: Developmentally Disabled Dialogue in Socially Engaged Art." *Museums & Social Issues* 9, no. 2 (October 2014): 109–23.

De Loisy, Jean. *Simple Shapes*. Exh. cat. Metz: Centre Pompidou-Metz, 2014. Published in conjunction with an exhibition of the same title, organized by and presented at the Centre Pompidou-Metz, Metz, June 13, 2014–January 5, 2015.

Esposito, Ursula. "L'heureuse saison des cassettes vidéo: les années soixante-dix et l'art vidéo en Italie." *Ligeia* 27, no. 133–36 (July–December 2014): 127–39.

Gallo, Francesca. "Informare, osservare, agire: riviste, performance e artisti." *Ricerche di storia dell'arte* 114, no. 3 (2014): 5–19.

Guercio, Gabriele. *De Dominicis. Scritti sull'opera e riflessioni dell'artista*, 2nd rev. ed. Turin: Umberto Allemandi, 2014.

Lancioni, Daniela. "Perché Jannis Kounellis ha consegnato la realtà della vita alla fissità del quadro?" *Ricerche di storia dell'arte* 114, no. 3 (2014): 46–60.

2015

Bonazzoli, Francesca. "De Dominicis, il 'mago' che si ispirava a Gilgamesh." *Il Corriere della Sera*, September 19, 2015.

Bruciati, Andrea, ed. *Qui non si canta al mondo delle rane. Gino De Dominicis.* Exh. cat. Cinisello Balsamo (Milan): Silvana Editoriale, 2015. Published in conjunction with an exhibition of the same title, organized by and presented at the Fondazione Menegaz, Castelbasso, July 26–September 6, 2015.

Farrell, Robyn. "Network(ed) TV: Collaboration and Intervention at Fernsehgalerie Gerry Schum and Videogalerie Schum." *Afterimage* 43, no. 3 (November/December 2015): 12–19.

Guercio, Gabriele. *L'arte non evolve. L'universo immobile di Gino De Dominicis.* Monza: Johan & Levi, 2015.

Nickas, Bob, ed. *69/96.* Exh. cat. Zurich: Edition Patrick Frey, 2015. Published in conjunction with an exhibition of the same title, organized by and presented at the Alte Fabrik, Zurich, February 28–March 30, 2015.

2016

Boatto, Alberto. *Ghenos Eros Thanatos e altri scritti sull'arte 1968–1985.* Rome: L'orma, 2016.

Bonazzoli, Francesca. "L'arte metafisica di De Dominicis. Un saggio su uno dei più misteriosi e ostici protagonisti del contemporaneo." *Il Corriere della Sera*, May 10, 2016.

Brandon, Claire R. "Spaces of Art in the Exhibition Age: Italy as a Laboratory for Global Exhibition Paradigms Since 1970." PhD diss. New York University, 2016.

Bruscia, Carlo. *Oltre il limite: in viaggio con la "Calamita Cosmica" di Gino De Dominicis (2000–2010).* Calcinelli di Saltara: Ideostampa, 2016.

Charans, Eleonora. "Work (and) behaviour: Gino De Dominicis at the 36th Venice Biennale: a case study and a methodology." In *Histoire(s) d'exposition(s). Exhibitions' Stories*, edited by Dufrene Glicestein, 45–54. Paris: Hermann, 2016.

Distefano, Natalia. "Roma, arte aperta. Tutti nell'ex Dogana." *Il Corriere della Sera*, April 28, 2016.

Fameli, Pasquale. "Il peso del vuoto. Emilio Prini ieri e oggi." *Intrecci d'Arte*, no. 5 (2016): 90.

Guercio, Gabriele. *L'Art n'évolue pas: l'univers immobile de Gino De Dominicis.* Paris: Ed. du Regard, 2016.

Madaro, Lorenzo. "Il mistero delle armi. 'Così svelo le opere segrete di Pascali e De Dominicis.'" *La Repubblica*, October 20, 2016.

Sassi, Edoardo. "Cosa mai conterrà quell'opera sigillata? 'Scrigno' svelato oggi all'Attico dopo 43 anni." *Il Corriere della Sera*, October 21, 2016.

Ventroni, Desdemona. "Firenze e … La Galleria Schema, crocevia delle neoavanguardie internazionali attraverso il bollettino 'Schema Informazione.'" In *Arte a Firenze 1970–2015: Una Città in Prospettiva*, edited by Alessandro Acocella and Caterina Toschi, 21–38. Macerata: Quodlibet, 2016.

Voso, Daniela. "Arte, marginalità del quotidiano, censura. I casi di Hans Haacke e Gino de Dominicis." *Piano b* 1, no. 1 (December 2016): 296–320.

2017

Arzel Nadal, Laurence. "An Exemplary Art Work." *Critique d'Art*, no. 48 (Spring/Summer 2017): 116–24.

Barilli, Renato, and Giada Pellicari. *Comportamento. Biennale di Venezia 1972 Padiglione Italia.* Exh. cat. Cinisello Balsamo (Milan): Silvana Editoriale, 2017. Published in conjunction with an exhibition of the same title, organized by and presented at the Centro Pecci, Prato, May 6–September 24, 2017.

Blunk, Julian. "Weshalb Pinocchio richtig lag: Gino De Dominicis' 'Calamita Cosmica' neben dem Mailänder Dom." In *Capriccio & Architektur*, edited by Stefan Burger and Ludwig Kallweit, 241–46. Berlin: Deutscher Kunstverlag, 2017.

Capasso, Angelo, ed. *Animalia.* Exh. cat. Rome: Pio Monti Arte Contemporanea, 2017. Published in conjunction with an exhibition of the same title, organized by and presented at the Galleria Monti, Rome, February 28–March 30, 2017.

Charans, Eleonora. "Tra esposizione e archiviazione. La videoarte di Gino De Dominicis." In *Crocevia Biennale*, edited by Francesca Castellani and Eleonora Charans, 225–34. Milan: Scalpendi Editore, 2017.

Di Lorenzo, Francesco, and Diana Lapucci. "'Intrusions' of contemporary art in places of worship: the 'Calamita Cosmica' in the ex church of Santissima Trinità in Annunziata in Foligno." *IN_BO. Ricerche e progetti per il territorio, la città e l'architettura* 7, no. 10 (July 2017): 215–35.

Ferraro, Alessandro. "Aneddoti e storie di una vita aliena." *Images Re-Vues*, no. 14. https://journals.openedition.org/imagesrevues/4119.

Guercio, Gabriele. "Our Lady of Warka: Gino De Dominicis and the Search for Immortality." In *Postwar Italian Art History Today: Untying "the Knot,"* edited by Sharon Hecker and Marin R. Sullivan, 73–92. London: Bloomsbury Publishing, 2017.

Luxembourg, Daniella, and Amalia Dayan, eds. *Gino De Dominicis. Works from the Collection of Guntis Brands.* Exh. cat. London: Luxembourg & Dayan, 2017. Published in conjunction with an exhibition of the same title, organized by and presented at Luxembourg & Dayan, London, October 4–December 8, 2017.

Melotti, Massimo. *Vicende dell'arte in Italia dal dopoguerra agli anni Duemila. Artisti, gallerie, mercato, collezionisti, musei.* Milan: Franco Angeli, 2017.

Risaliti, Sergio. *Ytalia. Energia pensiero bellezza. Tutto è connesso.* Exh. cat. Florence: Forma Edizioni, 2017. Published in conjunction with an exhibition of the same title, organized and presented at the Forte del Belvedere, Florence, June 2–October 1, 2017.

Sassi, Edoardo. "Addio a Claudio Abate, fotografo e testimone d'arte." *Il Corriere della Sera*, August 4, 2017.

———. "ANIMALIA ad arte. Da Pascali a Kounellis. In mostra alla Galleria Pio Monti 34 contemporanei." Exhibition review, Galleria Pio

Monti, Rome. *Il Corriere della Sera*, February 27, 2017.

Sgarbi, Vittorio. *Spoleto Arte*. Exh. cat. Milan: Cairo Editore, 2017. Published in conjunction with an exhibition of the same title, organized by and presented at the Palazzo Leti Sansi, Spoleto, July 1–August 30, 2017.

Zahm, Olivier. *Une avant-garde sans avant-garde: essai sur l'art contemporain*. Dijon: Les presses du réel, 2017.

2018

Bucci, Stefano. "Gino De Dominicis. L'arte estrema in bilico tra libertà e provocazione." *Il Corriere della Sera*, June 13, 2018.

Eastham, Ben. "Poor Art / Arte Povera: Italian Influences, British Responses, Estorick Collection, London 20 September–17 December." Exhibition review, Estorick Foundation, London. *ArtReview* 70, no. 1 (January/February 2018): 104–5.

Fumagalli, Sara, ed. *Black hole, arte e matericità tra informe e invisibile*. Bergamo: GAMeC Books, 2018. Exh. cat. Published in conjunction with an exhibition of the same title, organized by and presented at GAMeC, Bergamo, October 4, 2018–January 6, 2019.

Giaccone, Fausto. *Gino De Dominicis, Lo zodiaco*. Milan: Edizioni Nero, 2018.

Madaro, Lorenzo. "I cavalli di Kounellis tornano nell'Attico 49 anni dopo." *La Repubblica*, October 26, 2018.

Scarpa, Giuseppe. "Falsi De Dominicis. Vittorio Sgarbi sotto accusa." *La Repubblica*, November 30, 2018.

Sgarbi, Vittorio, ed. *GDD: genio della dimensione*. Exh. cat. Palermo: Ass. Babilonia, 2018. Published in conjunction with an exhibition of the same title, organized by and presented at the Palazzo Belmonte Riso – Museo d'arte contemporanea della Sicilia, Palermo, June 13–August 26, 2018.

———. "Niente dogmi l'arte è democrazia." *La Repubblica*, April 3, 2018.

Tonini, Bruno. *Gino De Dominicis – "Sicinimod ed" e altri documenti*. Gussago: L'arengario studio bibliografico, 2018.

Ziino, Giulia. "Oggi, domani è anche ieri. Tutto è contemporaneo." *Il Corriere della Sera*, October 28, 2018.

2019

Cirinei, Cecilia. "Paura del buio, il lato oscuro della bellezza." Exhibition review, Musja, Rome. *La Repubblica*, October 8, 2019.

Eccher, Danilo, ed. *The dark side. Chi ha paura del buio?* Exh. cat. Cinisello Balsamo (Milan): Silvana Editoriale, 2019. Published in conjunction with an exhibition of the same title, Musja, Rome, October 8, 2019–June 28, 2020.

Manganaro, Silvano. "Al Musja il lato oscuro di tutti noi." Exhibition review, Musja, Rome. *Il Giornale dell'Arte*, no. 401 (October 2019): 23.

Paglieri, Marina. "De Dominicis, La voglia di volare (e di essere anche immortale)." Exhibition review, GAM, Turin. *La Repubblica*, October 24, 2019.

Ruiz, Christina. "Enigmatic Gino De Dominicis subject of complex fakes investigation in Italy." *The Art Newspaper* 28, no. 309 (February 2019): 39.

Sacchettoni, Ilaria. "Falsificate le opere di De Dominicis." *Il Corriere della Sera*, March 11, 2019.

Sassi, Edoardo. "Il contemporaneo non fa più paura." *Il Corriere della Sera*, October 20, 2019.

2020

Byars, James Lee. "'L'inconsistance n'est pas l'insignifiance.'" *Beaux Arts Magazine*, no. 432 (June 2020): 42.

Gavarro, Raffaele. *L'arte senza l'arte. Mutamenti nell'era analogicodigitale*. San Marino: Maretti Editore, 2020.

Lemme, Fabrizio. "Mucciaccia vs l'Archivio De Dominicis. Archiviazione negata: è controversia giusdiziaria." *Il Giornale dell'Arte*, no. 406 (March 2020): 28.

Miliani, Stefano. "La terza via di De Dominicis. L'artista e i suoi 'compagni di strada.'" *Il Giornale dell'Arte*, no. 405 (February 2020): 5.

INDEX

Contributors

Marina Abramović is a Serbian artist based in New York. She studied at the Academy of Fine Arts in Belgrade and, in 1975, began a creative partnership with the German artist Ulay, with whom she performed internationally until 1988. Her work has been exhibited at Documenta 9 (1992); the XLVII Venice Biennale (1997), where she was awarded the Golden Lion; the Whitney Biennial (2004); and in retrospectives at the Van Abbemuseum, Eindhoven (1985); Musée National d'Art Moderne, Centre Pompidou, Paris (1990); Neue Nationalgalerie, Berlin (1993); Museum of Modern Art, Oxford (1995); and the Museum of Modern Art, New York, where she carried out her three-month performance *The Artist Is Present* in 2010. Her most recent exhibition, *Gates and Portals*, opened at Modern Art Oxford in 2022.

Jean-Christophe Ammann (1939–2015) was a Swiss curator and historian of contemporary art. He served as the director of the Museum für Moderne Kunst, Frankfurt, from 1989 to 2001; director of the Kunsthalle, Basel, from 1978 to 1988; director of the Museum of Art, Lucerne, from 1969 to 1977; and assistant director at the Kunsthalle, Bern, from 1967 to 1968. He co-organized Documenta 5 in 1972, co-curated the 1988 Carnegie International in Pittsburgh, and curated the German Pavilion at the XLVI Venice Biennale in 1995. He oversaw the catalogue raisonné of Alighiero Boetti and his writing has been published in numerous exhibition catalogues and art journals.

Andrea Bellini is a Swiss Italian curator and critic of contemporary art. Since 2012 he has been the director of the Centre d'Art Contemporain Genève, where he is also the artistic director of the Biennale de l'Image en Mouvement. He served as codirector of the Castello di Rivoli from 2009 to 2012, and curatorial advisor at MoMA PS1, New York, from 2007 to 2009, where he curated a Gino De Dominicis retrospective in 2008. He is curating the Swiss Pavilion for the LX Venice Biennale in 2024. He served as editor-in-chief of *Flash Art* and his publications include *Writing by Drawing: When Language Seeks Its Other* (Milan: Skira, 2020), *Roberto Cuoghi: 1996–2016* (Berlin: Hatje Cantz, 2017), and *Collecting Contemporary Art* (Geneva: JRP|Ringier, 2009).

Norman Bryson is an art historian and a professor emeritus at UC San Diego, where he has taught since 2003. He previously taught at King's College, Cambridge; the University of Rochester, Rochester, NY; Harvard University, Cambridge, MA; and the Slade School of Fine Art, University College, London, among others. His scholarship ranges from eighteenth-century French painting to contemporary art and theory, and his publications include *Vision and Painting: The Logic of the Gaze* (New Haven, CT: Yale University Press, 1983); *Tradition and Desire: From David to Delacroix* (New York: Cambridge University Press, 1984); *Visual Theory: Painting and Interpretation* (New York: HarperCollins, 1989), and *Visual Culture: Images and Interpretations* (Middletown, CT: Wesleyan University Press, 1994). Bryson was awarded a Guggenheim Fellowship in 1997.

Daniel Buren is a French artist who lives and works "in situ." Since graduating from the École Nationale Supérieure des Métiers d'Art, Paris, in 1960, he has exhibited at institutions including the Walker Art Center, Minneapolis; Kunsthalle, Düsseldorf; the Solomon R. Guggenheim Museum, New York; and the Centre Pompidou, Paris. His work, known for its 8.7 cm stripes of color, has been included in Monumenta, Paris (2012), and multiple iterations of the Venice Biennale (he was awarded the Golden Lion in 1986), and is installed permanently at the Guggenheim Museum Bilbao, the Tottenham Court Road station of the London Underground, and the MRT Circular Line Banqiao Station of the Taipei Metro, among other locations.

Germano Celant (1940–2020) was an Italian art historian and curator. He is known for coining the term "Arte Povera," first as the title of a 1967 exhibition (*Arte Povera – Im Spazio* at Galleria La Bertesca, Genoa) and then as the title of his 1969 book (published by Praeger). He went on to curate Arte Povera exhibitions at MoMA PS1, New York, and the Centre Pompidou, Paris, among other venues. He worked with Fondazione Prada, Milan, from 1995 to 2020, and the Solomon R. Guggenheim Museum, New York, from 1988 to 2008. He also assisted in Documenta 7 (1982) and curated the XLVII Venice Biennale (1997). Among hundreds of publications over the course of his career, he oversaw the catalogues raisonnés of Carla Accardi, Piero Manzoni, and Mimmo Rotella.

Laura Cherubini is an Italian critic and curator focusing on Italian art of the 1960s and 1970s. Since 1992 she has been a professor of contemporary art history at Accademia di Belle Arti di Brera, Milan, and has also taught at Sapienza Università and Luiss Guido Carli in Rome. She was head of contemporary art at the Instituto Nazionale per la Grafica, Rome, from 2005 to 2007, and curated *Dialogues with the City* at MAXXI, Rome (2008–9), and the Italian Pavilion at the XLIV Venice Biennale (1990), among others. In addition to regularly contributing to newspapers and journals, she has authored *Ettore Spalletti: Nerazzurro, Rosa Tenue* (Rome: Oredaria Arti Contemporanee, 2006) and *Trasparenze: L'Arte per le Energie Rinnovabili* (Rome: Edizioni Carte Segrete, 2010).

Ombretta Celeste is a freelance author based in Venice. Her writing, often published pseudonymously, addresses topics ranging from the visual arts to culture, politics, and climate change.

Andrea Cortellessa is an Italian art and literary critic and an associate professor of philosophy, communication, and performing arts at the Università degli Studi Roma Tre, Rome. He is known for his scholarship on Italian poetry, literature, and visual art of the twentieth and twenty-first centuries. He edited Fuoriformato, a series of publications on contemporary literature, from 2006 to 2018, cofounded the online magazine *Antinomie*, and currently codirects I Domani, a contemporary poetry series. He has published and edited several books on art and literature, including *Andrea Zanzotto. Il canto nella terra* (Rome: Laterza, 2021), *Giorgio de Chirico. La casa del poeta* (Milan: La nave di Teseo, 2019), and *Monsieur zero. 26 lettere su Manzoni, quello vero* (Rome: Italo Svevo, 2018).

Creighton Gilbert (1924–2011) was an American art historian, an expert on the Italian Renaissance, and a leading scholar on Michelangelo. He earned his PhD from New York University in 1955, with a dissertation on Girolamo Savoldo. He taught or held research positions at Indiana University, Bloomington; the Ringling Museum of Art, Sarasota, FL; Brandeis University, Waltham, MA; Harvard University, Cambridge, MA; Cornell University, Ithaca, NY; and Yale University, New Haven, CT, where he was a professor of the history of art from 1981 until the end of his career. He authored numerous essays, including the seminal "On Subject and Non-Subject in Renaissance Pictures" (1952), and published, among others, *Poets Seeing Artists' Work: Instances in the Italian Renaissance* (Florence: Leo S. Olschki, 1991); *Michelangelo: On and Off the Sistine Ceiling* (New York: George Braziller, 1994), *Caravaggio and His Two Cardinals* (University Park, PA: Penn State University Press, 1995), and *How Fra Angelico and Signorelli Saw the End of the World* (University Park, PA: Penn State University Press, 2003). Gilbert served as editor-in-chief of the *Art Bulletin* from 1980 to 1985. He gifted his art collection to the Fred Jones Jr. Museum of Art, Norman, Oklahoma.

Gabriele Guercio is an Italian art historian and essayist based in Milan. He has written extensively on modern and contemporary art, as well as the history of ideas on art. His publications include, among others, *Art as Existence: The Artist's Monograph and Its Project* (Cambridge, MA: MIT Press, 2006), *The Great Subtraction* (Brussels: ASA, 2011), *L'arte non evolve. L'universo immobile di Gino De Dominicis* (Milan: Johan & Levi, 2015), *Il demone di Picasso. Creatività generica e assoluto della creazione* (Macerata: Quodlibet, 2017), *Opere d'arte e nuovi inizi* (Macerata: Quodlibet, 2021), and *Antidestino. Quattro esempi dell'arte italiana, 1965–1983* (Naples: Cronopio, 2022).

Anselm Kiefer is a German artist living and working in France since 1992. He studied at the School of Fine Arts, Freiburg im Breisgau, and the Art Academy, Karlsruhe, in the 1960s, and became acquainted with Joseph Beuys, with whom he studied informally in Düsseldorf. His work was shown in the XXXIX Venice Biennale (1980) and Monumenta, Paris (2007). Kiefer has had solo exhibitions at the Metropolitan Museum of Art, New York (1998); Guggenheim Museum Bilbao (2000); and Fondation Beyeler, Basel (2001), among others. *Anselm Kiefer au Louvre* was held at the Musée du Louvre, Paris, in 2007; *Provocations* at the Met Breuer, New York, in 2017. His exhibition at Palazzo Ducale, Venice, opened in 2022.

Jannis Kounellis (1936–2017) was a Greek Italian artist. In 1956 he permanently relocated from Greece to Italy, where he became a central figure of the Arte Povera movement and was included in the eponymous exhibitions in 1967 and 1968. He represented his adopted country at the XLIII Venice Biennale (1988) and exhibited at institutions including the Galleria Nazionale d'Arte Moderna, Rome (2002); Neue Nationalgalerie, Berlin (2007); Museum of Cycladic Art, Athens (2012); and Fondazione Prada, Venice (2019).

Joseph Kosuth is an American artist. After studies at the Toledo Museum School of Design (1955–62), the Cleveland Institute of Art (1963–64), and the School of Visual Arts, New York (1965–67), he served on the faculty at SVA from 1967 to 1985 and continues to teach internationally. He was an originator of Conceptual art, cofounding and exhibiting at the Museum of Normal Art, New York, in 1967 and showing at Leo Castelli Gallery in 1969. He exhibited at Documenta in 1972, 1978, 1982, and 1992, at the Venice Biennale in 1976, 1993, and 1999, and in solo exhibitions at MoMA PS1, New York (1980), Palais des Beaux-Arts, Brussels (1990); the Louvre, Paris (2009); and MAMM, Moscow (2015), among many others.

Achille Bonito Oliva is an Italian art historian and critic; he has been a professor of contemporary art at Sapienza Università, Rome, since 1968. He coined the term "Transavanguardia" to describe the resumption of painting in Italian art in the 1970s and 1980s. He has curated numerous exhibitions of contemporary art, including *Contemporanea* at the Villa Borghese, Rome (1974); *Aperto 1980* (with Harald Szeemann) at the XXXIX Venice Biennale (1980); the XLV Venice Biennale (1993); the 3rd Dakar Biennale (1998); and the 1st Valencia Biennale (2001). His numerous publications include *Il territorio magico* (Florence: Centro Di, 1971), *L'ideologia del traditore* (Milan: Feltrinelli, 1976), *La Transavanguardia italiana* (Milan: Politi, 1980), *Conversation Pieces* (Turin: Umberto Allemandi, 1993), and *Lezione di boxe. Dieci round sull'arte contemporanea* (Rome: Sossella, 2004).

Luigi Ontani is an Italian artist who has been based in Rome since the 1970s. His work was shown at the Venice Biennale in 1978, 1986, and 1995, the Sydney Biennale in 1986, and the New Delhi Triennale in 1991. He has also exhibited at the Frankfurter Kunstverein, Frankfurt (1996); MoMA PS1, New York (2001); S.M.A.K., Ghent (2003); Kunsthalle Berne, Berne (2012); and the Accademia Nazionale di San Luca, Rome (2017).

Giovanni Pettinato (1934–2011) was an Italian historian of the ancient Near East and an authority on Sumerian and Mesopotamian languages and culture. He served as chair of Assyriology and ancient Eastern history at the University of Turin from 1970 to 1974, and chair of Assyriology at Sapienza Università, Rome, from 1974 to 2010. His many publications include *The Archives of Ebla: An Empire Inscribed in Clay* (Garden City, NY: Doubleday, 1981); *Ebla: A New Look at History* (Baltimore: Johns Hopkins University Press, 1991); and *La saga di Gilgamesh* (Santarcangelo di Romagna: Rusconi, 1992).

Emilio Prini (1943–2016) was an Italian artist involved with the Arte Povera movement. He participated in Documenta 10 (1997) and a posthumous retrospective of his work was held at Fondazione Merz, Turin, in 2019. His work has been exhibited at the Stedelijk Museum, Amsterdam; Kunstmuseum, Basel; Museum of Modern Art, New York; Museum of Contemporary Art, Chicago; Palazzo Grassi, Venice; Tate Modern, London; Walker Art Center, Minneapolis; Geffen Contemporary at MOCA, Los Angeles; and the Hirshhorn Museum and Sculpture Garden, Washington, DC, among others.

Marco Senaldi is an Italian academic theorist, critic, and curator. Based in Milan, he is currently a professor of media theory and aesthetics at the Accademia di Belle Arti di Brera, having previously taught at the IULM University of Milan and the Università degli Studi di Milano-Bicocca. He has curated exhibitions of contemporary art and media such as *Athos Ongaro – Abracadabra* at the Centro per l'arte contemporanea Luigi Pecci, Prato, 2011. His publications include *Enjoy! Il godimento estetico* (Rome: Meltemi, 2003), *Rapporto confidenziale. Percorsi tra cinema e arte visive* (Milan: Mimesis, 2012), and *Duchamp-Test: Marcel Duchamp et l'image idéomotrice* (Paris: Mimésis France, 2022).

Richard Shiff is an American art historian and theorist of modern and contemporary art. He is currently the Effie Marie Cain Regents Chair in Art and director of the Center for the Study of Modernism at the University of Texas at Austin. His many publications include *Cézanne and the End of Impressionism* (Chicago: University of Chicago Press, 1984), *Doubt* (Theories of Modernism and Postmodernism in the Visual Arts, vol. 3, New York: Routledge, 2008), *Between Sense and de Kooning* (London: Reaktion Books, 2011), and *Sensuous Thoughts: Essays on the Work of Donald Judd* (Berlin: Hantje Cantz, 2020), as well as many journal articles and exhibition catalogue essays.

Octavia Stocker is a British writer and critic whose work centers on media, literature, and feminism. She is currently an editor at Hoxton Mini Press in London and was previously an editor at Juxta Press, Milan.

Italo Tomassoni is an Italian critic and curator. He is a founder and the artistic director of the Centro Italiano Arte Contemporanea in Foligno. He previously taught at Sapienza Università, Rome, and the Accademia di Belle Arti, Perugia. In December 1998 he founded the Associazione Gino De Dominicis and the following year he co-curated (with Harald Szeemann) the first retrospective of De Dominicis's work at the XLVIII Venice Biennale. His publications include *Ipermanierismo* (Milan: Giancarlo Politi, 1985) and *Gino De Dominicis. Catalogo ragionato* (Milan: Skira, 2011).

Duccio Trombadori is an Italian writer, journalist, and curator whose interests range from legal philosophy and Marxism to contemporary art theory. He has taught at Sapienza Università, Rome, and served as editor of the cultural page of the newspaper *L'Unità*. Among his publications are a book of interviews with Michel Foucault, *Remarks on Marx* (Los Angeles: Semiotext(e), 1991), *Pier Paolo Pasolini. Figuratività e figurazione* (Rome: Edizioni Carte Segrete, 1992), and *De Dominicis amico pittore. Storia e cronistoria di un sodalizio* (Falciano, San Marino: Maretti Editore, 2012).

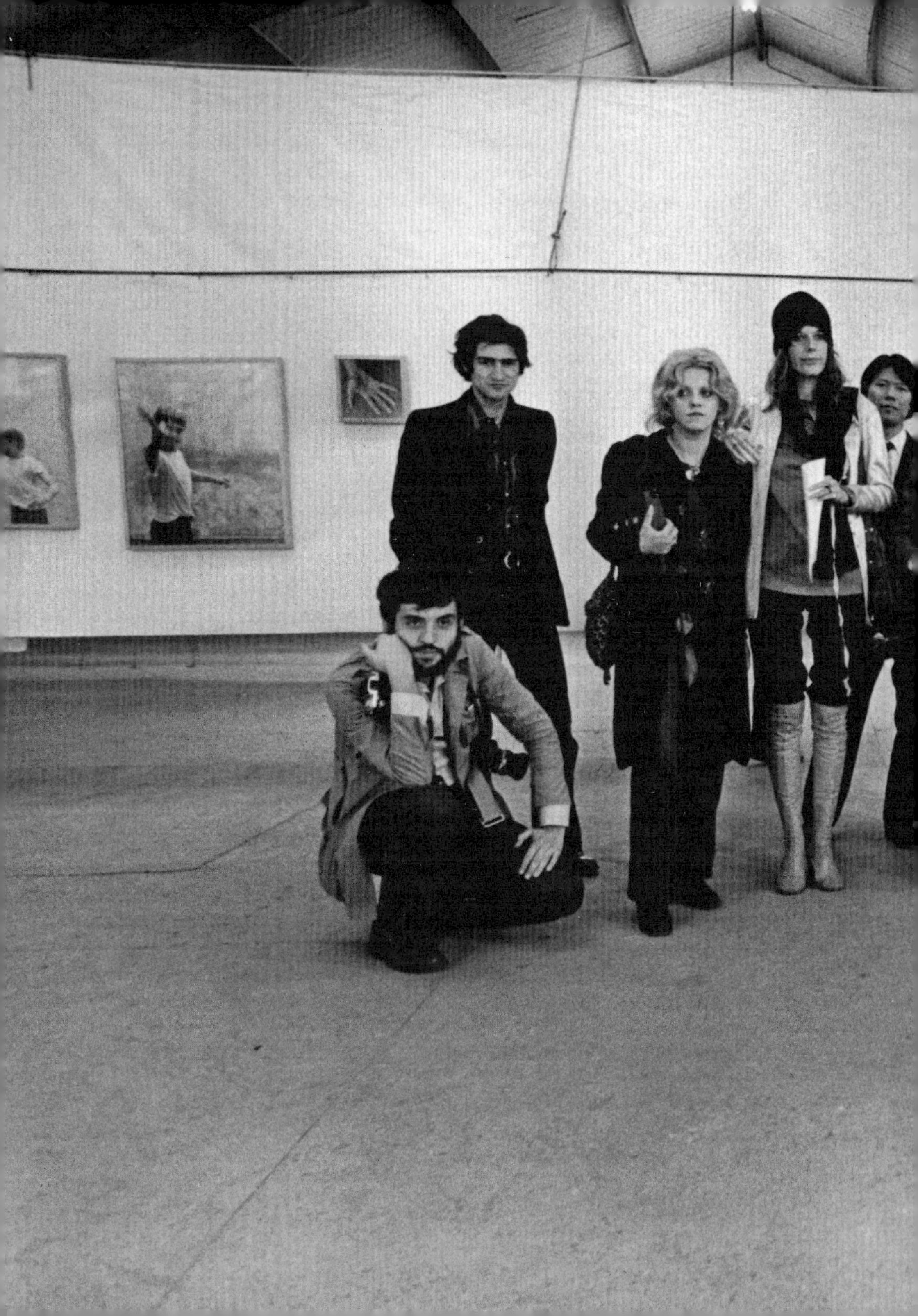

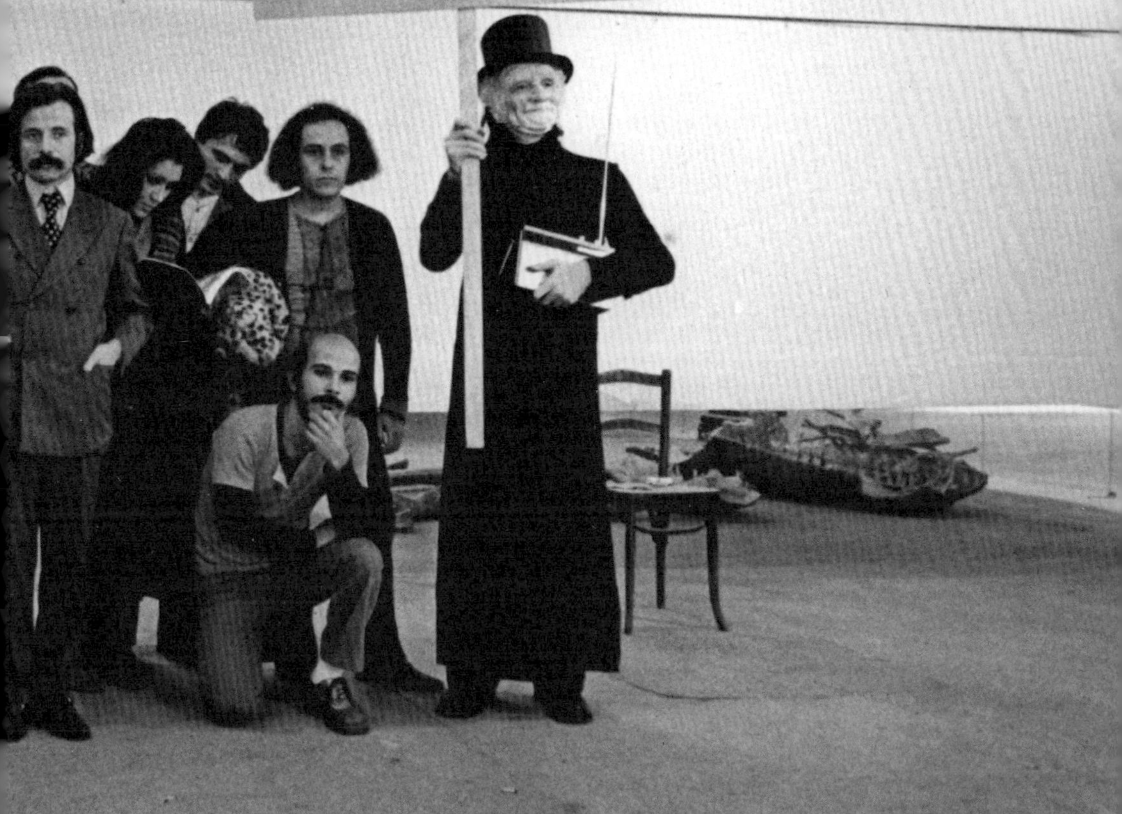

CHE COSA C'ENTRA LA MORTE?

Acknowledgments

First and foremost, I am grateful to the authors of the essays because it is they who have made this book possible at all. As a friend of mine, and as a friend of the artist and longtime supporter of his work, Lia Rumma has naturally played an essential role in the realization of this project. This book has benefitted enormously from Italo Tomassoni's knowledge and expertise, and the generosity with which both were given.

Karen Marta has enthusiastically endorsed the project from the outset; among her team, I am particularly grateful to Miles Champion for his comments and thoroughgoing copyediting of the text, and to Amy Peltz for her meticulous proofreading.

Barry Schwabsky's retranslations of De Dominicis's writings greatly improved them. It has been a pleasure to work with Michael Dyer, whose design not only captures the gist of De Dominicis's stance but succeeds in reflecting visually the intentions guiding the *Reader*.

I owe thanks as well to Francesco Ajello, Umberto Allemandi, Margherita Alverà, Maria Gloria Bicocchi, Todd Bradway, Lucia Coco, Arianna de Rosa, Anna Maria Farinato, Francesca Gallo, Olimpia Isidori, Emilio Mazzoli, Fabio Sargentini, and Nicola Trezza.

Gabriele Guercio
November 2021–January 2023

Gino De Dominicis
A Reader

Published by

Verlag der Buchhandlung
Walther und Franz König
Ehrenstraße 4
D – 50672 Köln

Consulting Editor and Producer:
KMEC Books
1 University Place
New York, NY 10003
karenmarta.com

Editor:
Gabriele Guercio
Consulting Editor:
Karen Marta
Managing Editor:
Todd Bradway
Assistant Editors:
Emma Tempest
Anton Haugen
Designer:
Michael Dyer/Remake
Scott Vander Zee
Copyeditor:
Miles Champion
Proofreader:
Amy R. Peltz
Translators:
Ombretta Celeste
Allison Grimaldi Donahue
Barry Schwabsky
Damion Searls
Jeremy Scott
Simon Turner
Andrea Vesentini

Printed and bound by
Lösch GmbH & Co. KG

Paper:
Holmen Trend 80 g/m²

Distribution:

Europe
Verlag der Buchhandlung
Walther und Franz König
Ehrenstraße 4
D – 50672 Köln
Tel: +49 (0) 221 / 20 59 6 53
verlag@buchhandlung-walther-koenig.de

UK & Ireland
Cornerhouse Publications Ltd. - HOME
2 Tony Wilson Place
UK – Manchester M15 4FN
Tel: +44 (0) 161 212 3466
publications@cornerhouse.org

Outside Europe
D.A.P. / Distributed Art Publishers, Inc.
75 Broad Street, Suite 630
USA – New York, NY 10004
Tel: +1 (0) 212 627 1999
orders@dapinc.com

ISBN 978-3-7533-0583-7
Printed in Germany

Back cover:
Senza titolo (Untitled), 1985. Chalk on wood,
28¾ × 14⅛ inches (73 × 36 cm). Silvio Sansone
Collection, Salerno [IT 259]

pp. 8–9:
Detail of *Senza titolo (Conversazione con macchia)*
(Untitled [Conversation with a Blotch]), 1971.
India ink on photographic paper, 19¼ × 24⅜ inches
(49 × 62 cm). Private collection, Rome [IT 136]

pp. 308–9:
Photo taken on the occasion of the 7th Paris
Biennial, Parc Floral-Bois de Vincennes, 1971.
Photographer unknown.
It features, among others, from left to right: Giuseppe
Penone, Mimma Pisani, Achille Bonito Oliva, Vettor
Pisani, Mimmo Germanà, and Gino De Dominicis